Family Life in Black America

Family Life. in Black America

Robert Joseph Taylor
James S. Jackson
Linda M. Chatters
EDITORS

SAGE Publications
International Educational and Professional Publisher
Thousand Oaks   London   New Delhi

For information:

SAGE Publications, Inc.
2455 Teller Road
Thousand Oaks,
California 91320
E-mail: order@sagepub.com

SAGE Publications Ltd.
6 Bonhill Street
London EC2A
4PU
United Kingdom

SAGE Publications India Pvt. Ltd.
M-32 Market
Greater Kailash I
New Delhi 110 048 India

Printed in the United States of America

Library of Congress Cataloging-in-Publication Data

Family life in Black America / edited by Robert Joseph Taylor, James
S. Jackson, and Linda M. Chatters.
  p. cm.
  Includes bibliographical references (p.) and index.
  ISBN 0-8039-5290-2 (cloth : acid-free paper). — ISBN
0-8039-5291-0 (pbk. : acid-free paper)
  1. Afro-American families. I. Taylor, Robert Joseph.
II. Jackson, James S. (James Sidney), 1944- . III. Chatters,
Linda M.
E185.86.F36 1997
306.85'089'96073—dc21   97-4776

This book is printed on acid-free paper.

97 98 99 00 01 02 03 10 9 8 7 6 5 4 3 2 1

Acquiring Editor:	Jim Nageotte
Editorial Assistant:	Kathleen Derby
Production Assistant:	Karen Wiley
Cover Designer:	Ravi Balasuriya
Print Buyer:	Anna Chin

Contents

Foreword
Andrew Billingsley   ix

Acknowledgments   xiii

1. Introduction   1
    Robert Joseph Taylor,
    Linda M. Chatters, and James S. Jackson

2. Recent Demographic Trends in
    African American Family Structure   14
    Robert Joseph Taylor, M. Belinda Tucker,
    Linda M. Chatters, and Rukmalie Jayakody

3. The Effects of Mate Availability on Marriage
    Among Black Americans: A Contextual Analysis   63
    K. Jill Kiecolt and Mark A. Fossett

4. Gender, Age, and Marital Status as Related to
   Romantic Involvement Among African American Singles   79
   M. Belinda Tucker and Robert Joseph Taylor

5. Life Stress and Psychological
   Well-Being Among Married and Unmarried Blacks   95
   Verna M. Keith

6. Religious Involvement and the Subjective
   Quality of Family Life Among African Americans   117
   Christopher G. Ellison

7. Multiple Familial-Worker Role Strain and
   Psychological Well-Being: Moderating Effects
   of Coping Resources Among Black American Parents   132
   Ruby L. Beale

8. Informal Ties and Employment Among Black Americans   146
   Robert Joseph Taylor and Sherrill L. Sellers

9. Families, Unemployment, and Well-Being   157
   Clifford L. Broman

10. Differences Among African
    American Single Mothers: Marital Status,
    Living Arrangements, and Family Support   167
    Rukmalie Jayakody and Linda M. Chatters

11. Child Rearing, Social Support, and Perceptions of
    Parental Competence Among African American Mothers   185
    Cleopatra Howard Caldwell and Lilah Raynor Koski

12. Strategies of Racial Socialization Among Black
    Parents: Mainstream, Minority, and Cultural Messages   201
    Michael C. Thornton

13. Instrumental and Expressive Family Roles
    Among African American Fathers   216
    Phillip J. Bowman and Tyrone A. Forman

14. Family Roles and Family Satisfaction Among Black Men   248
    Robert Joseph Taylor and Waldo E. Johnson, Jr.

15. Living Arrangements of African American
    Adults: Variations by Age, Gender, and Family Status   262
    Andrea G. Hunter

16. Husbands, Wives, Family, and
    Friends: Sources of Stress, Sources of Support   277
    Harold W. Neighbors

17. Changes Over Time in Support
    Network Involvement Among Black Americans   293
    Robert Joseph Taylor,
    Linda M. Chatters, and James S. Jackson

    References   317

    Name Index   351

    Subject Index   360

    About the Editors   369

    About the Contributors   371

Foreword

ANDREW BILLINGSLEY

W. E. B. Du Bois would be pleased with this new edited volume on *Family Life in Black America*. He would be encouraged by its comprehensivity, its fidelity to data, and the boldness with which its two dozen authors make the connection between the individual, the family, the community, and the larger society. Nearly 100 years ago, this pioneer sociologist set forth criteria for the scientific study of the African American experience—criteria, which have most often been "honored in the breach" by contemporary scholars. In a paper presented to the American Academy of Political and Social Science in 1898, Du Bois argued as follows:

> We should seek to know and measure carefully all the forces and conditions that go to make up these different problems, to trace the historical development of these conditions, and discover as far as possible the probable trend of further development. (Du Bois, 1898, p. 10)

More than any previous volume of its kind, *Family Life in Black America* honors the criteria laid down by Du Bois, by its bold reach toward comprehensivity. In this regard, the volume stands on the shoulders of the pioneering and perennial readers on African American families produced by Robert Staples (1994) and Harriette P. McAdoo (1996). Indeed, the reader of *Family Life in Black America* will find substantial enlightenment on a wide range of dimensions of black family life including maturation, mate selection, sexuality, procreation, infancy, childhood, adolescence, gender issues, young adulthood, cohabitation, parenting, grandparenting, and aging—it is like a fresh breeze of scholarship on the African American family, so often characterized by only one or two of its structural or functional dimensions. At the same time, this volume shows something of the diversity within African American families as well as the diversity among the forces that help to shape, limit, and enhance the family. There are four aspects of *Family Life in Black America* that especially appeal to me as major contributions to our understanding of this subject matter. First, each chapter is firmly anchored in empirical data, most often based on but not limited to the 1979-1980 data set from the National Survey of Black Americans, the most systematic and comprehensive survey of this population to date. Indeed, when some 20 years ago James Jackson, Belinda Tucker, and Gerald Gurin wrote a grant to the National Institute of Mental Health that launched this study, they surely could not have anticipated the success of their initiative in producing a steady stream of black scholarship and black scholars out of this one university setting. It is a record other universities have not been able or willing to match. This contribution to the study of life in black America is thus prodigious and enduring, of which this volume is a most recent and most excellent example. Scholars over the nation are indebted to them. A second major contribution of this volume is that it moves beyond the common tendency to focus on a limited range of issues and ideas to embrace a wide range of issues and ideas addressing both the problems and the promise of African American families, without being preoccupied with the former. It manages, in short, to avoid this limited focus by moving beyond the deficit perspective that still haunts the study of and policy perspectives on African American families. Increasingly in these days of turmoil, one hears sometimes from the most respectable sources the tired refrain that "Moynihan was right in 1965"—a view that ignores the variety and complexity of the internal and external forces shaping African American family life so prominently considered in *Family Life in Black America*. A third enduring feature of this book is its recognition of the social environment. Several of the authors who do so have clearly learned from the "ecological" studies of Margaret Beale Spencer (1985) and others. And, in this regard, social institutions and their impact on families receive welcome treatment. We have argued elsewhere it is not possible to have strong black families without strong black institutions. And although the authors in this volume do not yet reach that conclusion, they do massage the available empirical data in ways to show the relevance of such institutions as religion, the church, work, child care centers, institutions for the aged, and a wide range of social welfare institutions to a proper understanding of African American family life. Finally, this volume is well written. Many scholars will be aware of how difficult a feat this is to accomplish in a volume produced by more than one author, and often in single authored volumes as well. The challenge of weaving these separate chapters into an integrated whole, so that the authors all seemed to be "singing from the same sheet of music" as it were, must surely have been enormous. The editors of this volume deserve high praise for this feat, and the readers of it, whether students, or scholars, or policymakers, or community leaders, or professionals from a variety of fields, will be deeply in their debt.

Andrew Billingsley
Professor and Chair, Department of
Family Studies
University of Maryland,
College Park

To our families

Acknowledgments

We would like to acknowledge those individuals associated with the development of this edited volume. First and foremost, this book is a product of the Program for Research on Black Americans and benefits from the efforts of our talented faculty and staff. The support and encouragement of our colleagues at the PRBA represents an important personal and intellectual resource. Sally Oswald provided administrative support for this effort and was helpful in keeping us on track and mindful of deadlines. Analyses for a number of chapters were ably completed by Myriam Torres.

We were very fortunate to have had excellent support for the development and physical layout of the book itself. Ain Pili Boone developed the tables for each of the chapters. Karen Lincoln was pivotal in providing overall coordination of the individual chapters that comprise the book. She expertly developed the author biographical sketches, organized the many reference citations, formatted the individual chapters, and verified all table presentations for the volume. Her efforts were critical in executing this project. We gratefully acknowledge the National Institute on Aging, National Institute of Child Health and

Development and National Institute of Mental Health which supported work on various phases of this book.

Finally, we acknowledge the support and encouragement of our immediate and extended families. They remain a source of inspiration and are our constant companions in the shared experience of family. Robert Joseph Taylor would like to thank his siblings Mary Ann Greer [her children, Vicki and Andrea (spouse Lamont) and grandchildren, DeAndrea, R.J., Taylor, and Ellis], Harry W. Taylor, Jr. (his spouse, Jannie Grady Taylor, his daughter Joycelyn and grandson Jeffrey), and Donna Murray (spouse, Walter and children, Simone, Shawn and James). Linda Chatters would like to thank her siblings Trudy Patrick (spouse, Roger and son, Sean), Myrtle Harvey (spouse, Henry and children Adia and Henry, Jr.), and Owen Calvin Chatters. James S. Jackson would like to thank his siblings John, Larry (spouse, Janice and sons, Maurice, Sidney Paul and Alex), and Susan (spouse, Michael and children, Erica, Johnathan and Adrian).

Our extended families have also been a source of encouragement in our efforts. Robert Joseph Taylor and Linda Chatters would like to thank George Holt, (spouse, Edith, daughter-in-law, Carolyn, and grandchildren, George, Stephanie, David, Yvonne, Miles and Ruth); Ralph Holt; Phillip Morris [children, Phillip Morris II (spouse, Patricia) and Harriet Harrington (spouse, Reginald), grandchildren James, Tony, Kevin, Melissa and John Henry and great-grandchildren, Brian and Brianna, Alyssa, Michael, Meshell, and David], Robert and Jane Jackson (children, Robbie, Janeece, Jeanna, and Joy); Mrs. Jimmie Frazier [daughter, Emile Grant (spouse, Lee) and grandchildren, Angela and Candace). James S. Jackson would like to extend a thank you to his great-aunts Irene Frazier, Annie Lee Boyd, Jessie Mae Wilson, Nellie Wilson, and great-uncle, John Thomas Jackson, and to his aunts Nina Tatum and Geraldine Wilson. We extend a special thanks to our friend, Mrs. Adye Bel Evans, who always treated us just like family.

Finally, Robert Joseph Taylor and Linda Chatters thank their children, Harry Owen Chatters Taylor and Mary Louise Chatters Taylor. James S. Jackson extends a special thanks to his wife, Toni C. Antonucci and daughters, Ariana and Kendra. In countless ways, they bestow upon us the special rewards and blessings of family.

Robert Joseph Taylor
James S. Jackson
Linda M. Chatters

I

Introduction

ROBERT JOSEPH TAYLOR
LINDA M. CHATTERS
JAMES S. JACKSON

Over the past 20 years, American families—and black families—in particular, have undergone tremendous demographic and social transformation. Among a number of important changes, this period has seen significant increases in the rates of out-of-wedlock births, single-parent families (i.e., mother-only families), and childhood poverty (see Chapter 2, this volume, for a full discussion of these issues). Social science research, media reports, and social policy discussions of black families have focused their attention on these and other problems and challenges. Unfortunately, one consequence of a primary focus on the obstacles confronting black families is that the discussion of the state of black families is often framed within a "social problems" perspective. Certainly, an accurate appreciation of the challenges that confront black families is important and needed. As is often the case, however, a "problem focus" unnecessarily restricts one's viewpoint on black families and diverts attention from consideration of the important substantive issues affecting them. Furthermore, black families are often characterized as possessing few internal resources to deal with these challenges and come to be regarded in the public mind as simply problem families.

A recent manifestation of this process is evident in relation to discussions of urban poverty and the underclass. Over the past decade, research and social policy efforts have focused to a large degree on understanding the causes and consequences of long-standing poverty among primarily black and Latino urban residents. The family, and concerns about its structure (i.e., single-parent households) and functioning (i.e., welfare dependent, disorganized), have been a focus of much of these discussions. Similar to past debates, the locus of the problem of the underclass resides within the individuals themselves and their lack of appropriate values with respect to the family and work. Structural arguments concerning the causes of poverty (e.g., lack of jobs and viable workplace skills, restructuring of the labor market) have had a much less persuasive impact on public attitudes on this issue. The factors contributing to public perceptions about the causes of long-term poverty are numerous and complex. They are shaped, however, at least in part, by the fact that structuralist perspectives regarding the causes of poverty have been appropriated by groups pushing for reform (or abolishment) of the federal welfare system. This line of thinking states that welfare itself is the potent and overriding structural feature that causes and reinforces long-standing poverty. It is only recently (Danziger, Sandefur, & Weinberg, 1994; Wilson, 1996) that an appreciation for factors associated with the availability of jobs, the changing labor market, and workforce preparation (e.g., skills) has again gained attention.

Directed attention to the issues of the underclass debate is important for understanding the status and well-being of the group. One of the consequences of discussions of poverty and the underclass, however, is that the life experiences of black populations more generally are "homogenized." This is particularly the case with respect to discussions on the nature and functioning of families. Over the past several years, the predominant media image of black family life is urban and poor, with the added problems of teen pregnancy, drug addiction, and community violence. Although this characterization is most prominent in urban centers, it also affects more general perceptions of the family lives of blacks. To provide a more accurate picture, the current circumstances dictate that social science research and policy must employ a differentiated approach to the study of black families.

Current discussions of the problems that beset black families and their proposed remedies, in part, reflect a long line of social science and family policy research. Students of the black family will recognize that pejorative characterizations of black family life are not new. These negative characterizations arise, in part, from basic assumptions about the normative structure and functions of families. Furthermore, the particular perspective one adopts with respect to the origin of the problems facing families and whether families possess the capabilities to cope with these challenges, is critical to understanding and interpreting family phenomena. Two examples will help to illustrate these points.

A tradition of research focusing on simple race differences in family structure and function characterized black families as deviant from white, middle-class norms. The basic and unquestioned assumption was that there was a model family form that was preferred and regarded as ideal. The major contribution of black scholars of the family has been to question key assumptions of what is normative for families across cultural groups and to offer new paradigms and models for understanding the nature of black family life (Allen, 1978; Dilworth-Anderson, Burton, & Johnson, 1993; Dilworth-Anderson & McAdoo, 1988; Taylor, Chatters, Tucker, & Lewis, 1990; Wilson, 1986, 1989). In a similar vein, prior research and writings have described black families as pathological. The portrayal of black families as pathological is, in part, a consequence of identifying them with the social problems that they face. The label of pathology places the origin of the problem within the family and effectively precludes a perspective on black families as institutions that are capable of change and adaptation in response to both internal and external challenges and demands.

Certainly, more could be said regarding the scientific and political climate within which research on black Americans is conducted. Although such a discussion is beyond the scope of the present effort, a number of excellent review and theoretical works discuss these important issues in greater depth (Billingsley, 1992; Dilworth-Anderson et al., 1993; Hill et al., 1989; McAdoo, 1993; Staples & Johnson, 1993; Taylor et al., 1990; Tucker & Mitchell-Kernan, 1995a). Furthermore, within their respective substantive areas, individual chapters in this volume review the relevant theoretical models, issues, and controversies pertaining to black families.

One of the principal perspectives guiding the authors represented here and in the development of the National Survey of Black Americans data set on which this volume is based, is that black families are adaptive and resilient in the face of adversity. Consistent with the purpose and aims of the National Survey of Black Americans, this volume does not espouse a social problems perspective. We recognize, however, that adverse life conditions and circumstances that affect portions of the black population represent significant challenges and have potential negative consequences for the well-being of black families. To ignore the reality of these problems and their effects on black families would be intellectually dishonest and ethically irresponsible.

The perspective advanced here is that although black families face a number of social circumstances that constitute risks to their well-being, they also possess a number of strengths and resources that constitute protective factors that may offset these risks. The well-being and effective functioning of black families is dependent on an accurate assessment of not only the problematic circumstances they face, but the nature and types of resources and strengths that function to counterbalance these problems.

The approach taken in this volume is threefold. We believe that an accurate understanding of black families can be achieved by (a) examining them within the current context of demographic profiles and trends that affect basic family structure and function, (b) using a perspective that explores specific factors that serve to protect families, as well as identifying those factors that constitute risks to effective family functioning and well-being, and (c) giving special attention to the important substantive issues that have been ignored in the black family literature. Our approach to black families is comprehensive, both substantively and in relation to the institutions (e.g., churches, employment) and individuals (e.g., mothers, church members, friends) who affect family life and functioning. We believe that this approach provides a better understanding of the circumstances facing black families in relation to other important community institutions, as well as the varied ways that families function as resources to their individual members and within the broader social contexts in which they operate.

The volume opens (Chapter 2) with a brief overview of recent demographic trends that influence and shape contemporary black family life, including issues such as adolescent sexuality, contraceptive use, and pregnancy rates. Attention to the broader questions of demographic trends and context is evident in a number of the individual chapters in this volume. Furthermore, several chapters examine various challenges facing black families within the context of individual and family resources that may exert protective effects or mitigate the impact of adverse life circumstances. Chapters taking this approach include investigations of the amount of support received by single-mother families (Jayakody and Chatters), the role of the informal support network in finding employment (Taylor and Sellers), and the impact of unemployment on psychological well-being (Broman).

Throughout this volume, special attention is paid to family topics and issues that have been largely neglected in the literature on black Americans—for example, black men's performance in family roles (Bowman and Forman; Taylor and Johnson) and the impact of economic marginality among black men on marriage formation rates and patterns (Kiecolt and Fossett). Overall, this volume provides systematic and rigorous research that covers a broad profile of family life in black America and addresses substantive issues of importance to understanding black families. The collected chapters approach these concerns with an appreciation for the social and demographic realities faced by black families, as well as the personal and family factors that may function as assets or liabilities for overall well-being.

The National Survey of Black Americans

One of the strengths of this volume is that the chapters are based on the National Survey of Black Americans data set. The National Survey of Black Americans (NSBA) is the first survey derived from a multistage area probability sample of the adult black population in the United States. The NSBA was funded by the National Institute of Mental Health, with James S. Jackson, M. Belinda Tucker, and Gerald Gurin as the principal investigators. The NSBA was conducted in 1979-1980 and consists of 2,107 personal interviews. Containing over 2,000 items on a variety of topics (e.g., neighborhood, religion, employment and unemployment, group and racial identity, physical and mental health, family and friendships, political behavior, and numerous psychosocial issues), the NSBA remains the most representative and comprehensive survey of black American life. Jackson (1991) provides a detailed discussion of the sampling design, questionnaire items, interviewer training, coding, and methodological innovations employed in the creation of the NSBA.

Very little quantitative research on black family life was available prior to the introduction of the NSBA. Research during this period was characterized by the use of small and geographically restricted, nonprobability samples. Furthermore, this work did not employ multivariate analysis strategies, and demographic variation in family life on the basis of major status characteristics (e.g., gender, age, education, income, marital status) was only rarely investigated. Despite limited quantitative research, an established body of ethnographic work on the family life of black Americans (e.g., Aschenbrenner, 1975; Kennedy, 1980; Stack, 1974) provided a wealth of information about various aspects of family functioning among black Americans. Ethnographic studies, however, were limited by the lack of generalizability of research findings to the larger black population. The NSBA, in contrast, combines the advantage of a comprehensive focus, with the ability to generalize to the underlying population(s) of interest.

Another important strength of the NSBA is the ability to investigate within-group differences in family phenomena. This represents a major departure from previous research efforts in which race differences were a primary focus and were routinely investigated. Research focusing only on simple race differences typically provides little information beyond the fact that blacks and whites differ with respect to family phenomena. The investigation of within-group differences using the NSBA data can clarify how sociodemographic and other factors influence family phenomena among African Americans. Ultimately, the ability to examine within-group variation provides the opportunity to conduct more meaningful analyses exploring the role of racial status.

Family Research Based on the NSBA

The NSBA data sets have generated a considerable amount of research focusing on black families. A portion of this work concentrates on the structural characteristics and functional properties (e.g., social support) of immediate and extended family networks among various groups of black adults. This research investigates issues such as (a) the receipt of support from extended family members (Taylor, 1986, 1990), (b) the impact of household composition on family networks (Hatchett, Cochran, & Jackson, 1991), (c) availability of informal support when ill (Chatters, 1991; Chatters, Taylor, & Jackson, 1985, 1986), (d) intergenerational support exchanges (Chatters & Taylor, 1993; Taylor, Chatters, & Jackson, 1993), (e) the combined influence of family and church members as sources of informal support (Taylor & Chatters, 1986b), and (f) the prevalence of fictive kin in black extended families (Chatters, Taylor, & Jayakody, 1994).

Research based on the NSBA also examines family issues within the context of formal and informal help seeking in response to serious personal problems (i.e., Chatters, Taylor, & Neighbors, 1989; Greene, Jackson, & Neighbors, 1993; Jackson & Wolford, 1992; Neighbors & Jackson, 1984; Neighbors, Jackson, Bowman, & Gurin, 1983; Taylor, Neighbors, & Broman, 1989). Topics such as racial socialization (Bowman & Howard, 1985; Thornton, Chatters, Taylor, & Allen, 1990), gender relationships (Hatchett, 1991), families and well-being (Broman 1988b, 1991; Ellison, 1990), and the correlates of marriage and romantic relationships (Kiecolt & Fossett, 1995; Tucker & Taylor, 1989) are among the other issues that have been investigated within the NSBA.

In addition, a number of studies focus on discrete subgroups of the black population, including investigations of single mothers (Jayakody, Chatters, & Taylor, 1993), black women (Coleman, Antonucci, Adelmann, & Crohan, 1987), black men (Bowman, 1985, 1990; Taylor, Chatters, & Mays, 1988), and the family networks of elderly black adults (Antonucci & Jackson, 1990; Chatters et al., 1985, 1986; Gibson & Jackson, 1992; Taylor, 1985; Taylor &

Chatters, 1991). Finally, this volume, *Family Life in Black America,* is one of a series of edited volumes that is based on NSBA data. Other volumes based on the NSBA address black life in general (Jackson, 1991), focus on elderly blacks (Jackson, Chatters, & Taylor, 1993), and examine mental (Neighbors & Jackson, 1996a) and physical health (Gibson & Jackson, in press) within the black population.

Students of black families will be familiar with several other recent books that embody high standards of quality with respect to their conceptual and analytic approaches to the study of black family life. Staples and Johnson's (1993) *Black Families at the Crossroads: Challenges and Prospects* provides a solid review of research on black families. *Climbing Jacob's Ladder,* by Andrew Billingsley (1992), represents an exhaustive review of black family research that is coupled with useful qualitative and quantitative data. In addition, Tucker and Mitchell-Kernan's (1995a) edited volume, *The Decline in Marriage Among African Americans,* is a comprehensive and rigorous treatment of the dramatic decrease in marriage among blacks over the past 30 years. This volume empirically examines the correlates of the decline in marriage rates and its impact on both individual and community life among black Americans. As indicated here, the present volume is one of several recent efforts that attempts to make a rigorous and meaningful contribution to literature on black families.

Overview of Chapters

This volume is organized around several themes that unify and focus attention on either a relevant issue(s) or population group (e.g., men). The use of a common data set lends more consistency and similarity in focus than is found in most edited volumes. To limit redundancy, the principal introduction to the NSBA is provided in this chapter. Each of the chapters, however, presents additional information about the NSBA sample as it pertains to specific subsamples of NSBA respondents (e.g., mothers), including information on how the particular subgroup was derived (i.e., inclusion criteria).

Although the NSBA is the major data set used in this volume, other sources of information about black family life are used as well. For example, Taylor, Tucker, Chatters, and Jayakody (Chapter 2) describe demographic trends in black family structure using data from several data sources. Kiecolt and Fossett (Chapter 3) supplement their NSBA analysis with contextual variables derived from census data. The chapter by Bowman and Forman (Chapter 13) and the final chapter in this volume both use data from the NSBA Panel Study, which contains many of the items found in the original NSBA.

With respect to substantive focus, Taylor et al. (Chapter 2) provides an overview of research on recent demographic trends in black family structure. As a sample of adults, the NSBA does not address issues pertaining to children or adolescents, nor does it include items addressing reproductive behavior. Consequently, this chapter is augmented with information focusing broadly on research on children, adolescents, and reproductive behavior. With regard to children, research on living arrangements, foster care, child abuse, exposure to violence, and childhood poverty is examined. Demographic research on adolescents focuses on sexuality, contraceptive practices, pregnancy, abortion, and the consequences of childbearing for adolescent mothers and fathers. Furthermore, the chapter addresses a comprehensive set of issues related to family structure, including nonmarital childbearing, female-headed families, marriage and marital transitions, cohabitation, theories of the decline in marriage, interracial marriage, and extended family households. Information on the reproductive behaviors of adults focuses on topics such as sexuality and contraceptive practices. Two chapters explore the demographic correlates of marriage and romantic involvement among black Americans. Kiecolt and Fossett (Chapter 3) examine the effect of mate availability or sex ratio on marriage rates, using individual-level data from the NSBA and local-level contextual data (i.e., male-female sex ratio and level of public assistance) drawn from the U.S. census. They find that the higher the sex ratio (i.e., numbers of men in relation to the numbers of women) in a given community, the greater likelihood that black men and women will marry. Consistent with other research, their work demonstrates that increased economic marginalization experienced by black men is associated with decreases in the likelihood of marriage.

Research addressing the decline in marriage among African Americans provides important information on the nature and correlates of the marriage experience. Equally important areas of research, however, focus on individuals who, although they may not marry, are involved in stable, long-term romantic relationships. Tucker and Taylor (Chapter 4) investigate gender, age, and marital status differences in romantic involvement among single black Americans. They find that many of the factors associated with the likelihood of marriage, are also associated with the likelihood of being involved in a romantic relationship. Men, younger persons, and divorced respondents are more likely than their counterparts to currently be involved romantically or to want a main romantic involvement. The chapters by Kiecolt and Fossett and Tucker and Taylor together provide important information on the correlates of marriage and romantic involvement among black Americans.

Keith (Chapter 5) investigates the impact of stress on the psychological well-being of married and unmarried black adults. Her extensive analysis indicates that within each marital status group, those who have significantly more life problems are more likely to perceive their lives as being unhappy and less satisfying. Closeness to family members and having several close friends are both generally associated with greater well-being, although the strength of the relationship varies across marital status groups. Irrespective of marital status, however, the impact of stress on psychological well-being is buffered, to some degree, by family and friendship ties and demographic factors.

Ellison's (Chapter 6) investigation of the impact of religious involvement on the subjective quality of family life finds that church participation and perceived importance of religious socialization are significantly associated with family role performance, subjective family closeness, and satisfaction with family life. In contrast, frequency of private devotional activities is unrelated to subjective perceptions of family life. This analysis indicates that black adults who are religious report greater competency in family role performance, are more satisfied with their family lives, and indicate that their family members are subjectively close to one another. The discussion focuses on the varied ways that black church communities support and foster family life.

Several of the chapters in this volume focus on parental role perceptions and performance. Beale (Chapter 7) explores the impact of strain in family and work roles on psychological well-being among black parents. She finds that working black parents who experience strain in meeting the demands of family life and who are experiencing general role overload, report lower levels of family, job, and general life satisfaction. The effects of role strain, however, are partially offset by social resources (e.g., marital status, family closeness, religiosity). She argues that these results are supportive of a spillover hypothesis; that is, family problems significantly affect an individual's work life, even if the problems are not job-related. Howard and Koski (Chapter 11) examine the correlates of the mother role as perceived by young mothers with children, with a specific focus on the effects of child-rearing advice and social support on perceptions of parental competence. Their findings indicate that educational attainment, self-esteem, living arrangements, and social support in the area of child rearing all influence a mother's perception of herself as a competent parent.

Thornton's (Chapter 12) investigation of strategies and methods of racial socialization builds on his earlier research on the correlates of racial socialization practices among black parents (Thornton et al., 1990). In the present chapter, Thornton examines the specific types of racial socialization messages that black parents convey, distinguishing between three types: (a) mainstream experience, (b) minority experience, and (c) black cultural experience. His analysis finds that demographic and group identity factors have a significant influence on the type of racial socialization messages black parents convey to their children.

Over the past 10 years, researchers have given greater attention to the role of men in families. There is now a burgeoning literature on fatherhood, husband-wife relationships, and other normative family issues. Despite the emergence of several new books on the topic, however, the amount of work addressing these concerns among black men and their families remains limited. The majority of work on black men remains focused on social problems (e.g., adolescent fatherhood, out-of-wedlock paternity, child support enforcement, and street corner men) and reflects concern about teenage pregnancy and parenting, mother-only families, and the high rates of crime and incarceration among young black men. Attention to these issues is important and needed, but often comes at the expense of a more general understanding of black men's family relationships and roles.

Two chapters attempt to address this shortcoming in the literature by examining the familial roles and perceptions of black men. Bowman and Forman (Chapter 13) continue Bowman's program of research on black fathers. This chapter provides an exhaustive investigation of the instrumental and expressive family roles of the black father. These analyses examine the correlates of instrumental and family role functions (e.g., differences between mothers and fathers, married and unmarried fathers, poor and nonpoor fathers). The findings are discussed within the context of the roles of black fathers in the 21st century. Taylor and Johnson (Chapter 14) investigate the correlates of husband and father roles and perceptions of family life among black men. They find that, in general, black men generally perceive that they perform adequately in spouse and parental roles and are very satisfied with their family lives. Collectively, the programmatic work of Bowman, Taylor, and others will help bring attention to a critical and neglected topic in the black family literature and provide a more balanced understanding of the roles of black men in families.

Two chapters explore the interrelationships among employment, informal networks, and individual and family well-being. Taylor and Sellers's (Chapter 8) investigation of the role of informal networks in finding employment uses family, friendship, and racial composition factors as independent variables. They find that 60% of respondents report that they initially heard about their present job through friends or family members. Men, married respondents, persons with low levels of family income and occupational status, those with larger and more proximate family networks, and persons in jobs in which there is a high percentage of black workers are more likely to have found their present employment through a personal contact. Broman (Chapter 9) investigated the impact of unemployment on family network factors and psychological well-being. He finds that unemployed black adults report lower levels of family interaction and that they are unable to adequately meet their family's wants and needs. Furthermore, the unemployed report decreased levels of overall satisfaction with life.

The past three decades have seen dramatic changes in the family structure and living arrangements of black Americans. Currently, more than half of black families are headed by a single parent and more than half of black children live with their mothers only. Mother-only families also have higher levels of poverty than two-parent households (see Chapter 2 for more discussion of these issues). Given this demographic profile, the topics of household living arrangements and single-mother families deserve serious attention by black family researchers. Hunter's (Chapter 15) investigation of the living arrangements of black men and women reveals that living arrangements patterns are diverse and the majority of respondents reside in arrangements that depart from the "traditional" nuclear family. Furthermore, living arrangements vary by region, age, marital status, and gender. Hunter argues that the pathways leading to a particular household structure are diverse and, in part, reflect life cycle variations.

Jayakody and Chatters (Chapter 10) investigate the amount of support that single and married mothers receive from their families. Although a relatively large body of research using the NSBA examines the family support networks of black Americans, comparatively little research explicitly investigates the support networks of single mothers. This chapter augments earlier research on the types of assistance received by single and married mothers (Jayakody et al., 1993) and acknowledges that information about black single-mother families is limited because this family form is routinely depicted as a relatively homogeneous group. The present findings indicate that married mothers and mothers who reside with other relatives have a greater likelihood of receiving substantial amounts of help from their families. The investigation of within-group differences among single-mother families allows a more comprehensive understanding of the factors and circumstances that both promote and limit the availability and use of family resources.

Neighbors (Chapter 16) addresses several intriguing, yet often contradictory findings in the area of family social support and interpersonal stressors. Specifically, analyses of the NSBA document the extensive use of family, friends, and relatives in times of serious crisis. Family members or an acquaintance within the immediate social support network are, however, often identified as the source of interpersonal difficulties that result in significant mental distress (e.g., point of a nervous breakdown). This chapter explores why it is that the people that are relied on for help during a time of crisis are often the same individuals who, at other times, represent primary sources of stress in our lives. Neighbors finds that (a) interpersonal problems are the most frequently mentioned source of stress by NSBA respondents; (b) the vast majority of interpersonal problems are family-related—most involve a spouse (among the married) or a parent, child, or sibling; and (c) there are two types of interpersonal problems that cause people a significant amount of distress—negative crises that happen to respondent's significant other and interpersonal difficulties that involve the respondent and their significant other. These findings are useful for understanding how and in what ways respondents characterize interpersonal difficulties and the circumstances under which these problems represent risks for increased stress and reduced perceptions of well-being.

The final chapter in this volume is a departure from previous chapters in its examination of change in selected family and friendship variables among NSBA respondents. The analysis focuses specifically on friendship relationships and interaction, church support and family support, interaction and closeness. Change in these factors is noted from baseline (1979-1980) and in comparison to two successive panels of the NSBA data (1987 and 1992). These data allow an opportunity to examine the broad outlines of change in selected family and social relationship factors for this group of African Americans. Central to the task of the final chapter is the development of several conclusions regarding the state of African American families and an assessment of the impact of current societal and political developments on their status. Finally, a number of suggestions for future research are outlined that may contribute to a better understanding of family life among African Americans.

Summary

The main purpose of this volume is to examine empirically various facets of African American family life. As noted previously, continuing scholarly as well as political debate concerning the status of black families suffers from a constricted view of black family life. As a result, only a narrow range of research questions concerning black families have been addressed in the literature. This volume, along with other recent treatments, attempts to contribute to a more comprehensive understanding of black families through the use of a systematic approach to the conceptualization of relevant research questions and the employment of rigorous methodological and data analysis procedures.

The current volume on black family life reflects a coherent and comprehensive approach to this topic, using sophisticated analysis techniques that are based on a representative sample of African Americans. These features allow for the careful examination of a variety of factors that are thought to be of significance for understanding the status and functioning of black families. Of particular interest, the chapters reflect an orientation to family issues that moves beyond a "problem focus" to explore a variety of substantive issues that have been neglected. Finally, the quality of the data sets provides for an appreciation of the impact of relevant status characteristics such as income and education on the nature of black family life. The approach taken in this volume, to examine intragroup variability in black family life, has been a grievous omission in the literature.

Overall, we believe that this volume represents an important perspective on black family life that highlights the operation of the black family in response to the internal needs and challenges of its members. Furthermore, family status and functioning is contextualized with respect to the demands, barriers, and opportunities that operate within the larger social systems of neighborhood, community, and society within which families are embedded (Billingsley, 1992). This dual perspective is perhaps the most critical contribution made by this volume. It is our hope that the perspective taken here will encourage the adoption of a rigorous and conscientious approach in future empirical investigations of black family life.

2

Recent Demographic Trends in African American Family Structure

ROBERT JOSEPH TAYLOR
M. BELINDA TUCKER
LINDA M. CHATTERS
RUKMALIE JAYAKODY

Over the past three decades, American families have undergone a number of important demographic changes. Significant among these various trends are the following: overall declines in the rate of marriage and later ages at first marriage, a higher proportion of births to unmarried mothers, increases in female-headed households, larger percentages of children residing in female-headed families, and a higher percentage of children living in poverty (Jaynes & Williams, 1989; Wilson, 1987). Although these trends affect both blacks and whites, black families have been disproportionately affected by these demographic changes.

AUTHORS' NOTE: The authors would like to thank Kathleen Faller for helpful comments on an earlier version of this chapter.

This chapter is an update and expansion of the demographic section of an earlier article by Taylor, Chatters, Tucker, and Lewis (1990), which reviewed research on black families. This chapter broadly reviews a number of demographic trends that are associated with black family patterns and structure and is organized into five separate sections that are concerned with (a) children, (b) adolescents, (c) reproductive behavior, (d) changes in family structure, and (e) marriage patterns. The first section addresses the topic of children's status and well-being and examines research on living arrangements, foster care, childhood poverty, child abuse, and exposure to violence. Following this, the section devoted to adolescents examines sexuality, contraceptive practices, pregnancy, abortion, and childbearing and its consequences for adolescent mothers and fathers. The third section of the chapter addresses reproductive behavior among adults including sexuality, contraceptive behaviors, abortion, and fetal loss. The next section investigates broader issues of family structure including nonmarital childbearing, female-headed families, and single-father families. The final section of the chapter examines marital status patterns and transitions (e.g., marriage, separation, divorce, remarriage, cohabitation, widowhood, interracial marriage) and theories addressing the decline in marriage among black Americans.

Children's Well-Being

Living Arrangements of Children

The increase in the number of female-headed families has important implications for the living arrangements of black children (persons under the age of 18). Data for 1995 indicated that only 33.1% of black children lived with both parents, compared to 75.9% of white children and 66.3% of Hispanic children (U.S. Bureau of the Census, 1996b). Of children living with only one parent, the majority live with their mother; 52.0% of black children and 17.8% of white children live with their mother (U.S. Bureau of the Census, 1996b). The prevalence of single-father families is very low; only 3.4% of white children and 4.0% of black children reside with their fathers only (U.S. Bureau of the Census, 1996b). Overall, it's been projected (Bumpass, 1984) that 9 out of 10 black children are likely to spend some time during their childhood in single-parent households.

Analysis of census data from 1940 to the present indicates that black children are more likely to reside in the home of a grandparent(s) than are white or Hispanic children (Hernandez, 1993; U.S. Bureau of the Census, 1992e). In

1992, 12% of black children lived with their grandparents, compared with 4% of white, and 6% of Hispanic children (U.S. Bureau of the Census, 1992e). White and Hispanic children who live in their grandparent's home are more likely than black children to have both parents present in the same household. Of children living in their grandparent's home, 23% of white children and 26% of Hispanic children had both parents present; compared to only 2% of black children. Six out of 10 black children, 50% of white children, and 48% of Hispanic children who live with their grandparents have only their mother present. Furthermore, 35% of black children who reside with their grandparents live there without either parent present, whereas 21% of white and Hispanic children reside with grandparents only (U.S. Bureau of the Census, 1992b). In addition, 63% of families maintained by white grandparents had both grandparents present, compared to 35% of families maintained by black grandparents (U.S. Bureau of the Census, 1992a).

Foster Care

In the past decade, the number of children in out-of-home care (i.e., foster family homes, group homes, or institutional settings) has risen drastically from 270,000 in the early 1980s, to 429,000 in 1991 (Children's Defense Fund [CDF], 1992). Although the number of children in out-of-home care has grown rapidly, resources in the child welfare system have not kept pace. The child welfare system faces a number of significant problems including shortages of child welfare workers with adequate formal social work training. Child welfare workers typically have large and unmanageable caseloads and receive inadequate staff support. Similarly, foster parents receive meager reimbursement rates. Despite the fact that the needs of foster children are becoming more acute, foster parents are offered few supports and little special training to handle these challenges. As a result, children in out-of-home care often do not receive adequate and appropriate attention or sufficient specialized mental health, substance abuse, health, or educational services (CDF, 1992).

Black children are more likely than whites or Hispanics to reside with neither biological parent (Seltzer & Bianchi, 1988). Although the practice of informal adoption among black extended families absorbs many children, a disproportionate number of black children live in institutions, group homes, and with foster families. Research on foster care is limited by a lack of high-quality national data and the failure of many states and communities to keep current and reliable information. Available research, however, has noted several consistent findings (Jenkins & Diamond, 1985; Morisey, 1990). First, it has been estimated that black children are three times more likely than white children to be in foster care. Second, black children have a higher likelihood of being placed in foster care for reasons of child neglect (e.g., leaving children without adequate supervision, inadequate housing, nutrition). Last, black children remain in foster care for longer periods of time than do white children and, consequently, are more likely to undergo multiple placements. The developmental risks associated with long-term residence in the foster care system suggest that black foster care children are a high-risk group that deserves serious attention from both researchers and policymakers.

Childhood Poverty

The numbers of children in poverty is a very significant and revealing indicator of the status of children. Children in the United States are 2 to 13 times more likely to be poor than are children in Australia, Canada, France, Germany, Norway, Sweden, Switzerland, and the United Kingdom (CDF, 1992). Similarly, child poverty rates vary drastically by state, with Southern states generally having higher levels of poverty. Fully, one in five children in the United States is poor (20.8% in 1995; U.S. Bureau of the Census, 1996d). In 1995, 16.2% of all white children lived in families that had below poverty incomes compared to 41.9% of black children and 40.0% of Hispanic children (U.S. Bureau of the Census, 1996d). Although not evident in census data, research has shown that poverty among many white children may be a short-term occurrence, whereas black children have a high likelihood of living in chronic poverty (Duncan & Rodgers, 1988). The high incidence of poverty among black children is due to a variety of factors including the lower earnings of black men relative to white men, higher rates of female-headed households among blacks, and a decline in the real value of government cash transfers directed at children.

Hernandez's (1993) analyses involving indexes of relative poverty and luxury allow comparisons of the socioeconomic conditions of children from 1939 to the present. Although the relative poverty of black children decreased from 1939 to the present, half of all black children still reside in poverty, compared to 22.3% of white children (Hernandez, 1993, Table 7.4). Conversely, only 8% of black children presently live in luxury, compared to 24.7% of white children.

Children's living arrangements are strongly linked to the rates of childhood poverty. For instance, it has been found that about half of the growth in child poverty during the 1980s can be attributed to changing family structure (Eggebeen & Lichter, 1991). Hogan and Lichter's (1995) analysis indicates the following: (a) regardless of racial background, childhood poverty was highest among children who lived in mother-only families; (b) overall, childhood poverty was highest among black children regardless of living arrangements; and (c) black children who lived with their mothers only were four times more likely to be poor than black children who lived with both parents. It is important to note that simply changing the living arrangements of black children to resemble those of white children would reduce (by 44%), but not eliminate, the high rates of childhood poverty among blacks (Hogan & Lichter, 1995). The large proportion of black children living in poverty (especially long-term or chronic poverty) places them at risk for serious health problems, low educational achievement, and minimal labor market participation (Hogan & Lichter, 1995; Jaynes & Williams, 1989).

Child Abuse

The area of child maltreatment encompasses a number of different forms of behaviors and conditions. Child abuse is an overarching construct that generally includes physical abuse, neglect, sexual abuse, and emotional maltreatment (Tatara, 1991). Child neglect, the most pervasive form of child maltreatment and most likely to result in lengthy out-of-home placements, is defined as the failure to provide shelter, nourishment, health care, education, supervision, or clothing. Emotional maltreatment encompasses both emotional neglect and psychological abuse. Emotional neglect reflects a failure of the caretaker(s) to provide emotional support, whereas emotional abuse is abusive actions by adults that are detrimental to the psychological development of the child. By far, child sexual abuse receives the most amount of media and public attention and is a fast growing category of child abuse. In 1976, sexual abuse comprised only 3% of child maltreatment cases (American Humane Association, 1988), but by 1994, it represented 13.8% of the cases (National Child Abuse and Neglect Data System [NCANDS], 1996). Currently, there is very little quality research on child sexual abuse among black Americans, notable exceptions being work by Pierce and Pierce (1984) and Wyatt (1985).

The National Child Abuse and Neglect Data System (NCANDS) is one of the major sources of information on child maltreatment. Their data indicate that in 1994, child protective services agencies received reports of alleged abuse involving 2.9 million children, reflecting an increase from the 2.6 million children reported abused in 1990. The number of "substantiated" victims of child abuse increased from 798,318 in 1990 to 1,011,628 in 1994, an increase of almost 27%. Almost half of reported cases of abuse involve neglect (52.9%), 25.5% physical abuse, 13.8% sexual abuse, and 4.7% emotional maltreatment. Almost half of the victims of abuse were 8 years old or younger. In addition, from 1990 to 1994, child protective service agencies identified almost 5,400 children who died as a result of abuse or neglect.

With respect to perpetrators, 79.2% of acts of child neglect and abuse were committed by natural parents, stepparents, adoptive or foster parents, and 9.9% were committed by other relatives (NCANDS, 1996). Adoptive, foster, and stepparents were much more likely to have committed child sexual abuse than natural parents (Tatara, 1991). Individuals who are unrelated to the child account for only a small percentage of the cases of child abuse and neglect (Tatara, 1991, Table 7.4). It is important to note, however, that the percentage of child abuse cases committed by unrelated individuals is somewhat underestimated because child protective service agencies only handle child abuse cases that involve caretakers. Various law enforcement agencies have responsibility for cases of child abuse that are committed by unrelated persons.

The National Incidence Studies (NIS) are an additional source of information on child abuse. The NIS is a unique database because, in addition to information on children who were investigated by child protective services (CPS) agencies, it provides data on (a) children who were screened out by CPS without further investigation and (b) children who were seen by community professionals and not reported to CPS. To date, there have been three National Incidence Studies. One of the most important findings of the NIS documents that the actual incidence and prevalence of all forms of child abuse is much higher than is reflected in officially reported cases. The NIS-3 (collected in 1993), a representative sample of 5,612 community professionals, found a substantial increase in all forms of child abuse between 1986 and 1993. For example, the estimated number of seriously injured children rose from 141,700 in 1986, to 565,000 in 1993. Girls were three times more likely than boys to suffer sexual abuse, whereas boys were more likely to be emotionally neglected or to sustain a serious injury due to physical abuse. Family income was negatively associated with being a victim of abuse; children from poorer households had a much greater likelihood of being both seriously injured and neglected (NCANDS, 1996).

Several factors are consistently correlated with abuse and neglect (Hampton, 1991). Although most individuals who were abused in childhood do not become child abusers, being a victim of abuse as a child is a strong predictor of becoming a child abuser in adulthood. Social isolation from family, friends, and neighbors is also correlated with the likelihood that a family member will be abusive or neglectful. In contrast, persons with supportive networks are thought to be better able to cope with the stresses that may lead to abuse. In addition, they have others who are available to provide child care and parenting advice. Finally, high levels of stress, such as parental unemployment and illness may also contribute to child abuse and maltreatment (Hampton, 1991).

Statistics on child abuse and neglect indicate that black children are over-represented in official cases of abuse (Tatara, 1991). Hampton (1991) argues, however, that given similar injuries and circumstances, black children and poor children are more likely to be labeled abused than are children from white and more affluent families. Hampton's argument is partially substantiated by findings from all three National Incidence Studies, in which race was not found to be a significant predictor of child abuse and neglect. Poverty, however, was found to be a significant predictor of child abuse and neglect. In comparison to most studies of child abuse that focus solely on children in the child welfare system, the NIS data focuses on a much larger group of abused children. The absence of a race difference in the NIS data probably reflects the disproportionate number of black children who live in poverty, in conjunction with race-based differences in professional decision making as to whether a child enters the child welfare system. Although black children are much more likely to be in the child welfare and foster care system, the more comprehensive NIS data clearly indicate that black children are no more likely to be abused than are white or Hispanic children (for more detailed information on child abuse, please contact the National Clearinghouse on Child Abuse and Neglect).

High Poverty Areas and Exposure to Violence

Garbarino, Kostelny, and Dubrow (1991) and Garbarino, Dubrow, Kostelny, and Pardo (1992) examined the impact of violence on the psychological development of children in Mozambique, Cambodia, Israel and Palestine, and Chicago. They argue that the violence in many poor U.S. communities has escalated to the point that they are essentially urban war zones. For instance, Chicago's Robert Taylor Homes housing project, although comprising only 0.5% of Chicago's total population, accounted for 11% of that city's murders, 10% of its aggravated assaults, and 9% of its rapes. Similarly, Bell and Jenkin's (1991) analysis of 1,035 high school and middle school students in Chicago revealed that 39% of the students had personally witnessed a shooting, 35% had seen a stabbing, and 46.5% had been a primary victim of violence. On the basis of clinical evaluations, Garbarino et al. (1991, 1992) argue that the developmental experiences of children in war stricken countries and U.S. urban war zones are very similar. In particular, they found that many children in these areas suffer from posttraumatic stress disorder (PTSD) and display symptoms such as numbing, play reenactment of traumatic events, diminished future orientation, guilt, fear, lowered self-esteem, and impaired intimate relationships. The specific manifestation of PTSD symptoms are a function of age and the developmental level of the child. Bell and Jenkins (1991) argue that violence-exposed children evidence a decline in cognitive performance and school achievement. These problems may result from lowered levels of concentration due to distracting and intrusive thoughts concerning violent events.

The evidence suggests that children who live in dangerous neighborhoods are at risk for exposure to mental and physical stress and trauma that has important consequences for their development. The pervasiveness of violence means that homes and schools are not safe havens and avoiding dangerous situations becomes the critical concern when pursuing daily activities. Children may have to sleep on the floor to avoid random bullets and are often confined within their homes for fear of being assaulted. Furthermore, family members may, in some instances also be members of a gang. Consequently, the distinction between friend and enemy is often challenging and constitutes another source of stress in these children's lives. For some children, the consequences of repeated exposure to violence are devastating. It may undermine a child's basic trust in humanity and create a lifelong inability to develop close, trusting relationships. Some children may develop a sense of fatalism about their lives and come to expect more violence directed at them and premature death as a result of neighborhood violence (Bell & Jenkins, 1991). Many children who experience violence will identify with the aggressor by joining a gang and continue the cycle of violence (Bell & Jenkins, 1991; Garbarino et al., 1992).

Several studies suggest, however, that despite living in an urban war zone, many children are remarkably resilient and are able to successfully cope in this stressful environment. Resilient children tend to have high levels of efficacy and self-esteem, and tend to be affectionate, good-natured, flexible, and to exercise self-discipline (Anthony & Cohler, 1987). They are also more likely to have (a) a strong relationship with at least one parent or other significant adult, (b) supportive friends and extended family members, (c) parents who themselves constructively cope with their environment, and (d) a reassuring educational milieu (see Garbarino et al., 1992).

Play and art therapy have been found to be extremely useful tools in individual therapy with children who have undergone severe traumatic stress such as witnessing violence to family members or close friends. Through play, children can deal with complex psychological difficulties, and take control of an event by playing different roles or by altering reality. In play therapy with children, therapists can identify the psychological concerns of the child and help the child understand and cope with their feelings. Similarly, children's drawings represent the mental perceptions they have of their environment. By discussing their drawings with them, social workers, teachers, and parents can help children cope with their traumatic events and complex concerns.

Programs in high crime neighborhoods to address the problems of children living in these neighborhoods must also include assistance to social workers, educators, and other professionals. In particular, social workers in these settings need assistance in dealing with the intense emotions that they have about violence, loss, and the grieving process. Unless they can cope with these issues, they will be of limited assistance to the children and parents who need their help (see Garbarino et al., 1992 for an in-depth discussion of clinical intervention issues).

Adolescent Reproductive Behavior, Childbearing, and Parenting

Reproductive behavior is one of the few areas in which the personal and public spheres of human activity overlap (Forrest & Singh, 1990). Clearly, sexual activity, contraceptive practices, and abortion are personal and private matters. As is evident, however, by the public debate over various contraceptive methods and abortion, it is equally obvious that these topics engender a great deal of public concern and debate. From a social service perspective, reproductive behavior has implications with respect to providing services such as family planning and maternal and child health care. Furthermore, patterns of reproductive behavior are not static, but are influenced by temporal changes in social conditions, attitudes toward sexuality, and contraceptive technologies. Due to the evolving nature of reproductive behavior and the many ways in which data on reproductive behavior are used, it is imperative that social workers and other human service providers remain abreast with the most current research in this field (Forrest & Singh, 1990).

National surveys of the reproductive behavior of Americans have been conducted on a fairly regular basis since the 1955 survey, Growth of American Families (Forrest & Singh, 1990). More recently, the National Center for Health Statistics, has conducted the National Surveys of Family Growth (NSFG) in 1973, 1976, 1982, 1988, and 1990. The 1988 National Survey of Adolescent Males and the 1991 Survey of Men provides detailed information on the sexual behavior of men. With regard to abortion, the most reliable information is collected by the Alan Guttmacher Institute's (1992) survey of abortion clinics. This discussion of reproductive behavior will draw on these state-of-the-art national surveys.

Adolescent pregnancy, childbearing, and parenting are among the most significant family issues facing our society. Adolescent reproductive behavior and parenting deserves particular attention in this chapter, because it disproportionately affects African American youth and their families. First, we review Furstenberg's (1976) research on the family and cultural dynamics of adolescent sexuality and childbearing. Following this, we turn to a discussion of demographic research on adolescent sexuality, contraceptive practices, pregnancy, abortion, and childbearing. This section concludes with a discussion of the parenting experiences of adolescent mothers and fathers.

Adolescents in the United States are confronted with a culture that embodies contradictory attitudes and messages about sexuality. Music videos, movies, radio, and television all impart the message that sex is romantic and exciting—at the same time they are told that good girls should refrain from sex (Trussell, 1988). Furstenberg's (1976) research on adolescent sexuality and pregnancy provides insight into these conflicting attitudes and behaviors. Although his research was based on a sample of black girls, it is fairly generalizable to the larger population of American girls (Trussell, 1988). Furstenberg's work suggests that young black girls are aware of some of the difficulties involved in becoming a parent while still a teenager and endorse the idea of postponing sex until marriage. In their minds, however, sexual intimacy prior to marriage is allowable only when swept up in the heat of passion. The initial reactions of these young girls to pregnancy is usually negative, even among those who eventually carry the pregnancy to term. They express doubt that they are mature enough themselves to raise a child and are concerned that becoming a parent at this early age will negatively affect their educational and employment opportunities. They also believe, however, that they are not capable of changing their circumstances. As the pregnancy becomes accepted by family and friends, they become more positive about the upcoming birth. In some instances, adolescent mothers become unrealistically optimistic about their new roles as mothers and tend to underestimate the time demands of raising a child, the difficulties of completing their education, and the problems in maintaining a relationship with the child's father. In contrast, they tend to overestimate their future economic status (Furstenberg, 1976; Trussell, 1988). Furstenberg (1976) also explored the behaviors and attitudes of the parents of the adolescent mothers. He found that the parents of the teenage mothers did not actively discuss sexuality and sex education nor did they provide contraception. Although they emphasized that their daughters should not become pregnant, they offered minimal guidance in preventing pregnancy. On the whole, they tended to deny their daughters' sexuality and were shocked when they became pregnant (Furstenberg, 1976; Trussell, 1988).

Adolescent Sexual Activity

Data from the Alan Guttmacher Institute (AGI) indicate that half of unmarried adolescent females and 6 of 10 unmarried adolescent males have had sexual intercourse (AGI, 1993). Among adolescents, the likelihood of being sexually active increases with age. For unmarried 15-year-olds, 27% of women and 33% of men have had intercourse at least once. Among 19-year-olds, 75% of women and 86% of men have had intercourse. Furthermore, the first sexual experience of American youth is occurring at earlier ages. From 1982 to 1988, the percentage of 15-year-old unmarried women who had engaged in sexual intercourse increased from 19% to 27%. Levels of sexual activity among unmarried 15- to 19-year-olds demonstrate substantial race differences. Reporting having had intercourse are 81% of black males, 57% of white males, 59% of black females, and 48% of white females. During the 1980s, however, several racial and income differences in sexual activity declined because of increases in sexual activity among white teenagers and those with higher family incomes (AGI, 1993).

In a recent report on nonmarital childbearing, Moore (U.S. Congress, 1995) notes that, in some cases, sexual intercourse is coerced. In particular, among girls 14 years and younger there is some evidence that their first sexual intercourse is nonvoluntary. In addition, recent research that finds that almost 1 out of 5 adolescent mothers had a partner who was at least 6 years older (Landry & Forrest, 1995), indicates that there are substantial differences in status and power among many sexual partners (U.S. Congress, 1995). These differences are additional factors that may undermine contraceptive use and increase unwanted pregnancies (U.S. Congress, 1995).

Adolescent Contraceptive Use

Pleck, Sonenstein, and Ku's (1993) panel study of condom use among adolescent males found an initial increase in condom use between 1979 and 1988, later followed by a decline in use between 1988 and 1991. The decline in condom use was partially attributed to decreased concerns about HIV infection and an increased tendency to deny the seriousness of AIDS. Analysis of the 1982 and 1988 National Survey of Family Growth indicated an increase in the percentage of teenage women who use a contraceptive method at first intercourse, 47.9% in 1982 versus 65% in 1988 (Forrest & Singh, 1990). Despite this increase, 35.0% of adolescent women in 1988 did not use any contraception the first time they had sexual intercourse. Racial differences indicated that white adolescents (69%) were more likely than black adolescents (54.1%) to use contraception. White adolescent women were more likely to use a condom (51.1% vs. 34.8%) and withdrawal (9.6% vs. 3.1%), whereas black adolescent women were more likely to use the pill (15.7% vs. 7.1%) (Forrest & Singh, 1990). Compared to older women, adolescents are much more likely to experience a contraceptive failure in the first year of use (Jones & Forrest, 1992).

It takes sustained motivation to use contraceptives on a consistent basis or to abstain from sex. Moore (U.S. Congress, 1995) notes that a variety of factors undermine the motivation to prevent pregnancy including: overestimation of the risks of contraception, underestimation of the likelihood of pregnancy, ambivalence about sex and birth control, the cost of contraception, and a lack of career and educational opportunities. Consequently, a substantial number of sexually active adolescents eventually become pregnant.

Adolescent Pregnancy

Teenagers in the United States have one of the highest pregnancy rates in the Western world; twice as high as England, France, and Canada, and 3 times as high as Sweden (AGI, 1993). By the age of 18, roughly 24% of teenagers will become pregnant at least once and close to 40% will become pregnant by age 20 (AGI, 1993). Furthermore, nearly 1 in 5 teenagers who experience a premarital pregnancy will become pregnant again in a year. A total of 21% of white adolescents and 40% of minority adolescents will become pregnant by the age of 18. Similarly, 41% of whites and 63% of nonwhites will become pregnant by the age of 20.

A recent report by the National Center on Health Statistics (National Center on Health Statistics [NCHS], 1995c) calculates teenage pregnancy rates in two separate ways. Rates are calculated in the traditional method of the number of pregnancies per 1,000 teenage women, as well as the number of pregnancies per 1,000 sexually active women. The adolescent pregnancy rate was fairly constant from 1980-1988 (110.0 in 1980, 109.4 in 1988), but increased to 155.0 in 1991. The pregnancy rate for sexually active adolescents was 235 in 1980, 207 in 1988, and 209 in 1991 (NCHS, 1995c).

Black and Hispanic adolescent females have much higher pregnancy rates than white adolescent females. The 1991 adolescent pregnancy rate was 216.7 for blacks, 180.2 for Hispanics, and 84.7 for whites. Among sexually active teenagers, the pregnancy rate was 357 for blacks, 379 for Hispanics, and 61 for whites. In comparison to white adolescents, the higher pregnancy rates among blacks can be attributed to higher rates of sexual activity and less effective use of contraceptives. Among Hispanics, the higher rates of adolescent pregnancy result from less effective use of contraceptives (NCHS, 1995c).

A pregnancy can result in one of three outcomes, a live birth, an abortion, or a fetal loss. In 1991, only about half of all pregnancies among adolescents resulted in a live birth. Among black adolescents, 54.9% of all pregnancies ended in a birth, 37.2% in an abortion, and 8.0% in a fetal loss. Among white adolescents, 51.2% of all pregnancies ended in a live birth, 33.5% in an abortion, and 15.3% in a fetal loss (NCHS, 1995c, Table 6).

Adolescent Abortions and Fetal Losses

Among adolescents (aged 15 to 19) in 1991, black adolescents had an induced abortion rate of 80.5, compared to 40.4 among Hispanics, and 28.4 among whites (NCHS, 1995c, Table 5). Among blacks, the abortion rate was 54.9 among 15- to 17-year-olds and 115.7 among 18- to 19-year-olds (NCHS, 1995c, Table 5). Although black adolescents had a higher rate of abortions than white adolescents, they were equally likely to obtain an abortion when pregnant. It has been estimated that in 1991, 33.5% of the pregnancies of white adolescents and 37.2% of the pregnancies of black adolescents ended in an abortion (NCHS, 1995c, Table 6). Only 22.4% of the pregnancies of Hispanic adolescents ended in an abortion. This lower percentage is probably due to the higher rate of Catholicism among this group.

It has been estimated that in 1991, white adolescents had a fetal loss (mostly miscarriages) rate of 13.0, compared to 17.2 for black adolescents, and 33.1 for Hispanic adolescents (NCHS, 1995c, Table 5). Stated in another manner, 8.0% of the pregnancies of black adolescents, 15.3% of the pregnancies of white adolescents, and 18.4% of the pregnancies of Hispanic adolescents ended in a fetal loss (NCHS, 1995c, Table 6).

Consequences of Abortion

Very little research examines long-term differences between adolescents who bear children and those who terminate their pregnancies. Over a 2-year period, Zabin, Hirsch, and Emerson (1989) followed a group of 360 black female adolescents with similar socioeconomic status who had initially sought a pregnancy test. The study investigated whether those who subsequently received abortions were negatively affected by the experience. The relevant comparisons involved girls who obtained an abortion, with those who delivered a baby, and those who had a negative pregnancy test. The findings indicated that after 2 years, those who had an abortion (a) were more likely to graduate from high school or be in school at the appropriate grade level, (b) were less likely to have a subsequent pregnancy, and (c) did not experience psychological stress or anxiety. Their findings indicate that black adolescent females who had an abortion were doing as well or better than those who had a baby or had not been pregnant.

Adolescents' Attitudes Toward Childbearing

Several studies indicate that black adolescents have more positive attitudes about adolescent childbearing than their white counterparts. Black teenage girls are more likely than white teenage girls to favor having their first birth before the age of 20. Furthermore, they also report that the ideal age at first marriage is older than the preferred age for a first birth (Moore, Simms, & Betsey, 1989). Abrahamse, Morrison, and Waite's (1988) study of attitudes toward nonmarital childbearing among a national study of high school sophomore girls indicated that 41% of blacks and 23% of whites would or might consider having a child outside of marriage. Black sophomore girls who were willing to consider a nonmarital birth were also more likely to (a) report that they cut classes, (b) have high levels of absenteeism, and (c) have disciplinary problems in school. In addition, black teenagers who had lower expectations of completing a college education and those in urban war zones who felt that they may be killed at a young age may be more likely to consider a nonmarital birth.

Marsiglio's (1993) analysis of the 1988 National Survey of Adolescent Males asked respondents how they would feel if they became a father. Small race differences indicated that 10% of black males, as opposed to 5% of white males reported that fathering a child would make them feel like a real man. Similarly, blacks adolescents were more likely to indicate that they would feel pleased if they were a father now. Black adolescents who lived in better neighborhood conditions, however, were less likely to view fatherhood as a positive event. For instance, 15% of black males who lived in poor neighborhood conditions, as opposed to 5.1% of blacks males residing in very good neighborhood conditions, reported that they would be very pleased if they got a girl pregnant now (Marsiglio, 1993). Trussell (1988) suggests that the vast majority of unmarried adolescents who become pregnant do not actually intend to do so. The desire to avoid pregnancy is governed by an adolescent's present circumstances and their belief in the future. In large measure, for black adolescents who are in poverty, the benefits of postponing parenthood may not be apparent (Trussell, 1988).

Adolescent Childbearing

In 1994, the overall adolescent birth rate for girls aged 15 to 19 years was 58.9 (NCHS, 1996); for girls aged 15 to 17 years, the rate was 37.6; and for girls 18 to 19 years it was 91.5. In recent years, the birth rates have declined by 3% for both age groups, but they are still as high or higher than they were more than 20 years ago. Recently, it's been suggested that the steady increase in the adolescent birth rate that occurred during the late 1980s may have stopped. The 1994 birth rate for black adolescent girls aged 15 to 19 years (107.7) was more than double that of white adolescents (40.4) (NCHS, 1996, Table A). Since 1991, the birth rate for black adolescents decreased slightly, whereas among whites it has remained relatively stable. Among blacks, girls 10 to 14 years had a birth rate of 4.7, girls 15 to 17 had a rate of 78.6, and among 18- to 19-year-olds, the birth rate was 152.6 (NCHS, 1996).

Between 1992 and 1994, there was a 3% increase in the first birth rate for 15- to 17-year-olds (NCHS, 1996). In addition, in 1994, the first birth rate for older teenagers (aged 18 to 19 years) was 65.6, the highest since 1973. These rates are of concern because they indicate an increase in the proportion of young women who have become first-time mothers. From 1993 to 1994, however, there were considerable declines in the birth rates for second and third children among teenagers. In 1994, the birth rates (live births only) for second and third births was 6.1 and 0.8 among white adolescents, respectively, compared to 23.9 and 6.2 for black adolescents (NCHS, 1996).

In 1994, one quarter (24%) of all women who were first-time mothers were adolescents. Among whites, 18.6% of first births were to teenagers; among blacks, 40.6% were to teenagers (NCHS, 1996). Among blacks, 22% of all births were to adolescents and 31% of all births were to women 20 to 24 years of age. Consequently, among blacks, half of all births were to women 24 years and younger. Among whites, 9.5% of all births were to adolescents and 23% of births were to women 20 to 24 years of age (NCHS, 1996).

The majority of births to teenagers are to unmarried adolescents. In 1994, 95.3% of the births to black adolescents (aged 15 to 19) and 67.6% of the births to white adolescents were to unmarried females (NCHS, 1996, Table 14). These percentages are slightly higher than in 1989 when about half (56%) of white teenage births were to unmarried women, compared to 92% of births to adolescents blacks. This issue is discussed in more detail later in this chapter in the section on nonmarital childbearing.

Adolescent Mothers

A growing body of research has investigated the consequences of pregnancy for adolescent mothers. A National Research Council panel investigating teenage pregnancy and childbearing concluded the following:

> Women who become parents as teenagers are at greater risk of social and economic disadvantage throughout their lives than those who delay childbearing until their twenties. They are less likely to complete their education, to be employed, to earn high wages, and to be happily married; and they are more likely to have larger families and to receive welfare. (Hayes, 1987, p. 138; also cited in Hoffman, Foster, & Furstenberg, 1993a, pp. 5-6; Klepinger, Lundberg, & Plotnick, 1995, p. 23)

Many of the conclusions reached by the National Research Council were based on research conducted by Furstenberg, particularly his 17-year follow-up of a sample of adolescent mothers (mostly black) (Furstenberg, Brooks-Gunn, & Morgan, 1987). Furstenberg et al. (1987) found that many of the adolescent mothers in his sample resumed their education after the birth of the first child, usually 6 years or more following the birth of the child. Educational attainment for this group, however, was still significantly lower than for black women of comparable ages who had postponed childbearing (Furstenberg et al., 1987). Compared to mothers who have children later in life, early childbearers are less likely to find stable employment and are more likely to rely on welfare (Furstenberg, Brooks-Gunn, & Chase-Lansdale, 1989). These differences are most pronounced at younger ages, because many early childbearers recover from these interruptions later in life (Furstenberg et al., 1989). Rates of welfare use among respondents in the Furstenberg et al. (1987) sample decreased substantially as the women reached middle age. Racial variations in the labor force participation of black and white early childbearers indicate that black mothers accumulate more work experience than their white counterparts. Furthermore, differences in the work experiences of early and late childbearers are smaller among blacks than among whites (Hayes, 1987; Hofferth, 1987).

Other more recent work has reached the general conclusion that teenage childbearing has a negative impact on future socioeconomic achievement. Grogger and Bronars (1993) found that among black women, an unplanned teenage birth results in significantly lower rates of high school graduation and labor force participation and higher rates of poverty and welfare recipiency. Furthermore, they argue that the extent of these negative effects is more severe for black women. Ahn (1994) found that having a teenage birth results in a 50% decrease in the likelihood of completing high school. Klepinger et al. (1995) found that having a child before the age of 20 significantly reduces educational attainment by almost 3 years among whites, blacks, and Hispanics. In addition, Kalmuss and Namerow (1994) found that teenage mothers who have a second child 24 months after the first birth, also tend to have poorer educational and economic outcomes than young mothers who delay subsequent childbearing. Overall, this body of research indicates that early childbearing reduces the educational attainment of the mother, lowers her chances of marriage, increases her probability of receiving welfare, and reduces her family income.

This body of research findings indicating that teenage childbearing leads to poorer social and economic outcomes is intuitively plausible and has generally been accepted by both social scientists and the general public (Klepinger et al., 1995). A number of researchers, however, challenge these interpretations and conclusions. Geronimus (1991; Geronimus & Korenman, 1992, 1993), in particular, questions the degree to which teenage childbearing leads to negative social and economic outcomes. Geronimus speculates that early childbearing may be a positive adaptation to adverse economic and health conditions (see the exchange between Geronimus, 1991 and Furstenberg 1991, 1992). Geronimus and others argue that because teenage mothers disproportionately come from relatively disadvantaged socioeconomic backgrounds, teen mothers would likely fare poorly even if they delayed childbearing. Consequently, research on teenage childbearing may overstate the negative consequences of teen childbearing. Recent research that more fully addresses family background and individual differences between early and later childbearers indicates smaller, albeit still negative, effects of teenage childbearing (e.g., Ahn, 1994; Duncan & Hoffman, 1990; Hoffman et al., 1993a; Klepinger et al., 1995). Our assessment of this literature leads us to agree with Hoffman et al. (1993b) that early childbearing often causes harm to already disadvantaged women through a reduction of educational attainment and economic well-being (for a more exhaustive discussion of these issues see the exchanges between Geronimus & Korenman, 1993 and Hoffman et al., 1993a, 1993b).

Adolescent and Nonresident Fathers

Only in the past decade has research and policy related to pregnancy, childbearing, and child rearing focused on the involvement of men. The general absence of information on the role of men hampers a comprehensive understanding of teenage pregnancy and parenting (Lerman, 1986; Parke & Neville,

1987). The emergent literature on black adolescent fathers suggests a greater appreciation for the diversity of this population group in relation to the developmental aspects of adolescence (Parke & Neville, 1987) and their individual enactment of the fatherhood role. Black adolescent fathers, compared to other groups, have distinctly different patterns of fatherhood experiences (i.e., age at paternity, timing of fatherhood in relation to work and educational experiences, number of children, length of fatherhood experience, marital experience). Black adolescent fathers are more likely than Hispanics or whites to have had a nonmarital first birth and are least likely to live with that child (Marsiglio, 1987). Compared to other adolescent fathers, however, blacks are more likely to complete high school (Marsiglio, 1987). Adolescent fathers have a higher probability of living apart from their partner, child, or both than do nonadolescent fathers (Danziger & Nichols-Casebolt, 1988), and this is particularly the case among black adolescent fathers (Lerman, 1986; Marsiglio, 1987). Lerman (1986) found that early fatherhood (prior to age 18) is associated with subsequently living apart from one's child (black and Hispanic fathers become parents at earlier ages than whites). Absent fathers generally come from poorer family backgrounds than do young men who remain childless. For black youth, however, within-group differences in economic background are much smaller than among whites and Hispanics. Black fathers are least likely to marry even among those who live with their children. In addition, young black fathers who live with their children exhibit higher rates of employment than do absent black fathers and childless black men.

Mott (1990) conducted a detailed analysis of father-child contact among a sample of children aged 7 and younger who were born to mothers aged 14 to 25 years. His analysis indicated that overall, white children had higher levels of contact with their father than did black children. Due to the high rates of nonmarital fertility, black fathers were less likely to reside with their children than white fathers; about two-thirds of black children did not have their fathers in the home, as opposed to 28% for nonblack children. Among fathers who did not coreside with their children, black fathers were more likely to live nearby and had higher levels of visitation with their children than white fathers. The higher levels of visitation among nonresident black fathers, however, do not totally compensate for the fact that white children have higher levels of residence with their fathers, and consequently higher levels of contact (Mott, 1990). As children got older, there was some decline in contact between father and child. Finally, among both blacks and whites, father visitation was infrequent when the mother cohabited with a new partner.

Among children who did not live with their fathers, 6 out of 10 had someone who functioned as a father figure in their life. For black children, the father figure is much more likely to be the child's own biological father who visits frequently or some other nonspouse or nonpartner adult living in the household (e.g., uncle). For white children, the father figure is more likely to be a new spouse or partner. Although Mott's (1990) sample is only representative of young black children born to young mothers, it provides valuable insight into the frequency of contact between young children and their nonresident fathers.

Based on the assumption that the partners of teenage girls are teenage boys, much of the attention of research and policy focused on teenage males. It's generally expected that fathers tend to be 1 to 2 years older than the mother (which is consistent with age differences in marriage). Landry and Forrest (1995), however, found that fathers of babies born to adolescent mothers are especially likely to be older. In 1988, 42.4% of fathers of babies born to women aged 15 to 17 years were 20 to 24 years of age and 6.8% were 25 to 29 years of age. Similarly, almost 1 out of 5 mothers 15 to 19 years of age had a partner who was at least 6 years older. Landry and Forrest (1995) argue that programs and policies that aim to increase male involvement in the prevention of pregnancy and sexually transmitted diseases should focus on adolescent boys, as well as older males who are partners of teenage girls. Older male partners tend to be more developmentally similar to teenage fathers, than they are to their age peers (Landry & Forrest, 1995), and many have low levels of educational attainment and labor market participation. Landry and Forrest (1995) argue that, similar to those that help young mothers complete school, programs should be established for fathers to help them become more economically and personally involved in their child's life.

Sexual Prevalence and Contraceptive Use Among Adults

Male Sexuality and Condom Use

Historically, research on sexuality and contraceptive use has focused almost exclusively on women. In the past few years, researchers have begun to intensively examine the prevalence and frequency of male sexual acts and male contraceptive practices. The 1991 National Survey of Men (aged 20 to 39) revealed several race differences in male sexual practices (Billy, Tanfer, Grady, & Klepinger, 1993). Almost all men engaged in vaginal intercourse, but black men had more sexual partners (median 10.2 partners) over the course of their life than white men (median 6.6 partners). A higher percentage of black men (34.7%) than white men (21.8%) had 20 or more partners. White men (21.0%)

had a higher likelihood than black men (13.6%) of ever having anal intercourse. Similarly, white men were more likely to have both ever performed oral sex (78.8% compared to 42.8% for black men) and ever received oral sex (81.0% compared to 62.0% for black men).

Another study using the National Survey of Men found that among sexually active men, 38% of black men and 25% of white men used a condom in the 4-week period prior to the interview (Tanfer, Grady, Klepinger, & Billy, 1993). Among black men, being younger, unmarried, and unmarried without a regular partner increased the likelihood of using a condom. The majority of black men used a condom for birth control and protection against AIDS and other sexually transmitted diseases (Tanfer et al., 1993).

Women's Sexual Prevalence and Contraceptive Practices

Analysis of the 1988 National Survey of Family Growth revealed that among women 15 to 44 years of age, black women (81.5% and 51.5%, respectively) were more likely than white women (33.1% and 41.2%, respectively) to have had more than one sexual partner and 4 or more partners over the course of their lives (Kost & Forrest, 1992). There was no race difference in the percentage of women having six or more partners, although white women (9.0%) were more likely than black women (6.8%) to report having 10 or more partners. These racial differences can probably be attributed to marital status differences. Black women are less likely to be currently married than white women, and nonmarried women had more sexual partners than married women (Kost & Forrest, 1992).

A recent report by the National Center for Health Statistics (NCHS, 1995b) investigated the contraceptive practices of women aged 15 to 44 in the United States. This report used data from the 1982, 1988, and 1990 National Surveys of Family Growth. Information on the use of three new contraceptive methods (i.e., NORPLANT, Depo-Provera, and the vaginal pouch [female condom]) are not available because the survey was conducted before they were introduced in the United States (NCHS, 1995b).

In 1990, 60.5% of white women and 58.7% of black women indicated that they used contraceptives (NCHS, 1995b, Table 4). Among women who were presently not using a contraceptive method, 7.6% of black women and 7.7% of white women had intercourse within the past 3 months. Among women currently using a contraceptive method, the most common type was female sterilization (29.5%), closely followed by the pill (28.5%), condoms (17.7%), male sterilization (12.6%), diaphragm (2.8%), and the IUD (1.4%). Substantial black-white differences in the type of contraceptive used indicated that black women were more likely than white women to use female sterilization (41.0% vs. 27.3%). White women, however, were much more likely to use male sterilization (15.5% vs. 1.3%) (NCHS, 1995b, Table 4). Among black women, there were several notable changes in contraceptive use from 1988 to 1990. The percentage of black women who used condoms increased from 10.1% to 19.4%, whereas the percentage of black women using the pill decreased from 38.1% to 28.5%. In addition, the percentage of black women using female sterilization increased slightly from 1988 (37.8%) to 1990 (41.0%) (NCHS, 1995b, Table 4).

Mosher's (1990) analysis of the 1988 National Survey of Family Growth provides a more detailed picture of differences in contraceptive use among black women. Across all education levels, black women are more likely than white women to indicate that sterilization is their method of contraception. Among black women, however, there are strong educational differences in the type of contraceptive method used. For black women with less than a high school education, the majority use female sterilization (64%), 20% use the pill, and 6% use condoms. Contraceptive usage varies more among black women with 13 or more years of formal education, in which 35% use the pill, 31% use female sterilization, and 12% use condoms (Mosher, 1990).

An analysis of women's (aged 15 to 44) contraceptive use at first premarital intercourse (Mosher & McNally, 1991) revealed an increase in use from 47% in 1975-1979 to 65.4% in 1983-1988. The use of contraceptives at first premarital intercourse is an important indicator of early contraceptive use and, consequently, the risk of premarital pregnancy. For the period 1983-1988, a higher percentage of white women (69.8%) used a contraceptive method than black women (58.0%). Among those who used a contraceptive, black women were more likely to use the pill and white women were more likely to use a condom and withdrawal. Among black women, contraceptive use at first premarital intercourse rose from 34.9% in 1970-1974 to 58.0% in 1983-1988. In addition, among black women, Fundamentalist Protestants had a lower probability of using a contraceptive method (Mosher & McNally, 1991).

It is important to note that there are two objectives of contraception, that is, protection against unwanted pregnancies and protection against sexually transmitted diseases. Couples who place a high priority on minimizing both risks may use two contraceptive methods, because there is currently no method that maximizes protection against both (Cates & Stone, 1992).

Contraceptive Failure

Jones and Forrest (1992), using data from the 1988 National Survey of Family Growth, examined contraceptive failure during the first year of use. Their findings indicated that 26% of women using the rhythm method, 25% of women using spermicide-diaphragm, 15% of women using condoms, and 8% of women using the pill, accidentally became pregnant during the first year of use. Failure rates vary more by age, marital status, race, and poverty status than by method of contraception. This pattern suggests that the failure results from improper and irregular use, rather than from inherent limitations of the contraceptive method. High rates of contraceptive failure substantially contribute to the high levels of unintended pregnancy and abortion (Jones & Forrest, 1992).

An analysis of prior contraceptive use among a sample of abortion patients (Henshaw & Silverman, 1988) found that 91% had used a method of contraception in their lives and 51% were using one in the month in which they conceived. Blacks (41.8%) were less likely than whites (57.6%) to have used a contraceptive method during the month in which they became pregnant and slightly more likely to indicate never using a contraceptive (10.5% vs. 6.2%).

Pregnancy

There were an estimated 6.48 million pregnancies that ended in 1992. This represented a pregnancy rate of 109.9 pregnancies in 1992, which was 3% lower than the 1990 peak (NCHS, 1995c). Differences by age, race, and marital status in the pregnancy rate are only available for 1991. Pregnancy rates for women aged 20 to 24 have consistently been higher than any other age group. Overall, married women have a higher pregnancy rate (117.6) than nonmarried women (103.3), but nonmarried black women have a higher pregnancy rate than married black women (NCHS, 1995c, Table 4). Both black women (174.8) and Hispanic women (167.4) have a much higher pregnancy rate than white women (91.8) (NCHS, 1995c, Table 5) and these differences are evident across all age groups.

As noted previously, a pregnancy can result in a live birth, an abortion, or a fetal loss. Two-thirds (66.5%) of the pregnancies of white women (aged 15 to 44) ended in a live birth, 19.5% ended in an induced abortion, and 14% ended in a fetal loss (NCHS, 1995c, Table 6). Hispanic women have an almost identical distribution of pregnancy outcomes. Among black women, however, only half (50.1%) of all pregnancies ended in a live birth, 37.7% ended in an abortion, and 12.2% ended in a fetal loss (NCHS, 1995c, Table 6).

Attitudes Toward Abortion

Marsiglio and Shehan (1993) reviewed research indicating that blacks are generally less likely than whites to approve of legalized abortion. The lower level of approval by black adults has remained fairly stable over the past 20 years. In the more conservative climate of the 1980s, the attitudes of whites toward legal abortion declined to such a degree that in some studies there were no significant racial differences. There is some evidence that black men may be less approving of abortion than black women, and younger blacks may hold more favorable views of abortion than their older counterparts. The low approval of abortion by blacks has been attributed to (a) higher rates of religious participation, (b) lower socioeconomic status, (c) extended family networks that may provide support for women who bear children outside of marriage, and (d) racial group beliefs that may view abortion as a form of genocide.

Accessibility of Abortion Services

In many developed countries, abortion services are mainly performed in hospitals in the same manner as other minor surgical procedures (Henshaw, 1991). In the United States, however, abortion services have been concentrated in clinics. Although this system works for most women, some women face barriers in seeking abortions. Distance from clinics (27% of nonhospital abortion patients must travel more than 50 miles for services), personal harassment, costs, and the exclusion of women with special medical conditions (27% to 37% of nonhospital abortion clinics will not treat HIV-positive women), represent the most significant barriers (Henshaw, 1991).

Incidence of Abortion

Research by the Alan Guttmacher Institute provides some of the most accurate information on abortions (Henshaw, 1992). Over half of all pregnancies are unintended and one-half of those are terminated by an abortion. In 1988, there were 1.6 million abortions. The majority of women who had abortions were young. One-third of abortions were to women aged 20 to 24 years and 26% were to women under the age of 20 (Henshaw, 1992). Reasons given by women for obtaining an abortion include (a) having a baby would interfere with work, school, or other responsibilities; (b) inability to afford a child; (c) not wanting to be a single parent; or (d) having a baby would create problems with their husband or partner (Torres & Forrest, 1988).

Nonwhite (black and other races) women have much higher abortion rates than do white women (number of abortions per 1,000 women). In 1988, minority women obtained 565,000 abortions or 36% of all abortions. The nonwhite abortion rate of 57 per 1,000 women was 2.7 times the rate of white women (21 abortions per 1,000 women). Since 1980, the abortion rates of white women have remained relatively stable whereas abortion rates for nonwhite women have increased. In 1980, the abortion rate for nonwhite women aged 20 and under and 20 to 24 years were 70.4 and 95.6, respectively. For 1988, the abortion rates for nonwhite women aged 20 and under and 20 to 24 years were 80.1 and 108.5, respectively. Similar to their white counterparts, among nonwhites, younger women had a higher likelihood of having an abortion, with 57% of all abortions among nonwhites occurring among women under the age of 25.

There is an important interaction between race and marital status in obtaining an abortion. Across whites and nonwhites, unmarried women have a higher probability of obtaining an abortion. Married nonwhite women, however, have a higher likelihood of obtaining an abortion than married white women. For instance, in 1987 the abortion rate for unmarried white women (38.2) was 5.5 times that of married white women (6.9), whereas the rate among unmarried minority women (71.1) was 2.6 times that of married minority women (27.6) (Henshaw, Koonin, & Smith, 1992). Racial differences in rates of abortion among married women could be due to the racial differences in female labor force participation (Trent & Powell-Griner, 1991). Married black women have substantially higher rates of labor force participation than married white women; married black women have a greater likelihood of being the primary source of family income (Trent & Powell-Griner, 1991).

Using published and unpublished reports by the Centers for Disease Control and Prevention (CDC) and the Alan Guttmacher Institute, a recent report by the National Center for Health Statistics (NCHS, 1995c) estimated the rate of induced abortions. This report provided some of the first information on abortion that distinguished between blacks and Hispanics and other nonwhite groups. Data in this report indicated that the abortion rate declined 12% (from 29.4 to 25.9) between 1980 and 1992 (NCHS, 1995c). The decline in abortions largely reflects changes in the age distribution of women in the childbearing years. Between 1980 and 1992, the proportion of women aged 18 to 29 (the ages at which abortion rates are highest) obtaining abortions declined from 47% to 39%. Among white women, the abortion rate in 1991 was 17% lower than the rate in 1980; the abortion rate for all other women declined by 6% during the same period.

In 1991, the abortion rate for black women was 65.9, compared to 36.2 for Hispanic women, and 17.9 for white women. An estimated 37.7% of the pregnancies of black women ended in an abortion, compared to 19.5% of the pregnancies of white women and 21.6% of the pregnancies of Hispanic women. Among pregnant black and white adolescents, the likelihood of having an abortion was fairly similar (see previous section on abortions among adolescents). There are, however, some major divergences in abortion rates among women in their 20s and 30s. Among older whites, the percentage of pregnancies that were terminated by an abortion was substantially smaller than among adolescents. For white women in 1991, the percentage of pregnancies terminated by an abortion was 33.5% among adolescents, 14.2% for 25- to 29-year-olds, 12.0% for 30- to 34-year-olds, and 15.6% for 35- to 39-year-olds (NCHS, 1995c, Table 6). Among blacks, however, the percentage of pregnancies terminated by an abortion remains relatively constant across age groups. For instance, the percentage of pregnancies terminated by an abortion was 37.2%, 37.1%, 33.0%, and 36.0% among adolescents, 25- to 29-year-olds, 30- to 34-year-olds, and 35- to 39-year-olds, respectively (NCHS, 1995c, Table 6).

The high rate of abortions among minorities is due to several factors. Overall, minority women are more likely to not use a contraceptive method, to experience contraceptive failure, and, consequently, to have a higher number of unplanned pregnancies. The higher rate of unplanned pregnancies among non-whites results in both a higher rate of abortions and more unplanned births (Henshaw et al., 1992). Race differences in abortion rates are, in part, accounted for by economic status differences, because poorer people tend to have higher abortion rates (Henshaw et al., 1992).

Fetal Loss

Between 1980 and 1992, the fetal loss rate rose 7% from 14.1 to 15.1. This increase reflects a shifting age distribution of women of reproductive age, to ages at which fetal losses are relatively more likely. Most of the fetal losses are miscarriages; relatively few are stillbirths occurring late in pregnancy. Fetal loss early in pregnancy is often not detected. Estimates in the National Center for Health Statistics (1995c) study are of fetal losses from recognized pregnancies. The fetal loss rate in 1991 was 12.9 for white women, 21.3 for black women, and 23.2 for Hispanic women (NCHS, 1995c, Table 5). The percentage of pregnancies ending in fetal loss was fairly consistent across racial groups; 14% of pregnancies end in a fetal loss among whites, 12.2% among blacks, and 13.8% among Hispanics.

Changes in Family Structure

Nonmarital Childbearing

One of the major trends affecting family structure over the past few decades among both blacks and whites is the dramatic increase in the number of births to unmarried women (Farley & Allen, 1987a; Garfinkel & McLanahan, 1986; Jaynes & Williams, 1989; McLanahan & Casper, 1995; U.S. Congress, 1995; Waite, 1995). The number of nonmarital births increased from 89,500 in 1940 to 1,289,592 in 1994 (NCHS, 1996; U.S. Congress, 1995). The nonmarital birth rate, which measures the proportion of unmarried women who have a birth each year, has also increased. The rate rose from 7.1 births per 1,000 unmarried women in 1940 to 46.9 in 1994 (NCHS, 1996; U.S. Congress, 1995).

When discussing nonmarital births, it is important to keep in mind the distinction between nonmarital and teenage childbearing. Nonmarital births refer to births occurring to a woman of any age who is currently unmarried. Teenage childbearing refers to births occurring to teenage women regardless of marital status. Nonmarital births are often discussed as if they were the first births occurring to teenage women, however, there is no typical nonmarital birth. Moore (U.S. Congress, 1995) notes that a nonmarital birth can be first, second, or higher-order births. Nonmarital births can precede a first marriage; they can occur to a parent who never marries; they can occur to a parent whose marriage has ended; or they can occur to a woman who may have previously had one or more births within marriage (U.S. Congress, 1995). In 1993, only 30% of all nonmarital births occurred to teenagers, 35% of nonmarital births were to women aged 20 to 24; 35% were to women 25 and older. Adolescents, however, accounted for about half of all first births to unmarried women (U.S. Congress, 1995). In addition, more than a quarter of nonmarital births occur to cohabiting couples (U.S. Congress, 1995).

Over the past decade, nonmarital childbearing increased more for white women than it did for black women. In 1994, there were 794,261 births to unmarried white woman and 48,315 births to black unmarried women (NCHS, 1996). For white unmarried women, the birth rate in 1994 was 38.3 per 1,000, which is 112% higher than in 1980. In contrast, for black unmarried women, the 1994 birth rate was much higher at 82.1; but this reflects only a 2% higher increase in the rate from 1980. The larger increase in birth rates for white compared to black women resulted in an overall decline in the racial difference in nonmarital birth rates. In 1980, the rate for black women was 4.5 times the rate for white women; in 1994 this differential fell to 2.1 (NCHS, 1996).

For both black and whites, the proportion of all births to unmarried women has substantially increased. Between 1940 and 1994, the nonmarital birth ratio rose from 38 to 326 per 1,000 births. Expressed as a percentage, this means nonmarital births have risen from 3.8% to 32.6% of all births (NCHS, 1996; U.S. Congress, 1995). The increase in the proportion of births to unmarried black women has been particularly dramatic. In 1994, 25% of births to white women and 70% of births to black women were to unmarried mothers (NCHS, 1996, Table 16). The percentage of unmarried births among black women ranges from 95% among adolescents to about 45% among women in their 30s. Consequently, almost half of children born to black women in their 30s are born to an unmarried mother. In contrast, in 1960, the proportion of births to unmarried women among blacks was only 22% (Farley & Allen, 1987a; Jaynes & Williams, 1989). This increase in the percentage of births to unmarried black women resulted from two demographic changes (Farley & Allen, 1987a; Jaynes & Williams, 1989; McLanahan & Casper, 1995; Waite, 1995). First, a greater percentage of black men and women never marry and, for black women who do marry, the age at which they marry has risen and the overall length of time that they are married has shortened (see Marital Patterns section). Consequently, among black women, the length of time in which a nonmarital pregnancy can occur has increased, whereas the period of marital childbearing has shortened. Second, there has been a greater decline in the fertility rate of married black women compared to unmarried black women. The fertility rate of married black women reached an all-time low of 66.9 in 1994 (NCHS, 1996). This difference in fertility rates results in an increase in the percentage of total births to unmarried black women. Therefore, it is erroneous to interpret the increase in the percentage of births to unmarried black women as a rise in their birthrate. In reality, the birthrates of unmarried black women actually declined during the 1970s, and despite some fluctuation during the 1980s, it is almost the same in 1994 as it was in 1980 (Farley & Allen, 1987a, Table 4.1; NCHS, 1993, 1995c).

The increase in nonmarital childbearing is partially due to a decline in the propensity of couples to marry before the birth of the child. Unmarried women who become pregnant had a higher likelihood of marrying before the birth of the child in the 1960s as opposed to the 1980s. For instance, among births to women aged 15 to 34 years old in 1985-1989, 40% were either born or conceived prior to the woman's first marriage, up from 27% in 1960-1964 (U.S. Bureau of the Census, 1991a). Black women are consistently less likely than white women to marry because of a pregnancy. Between 1960 and 1964, about one-third of black women aged 15 to 34 years old who had a premaritally conceived first birth, married before their child was born. This proportion fell to less than 1 in 10 black women between 1985-1989. Between 1960 and 1964, 61% of white women married before their child was born; this figure fell to 34% between 1985-1989 (U.S. Bureau of the Census, 1991a). Consequently, if unmarried pregnant women had married at the same rate in the mid-1980s as they did in the 1960s, the increase in nonmarital births would have been relatively small (U.S. Congress, 1995).

Among whites, a decreasing incidence of adoption has served to increase the number of unmarried women raising children (Bachrach, Stolley, & London, 1992; U.S. Congress, 1995). Between 1965 and 1972, 19% of premarital births were relinquished for adoption, whereas by 1982-1988, only 3% of premarital births were given up for adoption (Bachrach et al., 1992). Among blacks, however, in both the 1960s and the 1980s only 1% or 2% of premarital births were given up for formal adoption.

Nonmarital childbearing is preceded by a series of decisions, including decisions about sexual activity, contraceptive use, abortion, marriage, and adoption. With premarital sex becoming more common among adolescents and young adults, coupled with delayed marriage and increasing rates of marital disruption, the size of the population at risk of having a nonmarital child has increased substantially (U.S. Congress, 1995). Increases in nonmarital childbearing has directly contributed to the high rate of female-headed households.

Female-Headed Families

From 1960 to 1990, there has been an increase among both white and black women in nontraditional family statuses (i.e., dual-earner couples, single-mother families). Black and white women differed primarily in terms of the type of nontraditional family roles they occupied: Whereas white women were primarily in dual-earner families (46% white vs. 26% black), black women were primarily in single-mother families (26% black vs. 7% white) (prevalence of single motherhood as a percentage of all women not of all mothers) (McLanahan & Casper, 1995).

The increase in single-mother families has been one of the most dramatic changes in American families in the past few decades. In 1991, single-mother families accounted for 25.5% of all family groups with children under 18 (U.S. Bureau of the Census, 1992a). Among whites, 19.5% of families were female headed, in comparison to 57.5% of black families, and 29.8% of Hispanic families (U.S. Bureau of the Census, 1992a). Explanations for the increased incidence of single parenthood differ by race. The major source of growth for white women was an increase in the number of formerly married mothers due to increased divorce and decreased remarriage rates. Although this explanation is also true for black women between 1960 to 1970, it does not apply to the growth experienced by this group since 1970. Since 1970, the major source of growth for black women was an increase in the number of never married mothers due to decreases in marriage (McLanahan & Casper, 1995; Waite, 1995; Wojkiewicz, McLanahan, & Garfinkel, 1990). Bumpass and Raley (1995) note that time spent as a single-parent family is longer among blacks than among whites as a consequence of both the lower marriage and remarriage rates and a higher proportion of single-parent periods that commence with a nonmarital birth.

McLanahan and Casper's (1995, pp. 23-25) profile of black single mothers suggest that the typical black single mother is in her early 30s, a high school graduate, and in the labor force. Only 4% were teenagers, less than a third were high school dropouts, and only 37% were not in the labor force. Important education and work experience differences are found among black single mothers. Never married mothers have higher levels of unemployment and are less likely than divorced-separated mothers to complete high school. Among both blacks and whites, never married women tend be more economically vulnerable as a consequence of being younger, less educated, and less likely to be employed. This is a critical distinction because black as opposed to white single mothers are more likely to be never married (McLanahan & Casper, 1995, pp. 23-25). In addition, consistent with declining rates of marriage among black Americans, black women with college degrees were more likely to be single mothers in 1990 than in 1980 (McLanahan & Casper, 1995, p. 26).

High rates of female-headed households are associated with high rates of poverty and economic instability. In both 1994 and 1995, over half of black single-mother households with children under 18 years had incomes below the poverty level (53.2% in 1995, 53.9% in 1994; U.S. Bureau of the Census, 1996e). White single-mother families with children under 18 also had a high poverty rate (35.6% in 1995), although not as high as their black counterparts (U.S. Bureau of the Census, 1996e).

Among both black and whites, married-couple families have the lowest levels of poverty, followed by single-father families and single-mother families. Among blacks, the 1995 poverty rate for families with children under 18 years was 9.9% for married-couple families, 23.4% for single-father families, and 53.2% for single-mother families. An examination of 1994 median incomes for all families (with and without children under 18) similarly demonstrates the advantage of married couples. Among black adults, married couples had a median income of $40,432, compared to $20,977 for single-male households, and $13,943 for single-female households (U.S. Bureau of the Census, 1996a).

Employment status, in conjunction with marital status, is strongly associated with standard of living. McLanahan and Casper's (1995) examination of 1990 census data indicates that among blacks, the poverty rate for married couples with children in which both spouses were employed was only 6% compared to 73% in single-mother families in which the mother was a homemaker. They argue that, controlling for other factors, married women fared better than single women and employed mothers fared better than homemakers. In an international comparison, McLanahan and Casper (1995) found that married-couple families in which the wife is employed have the lowest poverty rates in nearly all countries examined (i.e., Netherlands, Germany, Sweden, Italy, United Kingdom). Families headed by nonemployed single mothers, however, have the highest poverty rates. In addition, single mothers with children in the United States fare much worse relative to most other countries.

Jaynes and Williams (1989, p. 525) and McLanahan and Booth (1989) have identified several mechanisms that explain the disproportionate level of poverty among black female-headed families. First, many black families rely on the income of two employed adults to remain out of poverty. Simply due to its reliance on a sole wage earner, a single-parent family has a higher likelihood of being poor. Second, because black women have lower incomes than black men (Farley & Allen, 1987a) among single-parent families, those with a female head are more likely to be poor than those with a male head. Third, young black women who form single-parent households generally come from poor households and often lack the skills to generate high earnings. Fourth, due to the scarcity of inexpensive child care and lack of health insurance associated with lower status occupations, many black single mothers of young children cannot earn enough from employment to justify working outside the home. Fifth, Aid to Families With Dependent Children (AFDC or welfare) and food stamps accounted for 28% of the income for black female-headed households (Garfinkle & McLanahan, 1986, Table 2); AFDC benefits are recognized to be woefully inadequate. Sixth, child support and alimony payments to single mothers are meager, accounting for only 3.5% of the income of black single mothers (McLanahan & Booth, 1989). Finally, the birth of a child may disrupt the educational or job experiences of the mother and reduce future earnings potential.

Coresident Living Arrangements of Female-Headed Families

Coresident living arrangements, or household extendedness, is more common among blacks and female-headed households. Cross-sectional estimates reveal that about 7% of non-Hispanic white male-headed households and 19.6% of black male-headed families were extended. Among female-headed households, 16.5% of white and 28.2% of black families were extended (Angel & Tienda, 1982; Tienda & Angel, 1982). Data from the 1980 census reveals that black families are more than twice as likely to be extended as white families (Sweet & Bumpass, 1987). Findings from both cross-sectional studies (e.g., Sweet & Bumpass, 1987) and longitudinal designs (e.g., Beck & Beck, 1989) have found that blacks generally are more likely than whites to live in extended family households. Several benefits of residing in extended families have been found such as higher levels of employment among single mothers and the ability to care for an impaired family member. Limitations of residing in an extended family household have also been found such as a lack of privacy and conflicts over child rearing (see Jayakody, 1996 for an extensive discussion of these issues).

Welfare and Black Family Structure

There has been an increasing interest in the economic and demographic literature on the impact of welfare (i.e., AFDC, food stamps, Medicaid, public housing) on family structure (i.e., nonmarital childbearing, divorce, marriage, female-headed households). Research in this area has been particularly concerned with whether the welfare system discourages marriage and encourages female-headed families. Because AFDC benefits are paid to female heads of families with children with no spouse present, there are strong incentives to delay marriage, dissolve a marital union, and have children outside of marriage (Moffit, 1992). Moffit's (1992) impressive review of this literature indicates that none of the studies found a strong relationship between welfare benefits and family structure. The large increases in female-headed households, and nonmarital childbearing evidenced among black families in the past 30 years are not due to welfare benefits, and, consequently, reductions in welfare benefits will not reverse these trends.

Intergenerational Consequences of Female-Headed Households

Several studies have suggested that there are important intergenerational consequences with regard to the subsequent socioeconomic and marital status of children who live with mother-only families compared with two-parent families. These studies indicate that among black children, those who live with their mothers generally do less well on several social indicators than those who live with two parents. Some evidence suggests that black children who reside with one parent are less likely to be in school at the age of 17 and less likely to graduate from high school (McLanahan, 1985). Daughters of black single mothers were at higher risk of establishing a female-headed household by the age of 16, than daughters of two-parent black households (McLanahan, 1988). This risk was increased if the marital disruption of the parents occurred when the child was older (15 to 16) as opposed to younger (12 or less). Controls for income reduced, but did not eliminate the risk of a daughter establishing a single-parent household (McLanahan, 1988). In another analysis (McLanahan & Bumpass, 1988), black daughters who spent part of their childhood in a single-parent family because of marital disruption (i.e., divorce, separation) or because the parent never married, were 36% more likely to have a teenage birth, 52% more likely to have a premarital birth, and 32% more likely to have a marital disruption. The effects of residing in a single-parent family on these various outcomes were much more pronounced among whites than blacks. In addition, Hogan and Kitagawa (1985) found that black adolescent girls from single-parent families were more likely to be sexually active and to have pre-marital births than adolescents from two-parent households.

In a summary of this body of research, McLanahan (McLanahan & Casper, 1995, p. 7) indicates that both black and white children who grow up in single-parent households are, on average, less successful in adulthood than children who grow up with both parents. Even when controlling for differences in parents' socioeconomic status, children of single parents have higher rates of teenage and single motherhood, lower levels of educational attainment, and lower rates of labor force participation. Having a low income accounts for about half of the disadvantage associated with single parenthood; most of the rest is due to too little parental involvement and supervision and high levels of residential mobility.

Crime and Female-Headed Households

Several studies in the criminal justice literature purport that the increase in female-headed households has led to an increase in crime, in particular juvenile offenses (Matsueda & Heimer, 1987; Sampson, 1987). This body of work asserts that part of the overrepresentation of blacks in crime may be explained by the high rate of female-headed households, in particular the lack of a father in households. Single parents may devote less time to supervision and punishment and may be less effective in supervising general youth activities such as "hanging out" that encourage serious delinquency. In addition, one parent may also be less effective than two in observing and questioning strangers and watching over neighbors' property (Matsueda & Heimer, 1987; Sampson, 1987).

Several other studies, however, indicate that there is no relationship between crime and female-headed households. For instance, Austin's (1992) longitudinal analysis of FBI arrest data from 1971 through 1986 found that the increase in female households did not lead to a corresponding increase in juvenile crime. Other work has emphasized that studies that have linked female-headed households with crime ignore the role of extended family members. For instance, Ensminger, Kellam, and Rubin (1983) indicate that mother-grandmother, mother-aunt, and mother-father families are associated with less delinquency among adolescent boys than families in which the mother is the only adult present.

There may be a relationship between female headship and juvenile crime, but this relationship may be more indirect than direct. As stated earlier, female-headed households have a greater likelihood of being poor and poor blacks have a high likelihood of living in central cities where a high percentage of the residents are poor (Ellwood, 1988; Jaynes & Williams, 1989; Wilson, 1987). Neighborhoods that have a high concentration of poverty are characterized by gang activity, high levels of crime, high rates of adolescent pregnancy, and low-quality public schools. Consequently, family structure may be indirectly associated with crime to the degree that female-headed households are poor and live in high-poverty and high-crime neighborhoods.

Single-Father Families

A small, but growing body of research examines single-father families. Overall, the proportion of children who live in single-father families is very small—less than 4% in 1995 (U.S. Bureau of the Census, 1996b). This reflects approximately 13% to 15% of children who lived in single-parent families (Eggebeen, Snyder, & Manning, 1996; McLanahan & Casper, 1995). Although small, single-father families have increased substantially since 1960 when a little more than 1% of all families were headed by a single father. Much of the increase in father-only families took place during the 1980s, when the percentage of children in single-father families increased by 81% (Eggebeen et al., 1996). It has been estimated that about half of the growth in single-father families is a consequence of cohabitation, and half reflects a real change of exclusive coresidence with fathers (Garasky & Meyer, 1996). Black children are slightly more likely to reside in single-father families than white children (Eggebeen et al., 1996).

Eggebeen et al.'s (1996) review of the literature on single fathers indicates that single fathers have a distinct demographic profile from both men in married-couple families and women in mother-only families. Single-father families tend to fare better than single-mother families, but worse than married-couple families in terms of rates of poverty and labor force participation. Single fathers generally are not as young as single mothers, but are younger than married fathers. Lastly, single fathers are more likely than married fathers, but less likely than single mothers to live in extended family households.

McLanahan and Casper's (1995) demographic profile of black single fathers indicated that in 1990, over half (52%) of black single fathers were never married, 32% were high school dropouts, 31% completed at least some college, 65% were employed, and 29% were cohabiting. One of the major differences between black and white single-father families is that, consistent with the black-white differences in marriage, black single fathers were more likely to be never married (52% black vs. 19% white), whereas white single fathers were more likely to be divorced or separated (white 72% vs. black 42%). Fully 8 out of 10 single black fathers reported that they resided in either a subfamily (40%), a cohabiting relationship (29%), or with a related adult (e.g. brother, sister; 11%). Consequently, the majority of single black fathers did not have the sole responsibility for child rearing (McLanahan & Casper, 1995).

An examination of recent census data indicates that black single-father families with children under 18 had a slightly higher poverty rate (23.4% in 1995) than their white counterparts (18.4%; U.S. Bureau of the Census, 1996e). From 1994 to 1995, there was a large 11% decrease in the poverty rate among black single-father families with children under 18 years (1994 at 34.6% vs. 1995 at 23.4%). It is only by virtue of this decrease in the poverty rate among black single-father families that their poverty rates were comparable to white single-father families in 1995.

Marital Patterns of Black Americans

Marriage is a fundamental feature of family structure and is an area that has undergone quite dramatic change among African Americans in recent decades. This section reviews changing marital status patterns among black Americans and includes discussions of marriage (including interracial marriage), separation, divorce, widowhood, and remarriage. This discussion also presents theories regarding the nature of changing marital patterns.

Marriage

Examination of African American marital trends should be viewed within the context of the very significant recent changes that have characterized

American patterns of family formation more generally. Since 1900, marriage behavior in the United States has fluctuated greatly, with the 1950s, a period characterized by early marriage and greater marital prevalence, being especially aberrant (Cherlin, 1992). Yet, the reversals since that time have been dramatic (Waite, 1995). During this period there has been an increasing divergence in the marital status profiles of black and white adults. In 1950, black adults were more likely than white adults to be unmarried, but these differences were modest. Since 1950, the percentage of adults who are unmarried has increased among both blacks and whites. The growth in the proportion of black Americans who are unmarried, however, was very dramatic. In 1993, 61% of black women and 58% of black men were not currently married, compared with 41% of white women and 38% of white men. Among black adults, a great portion of the decline in marriage occurred because of a dramatic increase in the proportion of never marrieds. In 1993, 46% of black men and 39% of black women had never married. Among whites, however, the increase in the proportion of unmarried adults was the result of increases in divorce and declines in remarriage.

The marriage gap between blacks and whites is just as evident among both childless and women with children. Among women 18 to 55 years of age, regardless of parental status, white women are twice as likely as black women to be married (McLanahan & Casper, 1995). McLanahan and Casper (1995) argue that because the marriage differential between white and black women is equally high for nonmothers as for mothers, whatever is causing black women to forego marriage is affecting all women, not just mothers. This finding contradicts the argument that welfare benefits are a major cause of the racial difference in marriage. Although welfare might explain why women with children may forego marriage, it fails to explain why childless women would behave in a similar fashion (McLanahan & Casper, 1995, p. 19). (See Tucker and Mitchell- Kernan, 1995a for a more detailed analysis of family formation trends from 1940 to 1990.)

Separation, Reconciliation, and Divorce

Black Americans are much more likely than whites to have a marital disruption through either a separation or a divorce. Furthermore, black husbands and wives separate sooner than white husbands and wives, but take more than twice as long to divorce (NCHS, 1995a). Sweet & Bumpass (1987) provide a detailed analysis of black-white differences in the length of separation. Whereas 63% of whites divorce within a year of separating and 84% divorce within 2 years, only 28% of blacks divorce within a year of separating and only

42% do so 2 years later. Even after 4 years, almost half of all separated black women are not divorced. Some suggest this race difference reflects differing proportions of the population able to afford the cost of divorce, or differences in the proportion of the population with substantial economic assets to divide. This black-white difference, however, is unaltered when education and other variables are controlled (Sweet & Bumpass, 1987). Sweet and Bumpass argue that individuals who have low probabilities of remarriage have less incentive to finalize a marital separation with a divorce. Because black women are more likely to separate, and because they remain separated longer, at any one time there is a greater proportion of black women who are currently separated than white women (Cherlin, 1992).

Recently, researchers have begun to examine the issue of marital reconciliation after a separation. Wineberg and McCarthy (1993), using data from the National Survey of Families and Households, found that among women whose first marriage had ended, about 30% reported that at some stage in the process of dissolving the marriage they separated and reconciled before dissolving the marriage. In addition, multiple reconciliations are not unusual, with more than half of the women who attempted a reconciliation having at least two reconciliations. Among currently married women, about 9% of whites and 14% of blacks had separated and reconciled in their marriage (Wineberg & McCarthy, 1993). In a more recent analysis, Wineberg (1996) found that approximately one-fourth of black women attempting a marital reconciliation were still married a year after the reconciliation began.

There has been a slow, steady increase in the annual rate of divorce since about 1860. The 1950s were a departure from this long-term trend, showing annual divorce rates lower than what would have been expected given the long-term rise. Then, starting in 1962, the divorce rate rose sharply and continued to increase until the late 1970s. Although the rising divorce rates of the 1960s and 1970s were in keeping with the long-term trend, they were higher than would have been predicted (Cherlin, 1992). By 1982, the divorce rate had leveled off and even shown a slight decline, the first decline since 1962 (Thornton & Freedman, 1983). McLanahan and Casper (1995) argue that the leveling off of the divorce rate in the 1980s is based on three factors: (a) the increase in the average age at first marriage; (b) the baby boom cohorts had reached middle age and passed through the period in which they had the highest likelihood of getting a divorce; and (c) due to an increase in cohabitation, the couples who did marry were likely to be the most committed. Consequently, the leveling of the divorce rate in the 1980s was not necessarily an indicator of greater marital stability (McLanahan & Casper, 1995).

In 1990, there were 1.182 million divorcing couples (NCHS, 1995a). This was the highest number of divorces since 1985 (1.19 million), but lower than the peak number in 1981 (1.213 million). Approximately 2% of the population divorced in 1990. The 1990 divorce rates for black men and women were nearly 30% and 20% higher, respectively, than for white men and women. The divorce rate was 22.6 for black men, 22.8 for black women, 19.1 for white men, and 19.1 for white women (NCHS, 1995a, Table 13). One analysis indicated that even among women who attended college and who neither married early or had a premarital birth, the risk of divorce was twice as high for blacks as for whites (Martin & Bumpass, 1989). The higher rates of divorce among black adults are reflected in their current marital status. In 1995, 11.6% of black women were divorced, compared to 9.6% of white women, 7.8% of black men, and 7.6% of white men (U.S. Bureau of the Census, 1996c).

Divorce is more frequent among couples who are under the age of 40 than for older married men and women (NCHS, 1995a). Among whites, the divorce rates were at their peak for 15- to 24-year-olds and declined steadily with increasing age. Among blacks, the divorce rate peaked at 25 to 29 years of age and steadily declined with decreasing age. This delayed peak among blacks probably reflects the older age of blacks at the time of marriage, in conjunction with the longer length of separation among black adult couples (NCHS, 1995a).

Black wives are more likely than white wives to get sole custody of their children (aged 17 and under; NCHS, 1995a). In 1990, roughly 87% of black wives received sole custody, 5% received joint custody, and in 6% of the cases the husband received sole custody. For white wives, however, 71% received sole custody, 17% joint custody, and the husband received sole custody in 10% of the cases. In 2% of divorce cases of black and white couples, neither the wife nor the husband was granted custody (NCHS, 1995a, Table 20). The increase in divorce in conjunction with both the delay and decline in marriage has led to a dramatic rise in the ratio of divorced to married people among both whites and blacks. In 1960, there were 62 divorced blacks for every 1,000 married black men and women. By 1990, this number had risen fourfold to 282 (McLanahan & Casper, 1995, Figure 1.2). In addition, the ratio of divorced to married people is twice as large for blacks (282) as for whites (133). McLanahan and Casper further argue that the increase in the divorce ratio may have a feedback effect on marriage. They argue that by increasing the opportunity that divorced people may interact with single and married people, a high divorce ratio makes divorce more acceptable and marriage more uncertain.

Remarriage

There are large race and gender differences in the likelihood of remarriage. Men are more likely to remarry than women, and whites are more likely to remarry than blacks. Of the four race-gender groups, white men have the highest probability of remarriage followed by white women, black men, and black women. Sweet and Bumpass (1987) found that almost three out of four white women compared to only one-third of black women are remarried within 10 years of separation. Black women who (a) are separated when they are older than 35, (b) have 3 or more children, and (c) have less than 12 years of formal education, have a decreased probability of remarrying than their counterparts (Smock, 1990). The vast majority of black women who have not completed high school have not remarried after 10 years of separation from their spouse. Only among black women who have attended college is remarriage somewhat common and even this group has a lower probability of remarrying than white women (Smock, 1990).

As noted earlier, the probability of remarriage declines appreciably among those who separate when they are older. These age differences are more pronounced among women than men. Older men are more likely to be remarried than older women. This is due in part to the tendency for men to marry women who are younger than themselves, which in turn creates an increasingly disadvantageous marriage market for women as they age (Sweet & Bumpass, 1987).

Cohabitation

Since the mid-1960s, marriage rates have been in decline, and more recently, rates of remarriage have also decreased. These trends (i.e., declines in rates of marriage and remarriage) do not mean, however, that individuals are not involved in domestic unions. The sharp declines in marriage and remarriage have been offset by an increase in rates of cohabitation—couples of the opposite sex sharing a household, who are not married to each other, and who have a marriage-like relationship (Bumpass, Sweet, & Cherlin, 1991). Currently, young people establish cohabiting households at ages that are roughly comparable to those at which previous generations entered into marital unions, although cohabiting couples tend to be slightly older (Bumpass, 1990). During the past 25 years, cohabitation has been transformed from a rare and socially disapproved behavior to a central feature of the life course (Thornton, 1988) that is experienced by the majority of people. Cohabitation has increased among persons of all ages and marital statuses, especially among the young and divorced (Thornton & Freedman, 1983), and has become a central feature of the life course of many Americans. In the late 1980s, almost half of first marriages were preceded by cohabitation (Bumpass & Raley, 1995). Consequently, any discussion of marriage in contemporary American society must address the issue of cohabitation (Waite, 1995).

McLanahan and Casper's (1995) analysis indicated that in 1960 and 1970, about 2% of unmarried adults were cohabiting. After 1970, the percentage of cohabiting couples increased rapidly. Between 1980 and 1990, it grew from 5.3% to 7.9% among unmarried men and from 4.3% to 6.6% among unmarried women. Among single mothers, 7% of white and Hispanic single mothers and 5% of black single mothers were cohabiting in 1990.

Examining data from the first two waves of the National Survey of Families and Households (1987-1988 and 1992-1994), Waite (1995) suggests that even during this short period there were substantial increases in cohabitation. In the late 1980s, about 7% of persons 25 to 29 years of age lived in a cohabiting relationship. By the early 1950s this figure had risen to about 13%. During the prime ages of union formation—ages 25 to 34—between 20% and 24% of unmarried adults are cohabiting.

In one of the first major studies of cohabitation, Bumpass and Sweet (1989) found that one-sixth of the population 19 years and over had cohabited before marriage, and about a quarter had cohabited at some point in time. Of persons marrying between 1980 and 1984, 34% had lived with their spouse before marriage and an additional 5% had lived with someone else in addition to their spouse (Bumpass & Sweet, 1989). Of couples who began their cohabitation between 1975 and 1984, 60% of cohabiting relationships were likely to result in marriage. If cohabitation leads to marriage, it does so rather quickly. About a quarter of cohabiting couples marry within a year and about half marry within 3 years (Bumpass & Sweet, 1989). Even though cohabitation is an important transition state, marriage still represents the bulk of union experiences (Thornton, 1988).

Census data indicates there were approximately 3.3 million cohabiting couples in 1992, and one-third of these households had children under 15 years of age present (U.S. Bureau of the Census, 1992e). The majority of partners in cohabiting relationships have never been married (57%), 33% are divorced, 6% are married with spouse absent, and 4% are widowed (U.S. Bureau of the Census, 1992e). Part of the increase in the number of unmarried-couple households can be attributed to the changing age structure of the population. That is, there was an increase in the number of young adults (who are more inclined to cohabit) in the population compared to other age groups. Increases in rates of cohabitation can also be attributed to more accurate reports of living situations (i.e., admission of unmarried status). The overall increase, however, is far too large to be explained by these factors alone (Cherlin, 1992). Other plausible explanations are that increases in cohabitation are linked to high divorce rates. Due to high divorce rates, couples may decide to "try out" a relationship before committing to marriage. Alternatively, couples may be more likely to cohabit because of a weakening of societal restrictions against living together. Related to this, a common assumption about cohabitation is that it occurs mainly among college students. Individuals with lower levels of education, however, are more likely to cohabit than college students (Bumpass & Sweet, 1989).

There is a considerable debate as to whether cohabitation is a precursor to marriage, a substitute for marriage, or simply a more serious boyfriend-girlfriend relationship (McLanahan & Casper, 1995). Cohabiting unions are less stable than legal marriages and of much shorter duration (Bumpass, Sweet, & Cherlin, 1991). For instance, about 1 of 10 cohabitors do not plan to marry their current partner (McLanahan & Casper, 1995). Census data revealed that among women between the ages of 15 and 44, 33.6% of whites and 35% of blacks had cohabited. For white women, 54.4% of their first cohabitation experiences resulted in marriage, 10.3% of the relationships were still intact, and 35.4% of cohabiting relationships had ended. Among black women, 42.1% of the first cohabitation experiences ended in marriage, 9.2% were still intact, and 48.7% were terminated (NCHS, 1988). Cohabitors tend to move rather quickly into either marriage or disruption of the partnership. Consequently, although a sizable proportion of adults have cohabited, cohabitation appears to be a relatively short-lived stage in the life cycle for most adults (Waite, 1995).

One might assume that marriages preceded by cohabitation would be less likely to dissolve because of terminations of unsuitable matches before marriage, as well as the generally older age at marriage. The proportion of couples separating or divorcing within 10 years of marriage, however, is a third higher among those who lived together before marriage than among those who did not (Bumpass & Sweet, 1989). This does not mean that cohabitation leads to higher divorce rates. Rather, men and women who cohabit have less traditional views of marriage and are more approving of divorce (Axinn & Thornton, 1992).

McLanahan and Casper (1995) found that for both blacks and whites, cohabiting couples (aged 30 to 34) have less traditional relationships than married couples. Women in cohabiting relationships were more likely than married women to (a) have more education than their partners, (b) be the primary breadwinners, and (c) be considered the head of the household. Black cohabiting couples were, however, much more likely than white cohabiting couples to have children (McLanahan & Casper, 1995, Table 1.8). McLanahan and Casper argue that because parenthood is becoming relatively common among black cohabiting couples, it may suggest that, in black communities to a greater extent than is the case in white communities, cohabitation has become a substitute for marriage.

Recently, it has been argued that any measure of marital status should include cohabitation. When cohabitation is not assessed, families in which both parents share a household, but are not married are erroneously classified as single-parent families (i.e., children born to cohabiting couples are in two-parent families). This misclassification was an inadvertent consequence of survey procedures that were developed before the increase in cohabitation (Bianchi, 1995; Bumpass & Raley, 1995). Bumpass and Raley (Bumpass & Raley, 1995; Bumpass, Raley, & Sweet, 1995) argue forcefully for the inclusion of cohabitation in marital status designations and that cohabitation, in conjunction with divorce and nonmarital childbearing, is changing the family experience. Furthermore, traditional definitions of families limit our understanding of contemporary family life. For example, step families that are defined solely in terms of marriage underestimate the true extent of the step family experience. Children whose biological parents have divorced become members of a step family when their mother begins a cohabiting relationship. Children within cohabiting households, whether after a nonmarital birth or a marital dissolution, are likely to spend less time in a true single-parent family than we would expect from changes in marital status alone. One-third of white mothers and more than half of black mothers will share a household with their children and a partner who is not the children's father. When step families that are defined by nonmarital cohabitation are included in the figures for step families generally, about one quarter of white children and two-fifths of black children will live in a step family. Despite the lower rates of marriage and remarriage for blacks compared to whites (Bumpass, Raley, & Sweet, 1995), a higher proportion of black mothers and children will spend some time in a step family.

Widowhood

Sweet and Bumpass (1987) provide some of the most detailed information on the correlates of widowhood. Their analysis of 1980 census data (Table 5.14) revealed that women are more likely to be widowed than men and black women had a much higher incidence of widowhood than white women. Among women aged 40 to 44 years, 9.0% of black women's first marriage ended in widowhood as opposed to 3.7% for white women. Similarly, among women aged 50 to 54, 55 to 59, 60 to 64, and 65 to 69, the percentage of black women whose first marriage had ended in widowhood was 20.0%, 25.2%, 34.3%, and 45.7%, respectively; corresponding percentages for white women were 10.5%, 16.5%, 25.4%, and 36.5%. The present rates of widowhood are consistent with these patterns. Data from the 1995 current population surveys reveal that black women between the ages of 35 to 44, 45 to 54, and 55 to 64 years are twice as likely as white women to be widows. The respective percentages of black women who were widows was 2.4% (age 35 to 44), 8.3% (age 45 to 54), and 24% (age 55 to 64). This compares to 1.0%, 3.4%, and 11.2% among white women (U.S. Bureau of the Census, 1996c). These large racial differences in widowhood are due to a combination of the higher incidence of male mortality among blacks and the much larger age differences between spouses among blacks than whites.

Corresponding education differences in the rates of widowhood among black adults reflect the fact that mortality rates are inversely associated with educational level. Sweet and Bumpass (1987) found that for black women with 16 or more years of education, the percentage whose first marriage ended in widowhood among those aged 45 to 49, 55 to 59, and 65 to 69 years, was 8.5%, 18.7%, and 36.6%, respectively. Corresponding percentages for black women with less than 9 years of education were 18.0%, 29.7%, and 48.8%. In addition, consistent with research on remarriage, black middle-aged widows have a lower rate of remarriage than their white counterparts (Smith, Dick, & Duncan, 1991).

Marriage and Elderly Adults

The outlook for marriage in older age among presently younger cohorts of black adults is fairly bleak. As noted earlier, blacks in general marry later, have higher rates of separation, divorce, and widowhood, and are less likely to remarry. Although being unmarried is not unusual among elderly white women, it is almost normative among elderly black women. Being unmarried in older age has implications for informal social support networks, living arrangements, and income adequacy. For instance, spouses are a critical component of the informal support networks of elderly blacks and married elderly have larger networks than unmarried elderly (Chatters, Taylor, & Jackson, 1985). In addition, middle-aged and older black female heads of households may have heavy family responsibilities because their own daughters have children out-of-wedlock and continue to need support (Worabey & Angel, 1990). With regard to living arrangements, in the past few decades increasing percentages of elderly black women live alone. This increasing tendency to live alone may lead to greater institutionalization, because living alone is an important predictor of nursing home use (although to date few elderly blacks live in nursing homes). Last, although older blacks generally suffer from a high degree of poverty, married couples have a lower incidence of poverty than their unmarried counterparts (Taylor & Chatters, 1988). In particular, older black women who live alone have an exceptionally high incidence of poverty, with more than half of this group living in poverty (Taylor & Chatters, 1988). Higher rates of marital disruption, increased longevity, and differential morality between men and women ensure that the population of elderly black women will continue to grow (Worobey & Angel, 1990). This increase in the percentage of single women among future cohorts of older blacks may signal corresponding decreases in the size of informal support networks, and increases in poverty, living alone, and nursing home use (see Tucker, Taylor, & Mitchell-Kernan, 1993).

Interracial Marriage

Until recently, interracial marriage involving African Americans has been relatively rare, a situation owing in part to laws against marriage between whites and other races, which existed at one time in most U.S. states until banned by a 1967 Supreme Court ruling. Over the past several decades, however, substantial increases in interracial marriage have been evident. In 1970, interracial unions represented less than 1% of all marriages involving black men or women (U.S. Bureau of the Census, 1986). By 1994, the *Current Population Survey* indicated that the interracial marriage percentage among blacks had increased to 7.7% (U.S. Bureau of the Census, 1994a, 1994b). The census bureau (1992a, 1992b) cautions that sampling variability may be high for surveys of small groups. Nevertheless, these overall figures overshadow significant geographic variation in intermarriage. In 1980, intermarriage rates among blacks ranged from .6% among black females in the South to 12.3% among black males in the West (U.S. Bureau of the Census, 1985). Furthermore, outmarriage in the West has risen dramatically, such that one out of every six black men in the West who first married between 1970 and 1980 married a woman of another race (Tucker & Mitchell-Kernan, 1990; U.S. Bureau of the Census, 1985). Although regional marital characteristics data from the 1990 census have not yet been released, we would expect significant increases in intermarriage in all major regions of the country.

Overall, as well as by region, black female intermarriage remains about one quarter the male level. Lieberson and Waters (1988) used 1980 census data to calculate odds ratios representing the tendency to marry in one's ethnic group versus marrying out of one's ethnic group (i.e., percentage in/percentage out) and determined that black women have the highest overall odds of any ethnic group in the United States of marrying someone of the same race when they marry for the first time: 32,998 (compared to 3,468 for Puerto Rican women; 743 for Mexican women; and 16 for American Indian women). The odds, however, of black women under 25 years of age marrying a black man drops to 8,602 (in contrast to a ratio of 115,660 for black women aged 55 to 64 years), demonstrating a substantial increase in interracial marriage among younger cohorts.

Tucker and Mitchell-Kernan (1990) examined structural factors associated with black interracial marriage using 1980 census data for Los Angeles County (where black outmarriage is relatively high). They found that the predictors of interracial marriage were virtually identical for men and women. Interracially married blacks compared to those who married within the race tended to be younger, more likely to have been married previously, and had greater spousal age differences (both younger and older). In addition, interracial marriage seemed to be associated with living away from your place of birth coupled with having been raised in a more racially tolerant region of the country. These findings suggested that social control factors (from the community of origin) still strongly supports African American marriage within the race. Schoen and Wooldredge (1989), examining marriage choices in North Carolina and Virgina, found a greater likelihood of intermarriage among higher-educated black men, which the authors viewed as support for the disputed, but long-standing, notion that black grooms exchange higher socioeconomic status for their white bride's higher racial "caste" status (Davis, 1941; Merton, 1941).

Interracial marriage has implications for mate availability, particularly in the West where outmarriage among black men is relatively high and greatly exceeds the female rate. More recent evidence from a representative survey of southern California residents suggests that one response to greater outmarriage and interracial dating among black men may be an increased level of interracial dating among black women. Tucker and Mitchell-Kernan (1995b) found that nearly 90% of African American male respondents had dated interracially at least once (compared to two-thirds of white males and 80% of Latinos). Although women were less inclined to date outside their ethnic group than men, over 60% of black women had also dated interracially, compared to just over half of white women and Latinas. Moreover, interracial dating was associated with lower levels of loneliness in black women. These results suggest that as black women find themselves in situations where the availability of black men is constrained (due to demographic shortages, financial barriers, or interracial marriage and dating), they may begin to look elsewhere for partners.

Theories of Causation of the Declining Rates of Marriage

Rapidly changing patterns of marriage and marital dissolution among African Americans, particularly women, have spawned a renewed focus on the determinants of marriage behavior. Tucker and Mitchell-Kernan (1995a) recently reviewed work on the two dominant conceptual themes guiding research in this area: the impact of sex ratio imbalances on family formation behavior and the impact of the decreasing economic viability of black men on marriage. A summary of their observations follows.

Gender Imbalance

Since the 1920s, there has been a gradual significant decline in the overall African American sex ratio (i.e., number of men per 100 women). This change, which has been more dramatic in recent decades, has been cited by a number of theorists as a factor in black marital decline (Jackson, 1971; McQueen, 1979; Staples, 1981a, 1981b; Tucker & Mitchell-Kernan, 1995a), and has led some to consider the issue of broader mate selection standards among black women (Spanier & Glick, 1980). This growing disparity between the number of males and females is caused by higher male mortality across the life span, coupled with increased female longevity. Guttentag and Secord (1983) presented the controversial argument that societies evidencing different sex ratios exhibited strikingly different patterns of social organization and marital values. Shortages of men, in particular, were associated with more singlehood, divorce, "out-of-wedlock" births, adultery, and transient relationships; less commitment among men to relationships; lower societal value on marriage and the family; and a rise in feminism. They also suggested that the extended male shortage in the African American population is a major contributor to black marital decline and increasing extramarital childbearing. Secord and Ghee (1986) argue further that an imbalanced black marriage market destabilizes existing relationships, because viable alternatives are readily available to the gender that is in short supply.

Skepticism about the degree to which sex ratios have fueled African American marital decline has been voiced. For example, Epenshade (1985) noted that black sex ratios have declined since 1920, whereas marital decline began in the 1960s. Yet, there is empirical evidence of an association between sex ratios and black marital behavior (e.g., Darity & Myers, 1995; Kiecolt & Fossett, 1995; Sampson, 1995; Tucker, 1987).

Economic Conditions

Observers of black family formation trends have also focused on the declining economic condition of African American males. With the decline in the industrial sector, which provided opportunities to men without higher education, many black males are less attractive as potential husbands and less confident about their ability to support a family (Darity & Myers, 1986/1987; Wilson, 1987). There is empirical support for this hypothesis (Darity & Myers, 1995; Lichter, LeClere, & McLaughlin, 1991; Lichter, McLaughlin, Kephart, & Landry, 1992; Testa, Astone, Krogh, & Neckerman, 1989; Tucker & Taylor, 1989). Yet it is clear from these studies and others (notably Mare & Winship, 1991) that socioeconomic factors do not completely explain the substantial marital decline of the past 30 years.

Other economic explanations for marital decline have been offered, including the growing disparity between black male and female income levels and the increased economic independence of women generally. Empirical support for these theories has been rather equivocal, however. For example, the most economically independent women, black women that is, those who are most highly educated, tend to be more likely to marry than less educated women.

Tucker and Mitchell-Kernan (1995a) concluded that there is strong evidence, at both individual and aggregate levels, implicating both sex ratios and male employment as factors in African American family formation. There is also evidence that the effects of sex ratio and employment on black family structure are more pronounced under conditions of impoverishment. That is to say, the lower the sex ratio and the lower the male employment rate the higher the rate of female-headed families with children and in poverty (Sampson, 1995). One of the studies included in their book examined the marital process and found provider role anxiety to be a major contributor to marital instability among blacks (Hatchett, Veroff, & Douvan, 1995). As the authors recently observed, "It seems likely that the historically unstable economic situation of black couples, within a culture that exalts male economic dominance, has placed special strains on black marriage, thereby contributing to the very high divorce rate noted above" (Tucker & Mitchell-Kernan, 1995a). Although the gender imbalance and economic arguments have dominated discussions about recent changes in black marriage behavior, it seems likely that other societal phenomena are implicated in changes that have taken place, as well. These include the greater availability of contraceptives and abortion and broad society-wide shifts in cultural values related to family formation.

Conclusion

The volume of data reported in this chapter makes the development of a conclusion section a formidable task. Several general concluding remarks can be offered, however, relating to the areas of human services practice, social policy, and family research. Several of these comments are drawn from examples presented in the body of the chapter. These concluding remarks serve to underscore general features and themes of this research in ways that may facilitate a broader understanding of the status and functioning of black families.

The vast demographic changes affecting American families over the past 30 years (i.e., cohabitation, nonmarital births, delays in marriage formation, marriage dissolution, remarriage, and blended families) have occasioned a fundamental rethinking of assumptions about the family, particularly with regard to structure and membership. Theories that are grounded in minority family experiences (e.g., blacks and Latinos) have traditionally considered issues of plurality and diversity in family structure. In contrast, changing demographic profiles of the "typical" American family (i.e., white, middle class) are only now transforming the notion of what constitutes family within mainstream family theory. Family researchers, human services practitioners, and social policy analysts are finding that even among white Americans, the "typical" family is elusive.

This review of the literature demonstrates that family phenomena are related to one another in subtle and complex ways. A number of the issues addressed in this chapter are either direct or indirect consequences of the declining rates of marriage among black Americans. Fewer marriages among blacks lead to higher rates of nonmarital childbearing and female-headed households. As noted previously, increases in female-headed households lead to lower percentages of children living with both parents, increases in the percentage of children living in households with below poverty level incomes, and potentially higher rates of child neglect and foster home use.

It is important to recognize, however, that if the family and employment patterns of blacks more closely resembled those of whites, several of the concerns identified in this review would be reduced, but not completely alleviated. Hogan and Lichter (1995) indicate that even if black children lived in two-parent families in the same proportion as whites and had parents exhibiting work patterns (e.g., duration and stability of work histories) similar to those of whites, black poverty rates would still be double those of whites (20% vs. 11%). Consequently, the remaining differential in poverty rates is attributable to the persistent effects of racial discrimination and stratification of the labor market. Under conditions of comparable family and work patterns, however, the poverty rate for black children would be only one half of what it actually was in 1990 (Hogan & Lichter, 1995). Government efforts to address racial disparities in education and job opportunities have been successful in reducing these differences and improving the social and economic well-being of black families and children. Continued focus on these approaches offers viable strategies for addressing these persistent differences in the status of black and white families.

This chapter has discussed a number of problematic issues and concerns facing poor black families that deserve our continued efforts for resolution. Whereas recent social policy debate has centered on national- and state-level initiates to reform welfare, human services have provided a number of local, community-level programs involving social workers and other helping professionals that have been shown to be quite effective. For instance, Project Redirection, a 5-year follow-up of those who had participated in a comprehensive program of services for teenage mothers demonstrated several long-term benefits (Polit, 1989). In comparison to a group of young mothers who did not participate, program participants had better employment records, higher average earnings, and lower levels of welfare dependency. Participation in this program also improved parenting skills, as indicated by higher scores on a parenting evaluation and an increased likelihood to breast feed their infants and to enroll their children in a Head Start Program. In addition, the children of program participants had higher levels of cognitive, social, and emotional development than their comparison group counterparts. Project Redirection is one example of the many successful programs that have assisted black adolescent mothers (Polit, 1989).

This review of the status and functioning of black families also demonstrates the successes of national programs and policies directed to poor families. Recognizing that many of the problems encountered by black children and adolescents are influenced by state and national policies, social workers have been effective advocates for social policies that benefit black children and adolescents. For example, child poverty rates would be much more severe in the absence of programs such as Head Start, Food Stamps, Medicaid, and Low-Income Energy Assistance (Danziger & Danziger, 1993). Although conservative rhetoric blames poverty on government programs that foster dependency, the European experience suggests that the high child poverty rate in the United States results from spending too little on children (Danziger & Danziger, 1993).

Improving the social situation of black children and adolescents calls for an integrated set of programs, including subsidies to working poor families, greater access to subsidized day care and health care, expanded support services for children and their parents, and the provision of employment op-portunities for those unable to find jobs (Danziger & Danziger, 1993). Conse-quently, those who care about families should advocate a comprehensive set of policies that support poor black mothers and fathers in their efforts to take greater responsibility as parents and workers. Program supports of this type provide parents with the skills and resources that allow them to better provide for the emotional and financial support of their children (Danziger & Danzi-ger, 1993).

This chapter has investigated a number of major demographic trends that black families have undergone over the past 30 years. Several of these demo-graphic trends reflect and give rise to important social problems that currently confront wide segments of the black population. Any comprehensive review of the literature must include a critical discussion of these issues and their im-plications for the structure and functioning of black families. It is equally im-portant, however, to understand that the discussion of the social problems that affect the family lives of black Americans represents only a portion of the rele-vant literature. An exclusive focus on the social problems besetting black families effectively limits our understanding of the full range of family phe-nomena that occurs within black families. Furthermore, it is important to rec-ognize that black Americans have confronted racial and economic discrimina-tion and other adverse societal conditions throughout their history in the United States. The black legacy of endurance and survival against incredible odds is rooted in the primary institutions of family and community. A compre-hensive understanding of black families must concern itself not only with how this institution has maintained itself, but also the means by which black fami-lies impart specific strategies to its members to ensure their resiliency and ad-aptation. In keeping with this, the remaining chapters in this book examine many diverse aspects of black family life including the provision of social sup-port, the socialization of children, and psychological well-being.

3

The Effects of Mate Availability on Marriage Among Black Americans

A Contextual Analysis

K. JILL KIECOLT

MARK A. FOSSETT

In recent decades, patterns of first marriage in the United States have changed dramatically as shown by older ages at first marriage, lower marriage rates, higher rates of divorce and separation, and a greater prevalence of female-headed families. Although the trends are similar among blacks and whites, they are more pronounced among blacks (Bennett, Bloom, & Craig, 1989; Walker, 1988). Structural explanations for these changes in marriage and family structure emphasize shortages of men (Darity & Myers, 1984; Guttentag & Secord, 1983; Heer & Grossbard-Shechtman, 1981; Jackson, 1971; Lichter, McLaughlin, Kephart, & Landry, 1992; South & Lloyd, 1992; Tucker, 1987; Wilson & Neckerman, 1987), men's declining economic circumstances (Landale & Tolnay, 1991; Lichter et al., 1992; Oppenheimer, 1988; Tucker & Taylor, 1989; Wilson & Neckerman, 1987), and women's relative economic independence (Becker, 1973; Lichter et al., 1992; Preston & Richards, 1975; White, 1981). These factors, too, differ for blacks and whites. The shortage of men is especially acute among blacks, because of higher rates of mortality and institutionalization of black men (Espenshade, 1985; Jackson, 1971; Passel & Robinson, 1985; Spanier & Glick, 1980). Unemployment and underemployment are much higher among black men than among white men (e.g., Horton & Burgess, 1992; Wilson & Neckerman, 1987). Finally, because gender inequality in education, employment, and occupation is less pronounced among blacks than among whites, black women are relatively more economically independent than white women (Farley & Bianchi, 1987).

Most previous studies of the effects of mate availability on marriage have investigated marriage prevalence or marriage rates aggregated over metropolitan areas, nonmetropolitan counties, labor market areas, or states (e.g., Fossett & Kiecolt, 1990, 1991, 1993; Lichter, LeClere, & McLaughlin, 1991; South & Lloyd, 1992). Only a few studies have linked mate availability in local areas to marriage at the individual level. One finds that the more women available in local marriage markets, the younger the ages at which men first marry (Lloyd & South, 1996). Another study finds that a shortage of men in local marriage markets delays women's transitions to first marriage (Lichter et al., 1992). In this study we conduct an individual-level contextual analysis of how the supply of available men affects African American men's and women's marital status and family structure, using data from the National Survey of Black Americans (Jackson, Tucker, & Gurin, 1980) and the U.S. census.

Influences on Marriage and Family Structure

Imbalances in the numbers of men and women (the sex ratio) are predicted to affect entry into marriage (Becker, 1973; Guttentag & Secord, 1983; Heer & Grossbard-Shechtman, 1981). Both the sex ratio hypothesis (Guttentag & Secord, 1983; Heer & Grossbard-Shechtman, 1981) and marital search theory (e.g., England & Farkas, 1986; Oppenheimer, 1988) address this relationship. Marital search theory considers only how imbalances in the sex ratio constrain marriage. This theory predicts a positive relationship between the sex ratio and marriage for women, and a negative relationship for men. That is, whenever men or women are in short supply, they should be more likely to marry and to marry at younger ages. By definition, members of the scarcer gender have more potential matches, and thus tend to have greater "search efficiency"—a higher likelihood of finding a good match for the costs they incur while searching (Oppenheimer, 1988).

The sex ratio hypothesis, in contrast, considers how imbalanced sex ratios interact with gender inequality to affect marriage patterns. The theory assumes that members of the scarcer gender, whether men or women, have a bargaining advantage in male-female relationships because they have more potential mates (Guttentag & Secord, 1983; Heer & Grossbard-Shechtman, 1981). More importantly, how members of the scarcer gender use their advantage depends on their relative structural power, and their control of political and economic resources (Guttentag & Secord, 1983). Men have more structural power than women, and they depend less on marriage for financial support.

Consequently, how imbalanced sex ratios affect marriage depends on whether men or women are scarce. The sex ratio hypothesis predicts that the effects of the sex ratio on marriage will be linear and positive for women, and weaker and curvilinear for men (Cox, 1940; Guttentag & Secord, 1983; Heer & Grossbard-Shechtman, 1981). Because women depend more on marriage for financial support, they are predicted to use their bargaining advantage when potential mates are plentiful to marry and to marry higher-status mates than they could otherwise attract. Thus, the sex ratio should be positively related to women's likelihood of marrying.

In contrast, the sex ratio is expected to be curvilinearly related to men's likelihood of marrying. When the sex ratio is below 100 (men are scarce), the relationship is expected to be positive. When the sex ratio is above 100 (men are in oversupply), the relationship is expected to be negative. This implies that men should be most likely to marry when the sex ratio is approximately balanced (i.e., near 100). The rationale is as follows. The farther the sex ratio is above 100, the less likely that men should be to marry because women are increasingly scarce. The farther the sex ratio is below 100 (men are in short supply), the less likely men should be to marry because they need not offer commitment to gain companionship and sexual relationships outside marriage (Guttentag & Secord, 1983). Thus, when sex ratios are below 100, both men and women are predicted to be less likely to marry; men because the surfeit of women enables them to avoid or postpone traditional familial responsibilities (Staples, 1985), and women because men are scarce and also more reluctant to marry.[1]

Mate availability also should be related in the same way to the likelihood that people are married at a given time, because effects of mate availability are predicted among married people as well. Low sex ratios are hypothesized to weaken husbands' commitment to marriage (Heer & Grossbard-Shechtman, 1981) by decreasing the value that men place on marriage (Becker, 1973). Under these conditions, husbands are hypothesized to provide fewer "benefits" to wives (Heer & Grossbard-Shechtman, 1981), resulting in lower marital satisfaction for women than for men (Guttentag & Secord, 1983). Ultimately, this imbalance is predicted to heighten the risk of separation and divorce (Guttentag & Secord, 1983; Heer & Grossbard-Shechtman, 1981).

Previous Research

Numerous studies show a relationship between mate availability and marriage (Cox, 1940; Guttentag & Secord, 1983; Jackson, 1971; Tucker, 1987; Wilson & Neckerman, 1987). A study using individual-level data indirectly supports the notion that mate availability (as indexed by age) affects whether black men and women are married (Tucker & Taylor, 1989). Local mate availability is positively related to female marriage prevalence in metropolitan areas (Fossett & Kiecolt, 1991, 1993; Preston & Richards, 1975; White, 1981), cities (Cox, 1940), nonmetropolitan Louisiana counties (Fossett & Kiecolt, 1990), and states (South & Lloyd, 1992). It also is positively associated with black and white women's entry into marriage (Landale & Tolnay, 1991; Lichter et al., 1992) at the individual level.

Studies of how mate availability affects men's marriage patterns show weaker effects, as the sex ratio hypothesis predicts. The findings do not clearly support either the hypothesis from marital search theory of a negative, linear relationship or the sex ratio hypothesis of a curvilinear relationship. Of four studies of men's marriage prevalence that modeled a curvilinear relationship, three found one: in U.S. cities (Cox, 1940), in nonmetropolitan Louisiana counties (Fossett & Kiecolt, 1990), and in metropolitan areas (Fossett & Kiecolt, 1993). The other study found instead that the greater the surfeit of men, the later the ages at which white and, to a lesser extent, black men marry (Lloyd & South, 1996). Thus, studies at the individual level support marital search theory.

A few studies, however, find inconsistent effects (Lichter et al., 1991) or no effects (O'Hare, 1988; White, 1981) of the sex ratio on women's marriage prevalence and on changes in marriage "propensity" among blacks and whites (Schoen & Kluegel, 1988). The discrepancies in previous studies probably are attributable to differences in measurement of mate availability, populations studied, and units of analysis. On balance, however, it appears that mate availability influences women's and men's marital behavior.

Not just the supply of men, but the supply of economically attractive men may influence marriage (Lichter et al., 1991; O'Hare, 1988; Oppenheimer, 1988; Tucker & Mitchell-Kernan, 1995c; Wilson & Neckerman, 1987). Wilson and Neckerman (1987) assume that men not in the labor force tend not to be viewed as viable candidates for marriage, and they exclude men who are not employed from estimates of mate availability in their "male marriageable pool index." Independent of the supply of men, men's labor market opportunities are positively related to men's and women's marriage prevalence (Fossett & Kiecolt, 1993; Lichter et al., 1991; South & Lloyd, 1992; Wilson & Neckerman, 1987) and to women's entry into marriage (Lichter et al., 1992).

At the individual level, men's labor market position is expected to influence their marital status. Commonly used indicators include education (a proxy for long-term labor market status), employment status, and income. Research on African American men shows that education (Tucker & Taylor, 1989; but see Lloyd & South, 1996) and income (Lloyd & South, 1996; Teachman, Polonko, & Leigh, 1987; Tucker & Taylor, 1989) are positively associated with marriage. Tucker and Taylor (1989) suggest that many black men do not marry until they can fulfill the provider role, and they review evidence that women consider men's earning capacity in choosing a mate.

The hypothesis of "women's economic independence" (Becker, 1973; Farley & Bianchi, 1987) suggests that the better the women's labor market position, the more likely that women will delay marriage or be unmarried. Women who have less need to marry for financial support can set higher standards for an acceptable match (England & Farkas, 1986) or more easily leave an unsatisfactory marriage. Consistent with this hypothesis, compared to less educated women, more educated women are less willing to marry a man who cannot hold a job (South, 1991). Educational attainment is positively related to age at marriage, and the relationship is stronger among women than among men (Marini, 1978). The higher women's average economic status in metropolitan areas, the lower men's and women's marriage prevalence when men's average economic status is controlled (Fossett & Kiecolt, 1993). Tucker and Taylor (1989) find that income is negatively associated with being married among black women, but note that the effect is probably reciprocal.

Other evidence is accumulating, however, which contradicts the hypothesis of women's economic independence. School enrollment and the age at completing school, rather than educational attainment per se, may delay marriage (Oppenheimer, Blossfeld, & Wackerow, 1995, p. 167). Education is positively related to being married among African American women (Tucker & Taylor, 1989), and women's education, employment, and earnings are positively related to entry into marriage (Goldscheider & Waite, 1986; Lichter et al., 1992, pp. 789, 791). Moreover, marriage prevalence is far lower for black women with less than a high school education than for other black women (Albrecht, Fossett, Cready, & Kiecolt, 1995). Women's labor market prospects may increase their attractiveness as potential mates (Mare & Winship, 1991; South, 1991), as well as enable couples to marry (Goldscheider & Waite, 1986) in times when men's labor market prospects are unpredictable (Oppenheimer, 1988).

The level of public assistance such as Aid to Families With Dependent Children (AFDC) also may be negatively related to being married, because it provides women with another alternative to financial support from marriage

(Farley & Bianchi, 1987). Public assistance may increase single mothers' likelihood of forming separate households and reduce their financial incentive to marry or remarry (discussed by Kosterlitz, 1992). It also may diminish men's likelihood of marrying by decreasing their sense of obligation to support their children financially. Public assistance may lead couples to postpone or forego marriage to maximize household income in the short term, and it may increase their likelihood of leaving an unsatisfactory marriage. The level of public assistance is negatively associated with marriage in local areas and at the state level (Fossett & Kiecolt, 1993; Lichter et al., 1991; South & Lloyd, 1992), and it is slightly positively associated with the proportion of female-headed families among African Americans over time (O'Hare, 1988). The level of public assistance in the local area is negatively related to marrying for both black and white men (Lloyd & South, 1996).

Population size also is expected to be negatively related to the likelihood of marrying and being married, presumably because norms supporting traditional family structure are weaker in urban areas (Lichter et al., 1991). Population size is negatively associated with marriage prevalence (Fossett & Kiecolt, 1993; Lichter et al., 1991, p. 847) and with the likelihood of being married (Tucker & Taylor, 1989). Women in nonmetropolitan areas marry at younger ages than their counterparts in metropolitan areas (McLaughlin, Lichter, & Johnston, 1993), independent of the effects of mate availability.

Based on previous research, we predict that the sex ratio will be positively related to ever having married and to being married among women. It should be curvilinearly related to ever having married and being married among men. Education, employment, and income are expected to be positively related to marriage among men, but not necessarily among women. It is difficult to predict how women's economic independence (education, employment, and income) will affect their marital status, because demand factors (the value of these assets to potential mates) also must be considered. The level of public assistance and residence in a metropolitan area are predicted to be negatively related to ever having married and to being married for men and women.

Method

Sample

Individual-level data for the analysis are drawn from the 1980 National Survey of Black Americans (Jackson et al., 1980), a representative, national sample of 2,107 blacks 18 years of age or older in the continental United States.

Only respondents aged 18 to 44 are included in the analysis, because these are the ages at which the predicted effects of the sex ratio on marriage and family structure should be the strongest. Of these respondents, 13 respondents from a county for which contextual data are not available are excluded from the analysis. Five additional respondents from a county with an extreme value on the sex ratio (192.3) also are excluded, for a sample size of 1,180.[2]

The contextual variables for the analysis are calculated using published data from the 1980 U.S. census (U.S. Bureau of the Census, 1980, 1982) for each place (metropolitan area or nonmetropolitan county) in the sampling frame of the National Survey of Black Americans. The contextual data are merged with the data on respondents to the National Survey of Black Americans.

Measures

The dependent variables in the analysis are (a) whether respondents have ever married and (b) whether they are married and living with a spouse, based on the question, "Are you married, divorced, or separated, or have you never been married?" Respondents are categorized as ever married if they are married, divorced, separated, or widowed. Respondents are categorized as currently married if they are legally married and living with a spouse. The sex ratio, an indicator of mate availability in marriage markets, is best measured at the local level (Freiden, 1974; Goldman, Westoff, & Hammerslough, 1984; Lichter et al., 1991), because people usually choose mates who live nearby. The sex ratio varies widely across metropolitan areas, cities, and nonmetropolitan counties (Cox, 1940; Fossett & Kiecolt, 1990, 1991, 1993; Goldman et al., 1984; Passel & Robinson, 1985). We calculate the sex ratio by taking the log of the ratio of men in the labor force to noninstitutionalized women aged 16 and older in the respondent's local area (metropolitan area or nonmetropolitan county, as appropriate; U.S. Bureau of the Census, 1980). Inmates of institutions are excluded because they do not participate in local marriage markets. Also, because most inmates are men, including them could distort the sex ratio in areas with small populations. Men not in the labor force also are excluded because of their disadvantage in the marriage market (Wilson & Neckerman, 1987).[3]

We take the natural log of the sex ratio because it is "asymmetric" in its natural metric; that is, it varies from 0-100 below 100 and to infinity above 100. Taking the natural log makes the measure symmetric and slightly improves its correlations with the dependent variables. Although this measure is simple, it explains marital status as well or better than measures of the sex ratio based on more detailed age data, such as age-specific measures or availability ratios, from which inmates of institutions cannot be excluded using standard census sources (see discussion in Fossett & Kiecolt, 1991).

Respondents' labor market position is measured by their education, their employment status, and their earnings from the previous year. Because preliminary analyses showed nonlinear effects of education, education is measured by a set of three dummy variables identifying respondents who have completed high school, respondents who have completed 1 to 3 years of college, and respondents who have at least a 4-year college degree. Respondents with less than a high school education comprise the omitted reference category. Employment is coded 1 if a respondent is employed, 0 otherwise. Income is measured by the midpoint of each income category, in thousands of dollars. Age in years also is included in the models, as is the square of age, because the relationship between age and marital status is nonlinear (Tucker & Taylor, 1989).

The level of public assistance is indicated by the average AFDC payment per family per month in each respondent's local area (U.S. Bureau of the Census, 1982). Data on SMSAs are used for respondents in SMSAs. State-level data are used for residents of nonmetropolitan counties, because data for counties are not available. Payments vary little within states, however, because amounts are set by state governments. Residence in an urban area is measured by a dummy variable coded 1 if a respondent lives in a metropolitan area, 0 otherwise. We use residence in a metropolitan area instead of population size as an indicator of urbanization because the latter is collinear with level of AFDC payments.[4]

Results

Table 3.1 presents descriptive data for the variables in our analyses. As the table shows, the mean sex ratio of black men in the labor force to noninstitutionalized black women aged 16 and older is 56.64, indicating a deficit of African American men in the labor force in most areas. The sex ratio for places in the analysis (excluding the outlier mentioned above) ranges from 37 to 125, and the standard deviation of nearly 8 indicates that it varies widely across areas. The amount of variation in the sex ratio resembles that found in previous studies of metropolitan areas (Passel & Robinson, 1985), cities (Cox, 1940), and nonmetropolitan counties (Fossett & Kiecolt, 1990).

Women are more likely than men to have ever been married. Consistent with previous research (Tucker & Taylor, 1989), however, men are more likely than

Table 3.1 *Descriptive Statistics for Variables Used in Analysis of Ever-Married and Currently Married Status*

Variable	Percentage	μ	SD
Ever married			
Men	60.0		
Women	66.0		
Total	63.7		
Currently married			
Men	46.9		
Women	35.5		
Women with children < 18	37.9		
Total	39.8		
Female	62.0		
Education			
Less than high school	9.7		
High school graduate	25.9		
Some college	37.0		
College graduate and more	27.5		
Employed	64.6		
Residing in metropolitan area	84.4		
Ratio of men in labor force to noninstitutionalized women		56.64	8.00
Average AFDC[a] payment per recipient child		230.45	94.96
Respondent's income (in thousands)		8.22	7.01
Age		29.933	7.26

a. AFDC = Aid to Families With Dependent Children.

women to be currently married. Probably this is because of men's higher re-marriage rate.

Marital Status

We test for effects of mate availability, level of public assistance, metropolitan residence, respondents' labor market position, and age on whether respondents have ever married and whether they are currently married. Because these dependent variables are dichotomous, the models are estimated using logistic regression. We perform separate analyses by gender because some of the effects were predicted to differ for men and women. The model for men initially included the square of the sex ratio because a nonlinear effect of the sex ratio on marital status was predicted. We dropped the squared term because it did not improve the fit of the model. In addition, because most effects are in the same direction for men and women, we perform pooled analyses that combine both men and women. This increases the efficiency of the parameter estimates and enables us to test whether the effects differ significantly by gender.

The left side of Table 3.2 shows the results of the logistic regressions of whether men and women have ever married. The sex ratio is positively related to whether women, but not men, have ever married. In the pooled analysis of men and women, the sex ratio does not affect whether respondents have ever married. This indicates that the sex ratio affects only whether women have ever married.

Average AFDC payment per recipient child in the respondent's local area has a negative effect on the likelihood of ever having been married, and the effect does not differ by gender. Residence in a metropolitan area is not related to ever having married for either men or women.

Education is significantly related to whether respondents have ever married, and the relationship is curvilinear. Compared with men and women with less than a high school education, men and women with 1 to 3 years of college are slightly more likely to have married, whereas men and women with college or graduate degrees are less likely to have married.

Being employed does not influence whether men and women have ever married. Income is strongly and positively related to whether men, but not women, have ever married. Although income has significant effects in pooled analyses of men and women, the pattern of interaction by gender indicates that income has stronger effects on whether men have ever married.

Consistent with previous research (e.g., Tucker & Taylor, 1989), age is strongly and positively related to the likelihood of having married for both men and women. The significant negative coefficient for the squared term indicates that the relationship levels off with age.

The right side of Table 3.2 presents a logistic regression of whether men and women are currently married on the contextual variables and individual characteristics. The sex ratio is positively related to whether women, but not men, are currently married. In the pooled analysis, the sex ratio has a positive, significant effect on whether men and women are currently married, and the interaction of the sex ratio with gender is not significant. Nevertheless, we cannot

Table 3.2 Coefficients from the Logistic Regression of Ever-Married and Currently Married Status on Mate Availability by Sex

	Ever Married						Currently Married					
	Men		Women		Total		Men		Women		Total	
	Coefficient	RM[a]	Coefficient	RM	Coefficient	RM	Coefficient	RM	Coefficient	RM	Coefficient	RM
Ln sex ratio	.191	6.013	1.523*	2.881	1.014	1.209	−.137	1.588	1.794**	2.759	1.034*	.872
Public assistance	−.004**	.996	−.003**	.997	−.004***	.996	−.004**	.997	−.002*	.998	−.003***	.997
Metropolitan area	.319	1.376	.062	1.064	.131	1.140	−.185	.831	−.635*	.530	−.506*	.603
Education												
High school graduate	−.011	1.011	.359	1.431	.256	1.292	.151	1.163	.451*	1.570	.366*	1.442
Some college	.602	1.825	.280	1.323	.420*	1.522	.566	1.164	.320	1.376	.418*	1.519
College graduate +	−.863	.422	−.921*	.398	−.956**	.460	−.616	.540	.238	1.269	−.169	.845
Employed	.459	1.582	−.008	.992	.078	1.081	.787**	2.197	.192	1.212	.229	1.258
Income	.075**	1.078	.037	1.038	.058**	1.060	.091***	1.095	−.009	.992	.047***	1.048
Age	.952***	2.590	.723***	2.061	.811***	2.250	.878***	2.407	.339***	1.404	.515***	1.673
Age-squared	−.012***	.988	−.009***	.991	−.010***	.990	−.013***	.988	−.004**	.996	−.007***	.993
Intercept	−17.655***		−18.265***		−18.258***		−14.988***		−13.328***		−12.988***	
Model chi-square	213.249		240.433		447.556***		157.742		71.454		200.601***	
N	417		676		1093		417		676		1093	

a. The numbers in the RM column are odds ratio multipliers.
*p < .05; **p < .01; ***p < .001.

confidently conclude that the effect is significantly differently from zero for men.

Average AFDC payment per recipient child in the respondent's local area has a negative effect on the likelihood of being currently married for men and women. Residence in a metropolitan area is negatively related to being currently married for women, but not for men. In a pooled analysis of men and women, metropolitan residence has a negative effect on being currently married.

Education is only weakly related to being currently married. The set of dummy variables reaches significance for the sample as a whole, but not for men and women separately. Compared with men and women with less than a high school education, men and women with a high school education and those with 1 to 3 years of college are slightly more likely to be currently married, whereas men and women with college degrees are not. The only effect of education that differs by gender is that men with 1 to 3 years of college are significantly more likely than their female counterparts to be currently married ($p <$ 0.05). Men who are employed are more likely to be currently married than men who are not. On this they differ significantly from women ($p < 0.01$), for whom employment status is not related to being married (results not shown). Income also is strongly and positively related to whether men are currently married. Although income is not significantly related to being currently married among women, it has significant effects in pooled analyses of men and women. In models that include an interaction term for income and gender, the effect of income on whether respondents are currently married is significantly stronger for men than for women ($p < 0.001$). Consistent with previous research (e.g., Tucker & Taylor, 1989), age is strongly and positively related to the likelihood of being currently married for both men and women, and as with ever-married status, the effect levels off with age.

Family Structure

Table 3.3 reports a logistic regression analysis of how mate availability and labor market position affect family structure, as indicated by whether women who have children under age 18 at home are currently married. The higher the sex ratio, the higher the likelihood that women with children are currently married. Public assistance and urban residence are negatively related to being currently married. The effect of education is significant and curvilinear. Compared to women who have not finished high school, women with high school

Table 3.3 *Logistic Regression Coefficients From the Logistic Regression of Currently Married Status on Mate Availability for Women With Children Under 18 Years Old*

	Currently Married	
	Coefficient	*Exp(B)*[a]
Ln sex ratio	2.256**	9.543
Public assistance	−.003*	.997
Metropolitan area	−.726*	.484
Education		
High school graduate	.603*	1.828
Some college	.759**	2.137
College graduate and more	.523	1.686
Employed	.117	1.124
Income	−.005	.995
Age	.136	1.146
Age squared	−.001	.999
Intercept	−11.731**	
Model chi-square	47.277***	
N	541	

A. Odds ratio multipliers
$*p < .05; **p < .01; ***p < .001.$

degrees and with some college are more likely to be currently married, but women with college degrees are not.

Discussion

This study has investigated the effects of mate availability in local areas and individuals' labor market position on the marriage patterns of black Americans. Consistent with theory and with previous studies, we find that the higher the community sex ratio, the higher the likelihood that black women have ever married and that they are currently married. For men, we find no effect of the sex ratio on being ever married and a weak effect on being currently married. Previous studies of marriage prevalence at the aggregate level also have found weaker effects for men than for women (Cox, 1940; Fossett & Kiecolt, 1990, 1993).

Our findings also support arguments that men are more likely to marry and to be married when their labor market position is more favorable (Lichter et al., 1991; Oppenheimer, 1988; Wilson & Neckerman, 1987). Moreover, the effects of men's labor market position are stronger than the effects of women's labor market position. Employment and income have significantly larger effects on whether men than women are currently married (results not shown). Of course, in a cross-sectional analysis, the relationship between income and current marriage for women may be weak, because although employment may enable some women to marry, marriage also may enable women to leave the labor force or to work part-time (Tucker & Taylor, 1989, p. 661). On balance, the findings concerning employment and income support previous arguments that marriage and family structure are more strongly linked to men's than to women's labor market position (Oppenheimer, 1988; Wilson & Neckerman, 1987).

In contrast to employment and income, education has a different relationship to marriage. Education has a curvilinear effect on whether respondents have ever been married, in that men and women with college degrees are less likely to have been married than men and women with less education. The finding for women may indicate support for the hypothesis of women's economic independence (Becker, 1973; Farley & Bianchi, 1987). Alternatively, it may indicate a shortage of potential mates for more educated black women (Goldman et al., 1984; Guttentag & Secord, 1983), because of the norm that women should marry men with equal or greater education. Like Lichter et al. (1992), however, we find that the effects of the sex ratio on marriage do not differ by women's level of education (results not shown). The finding that men with college degrees also are less likely to have ever married is not readily explainable, but also has been found by Lloyd and South (1996).

The level of public assistance is negatively related to ever having married and being currently married among men and women, and among women with children under 18 years of age. These findings are consistent with those of recent aggregate-level studies (e.g., Fossett & Kiecolt, 1993; Lichter et al., 1991; South & Lloyd, 1992) as well as an individual-level contextual study of black and white men (Lloyd & South, 1996). The findings may indicate that AFDC payments create expectations that financial resources other than earnings are available to women that influence men's and women's decisions concerning marriage. For example, the current structure of welfare benefits exacts a penalty for marriage for some AFDC recipients (Kosterlitz, 1992). Any policy responses to an undesired welfare effect, however, must take into account low sex ratios of African Americans. Policymakers may advocate alternatives to the present system that would encourage rather than discourage marriage, on the grounds that "marrying another wage earner, not solo employment, is the surest route off the welfare rolls" for women (Garfinkel as cited in Kosterlitz, 1992). Yet, our findings suggest that marriage is simply not a viable option for many African American women given the shortage of African American men. Another explanation for the effect of AFDC payments on marital status also is possible. The level of public assistance may be a proxy for other, unmeasured variables. If so, a task for future research is to identity those variables so that models can be more correctly specified.

Still needed are studies that investigate the effects on marital behavior not only of contextual effects and individual characteristics, but also of attitudes and beliefs. Previously, this question has been framed in terms of distinguishing the effects of preferences for marriage from those of market constraints or opportunities (Goldscheider & Waite, 1986; Staples, 1985). The evidence to date suggests that mate availability influences behavior even in the absence of an effect on attitudes or an effect of attitudes on behavior, and regardless of people's awareness of them (Guttentag & Secord, 1983). Behavior is partly a function of the opportunity structure, irrespective of attitudes. For example, preferences for traditional gender roles (Lichter et al., 1992) are positively associated with women's entry into marriage, but this effect is far weaker than the effect of the sex ratio.

Nevertheless, discovering the role of attitudes and beliefs that may intervene between mate availability and marital behavior requires more than ascertaining "preferences" for marriage. It also involves discovering how structural factors shape perceptions of marital and labor market opportunities and how such perceptions in turn influence the length of time people search for a mate and their criteria for an acceptable match (Oppenheimer, 1988; Tucker & Mitchell-Kernan, 1995c). Thus, many intriguing social psychological aspects of these theories remain to be tested.

Notes

1. Guttentag and Secord (1983) emphasize that the sex ratio influences individuals' experiences in the marriage market, as well as their attitudes and expectations concerning mate selection, regardless of whether they are aware of it. Other aspects of social structure (e.g., city size) also influence attitudes and behavior without people's awareness (reviewed by Kiecolt, 1988). Nevertheless, evidence from the popular press suggests that the public has long been somewhat aware of the sex ratio (Churchill, 1946; "Marriage: 800,000," 1947).

2. When residents of this county are included in the analysis, the effects of the sex ratio are nearly the same.

3. It is well known that the differential undercount of black men biases sex ratios downward. Nevertheless, the undercount is not problematic for comparative studies. Intercommunity

variation in the sex ratio is substantial, and it is scarcely affected by adjustments for undercount. Adjustments for undercount increase the sex ratio by several percentage points on average. But adjusted and unadjusted sex ratios are highly correlated (r is at least 0.98), and they have the same effects on family formation and family structure (Fossett & Kiecolt, 1991).

4. Region (a dummy variable for Southern residence), another variable that is positively related to marriage (e.g., Fossett & Kiecolt, 1993; Lichter et al., 1992; Tucker & Taylor, 1989), had to be dropped from the models because of its high correlation with the level of AFDC payments ($r = 0.84$).

4

Gender, Age, and Marital Status as Related to Romantic Involvement Among African American Singles

M. BELINDA TUCKER
ROBERT JOSEPH TAYLOR

Unmarried African Americans are uniquely positioned in American society, relative to single persons in other U.S. ethnic groups. Singles comprise a greater proportion of the total black population, are more evenly representative on the basis of age and gender, and are more likely to have children than singles in other groups. These unique characteristics are due to rapid changes in family formation patterns over the past two decades that have been observed generally in the U.S. population, but are more pronounced among African Americans (Tucker & Mitchell-Kernan, 1995e). Black women and men now marry later and less, are more likely to divorce, and are more likely to have nonmarital births than in previous times (Tucker & Mitchell-Kernan, 1995e). In 1990, one third of black women and 43% of black men had never married (U.S. Bureau of the Census, 1991). African American women are also less likely than other groups of women to remarry after divorce or widowhood (U.S. Bureau of the Census, 1992d). One consequence of these changes is that blacks, relatively to other groups and to previous times, will spend a substantially greater proportion of their lives as singles. Because of this fact, singlehood may be perceived by African Americans as a more normative experience.

Of course, being unmarried does not mean that one does not have a partner, although few studies examine the extent of romantic involvement or partnering outside of marriage. In a rare study of black singles, Staples (1981b) examined dating and sexual behavior, among other issues. Although not based on a representative sample and focused specifically on the middle class, the study raises compelling issues about the role of singles in African American communities. In particular, he noted the range of living arrangements and lifestyles evident among persons who are single. Furthermore, Staples found that most respondents did not view singlehood as a choice, but as a response to societal constraints.

Our previous research indicates that the decline of marriage among blacks is not indicative of a reluctance to enter into relationships and that, with the exception of elderly women, romantic involvement among unmarried blacks is quite high (Tucker & Taylor, 1989; Tucker, Taylor, & Mitchell-Kernan, 1993). Although there has been considerable work focused on understanding the structural factors associated with marital status, we know little of the indicators of relationship status among unmarried persons. To begin to address this omission, this study examines how gender, age, and marital status are related to whether African American singles are romantically involved, and whether those without partners are desirous of involvement.

Conceptual Perspectives

Discussion of the structural correlates of relationship status has been almost exclusively in regard to marriage and cohabitation. Therefore, theory development has focused on predictors of marriage and, in the case of cohabitation, why persons would choose to simply live together, rather than marry (i.e., the negation of marriage). Explaining romantic involvement, without regard to living arrangements, has been largely a task of psychologists who tend to explore intrapsychic dynamics and individual attributes related to the formation and maintenance of close personal relationships (Duck & Gilmore, 1981; Kelley, 1983). Sociological discussions of intimate relationships have been somewhat limited, and focused primarily on role functions (see critique by Blumstein & Kollock, 1988). Neither discipline has told us much about structural predictors of relationship formation.

Despite the relative absence of structural conceptualizations of romantic involvement (other than role-centered work), certain of the predominant theories of marriage are relevant to the focus of this chapter—that is, the relationship of gender, age, and marital status to romantic involvement. Two predominant lines of research explore links between marriage behavior and demographic and economic forces. One direction of inquiry concerns the impact on marriage of imbalances in the number of men relative to women in communities and societies. The other body of research examines nuptiality in relation to various economic factors, including declines in male economic viability, increased female economic independence, and a decreasing gap in the male-female salary differential.

A limited, but developing, literature has examined the relative merits of these two perspectives for explaining recent changes in marital behavior. Findings have been somewhat inconsistent, with some support for both the availability and economic perspectives, a few studies supporting only one of the two theories, and several investigations finding no support for either (see Tucker & Mitchell-Kernan, 1995d for a review). This inconsistency in findings may be due, in part, to widely contrasting research strategies and definitions of concepts (Tucker & Mitchell-Kernan, 1995d). Furthermore, the goals of these studies have not been entirely compatible. Some have been concerned with changing patterns of marriage generally, whereas others have been focused on explaining the increasing differences between African American and white marriage behavior. There is also an implicit expectation that a single theory will provide the definitive explanation for the dramatic changes in family formation patterns that have occurred in recent decades. Our more limited interest is in discovering whether or not these theories contribute meaningfully to our understanding of these changes. With respect to understanding diverging African American and white marriage behavior, Lichter, McLaughlin, Kephart, and Landry (1992), summarize one of the most comprehensive studies on the subject by concluding that "marriage market factors contribute more in 'explaining' the race effect than most other factors frequently considered in previous research" (p. 27).

Although both lines of thought have implications for romantic involvement as well as marital behavior, the economic theories would appear to have more direct relevance for marriage, because the economic obligations of marriage are widely acknowledged. Nonmarital romantic involvement is of a more experimental nature and is less bound by the formal rules of mate selection, including provider expectations for males. In contrast, mate availability considerations will necessarily affect nonmarital romantic partnerships as well as marriage. Moreover, given the focus of the present study, theories of mate availability include differential predictions of mating opportunity as a function of location in the social structure.

Mate Availability

The mate availability perspective has been informed by several lines of theory and research, all directed toward understanding causes, correlates, and consequences of constrained mate availability and marital opportunity. In general, the focus has been on populations and groups, rather than individuals. Demographers contend that a "marriage squeeze," a decrease in the availability of marriage partners among female members of the "baby boom," has led to delays in marriage and lower marriage rates, particularly for women (Glick, Heer, & Beresford, 1963; Rodgers & Thornton, 1985; Schoen, 1983). This shortage of partners is due to the gradual increase in birth rates following World War II, coupled with the tendency of women to marry slightly older men. Baby boom women were therefore seeking husbands from older but smaller cohorts. Although this marriage squeeze affected all races, it exacerbated the impact of the mortality driven decline in African American sex ratios (i.e., the number of males per 100 women), evident since the 1920s (Cox, 1940; Jackson, 1971; McQueen, 1979; Staples, 1981a, 1981b; Tucker & Mitchell-Kernan, 1995c), and leading, in the opinion of some, to a broadening of mate selection standards among African American women (Spanier & Glick, 1980).

Guttentag and Secord (1983) argued that imbalanced sex ratios throughout time have had major societal consequences, with male shortage leading to higher rates of singlehood, divorce, "out-of-wedlock" births, adultery, and transient relationships; less commitment among men to relationships; lower societal value on marriage and the family; and a rise in feminism. They cite imbalanced sex ratios as a factor in black marital decline and an increasing nonmarital birth rate. Some have challenged this interpretation. For example, Epenshade (1985) noted that although black sex ratios have declined since 1920, marital decline has only been evident since the 1960s. Yet, relationships between sex ratios and marriage behavior have been demonstrated. Low sex ratios (i.e., relatively fewer males) have been statistically associated with delays in marriage, higher rates of singlehood (among women in particular), more female-headed households, the percentage of marriage couples with school-age children, and marital dissolution (Kiecolt & Fossett, 1995; Lichter et al., 1992; Sampson, 1995; Schoen, 1983; Secord & Ghee, 1986; Tucker,

1987). Although South (1988) has demonstrated that sex ratio effects can be moderated by women's economic power.

We believe that the inconsistencies noted by Epenshade (1985) may stem, at least in part, from the narrow focus on the demographic variable of sex ratio, rather than the range of issues related to an individual's potential for relationship formation. As we have argued elsewhere (Tucker & Mitchell-Kernan, 1995c), we believe that individual preferences and attributes, as well as sociocultural imperatives, ultimately affect relationship occurrence. In the case of African Americans, male availability, as well as suitability, for marriage have been especially compromised in recent decades as increasing differential mortality has been compounded by decreasing economic viability (Darity & Myers, 1987/1988; Wilson, 1987).

Guttentag and Secord (1983) made propositions concerning how sex ratio imbalance would affect romantic involvements. Using social exchange theory, they argued that when imbalance exists, the sex in greater supply has more difficulty finding a partner and may find relationships less satisfying, because the other partner has more potentially satisfactory alternatives. The partner in greater supply is therefore more dependent and more committed to the relationship than the partner in less supply. Jemmott, Ashby, and Lindenfeld (1989) found that a perceived shortage of the opposite sex was related to greater commitment in relationships.

Relationship Opportunity and Social Structural Position

How do mate availability conceptualizations help us to understand the potential for relationship involvement among various subgroups of single persons? Based on availability determinations, among African Americans, older women would be especially disadvantaged in the relationship market. As we have discussed elsewhere (Tucker et al., 1993), this is due to a number of factors including the longer life span of black women relative to men, the higher rate of marital dissolution among black women, the lower remarriage rate of black women relative to black men and women of other race, and the tendency for older men to marry much younger women.

There would be other areas of differential advantage in relationship opportunities. Due to the overall shortage of African American men relative to women, men in general would be advantaged in the relationship market. Due, however, to cultural norms and different demographic patterns at younger ages, the situation among younger African Americans could be quite different. That is, sex ratio discrepancies at the youngest ages are slight, and because societal preferences allow younger women to seek mates of all ages whereas younger males are largely confined to even younger women, younger black women could have an advantage over younger men in the romantic relationship market.

There has been little discussion of the impact of marital status on relationship opportunity, although it seems clear that women who have been previously married are more disadvantaged than previously married men when seeking new relationships. This assessment is based on the fact that men are substantially more likely to remarry after divorce and widowhood than are women (Glick, 1984; Ross & Sawhill, 1975). The differential is even greater for blacks who have lost their spouses through death, with widowers being 4 times more likely to remarry than widows (Sweet & Bumpass, 1987). Formerly married women are also particularly disadvantaged in relationship formation due to the fact that they are more likely to have children to care for and are therefore less attractive to available men. Marital status may not serve as an additional disadvantage for men, because men grow scarcer numerically with age, and because older men may be better off financially than younger men (thereby enhancing their attractiveness).

Previous Research

In a previous article (Tucker & Taylor, 1989), we examined the structural correlates of relationship status in a national sample of African Americans. The study demonstrated that, in this general sample, the factors associated with marriage, as opposed to romantic involvement, were distinctive. Less economically equipped males, older women, and the lesser educated in general were less likely to be married. We interpreted these findings as being indicative of differential marital opportunity, wherein males who were less capable of fulfilling the provider role and older women disadvantaged in the marriage market in this culture. The study also revealed very distinctive patterns on the basis of gender and age. Compared to men, single women aged 55 and over were highly unlikely to be involved romantically. Particularly striking was the fact that older women, who were neither married nor involved in a relationship, were overwhelming uninterested in having a romantic involvement. In a separate article focused solely on sample members age 55 and older (Tucker et al., 1993), we noted that there are a good many disincentives associated with intimate relationships for older women. Focus group discussions we conducted with older African American women revealed that they feared that marriage and romantic involvements would compromise them financially. In addition, older women felt that relationships with even older men would be unduly burdensome, because the women would be expected to serve the men as well as care for them, should they become infirm.

It seems clear from our previous work that both gender and age are key correlates of romantic involvement and desire for romantic involvement. The present study is an attempt to further delineate that association, through explicit consideration of possible interactions between the two variables, as suggested by mate availability conceptualizations. Because marital status is a structural indicator that could influence the association between gender and age and romantic involvement, we have added that variable to the analysis as well.

Method

Sample

The analyses were conducted on the National Survey of Black Americans (NSBA) data set. The NSBA was conducted in 1979-1980 by the Program for Research on Black Americans at the Survey Research Center, Institute for Social Research, University of Michigan, and is the first nationally representative cross-sectional survey of the adult (18 years and older) black population living in the continental United States. The sample consisted of 2,107 men and women, representing a response rate of nearly 70%. A more detailed description of the sample is presented by Neighbors (1986). The present analyses are based on the 1,210 respondents who reported that they had never been married or were either divorced, separated, or widowed. As shown in Table 4.1, the resulting sample was 30% male and 70% female.

Dependent and Independent Variables

Two dependent variables were used in these analyses: (a) having a main romantic relationship and (b) wanting a main romantic relationship. Both of these variables were derived from a question measuring marital status. Respondents were first asked, "Are you married, divorced, separated or have you never been married?" Those who responded that they were not married were asked the follow-up question: "Do you have a main romantic involvement at this time?" Persons responding "no" were asked the additional question, "Would you like to have a romantic involvement at this time?" Gender, marital status, and age were the independent variables used in these analyses.

Table 4.1 *Bivariate Analysis of Gender, Marital Status, and Age on Having a Main Romantic Involvement*

| | Have Main Romantic Involvement | | | | |
	Yes (%)	No (%)	N	χ^2	Gamma
Gender					
Male	49.1	58.1	369	11.15***	.21***
Female	38.8	61.2	841		
Marital status					
Divorced	47.9	52.1	240	86.48***	
Separated	38.2	61.8	204		
Widowed	20.9	79.1	302		
Never married	53.8	46.2	461		
Age					
18 to 25	51.2	48.8	303	135.38***	−.38***
26 to 34	53.5	46.5	243		
35 to 54	52.1	47.9	311		
55 to 64	23.7	76.3	135		
65 and older	11.7	88.3	213		

$*p < .05; **p < .01; ***p < .001.$

Data Analysis

Log-linear analysis was used to examine the combined influence of the independent variables on each of the two dependent variables. This procedure models cell frequencies using the multinomial response model. Through log-linear analysis, we can explicitly test for interactions among our independent variables.

Results

Have Main Romantic Relationship

Four out of 10 respondents (41.9%) reported having a main romantic involvement (MRI) at the time of the interview. Gender, marital status, and age each had a significant bivariate relationship with whether respondents had a main involvement (see Table 4.1). Men were more likely than women to have a

Table 4.2 *Odds Ratios Describing the Effects of Gender, Marital Status, and Age on Having a Main Romantic Involvement*

	Odds Ratios
Gender	
Male/female	1.50
Marital status	
Divorced/separated	1.49
Divorced/widowed	3.46
Divorced/never married	.79
Age	
Young/middle	1.00
Young/old	5.46
Gender and age	
Young: male/female	.78
Middle: male/female	1.34
Old: male/female	7.06

NOTE: Preferred model—[HGA] [HMA] [GMA]; LRX(9df)^2 = 13.23, p = .15.

MRI. Although half of men had relationships, less than 40% of women were romantically involved. Among marital status groups, a higher percentage of never married respondents had a MRI, followed by divorced, separated, and widowed respondents. Age was negatively associated with the dependent variable: Older respondents were less likely to have a MRI than younger respondents.

A log-linear analysis was conducted to examine the combined influence of gender (G), marital status (M), and age (A) on having a MRI (H). The log-linear model that best fit the data is [HGA] [HMA] [GMA]. This model indicates the presence of an interaction between gender and age on having a MRI and an interaction between marital status and age on having an MRI. Tables 4.2 and 4.3 present the odds ratios associated with the relationships specified by the best fitting model. As indicated in Table 4.2, men were 50% more likely than women to have a MRI. There is no difference in the likelihood of young and middle-aged respondents to have a romantic relationship, but young respondents were 5 1/2 times more likely than older respondents to have a MRI.

Among marital status groups, divorced respondents were nearly 50% more likely than separated, and 3 1/2 times more likely than widowed respondents to have a MRI. Divorced respondents, however, were 21% less likely to have a MRI than their never married counterparts. Please note that the odds ratios representing these bivariate relationships are consistent with the findings

Table 4.3 *Odds and Odds Ratios Describing the Effects of the Interaction Between Age and Marital Status on Having a Main Romantic Involvement*

Age and Marital Status	Odds	Odds Ratios	
Young			
Divorced	1.32		
Separated	.39	Divorced/separated	3.38
Widowed	2.33	Divorced/widowed	.56
Never married	1.20	Divorced/never married	1.10
Middle aged			
Divorced	.96		
Separated	1.20	Divorced/separated	.80
Widowed	.93	Divorced/widowed	1.04
Never married	1.43	Divorced/never married	.67
Old			
Divorced	.39		
Separated	.30	Divorced/separated	1.29
Widowed	.14	Divorced/widowed	2.66
Never married	.28	Divorced/never married	1.35

NOTE: Preferred model—[HGA] [HMA] [GMA]; LRX(9df)^2 = 13.23, p = .15.

presented in Table 4.1. Table 4.2 also presents the odds ratios of the interaction between gender and age on having a MRI. Although men were generally more likely to have a MRI than women, among the youngest group, men were 22% less likely to have a MRI. Thereafter, however, the male advantage intensifies. Middle-aged men were 34% more likely and older men were 7 times more likely than women to have main romantic relationships.

Table 4.3 presents the odds and odds ratios of the interaction between marital status and age on having a main romantic relationship. An examination of the odds indicates that among the youngest group of respondents, those who had been widowed had the greatest likelihood of having a relationship, followed by divorced, then never married, then separated respondents. These differences are reflected in the odds ratios, which indicated that divorced respondents were over 3 times more likely to have a MRI as those who were separated, half as likely as widowed respondents, and only 10% more likely than never married respondents. Marital status differences in having a MRI were not large among middle-aged respondents, with never marriedrespondents being somewhat more likely to have a MRI than their counterparts. Among older respondents, the divorced were slightly more likely than separated and never married respondents to have a MRI and 2 2/3 times as likely as widowed respondents to be in a romantic relationship.

Table 4.4 *Bivariate Analysis of Gender, Marital Status, and Age on Wanting a Main Romantic Involvement*

	Want a Main Romantic Involvement				
	Yes (%)	No (%)	N	χ^2	Gamma
Gender					
Male	45.9	54.1	185	18.79***	.36***
Female	28.4	71.6	497		
Marital status					
Divorced	60.7	39.3	122	71.75***	
Separated	28.7	71.3	122		
Widowed	17.0	83.0	230		
Never married	37.5	62.5	208		
Age					
18 to 25	38.2	61.8	144	63.47***	−.34***
26 to 34	45.0	55.0	111		
35 to 54	49.7	50.3	143		
55 to 64	25.7	74.3	101		
65 and older	12.6	87.4	182		

*$p < .05$; **$p < .01$; ***$p < .001$.

Desire for Relationship

Of those respondents who did not have a main romantic involvement, one third stated that they would like to have one. As shown in Table 4.4, bivariate analyses indicate that gender, marital status, and age were each significantly associated with whether respondents wanted a MRI. Males were more likely than females and divorced respondents were more likely than other marital status groups to desire a romantic involvement. Age exhibited a curvilinear associational pattern: Compared to other age groups, a higher percentage of middle-aged respondents (35 to 54 years) indicated that they wanted a MRI. Log-linear analyses of the combined influence of gender (G), marital status (M), and age (A) on wanting a main romantic involvement (W) indicates that the best fitting model is [WGA] [WM] [GMA]. This model indicates the presence of (a) a bivariate relationship between marital status and wanting a MRI and (b) an interaction between gender and age on wanting a MRI. Table 4.5 presents the odds ratios derived from the log-linear model and indicates that, among single persons who were not involved in primary romantic relationships, men were twice as likely as women to desire such a relationship.

Table 4.5 *Odds Ratios Describing the Effects of Gender, Marital Status, and Age on Wanting a Main Romantic Involvement*

	Odds Ratios
Gender	
Male/female	2.16
Marital status	
Divorced/separated	3.82
Divorced/widowed	7.77
Divorced/never married	4.41
Age	
Young/middle	.71
Young/old	3.33
Gender and age	
Young: male/female	1.01
Middle: male/female	1.71
Old: male/female	6.29

NOTE: Preferred model—[WGA] [WM] [GMA]; LRX(9df)^2 = 21.98, p = .11.

Divorced respondents were more likely than all other marital status groups to desire a relationship: 7.8 times as likely as widowed, 3.8 times as likely as separated, and 4.4 times as likely as never married persons. Younger respondents were only one third as likely as middle-aged respondents, but 3 1/3 times as likely as older respondents to desire a MRI. These results are also consistent with the bivariate associations presented in Table 4.4. The odds ratios that represent the interaction between gender and age on wanting a MRI indicate that among the young, there is no gender difference in desire for a relationship. Middle-aged men, however, were 71% more likely than middle-aged women to want an MRI, whereas older men were 6.29 times as likely as older women to want a romantic relationship.

Discussion

Having a Romantic Involvement

Although the present research does not directly test mate availability conceptualizations, the results provide strong support for such interpretations. The analyses clearly indicate that, overall, being female and being older is associated with a decreased likelihood of romantic involvement among single African Americans. Because the black population exhibits a shortage of males generally, and because one's ability to compete for mates declines at the oldest ages, such overall patterns of romantic involvement would be expected. It is interesting to note that there is no difference whatsoever (i.e., odds ratio = 1.00) in likelihood of romantic involvement among young versus middle-aged respondents. The drop-off in the chances of being involved begins with the oldest age cohort.

Consideration of the number of males versus females for different age cohorts in the black population, however, would suggest that these overall patterns would not be observed across age groups. In particular, a different pattern should be apparent at the youngest ages, where no shortage of males is evident and at which point women (more so than men) are able to seek mates from older age groups. Indeed, our data do reveal that young African American males are somewhat disadvantaged, compared to young women, in the relationship market. This striking difference in relative advantage by gender at different points in the life span is perhaps the clearest evidence for the centrality of availability concerns.

Our previous analyses with the total NSBA sample and with respondents age 55 years and older demonstrated that older women were less likely to be either married or romantically involved than older men. The present study, using log-linear analysis, and focusing solely on the issue of romantic involvement among singles, demonstrates more clearly the degree to which being female and older decreases likelihood of involvement. The finding that older men were over 6 times more likely than women to be romantically involved is quite remarkable. In fact, the difference is so striking that it would appear that sheer availability of mates could not be the most compelling predictor of involvement. Let us explore this concern a bit further.

First, although deficiency of men at older age is a significant factor in chance for involvement, the sex ratio difference does not match the difference in likelihood of involvement. In 1990, the sex ratio for U.S. blacks aged 65 and over was 61.0 (i.e., just over 60 men for every 100 women). Although the sex ratio declines further through the later ages, even at the very oldest age levels—85 years and up—does the sex ratio fall to 41.0, roughly two women to every man (U.S. Bureau of the Census, 1992c).

Second, even when we consider the tendency of older men to marry younger women, one might argue that availability concerns could not be the central factor, because the mean groom-bride age differential does not eliminate older women as potential partners. Calculating mean groom-bride age differences by age of groom, Goldman, Westoff, and Hammerslough (1984) noted that as male age at marriage increased, the spousal age difference increased substantially. Yet even at age 65, grooms were on average 9 years older than their brides (compared to a one year difference at age 20). So a man in his seventies would be highly likely to marry a woman over the age of 55. Still, this could be a more salient factor among African Americans, because spousal age disparity tends to be greater for blacks than whites, with 16% of all black marriages involving a husband who was 6 or more years older than his wife (Sweet & Bumpass, 1987, Table 2.13).

Although these two factors make it appear that constrained mate availability is not the central driving force behind involvement differentials in older ages, we must consider how imbalanced availability both directly and indirectly influences relationship behavior. Based on the evidence presented here and focus group results that we have presented elsewhere (Tucker et al., 1993), it seems likely that older African American women are deliberately opting out of the relationship market for reasons of personal well-being. As stated earlier in this discussion, some older women see a relationship as a threat to their economic security and an unreasonable demand for services. It is likely that the need for companionship has not diminished, but that many women feel that the cost of male romantic companionship is simply too high. Other research we have conducted that addresses the issue of mate availability (Tucker, 1987) more explicitly suggests that male expectations for relationships are higher among men who believe that they are in short supply. This is exactly what Guttentag and Secord (1983) predicted on the basis of social exchange theory. That is, persons in short supply can afford to be more demanding in relationships. Because older black men undoubtedly see themselves as being in short supply, older black women may be responding to their elevated expectations by opting out of the relationship market altogether. Obviously, there is need for additional research that is focused directly on this issue.

The impact of marital status on romantic involvement differs considerably as a function of age. Widowhood is associated with a greater likelihood of involvement among the young, but less involvement among respondents in the middle-aged and older cohorts. It may be that the impact of the death of a spouse is greater in middle and older cohorts because the investment in the relationship is likely to have been greater. Among the oldest group of respondents, the odds of being involved were very similar across marital status. This could reflect the high likelihood of uninvolvement among women, regardless of marital status, coupled with the fact that a male shortage among older men would make marital status less relevant.

Wanting a Romantic Involvement

Many of the associations observed for involvement in romantic relationships were also apparent in desire for romantic involvement. Men who are not in relationships were more desirous of a romantic involvement than were women without partners. It is noteworthy, however, that the majority of both women and men who were neither married nor involved in a romantic relationships did not desire to be in relationships.

Staples (1981b) distinguishes between singlehood for structural reasons versus personal preference. Although a reported disinclination to be in relationships could, for some, be a matter of "sour grapes," clearly many African Americans are not involved in intimate relationships by choice. In fact, less than half of all single men in our sample (48%) were either in relationships or were desirous of being in a relationship. Only one third (35%) of single women were romantically involved or desirous of involvement.

Overall, those who were middle age or approaching middle age (ages 26 to 34, 35 to 54) were most interested in romantic involvement. It may be that societal supports for singlehood are most absent during these periods. Young adulthood is a time when the freedom of singlehood is not only expected but encouraged. Parents worry when offspring get "tied down" with one partner "too soon." By the same token, the prevalence of singlehood during the oldest age groups (i.e., 55 to 64, 65+), whether because of widowhood or imbalanced sex ratios, makes the experience somewhat normative—especially for women. Therefore, singles would not feel particularly out of place. Also, the age groups 26 to 54 are those that are more focused on parental roles. Despite the recent emphasis on singlehood as a valid experience, the predominance of family and child-rearing concerns among persons of these ages, could make single persons feel left out.

The interaction patterns reemphasize certain of the mate availability interpretations presented in connection with having a romantic involvement. That is, there was no gender difference in the desire for romantic involvement among the youngest respondents. Older males, however, were over 5 times more likely to want a relationship than older women. Again, the proportionate difference far outweighs that sex ratio imbalance and the tendency for older men to marry significantly younger women. It seems likely that there is a differential cost and reward structure for relationships among older women and men. To cite again the women in our focus groups, men are likely to be served in such relationships, whereas women are likely to be required to serve.

Divorced persons are by far the most desirous of romantic involvement. Most of those who are not in relationships want to be in one. On one level, it could be argued that those who have been through divorce would be least likely to want such entanglements. On the other hand, those who have tried marriage have demonstrated a need for an intimate relationship.

Conclusions

This study raises a number of important issues concerning the welfare of African American singles. Despite the possible structural impediments to relationship formation (e.g., economics, sex ratio imbalance), it seems likely that singlehood has become an acceptable lifestyle choice for many blacks. Due, in part, to the substantial changes in family formation patterns and living arrangements among African Americans, singlehood has become a very normative experience. This means that single persons are an integral part of the social fabric of African American communities. The absence of stigma, coupled with social acceptance, should serve to bolster the psychological health of single persons.

There is one methodological caveat, however. Although the questionnaire in this study did not specify gender when the inquiry about romantic involvement was made, it is possible that gay males and lesbians did not report same-gender relationships. This could be true even today, but was certainly more likely to have been the case in 1979-1980 when these data were collected. Therefore, our "single" figures are certainly biased upward by the underreporting of homosexual relationships.

Focusing specifically on heterosexual partnerships, then, it is clear that the group most likely to be uninvolved are older women. Although such women may be free of the demands of older men who were probably socialized to hold traditional notions of gender roles, our concern is whether older African American women have sufficient sources of support, given the absence of spouses and romantic partners.

This research, conducted on a representative national sample of blacks, provides a more refined determination than heretofore available of the way that gender, age, and marital status are related to romantic involvement among singles. It is clear, however, that our understanding of the experience of singlehood among African Americans today is woefully inadequate. Single parenthood has received the lion's share of the attention on singles, but an emphasis on single persons who do not have children in the home is virtually absent. We need to know more about the consequences of the normalization of singlehood for both community and individual well-being. How has society at large addressed the reality of increased singlehood? How do single African Americans receive adequate support, particularly during those stages of life when singlehood is, apparently, less acceptable? Given the increasing centrality of singlehood in the lives of blacks, it is clear that an understanding of the lives of single persons is essential for an understanding of African Americans more generally. This is a critically needed research agenda for the 1990s.

5

Life Stress and Psychological Well-Being Among Married and Unmarried Blacks

VERNA M. KEITH

A growing collection of studies indicates that married blacks have higher levels of psychological well-being than unmarried blacks (Broman, 1988a; Jackson, Chatters, & Neighbors, 1986; Williams, Takeuchi, & Adair, 1992; Zollard & Williams, 1987). Documenting marital status differences in subjective well-being has been an important step in advancing our understanding of the determinants of mental health in the black population. If knowledge in this area is to move forward, however, researchers must begin to identify factors that enhance or diminish well-being within each specific marital group. Research of this type is especially critical for the black community given current patterns in marital formation and dissolution. U.S. Bureau of the Census (1992e) data indicate that between 1970 and 1992, the proportion of blacks 18 years and older who were married declined from 64% to 43%, whereas the proportion never married increased from 20.6% to 37.4%. Even more alarming, marital dissolution through divorce more than doubled—from 4.4% to 10.8%—during this 20-year period, surpassing disruption through widowhood, which declined from 11.0% to

95

8.8%. These figures, along with other analyses (see Glick, 1988; Norton & Moorman, 1987), suggest that an increasingly larger proportion of black Americans will never marry or will divorce in the event that they do marry. Increases in the proportions occupying less psychologically advantaged marital positions sharpen the need to identify in greater detail factors that influence well-being within these groups.

Over the past 15 years, life stress has become an influential concept in general research on the determinants of subjective well-being (for review, see Thoits, 1983; Kessler, Price, & Wortman, 1985). According to the stress perspective, acute life problems (e.g., death of a relative) and ongoing strains (e.g., persistent economic difficulties) present demands that challenge the adaptive abilities of the individual. An accumulation of problematic life changes in a relatively short time span or experiencing difficulties over a long time period may erode positive psychological functioning. The stress framework also contends that differences in levels of well-being (within or across marital groups) may emerge in at least two ways (Kessler, 1979). First, some persons are exposed to more stressful life problems than others because of particular constellations of roles and economic resources. Second, and perhaps more important, some individuals are more psychologically responsive to stress because they are less likely to have psychosocial resources (e.g., social support and sense of mastery), which buffer or protect them from the injurious effects of stress. Given that the social and economic circumstances that give rise to stressors vary substantially within marital groups, the stress perspective should be useful for identifying who among the married, widowed, separated-divorced, and never married are most psychologically troubled.

This chapter investigates the effects of stress exposure and stress responsiveness on the psychological well-being of married, separated-divorced, widowed, and never married blacks. A major goal is to determine which social and economic factors increase the probability of experiencing stressful problems within each marital group. In addition, given that previous analyses of the general population have found that resources such as social support can modify the impact of stress on subjective well-being (for review, see Cohen & Wills, 1985; House, Umberson, & Landis, 1988), a second goal of the study is to assess whether family and friendship ties protect blacks from the damaging effects of stress and whether these supportive ties are equally protective for each marital group.

Previous Research

Marital Status and Psychological Well-Being

One of the most consistent findings in the mental health literature is that married persons report higher levels of psychological well-being than unmarried persons (e.g., Andrews & Withey, 1976; Campbell, Converse, & Rogers, 1976; Glen, 1975; Gove, Hughes, & Styles, 1983; Kessler & Essex, 1982; Veroff, Douvan, & Kulka, 1981). As Broman (1988a) points out, early studies of the relationship between marital status and well-being primarily reflected findings for the white population. Information on blacks was limited because small and unrepresentative samples of black respondents restricted sophisticated interracial and intraracial analyses. More satisfactory data has become available in recent years, and an emerging body of research indicates that, similar to the larger population, marital status has a significant impact on the mental health of black Americans.

This research has generally found that married blacks have higher levels of psychological well-being than those who are not married and has also shown that there are substantial differences among the unmarried (Broman, 1988a; Jackson et al., 1986; Williams et al., 1992; Zollard & Williams, 1987). Blacks who have experienced marital dissolution through separation or divorce seem particularly prone to unhappiness and psychological problems (e.g., Broman, 1988a; Williams et al., 1992), although Ball and Robbins (1986) reported that black males in broken marriages were more satisfied with their lives than their married counterparts. Never married blacks appear to have levels of subjective well-being either slightly below the levels for married blacks (Broman, 1988a; Williams et al., 1992) or intermediate between married and separated-divorced blacks (Jackson et al., 1986). Several studies have found no significant differences in levels of satisfaction and happiness among the married and widowed (Broman, 1988a; Jackson et al., 1986). Risks for clinical psychiatric disorders, however, are similar for the widowed and separated-divorced, and the risks are significantly higher for these groups than for the married and never married (Williams et al., 1992). Although Reskin and Coverman (1985) found no marital status differences in psychological distress, most of the evidence points to a significant marital status effect.

Determinants of Psychological Well-Being

Researchers have long noted that status positions and resources affect subjective evaluations of well-being (Campbell et al., 1976; Veroff et al., 1981). Findings from studies of black respondents reveal positive associations between subjective well-being and characteristics such as age; Southern, rural residence, or both; and education (e.g., Campbell et al., 1976; Jackson et al., 1986). Thus, in addition to marital status, these characteristics define other subgroups that have differential access to resources and, consequently, differing levels of well-being. Studies of marital status and subjective well-being among blacks have primarily focused on investigating the extent to which marital status remains predictive of well-being after adjusting for differences in these status positions and resources. As a consequence of this approach, factors that contribute to a more satisfying and happy life within each marital group and that allow researchers to identify subgroup variations have not been extensively investigated.

Although levels of psychological well-being are highest for the married, not all married persons experience the same levels of happiness and well-being (Gove et al., 1983). Research in the general population suggests depressive symptoms are greater for the married with low earnings and low education (Kessler, 1982; Ross & Huber, 1985). Accordingly, married blacks who are well-educated and have few financial problems can be expected to have a psychological advantage over married blacks who are less educated and who have low incomes. Another consideration is that whereas married and never married blacks may report similar levels of well-being, these outcomes may not be produced by the same factors. Some support for this argument is provided by Broman (1988a) who investigated marital status and life satisfaction among blacks. Broman's research revealed interaction effects between marital status and factors such as age, education, and urbanicity. Age, for example, was predictive of life satisfaction among all marital groups except the never married. Thus, previous work on the mental health of black Americans indicates that status positions and economic characteristics are predictive of well-being. The explanatory significance of a specific characteristic, however, may vary from one marital group to another.

Status Positions, Stress Exposure, and Well-Being

The question of why social and economic characteristics predict well-being among blacks, however, remains largely unanswered. Chatters (1988b) notes that status positions and resources can affect psychological well-being indirectly through modifying or intermediate factors. Existing research indicates that life stress is an important modifying factor because it is related to both psychological well-being and to status positions (see Chatters, 1988b; Kessler, 1979; Wheaton, 1980). Consistent with literature drawn from the larger population, research on blacks has found that as levels of acute and chronic stressors increase, levels of psychological distress also increase (Ulbrich, Warheit, & Zimmerman, 1989). Health problems (Broman, 1988a), as well as an accumulation of problems across many areas of life (Chatters, 1988b; Ellison, 1990), are also associated with lower levels of happiness and life satisfaction among black Americans.

Findings from research in the larger population suggest that unmarried persons are exposed to more acute life crises and enduring stressors than married persons (Kessler, 1979; Pearlin & Johnson, 1977). In addition to marital status, investigators have reported linkages between stress exposure and other social characteristics such as age, social class, parental status, and gender.

In general, younger adults report more acute stressors and more chronic strains than older adults (George, 1989; House & Robbins, 1983). Even among blacks aged 55 years and older, Chatters (1988b) found linear age gradations in exposure with older blacks reporting fewer stressors. Diminishing social roles and the problems attached to these roles that accompany aging is one explanation for differential exposure, although some researchers suggest that standard scales may underrepresent stressors unique to the elderly (e.g., Chiriboga, 1977). Socioeconomic standing is also a powerful predictor of stressful experiences. Lower status blacks experience more undesirable acute stressors (e.g., illness and death of family members, crime victimization, and so forth) and chronic economic problems than middle and upper status blacks (Ulbrich et al., 1989). Research on the general population indicates that unemployment, which may be initially classified as a short-term stressor, often leads to longterm problems such as poor health (Kessler, House, & Turner, 1987) and financial instability (Pearlin, Lieberman, Menaghan, & Mullan, 1981; Ross and Huber, 1985).

Parental responsibilities may also be stressful. Although Broman (1988a) found no direct relationship between parental status and subjective well-being among blacks, other research indicates that this relationship may be indirect. Children increase financial pressure on the family (Ross & Huber, 1985) and often create secondary problems such as overcrowding (Ross, Mirowsky, & Goldstein, 1990). Parenting seems particularly stressful for nonmarried persons (for review, see Ross & Mirowsky, 1990). Single parenting, for example, has been associated with chronic role strains among low-income black women (Thompson & Ensminger, 1989). Thus, parenting may have an indirect effect on well-being by increasing exposure to stressful life events and strains.

Researchers have long argued that women, especially married women, experience more stress than males because their roles are more demanding and less rewarding (e.g., Gove, 1972; Gove & Tudor, 1973). In a study of family life satisfaction, Broman (1988b) reported that married black women were more likely than married black men to perform household work and more likely to report being overworked. A study by Chatters (1988b) of older blacks also revealed that women reported more problems than men. It is important to note that the relationship between gender and stress exposure may not be consistent across all marital groups. Thoits (1987) found that married women were exposed to fewer fateful events than married men, but unmarried women experienced more events than unmarried men.

In summary, previous studies suggest that, in addition to being unmarried, being young, lower class, a parent, unemployed, and, in some instances, female are all associated with greater exposure to stressful events and chronic strains. Furthermore, because exposure to stress erodes positive feelings of subjective well-being, differential exposure may provide a link between status positions and psychological outcomes.

Stress Buffering—The Importance of Family and Friends

Investigators have long acknowledged that the relationship between exposure to stress and subjective well-being is less than perfect in the general population (Kessler, 1979; Thoits, 1983). Some individuals are more psychologically vulnerable or responsive to stress than others, even when exposed to similar levels of stress. A considerable body of research has established that persons who are enmeshed in strong family and friendship networks are less likely to succumb to the damaging effects of stress and, therefore, more likely to enjoy higher levels of mental health (for review, see Cohen & Wills, 1985; House et al., 1988). These networks protect members by providing them with emotional and tangible resources that can be used to alleviate or cope with problems and difficulties. Indeed, Kessler and Essex (1982) found that the strong emotional attachments provided by marriage buffered the effects of stress and largely accounted for why the married enjoyed better mental health than the unmarried.

Research in the black community has documented the existence of elaborate social networks that include extended family, friends, neighbors, and church members (e.g., Chatters, Taylor, & Jackson, 1986; Hays & Mindel, 1973; Stack, 1974; Taylor & Chatters, 1986b; Taylor, Chatters, & Mays, 1988). According to Taylor (1986), these networks provide a crucial system of mutual aid (e.g., financial support, emotional comfort and advice, and services). Several recent studies have demonstrated that family and friendship ties are significant for the subjective well-being of blacks. Ellison (1990) found that perceptions of close family relationships increased life satisfaction and happiness. A positive association between the number of close friends and happiness was also reported in this study. Some researchers have also found support for the buffering effect. In a study of depressive symptoms in a Southern black community, Dressler (1985) reported that the extended family buffered the effects of stress among males of all ages and older females. Brown and

Gary (1987) found stress buffering effects for perceived family support among black females of all ages.

It important to note that family and friendship resources may not be equally important across all marital groups. The dissolution of a marriage through separation or divorce may disrupt or create strained relationships between other family members thus reducing emotional closeness and mutual support. Under such circumstances, friendships may become a more important source of help and assistance. Research by Gertsel (1988) indicated that for both divorced men and women, relationships with kin were not always supportive and that many relied on nonkin for practical and emotional support. Thus, although family relationships may be an important buffering resource, it may be more important for divorced persons to have access to confidants that are not enmeshed in the family network.

Research Questions

A growing body of literature has documented the significance of marital status for the psychological well-being of black Americans. This study extends this line of research by investigating stress, buffering, and psychological well-being within and across marital groups. The study particularly addresses the following research questions: (a) Does the level of stress vary by marital status? (b) Do the determinants of stress differ for the married, separated-divorced, widowed, and never married? (c) Does stress have an impact on psychological well-being within each marital group? (d) Do family and friendship ties buffer the impact of stress within each marital group? (e) Are family and friendship ties equally effective for all marital groups?

Method

Data

NSBA respondents were classified into four marital status groups—married ($N = 760$), separated-divorced ($N = 379$), widowed ($N = 231$), and never married ($N = 388$). Separated and divorced respondents were combined because sample sizes precluded independent analyses of the two groups. The sample sizes reflect attrition due to missing data.

Dependent Variables

Psychological Well-Being. Two indicators were used to measure psychological well-being—personal happiness and general life satisfaction. Personal happiness, an affective dimension of well-being, measures a transient mood that is grounded in an individual's immediate experiences (Campbell, 1981). In this study, happiness is measured with a single item that asked respondents to indicate how happy they are. Responses were coded 1 (*not too happy*), 2 (*pretty happy*), and 3 (*very happy*). Life satisfaction, a more enduring cognitive dimension of well-being, involves an assessment of the gap between an individual's ideal, expected, and achieved status (Campbell, 1981). This indicator is measured with a single item that asked respondents how satisfied they are with their lives as a whole. Responses range from 1 (*very dissatisfied*) to 4 (*very satisfied*).

Independent Variables

Stress. Stressful problems are measured with a nine-item check list of negative life events occurring in the following areas—health, money, job, police, crime, racial difficulties, love life, problems with people outside the family, and children. Respondents were asked to indicate whether they had experienced any of these events within the past month. Each problem received a score of 1 and a simple summary score was computed. Events were not weighted by their readjustment value and no attempt was made to assess the stressfulness of the problem because past research indicates that these procedures do not increase explained variance (see Thoits, 1983).

Family and Friendship Ties. Perceived family closeness is used as a measure of family relations in the analyses. Scores for this item range from 1 (*not close at all*) to 4 (*very close*). The number of close friends that respondents could discuss personal problems with is used to measure friendship ties. Scores for this item ranged from 1 (*none*) to 4 (*many*).

Status and Resource Variables. Based on previous research, the following status and resource indicators were selected: age (years), gender (female coded 1), children (any children under 18 years of age residing in household, coded 1), employed (employed respondents coded 1), family income (8-point scale ranging from 1 *under $4,000 per year* to 8 *$30,000 or more per year*), education (18-point scale ranging from 0 *no years of completed schooling* to 17 *college graduate, additional years of schooling, or both*).

Control Variables. In addition to the status position and resource variables, two demographic factors that have been predictive of psychological well-being in previous studies (e.g., Broman, 1988a; Campbell, 1981) are included in the analyses—region of residence (South coded 1) and urban (coded 1 for residence in an urban area of any size).

Data Analysis

Ordinary least squares regression techniques (OLS) are used to estimate a series of separate models for married, separated-divorced, widowed, and never married blacks. To evaluate the stress buffering hypothesis, interaction terms are created by multiplying the stress score by the family closeness score and the stress score by the number of close friends. Wheaton (1985) refers to this form of stress buffering as a "moderator" effect. The moderator model of stress buffering makes no assumptions about causal relationships between stress and family-friendship ties. Rather, it indicates under what conditions the relationship between stress and psychological well-being is altered. In this analysis, a statistically significant interaction term reveals whether feeling close to one's family or having many close friends reduces or increases the impact of stress on well-being.

Results

Marital Status Differences in Status, Resources, Stress, Social Ties, and Well-Being

Table 5.1 presents means for each variable used in the analysis by marital status. For purposes of comparison, statistically significant differences between the married and the nonmarried are indicated. The results show that, compared to married blacks, separated-divorced blacks are more likely to be female, have fewer children residing in the household, less likely to reside in

Table 5.1 *Marital Status Differences in Status, Stress, Resource, and Well-Being*

Variable	Married	Separated/ Divorced	Widowed	Never Married
Age	43.63	42.68	63.87***	27.52***
Female (%)	.52	.72***	.83***	.58*
Children < 18 (%)	.62	.52***	.24***	.50***
Employed	.66	.64	.30***	.58***
South (%)	.55	.47*	.63*	.50*
Urban (%)	.75	.88***	.73	.82*
Education	11.24	11.17	8.50***	12.12**
Family income	12.32	9.73***	6.89***	10.03***
Stress	1.39	1.94***	1.17*	2.13***
Family closeness	3.52	3.39***	3.58	3.40**
Close friends	2.16	2.22	2.18	2.23
Happiness	2.23	1.97***	2.29	1.96***
Life satisfaction	3.14	2.92***	3.16	2.92***
N	760	379	231	388

Significant difference from married is denoted with asterisks: $*p < .05$; $**p < .01$; $***p < .001$.

the South, more likely to reside in urban areas, and have lower family income. Separated-divorced respondents have considerably higher levels of stress (means are 1.94 vs. 1.39) lower levels of happiness (1.97 vs. 2.23) and life satisfaction (2.92 vs. 3.14), and are somewhat less likely to feel closer to their families (3.39 vs. 3.52) than married blacks.

Widowed blacks differ significantly from married blacks on all status and control variables with the exception of urban residence. The widowed are older, more likely to be female, have fewer children in the household, are less likely to be employed, more likely to reside in the South, and have lower levels of education and family income. Consistent with the literature, the widowed report fewer stressors than married blacks (1.17 vs. 1.39), but there are no significant differences in family and friend relationships or in psychological well-being.

The never married differed from the married on all variables except number of close friends. Compared to married persons, individuals who have never married are younger, more likely to be female, have fewer children, are less likely to be employed, less likely to reside in the South, and more likely to reside in an urban area. The never married are better educated than the married but have lower incomes. Never married persons report experiencing more stress than the married (2.13 vs. 1.39), but are somewhat less likely to feel close to their families (3.40 vs. 3.52) and less likely to be happy (1.96 vs. 2.23) or feel satisfied with their lives (2.92 vs. 3.14).

In summary, married and widowed blacks experience the least amount of stress, followed by the separated-divorced and the never married, in that order. The married and widowed also report greater family closeness and higher psychological well-being than the other marital groups. There are no significant differences in number of close friends.

Factors Affecting Stress Exposure

Table 5.2 presents the results of analyses that were designed to evaluate the impact of status and resource variables on levels of stress for each of the marital groups. The control variables, Southern residence and rural residence, were also included in the analysis. Among the married, being older was associated with lower levels of stress, being female was associated with higher levels of stress, and having children had no effect. Married persons who were employed and resided in the South reported fewer stressors. Level of education had no significant impact on stress exposure, but higher family income reduced exposure to stressful problems.

Among separated and divorced blacks, being older and having higher family income were associated with reduced levels of stress whereas being female was associated with heightened exposure to problems. None of the other variables had a significant impact on stress exposure. For the widowed, being older and residing in the South, and having higher family income were associated with reduced stress. Among never married blacks, in contrast to the other marital groups, age and family income had no significant effect on stress exposure. Being employed and living in the South reduced exposure to stress in this group, but none of the other factors affected stress. In summary, given status and resource variables affect stress exposure to some degree in each of the marital groups. Factors affecting stress, however, are not consistent across all groups.

Table 5.2 The Effects of Stress and Supportive Resources on Happiness and Life Satisfaction by Marital Status[a]

	Married					Separated-Divorced				
	Stress	Family Close	Close Friends	Happiness	Life Satisfaction	Stress	Family Close	Close Friends	Happiness	Life Satisfaction
Age	-.028*** (-.264)	.003 (.059)	.005* (.097)	.007*** (.167)	.007** (.143)	-.038*** (-.284)	.001 (.017)	.003 (-.047)	.011*** (.234)	.001* (.141)
Female	.333*** (.103)	.040 (.029)	.128 (.086)	.027 (.022)	.014 (.008)	.527*** (.133)	-.051 (-.029)	-.060 (-.035)	.077 (.055)	.022 (.010)
Children < 18	.118 (.035)	-.069 (-.048)	.050 (.032)	.050 (.039)	.061 (.036)	.203 (-.133)	.027 (.017)	.042 (.028)	.098 (.077)	.065 (.034)
Employed	-.369** (-.108)	.103* (.071)	.092 (.058)	-.072 (-.055)	-.034 (-.020)	-.360* (-.097)	.140 (.085)	.084 (.053)	.087 (.066)	.091 (.046)
South	-.322** (-.099)	-.034 (-.025)	-.089 (-.060)	.015 (.012)	.067 (.040)	.092 (.026)	.133 (.084)	-.104 (-.068)	.052 (.041)	.171* (.089)
Urban	.455 (.120)	-.052 (-.033)	-.195** (-.114)	-.048 (-.034)	-.040 (-.021)	.034 (.006)	-.128 (-.052)	-.121 (-.031)	.129 (.065)	-.178* (-.059)
Education	-.001 (-.002)	.003 (.014)	-.013 (-.059)	-.001 (-.006)	-.001 (-.005)	.006 (-.011)	.014 (.057)	.010 (.041)	-.016 (-.078)	-.033* (-.106)
Family income	-.061*** (-.147)	.009 (.049)	-.005 (-.026)	-.000 (-.003)	-.006 (-.028)	-.042 (-.100)	-.004 (-.023)	.003 (.016)	.012 (.081)	.001 (.002)
Stress		.092*** (-.217)	.005 (.010)	-.124** (-.326)	-.110*** (-.217)		-.051* (-.115)	-.012 (-.027)	-.100*** (-.283)	-.136*** (-.252)
Family closeness				.078 (.087)	.139** (.116)				.002 (.003)	.034** (.028)
Close friends				.060* (.073)	-.033 (-.030)				.106** (.128)	.174** (.139)
R^2	.135	.074	.034	.196	.113	.157	.037	.019	.185	.143

a. Standardized coefficients appear in parentheses.
*$p < .05$; **$p < .01$; ***$p < .001$.

Table 5.2 (continued)

	Widowed					Never Married				
	Stress	Family Close	Close Friends	Happiness	Life Satisfaction	Stress	Family Close	Close Friends	Happiness	Life Satisfaction
Age	-.049***	-.005	.004	.018***	-.011	-.015	-.004	-.005	.001	-.004
	(-.454)	(-.097)	(.079)	(.384)	(.159)	(-.284)	(-.050)	(-.062)	(.015)	(-.041)
Female	-.132	.032	.071	.005	-.028	.104	-.032	-.149*	.051	.007
	(-.034)	(.017)	(.036)	(.003)	(-.011)	(.027)	(-.021)	(-.091)	(.037)	(.004)
Children < 18	-.056	.016	.017	.162	.170	.143	.103	.043	.094	-.029
	(-.016)	(.010)	(.010)	(.106)	(.078)	(.038)	(.066)	(.027)	(.069)	(-.016)
Employed	-.228	-.109	-.031	-.069	-.054	-.618**	.279**	-.063	-.087	-.063
	(-.072)	(-.070)	(-.019)	(-.049)	(-.027)	(-.162)	(.178)	(-.039)	(-.063)	(-.035)
South	-.361*	-.260**	.106	.086	.041	-.857***	.114	.139	.081	.115
	(-.120)	(-.177)	(.069)	(.064)	(.021)	(-.227)	(.073)	(.086)	(.059)	(.065)
Urban	-.273	-.012	-.143	-.080	-.120	.267	-.059	-.073	-.102	-.173
	(-.083)	(-.008)	(-.085)	(-.054)	(-.057)	(.055)	(-.030)	(-.035)	(-.058)	(-.075)
Education	-.017	.016	-.001	-.002	-.015	.026	.036*	.029	-.003	-.007
	(-.044)	(.082)	(-.006)	(-.012)	(.060)	(.034)	(.116)	(.088)	(-.009)	(-.019)
Family income	-.057*	.016	-.043**	.020	.002	-.030	-.008	.021*	.007	.016
	(-.144)	(.083)	(-.212)	(.114)	(.009)	(-.072)	(-.046)	(.119)	(.047)	(.084)
Stress		-.059*	.024	-.050*	-.183***		-.056*	-.043*	-.115***	-.132***
		(-.122)	(.049)	(-.113)	(-.286)		(-.138)	(-.101)	(-.320)	(-.281)
Family closeness				.191***	.115				.171***	.127*
				(.208)	(.087)				(.195)	(.111)
Close friends				-.060	-.078				.068*	.110*
				(-.068)	(-.062)				(.081)	(.100)
R^2	.188	.061	.043	.233	.157	.111	.090	.067	.209	.163

a. Standardized coefficients appear in parentheses.

*p < .05; **p < .01; ***p < .001.

107

Table 5.3 *Multiple Regression Estimates for Predictors of Happiness by Marital Status*

| | Married | | | | | | Separated-Divorced | | | | | |
| | Model 1 | | Model 2 | | Model 3 | | Model 1 | | Model 2 | | Model 3 | |
Variable	*b*	*β*	*b*	*β*	*b*	*β*	*b*	*β*	*b*	*β*	*b*	*β*
Age	.007***	.187	.007***	.174	.007***	.173	.011***	.239	.012***	.246	.012***	.241
Female	.031	.025	.020	.016	.023	.016	.075	.053	.082	.058	.090	.064
Children < 18	.043	.034	.045	.036	.045	.036	.106	.083	.103	.081	.098	.079
Employed	-.069	-.053	-.083	-.063	-.088	-.067	.104	.079	.097	.074	.099	.075
South	.006	.005	.015	.012	.014	.012	.036	.029	.047	.037	.047	.037
Urban	-.074	-.052	-.058	-.041	-.057	-.040	.125	.064	.142	.072	.138	.070
Education	-.001	-.006	.000	-.003	-.000	-.003	-.014	-.070	-.015	-.075	-.016	-.079
Family income	.000	.002	.000	.000	.001	-.004	.018	.073	.011	.071	.012	.072
Stress	-.144***	-.329	-.135***	-.310	-.214***	-.491	-.114***	-.282	-.112***	-.279	-.153***	-.380
Family close (FC)			.084**	.094	.060	.067			.000	.000	-.014	-.017
Close friends (CF)			.059*	.071	.037	.044			.101**	.122	.083	.101
Stress × FC					.012	.092					.006	.050
Stress × CF					.018	.095					.009	.059
Intercept	2.161		1.746		1.888		1.464		1.218		1.325	
R² adjusted	.16		.18		.18		.15		.16		.16	
R²	.17		.19		.19		.17		.18		.18	

+*p* < .10; *p* < .05; **p* < .01; ***p* < .001.

Table 5.3 (continued)

	Widowed						Never Married					
	Model 1		Model 2		Model 3		Model 1		Model 2		Model 3	
Variable	b	β	b	β	b	β	b	β	b	β	b	β
Age	.020***	.373	.019***	.397	.019***	.397	.000	.000	.000	.015	.001	.021
Female	.009	.006	.007	.004	.004	.002	.027	.020	.044	.032	.001	.021
Children < 18	.167	.109	.165	.107	.161	.105	-.080	-.075	-.101	-.075	-.103	-.076
Employed	-.087	-.061	-.068	-.048	-.068	-.048	-.054	-.039	-.100	-.073	-.104	-.076
South	.134	.100	.090	.067	.090	.069	.110	.081	.078	.058	.076	.056
Urban	-.071	-.048	-.077	-.052	-.072	-.049	-.120	-.068	-.115	.066	-.123	-.070
Education	.002	.013	-.001	-.006	-.001	-.006	.008	.030	.000	-.001	.000	-.001
Family income	.020	.114	.020	.113	.020	.111	.007	.052	.008	.051	.007	.049
Stress	-.059+	-.125	-.046	-.098	-.042	-.089	-.134***	-.334	-.122***	-.303	-.182*	-.453
Family close (FC)			.193***a	.210	.180*	.196			.175***	.200	.119+	.136
Close friends (CF)			-.061	-.070	-.049	-.056			.071+	.084	.090	.106
Stress × FC					.005	.038					.023	.197
Stress × CF					-.009	-.049					-.007	-.045
Intercept	1.016		.448		.447		2.163		1.496		1.649	
R^2 adjusted	.15		.20		.19		.13		.18		.17	
R^2	.19		.23		.23		.15		.20		.20	

a. Coefficient significantly different from the married.
$+p < .10$; $*p < .05$; $**p < .01$; $***p < .001$.

109

Stress, Buffering, and Personal Happiness

Table 5.3 presents results from the hierarchal regression analysis of personal happiness for each of the marital groups. It is important to note that prior to estimating Model 1, only the status-resource and control variables were entered into the regression equation. With the exception of age, none of these variables had a significant direct impact on happiness. Therefore, the results from the regression analysis, which included only status-resource and control variables, are not presented in Table 5.3.

Considering married persons first, Model 1 presents the effects of status position, resources, stress, and the control variables on personal happiness. The results indicate that age has a positive direct impact on happiness among the married whereas stress is associated with lower levels of happiness. Model 2 shows that family closeness and number of close friends are both associated with increased levels of happiness, although the effect for close family is stronger. There are no significant interaction effects between stress and either family closeness or number of close friends, as shown in Model 3. Thus, although these social relationships are significant for levels of happiness among the married, they do not buffer the effects of stress.

Among separated and divorced blacks, happiness increases with advancing age, but stress reduces feelings of happiness (see Model 1). Family closeness has no impact on personal happiness among separated-divorced blacks. Number of close friends, however, is associated with higher levels of happiness, but there is no support for stress buffering when the interaction terms are added in Model 3.

Turning to the widowed, increased age is again associated with higher levels of happiness. The impact of stress on personal happiness, however, is only marginally significant ($p = .10$). Among widowed blacks, feeling close to one's family is the strongest determinant of personal happiness, whereas number of close friends has no significant effect. Indeed, the relationship between close friends and happiness is negative and opposite of expectation. Neither of the interaction effects are significant for this marital group.

Among the never married, in contrast to the other marital groups, age has no effect on personal happiness. Stress has a significant negative effect and family closeness a significant positive effect among persons never married. Having close friends is only marginally significant and neither interaction effect is significant.

In summary, the findings show that stress reduces feelings of happiness in all marital groups. Although family and friend relationships do not meet the criteria for stress buffering, they do appear to exercise a positive, independent effect on happiness, but their relative importance varies from one marital group to another. For the married, both resources are important. For the widowed and never married, family closeness is important. Among the separated-divorced, having close friends is a key element in level of happiness. It is noteworthy that most of the status and resource variables had no direct effect on happiness in any of the marital groups. The analyses presented in Table 5.2, however, indicate that status and resource variables may operate indirectly through stress. Among the married, for example, gender; employment; Southern, rural residence, or both; and family income affected exposure to stress and stress affected personal happiness.

Stress, Buffering, and Life Satisfaction

Results of the analyses of life satisfaction are presented in Table 5.4. Similar to the findings for personal happiness, age has a positive effect on satisfaction in all marital groups except the never married. Higher levels of stress are associated with reduced life satisfaction in all marital groups. Similar to the findings for personal happiness, most of the status and resource variables did not affect life satisfaction directly.

Among married persons, family closeness increased levels of satisfaction. Although the relationship between number of close friends and life satisfaction was not significant, the sign of the relationship indicated that married persons with many close friends were less satisfied with their lives.

Among the separated and divorced, family closeness has no significant effect on life satisfaction. As the number of close friends increase, level of satisfaction increases. The results also indicate a significant interaction effect between stress and family closeness within this marital group. It should be noted that the relationship is marginal given the small increase in R^2. Interestingly, the sign of the interaction effect is negative. This finding suggests that the impact of stress on life satisfaction is more deleterious for separated-divorced persons who have strong emotional bonds with their families. To explore this relationship further, the effects of stress on life satisfaction for several levels of family closeness were computed. The results show that at one standard deviation below the mean level of family closeness, the relationship is $-.1288$. It is $-.1789$ at the mean and $-.2880$ at one standard deviation above the mean. Thus, close emotional ties to the family during times of stress appears to make matters worse.

Among the widowed, neither family closeness nor close friends had a significant effect on life satisfaction. Similar to the findings for personal happiness, the relationship between number of close friends and life satisfaction is

Table 5.4 Multiple Regression Estimates for Predictors of Life Satisfaction by Marital Status

	Married						Separated-Divorced					
	Model 1		Model 2		Model 3		Model 1		Model 2		Model 3	
Variable	b	β	b	β	b	β	b	β	b	β	b	β
Age	.008**	.148	.007**	.143	.008**	.141	.011*	.147	.011*	.156	.011*	.145
Female	.011	.006	.010	.006	.012	.059	.023	.011	.036	.017	.033	.016
Children <18	.045	.027	.057	.033	.055	.032	.087	.078	.083	.043	.066	.036
Employed	-.037	-.021	-.048	-.027	-.055	-.032	.128	.063	.113	.057	.093	.047
South	.062	.038	.064	.039	.064	.039	.151	.078	.164	.085	.185	.093
Urban	-.047	-.025	-.045	-.023	-.044	-.023	.185	.062	.216	.072	.229	.077
Education	.000	.001	-.001	-.003	-.007	-.023	-.030	-.097	-.032	-.104	-.030	-.096
Family income	-.004	-.022	-.006	-.029	-.007	-.031	-.002	-.007	-.002	-.009	.000	-.004
Stress	-.144***	-.248	-.130***	-.224	-.218*	-.376	-.161***	-.264	-.157***	-.257	-.032	-.052
Family close (FC)			.140**	.117	.123	.102			.029	.024	.184	.151
Close friends (CF)			-.034	-.031	-.069	-.063			.160***	.127	.077	.061
Stress × FC					.008	.045					-.066*	-.378
Stress × CF					.028	.114					.041	.170
Intercept	3.043		2.639		2.792		2.732		2.243		1.905	
R² adjusted	.09		.10		.10		.11		.12		.12	
R²	.10		.12		.12		.13		.14		.15	

*p < .05; **p < .01; ***p < .001.

112

Table 5.4 (continued)

| | Widowed | | | | | | Never Married | | | | | |
| | Model 1 | | Model 2 | | Model 3 | | Model 1 | | Model 2 | | Model 3 | |
Variable	b	β	b	β	b	β	b	β	b	β	b	β
Age	.012*	.170	.012*	.182	.012*	.180	-.004	-.056	-.003	-.045	-.004	-.049
Female	-.024	-.051	-.022	-.008	-.010	-.004	-.033	-.018	-.012	-.006	-.020	-.011
Children < 18	.182	.083	.181	.083	.185	.084	-.015	-.008	-.034	-.019	-.029	-.016
Employed	.047	.023	.057	.028	.057	.028	-.036	-.020	-.069	-.038	-.063	-.035
South	.068	.035	.046	.024	.039	.020	.136	.077	.103	.058	.100	.056
Urban	-.108	-.051	-.119	-.056	-.134	-.064	-.184	-.080	-.184	-.078	-.180	-.078
Education	-.011	-.042	-.013	-.050	-.012	-.048	.003	.007	-.005	-.015	-.004	-.011
Family income	.000	.000	.002	.007	.001	.007	.018	.092	.017	.086	.017	.085
Stress	-.187***	-.275	-.178***	-.263	-.268	-.397	-.152***	-.288	-.140***	-.264	-.139***	-.263
Family close (FC)			.118	.090	.128	.098			.138*	.120	.192*	.167
Close friends (CF)			-.083	-.066	-.124	-.099			.110***	.099	.039	.035
Stress × FC					.002	.012					-.022	-.143
Stress × CF					.038	.138					.034	.151
Intercept	2.730		2.443		2.507		3.297		2.671		2.636	
R² adjusted	.10		.11		.10		.11		.13		.13	
R²	.14		.15		.15		.13		.15		.16	

*p < .05; **p < .01; ***p < .001.

113

negative. Among the never married, both family closeness and number of close friends are associated with greater life satisfaction. There were no significant interaction effects for either the widowed or the never married.

Summary and Conclusions

The significance of marital status for the mental health of black Americans has been noted in previous research. The purpose of this study was to extend this line of research by identifying factors that enhance or diminish psychological well-being within specific marital groups—the married, separated-divorced, widowed, and never married. The importance of stressful life problems and family and friendship ties for the well-being of each marital group are of particular interest. The guiding argument is that within each marital group, differentials in status and resources affect exposure to stressful life problems, which, in turn, affects psychological well-being. The relationship between stress and well-being, however, may be moderated or buffered by family and friendship ties and these stress buffering resources may differ by marital status.

Findings from the descriptive analyses indicated significant marital status variations in levels of well-being, stressful life problems, ties to family, and indicators of status and resources. Consistent with previous research on black Americans (see Jackson et al., 1986), the married and widowed have the highest levels of happiness and life satisfaction and the separated-divorced and never married have the lowest levels. Stressful life problems are most prevalent among the never married, followed by the separated-divorced, married, and widowed in that order. Married and widowed blacks report more emotional closeness with their families, separated-divorced blacks the least, and never married blacks report intermediate levels. There are no significant marital status differences in the number of friends that respondents could confide in.

The analyses of the determinants of exposure to stressful life problems confirmed findings from the general stress literature. Within each marital group, stress exposure was conditioned to some extent by status and resource variables. Because factors such as age, gender, employment status, region of residence, and family income partially define the context of life experiences, they also condition exposure to problematic aspects of life. More important, a major finding of the present study is that the relevance of specific status and resource characteristics in determining exposure to stress differs for specific groups. Age and family income, for example, significantly affect the level of stress experienced by all marital groups except the never married. Only among the married and the separated-divorced is being female associated with significantly higher levels of stress than being male. Although space constraints preclude further consideration of these patterns, the results underscore the utility of conducting separate analyses for each marital group.

As anticipated, stress plays a major role in determining level of psychological well-being among black Americans. In general, as stressful life problems increased, happiness and life satisfaction decreased in all marital groups. The relationship between stress and life satisfaction, however, was only marginally significant among widowed blacks. These findings indicate that within each marital group, it is those who are facing negative life experiences that are most likely to be unhappy and unsatisfied. With the exception of age, status and resource variables had no significant impact on well-being in any of the marital groups. These findings, together with those discussed previously, lend strong support to the contention that stress acts as a modifying or intervening factor that links status and resources to subjective well-being (see Chatters, 1988b; Kessler, 1979).

The results indicate that being close to family members and having many close friends are also associated with happiness and life satisfaction, although the relative importance of these social ties varies across marital groups and indicators of well-being. Among married respondents, feeling that the family is close is associated with greater levels of happiness and life satisfaction. Having many close friends is also positively associated with happiness. Among separated-divorced blacks having many close friends increases subjective well-being, whereas family closeness has no significant direct effect. These findings are consistent with literature that suggests that friends become important sources of support during a marital breakup.

Both family closeness and having close friends are important for each indicator of well-being among the never married. For widowed blacks, family closeness is significant for determining happiness. Indeed, the relationship between stress and happiness becomes nonsignificant when family closeness is added to the regression model. Having lost an important social relationship on being widowed, their remaining family members may become even more important to them. Family and friendship ties did not generally buffer the effects of stress in these analyses, although they had independent effects in various marital groups. Family closeness did buffer the impact of stress on life satisfaction among the separated-divorced. The relationship was only marginally significant and should be interpreted with care. Unexpectedly, separated-divorced persons who feel close to their families experience lower levels of satisfaction during times of stress. Research by Taylor (1986) revealed a positive association between family closeness and received support. Perhaps separated and divorced blacks must rely extensively on the family network during times of stress. Although they may feel emotionally close to the family, they may also feel dependent, which may lead to lower satisfaction.

Overall, this research demonstrates the utility of examining determinants of psychological well-being within and across marital groups among black Americans. This approach facilitates identifying subgroups that may be more psychologically troubled than others. This study also suggests that the stress framework is useful for understanding mental health among blacks. Within each marital group, individuals who are most burdened by life problems are most likely to perceive their lives as being unhappy and less satisfying.

The analyses presented here included a limited number of stressful problems. Future research should include a more comprehensive list of acute events and also explore the effects of chronic life strains such as poverty. Marital status differences in levels of stress might indeed reflect differences in the relative representativeness of the items for each group. An examination of the impact of persistent marital strife on the well-being of married blacks would also be enlightening. Future studies of the mental health of blacks should also assess whether or not personal resources such as the sense of control operates to buffer the effects of stress within marital groups. Although this study examined only one type of stress buffering, the moderator form, researchers should examine other types suggested by Wheaton (1985).

6

Religious Involvement and the Subjective Quality of Family Life Among African Americans

CHRISTOPHER G. ELLISON

Introduction

The religion-family connection has received significant attention from social scientists in recent years. A growing body of research links religious participation and beliefs with various family attitudes and practices: the choice of
marital partners; the timing, duration, and stability of marital bonds; fertility-
related beliefs and patterns; gender roles; sexual attitudes and practices; and
child-rearing values and practices; as well as other dimensions of family life
(for reviews, see Marciano, 1987; Thomas & Cornwall, 1990).

To date, however, most of the research on the religion-family connection
has been based on data from predominantly white samples. The possible impact of religious factors on the family life of African Americans has been given
short shrift in the literature until very recently. This general pattern of neglect
is surprising for at least three reasons. First, religious institutions have traditionally played central symbolic and functional roles within the black community, and individual African Americans have engaged in comparatively high
levels of organizational and private religious practice (Levin, Taylor, & Chatters, 1994; Roof & McKinney, 1987; Taylor & Chatters, 1991b). Second, as

secular organizations have increasingly assumed the political functions once fulfilled primarily by the black church, a number of commentators have suggested that the main future contribution of religious institutions will be in enhancing the quality of African Americans' personal lives, specifically in mitigating the harmful effects of interpersonal and institutional racism (e.g., Gilkes, 1980; Mukenge, 1983). Third, scholars, policymakers, and community activists have expressed perennial concern over the status of African American families, including the high incidence of single-parent households, out-of-wedlock births, and other issues. Thus, given the prominence of religion and the widespread interest in families, it is surprising that researchers have largely neglected the relationships between these two pivotal institutions in the black community.

This chapter begins to fill this gap in the research literature by exploring the relationships between religious involvement and subjective assessments of the quality of family life among African Americans. After briefly outlining several theoretical links between aspects of public and private religious involvement and the perceived quality of family life, I explore this issue using data from the NSBA. Via a series of multivariate logistic regression models, I estimate the net effects of religious variables and covariates on three indicators of the subjective quality of family life: (a) positive evaluations of performance in family roles (i.e., as provider, spouse, parent); (b) perceptions of family closeness; and (c) satisfaction with family life. The concluding section of this chapter discusses the implications of these findings and suggests several important directions for future data collection and analysis.

Theoretical and Empirical Background

The Centrality of the Black Church

Religious institutions have traditionally been situated at the institutional and symbolic core of the African American community. Because the church has been the major institution controlled by African Americans in a largely hostile social and political environment, it has been called on to fulfill a wide range of functions within the black community (Frazier, 1964/1974). For instance, since the slave era, churches have promoted mutual aid (e.g., burial societies), educational uplift, and various other initiatives aimed at advancing the individual and collective welfare of African Americans (Lincoln & Mamiya, 1990; Mays & Nicholson, 1933; Nelsen & Nelsen, 1975). Furthermore, churches and clergy have traditionally assumed political leadership in black communities, providing information about issues and spurring community-wide mobilization (Ellison, 1991; Morris, 1984; Washington, 1985). Moreover, participation in religious clubs and organizations has frequently offered African Americans opportunities for social interaction and social status that have historically been unavailable in white-dominated society (Ellison & Sherkat, 1995). Given this history, it is reasonable to anticipate that religious participation may have important implications for the quality of family life among African Americans.

Congregations as Family Support Systems

One expects that public religious participation—that is, regular participation in religious services and other church activities—may be associated with positive subjective family closeness and satisfaction with family life among African Americans for at least three reasons. First, many black church communities promote informal and formal mechanisms of family support. African Americans derive substantial informal social support from coreligionists, and this support ranges from socioemotional support (e.g., companionship) to tangible aid (e.g., money, goods, transportation, child care, information) (Ortega, Crutchfield, & Rushing, 1983; Taylor & Chatters, 1988). In addition to these informal practices, various African American congregations sponsor a wide range of initiatives aimed at (a) reducing sources of potential stress for families, and (b) dealing with family problems effectively: youth and pregnancy prevention programs (McAdoo & Crawford, 1990), mental health counseling and referral (Williams & Griffith, 1993), health information programs (Eng, Hatch, & Callan, 1985), and programs for the elderly (Caldwell, Greene, & Billingsley, 1992), among many others. Levels of service provision are generally higher among African American congregations than among predominantly white churches (Chaves & Higgins, 1992; Taylor, Luckey, & Smith, 1990), and the commitment to service provision among African American congregations cuts across traditional denominational and theological boundaries within the black community (Caldwell et al., 1992; Lincoln & Mamiya, 1990).

Although these programmatic aspects of the church's support for families have received growing attention from scholars in recent years, other understudied facets of congregational life may also contribute to family solidarity and satisfaction. Religious groups are sustained by social networks (e.g., Cornwall, 1987), and participation in church-related activities often brings together individuals who share status characteristics (e.g., race, socioeconomic status), as well as religious convictions (Lewis, 1955; Ross & Wheeler, 1971; Williams, 1974). It is reasonable to expect that regular contact with like-minded others within religious contexts may reinforce basic role identities and role expectations, including those germane to the family. Indeed, informal interaction with coreligionists—along with the statements of church leaders from the pulpit, in Sunday School classes, and so forth—may buttress beliefs about the sanctity of marriage as an institution, and the essential validity and importance of parenting. Furthermore, such interaction may affirm common understandings of the "good" spouse, the "good" parent, and the "good" son or daughter (Ellison, 1993). At the same time, such informal interaction may help to reassure individuals that their performance in these familial roles is reasonable and appropriate, while facilitating the sympathetic exchange of advice on marital relations, child rearing, or other family issues among participants. In these ways, regular engagement by individual African Americans in congregational activities may enhance perceptions of the quality of family life. Finally, the rhetoric and discourse within many African American religious groups may center on the theme of "family" in several ways (Cooper-Lewter & Mitchell, 1986). Given the role of religious institutions as conservators of African American history and culture (Washington, 1985), it is not surprising that sermons and other official pronouncements may underscore the close historical and functional alliance between the institutions of church and family. Clergy and lay leaders in recent years have worked to stimulate awareness of the problems confronting contemporary African American families, and to emphasize the importance of family solidarity and integrity for the intergenerational transmission of religious values and African American culture (Roberts, 1980). In addition, many congregational events are structured to facilitate the collective recognition of the accomplishments of families and their members. Thus, the activities and rhetoric of many African American congregations may encourage an appreciation of the importance of family life, while providing supportive feedback to members in their efforts to build and maintain stable, happy families.

Private Religiosity and "Divine Relations"

In addition to the possible role of churches and church communities, one also expects that private devotional activities may contribute to positive perceptions of family life among African Americans for several reasons. Through prayer, meditation, and scriptural readings, individuals construct personal relationships with "divine others," in much the same way that they develop relationships with concrete social others (Pollner, 1989; Wikstrom, 1987). By identifying with figures portrayed in religious texts and other religious media, individuals engage in "role taking." Individuals may come to understand their own life circumstances, including family relations, in terms of a scriptural figure's situation, and they may begin to reconsider their situations from the point of view of the "God role"—that is, what a divine other would expect in terms of appropriate parental or spousal demeanor and deportment.

Devotional practices may promote positive assessments of the quality of family life for additional reasons. First, the Bible and other religious texts routinely extol the intrinsic virtue of love, compassion, and commitment, particularly toward family members. In addition, numerous scriptural passages are widely interpreted as offering specific guidance regarding spousal and intergenerational relationships. Furthermore, several studies of predominantly white samples suggest that private religious devotion helps family members to cultivate a sense of purpose and values centered on loving and caring (Scanzoni & Arnett, 1987) and on the needs and welfare of others (Larson & Goltz, 1989; Schumm, 1985).

Measures

Subjective Quality of Family Life

This study employs three main indicators of subjective assessments of family life. First, subjective family closeness is measured in terms of responses to the following item: "Would you say your family members are very close in their feelings to each other, fairly close, not too close, or not close at all?" The distribution of these responses is sharply skewed, with some 63% of the NSBA respondents reporting having *very close* family relationships. In light of the skewness, this item has been recoded dichotomously to identify those persons with *very close* family ties.

Second, family satisfaction is measured via responses to this item: "How satisfied are you with your family life, that is, the time you spend and the things you do with members of your family? Would you say that you are very satisfied, somewhat satisfied, somewhat dissatisfied, or very dissatisfied?" Like the indicator of family closeness, the distribution of this variable is positively skewed. Because nearly 55% of NSBA respondents express high satisfaction with their families, this item has been dichotomized to identify respondents who are *very satisfied* with their family life.

Third, this study also employs a measure of the self-rated performance of family roles. This indicator is constructed from the following items: (a) "Given the chances you have had, how well have you done in taking care of your family's wants and needs?" (b) "Given . . . how well have you done at being a good husband to your wife/wife to your husband?" (c) "Given . . . how well have you done at being a good father/mother to your children?" Items were recoded so that higher scores reflect more favorable self-evaluations. Like the other subjective evaluations of family life, these items are positively skewed. For instance, some 63% of respondents report that they have done *very well* in caring for their families, 74% of married respondents indicate that they have done *very well* in spousal roles, and more than 78% of NSBA parents feel they have performed *very well* in that role. The indicator used in this study is a dummy variable identifying those respondents (more than 42% of the sample) who report performing *very well* in all relevant familial roles.

Religious Involvement

Public religious participation is measured as the mean of an unweighted two-item index tapping (a) frequency of attendance at religious services and (b) frequency of participation in other congregational activities (alpha = .79). Responses range from 1 to 5, and they have been recoded so that higher scores reflect more frequent participation. Consistent with the accumulation of research findings over the years (for review, see Taylor & Chatters, 1991b), some 36.5% of NSBA respondents report attending religious services at least once per week. Approximately 28% indicated that they attended sporadically, usually a few times per month. Fewer than one in five African Americans reported attending services less than once per year (or never).

Private devotional activity is measured as the mean of an unweighted index constructed from three items tapping (a) frequency of reading religious books or other religious materials, (b) frequency of religious television or radio consumption, and (c) frequency of personal prayer (alpha = .65). Again, responses range from 1 to 5, and they have been recoded to insure that higher scores indicate more frequent devotional activity. Approximately 78% of the respondents report praying several times per week, 51% report reading religious books or materials at least once per week, and roughly 68% indicate that they watch or listen to religious broadcast media at least once per week. Thus, it is not surprising that mean scores on the index are relatively high (mean = 3.87 out of a possible 5).

Also of interest for the present purposes is a single item on the importance of religious socialization: "How important is it for black parents to send or take their children to religious services?" Responses range from *not important at all* to *very important,* and the distribution of answers to this item indicate that the intergenerational transmission of religious belief remains important to a large proportion of the African American adult population. Few participants in this national sample are inclined to disparage the importance of religious socialization for children. Indeed, given the dramatically skewed distribution of responses to this item, I have created a dummy variable to identify those persons (80% of respondents) who feel that such socialization is *very important* for children.

In addition to the items discussed previously, the NSBA dataset contains a substantial array of items gauging religious affiliation, experience, and belief. The results of ancillary analyses involving these items are summarized briefly later in this chapter.

Covariates

A thorough examination of the links between religious involvement and perceptions of family life must also consider the potentially confounding estimated effects of a number of sociodemographic factors and other controls: gender (1 = female), age (in years), marital status (1 = married), number of adults in the household (actual number), number of children in the household (actual number), and education (8-point summary scale). Because only small numbers of respondents are missing valid responses to these items, missing data on these items are handled via listwise deletion.[1]

Family income (17-point summary scale) is also included as a control variable in these analyses. Because a relatively large proportion of the NSBA respondents (roughly 12.9%) are missing data on personal income, these missing values are replaced with the valid sample mean, and a dummy variable is included to identify these cases. When this dummy variable did not surface as a predictor of the family attitudes of interest in this study, the dummy was omitted from subsequent multivariate models.

Frequency of contact with relatives is gauged via responses to the following item: "How often do you see, write, or talk on the telephone with family or relatives who do not live with you?" Approximately 64% of NSBA respondents report that they experience such contact at least once per week, with some 37% of respondents indicating that they are in touch with relatives *nearly every day—four or more times a week.* Thus, this item has been recoded as a dummy variable identifying individuals who are in contact with relatives at least weekly.[2]

Table 6.1 *Logistic Regression Estimates of Net Effects of Religious Involvement and Covariates on Positive Self-Reported Family Role Performance*

	Model 1			Model 2		
Variable	*b*	*SE*	*Odds Ratio*	*b*	*SE*	*Odds Ratio*
Age	.026***	.004	1.026	.026***	.004	1.026
Female	.115	.111	1.121	.126	.112	1.134
Education	−.068*	.031	.934	−.054	.032	.947
Income	.015	.013	1.015	.015	.013	1.015
Married	.031	.106	1.031	.047	.107	1.048
Number of adults	−.031	.052	.969	−.036	.052	.965
Number of children	−.012	.036	.988	−.010	.036	.990
Visits relatives at least weekly	.229*	.103	1.257	.244*	.103	1.276
Church participation	.136**	.052	1.146	.104*	.053	1.110
Private devotion	.087	.063	1.091	.029	.065	1.029
Religious socialization "very important"	—	—	—	.576***	.140	1.779
Intercept		−2.147			−2.355	
N		1,983			1,983	
Model χ^2/df			177.03/10			194.57/11
Dependent variable mean		.422			.422	
Pseudo R^2		.082			.089	

$*p < .05; **p < .01; ***p < .001.$

Findings

Key Multivariate Results

Table 6.1 presents multivariate logistic regression models (see Aldrich & Nelson, 1984) estimating the net effects of religious factors and covariates on the natural log of the odds of highly favorable self-evaluations of family role performance. Model 1 presents the estimated effects of the frequency of religious attendance, the frequency of devotional activities, and secular covariates. Model 2 adds the perceived importance of intergenerational religious socialization. Although full models are displayed, to conserve space this discussion centers only on the estimated net effects of the religious variables.

Table 6.2 *Logistic Regression Estimates of Net Effects of Religious Involvement and Covariates on High Subjective Family Closeness*

	Model 1			Model 2		
Variable	*b*	*SE*	*Odds Ratio*	*b*	*SE*	*Odds Ratio*
Age	.008*	.004	1.008	.008*	.004	1.008
Female	−.157	.111	.855	−.152	.111	.859
Education	−.014	.032	.986	.002	.032	.998
Income	.003	.013	1.003	.002	.013	1.002
Married	−.017	.106	.983	.006	.106	.994
Number of adults	.168**	.052	1.183	.166**	.053	1.181
Number of children	−.047	.035	.954	−.046	.036	.955
Visits relatives at least weekly	.974***	.101	2.649	.991***	.102	2.694
Church participation	.200***	.053	1.221	.173**	.053	1.189
Private devotion	.078	.061	1.081	.032	.062	1.033
Religious socialization "very important"	—	—	—	.438***	.129	1.550
Intercept		−1.491			−1.622	
N		1,991			1,991	
Model χ^2/df			160.28/10			171.80/11
Dependent variable mean		.598			.598	
Pseudo R^2		.074			.079	

*$p < .05$; **$p < .01$; ***$p < .001$.

In this regard, several empirical patterns merit attention. First, each increment in the ordinal measure of religious attendance is associated with a modest increase (of 11% in Model 2) in the odds of positive self-evaluation in the performance of family roles—as spouse and parent, and in taking care of the needs of other family members. Thus, in the full model (Model 2), NSBA respondents who report participating in congregational activities *several times per week* are approximately 55% more likely on average than those who report participating *less than once a year* to rate themselves very positively in their performance of family roles. This relationship persists despite statistical controls for sociodemographic, familial, and religious covariates. Second, the frequency of devotional activities appears to be largely unrelated to self-reported familial role performance. Third, the belief that it is *very important* for African American parents to take their children to church is associated with an increment of roughly 80% in the odds of perceiving one's family role

Table 6.3 *Logistic Regression Estimates of Net Effects of Religious Involvement and Covariates on High Family Satisfaction*

Variable	Model 1			Model 2		
	b	*SE*	*Odds Ratio*	*b*	*SE*	*Odds Ratio*
Age	.016***	.004	1.016	.015***	.004	1.015
Female	−.369**	.111	.691	−.363***	.112	.696
Education	−.172***	.032	.842	−.157***	.032	.855
Income	−.029*	.013	.971	−.031*	.013	.969
Married	.002	.105	.998	.014	.106	1.014
Number of adults	.110*	.051	1.116	.107*	.051	1.113
Number of children	−.009	.035	.991	−.007	.036	.993
Visits relatives at least weekly	.419***	.102	1.520	.443***	.103	1.557
Church participation	.177***	.052	1.194	.141**	.053	1.151
Private devotion	.167**	.062	1.182	.102	.064	1.107
Religious socialization "very important"	—	—	—	.623***	.132	1.865
Intercept		−.973			−1.171	
N		1,974			1,974	
Model χ^2/df		209.68/10			232.10/11	
Dependent variable mean		.525			.525	
Pseudo R^2		.096			.105	

*$p < .05$; **$p < .01$; ***$p < .001$.

performance favorably. Furthermore, the inclusion of this variable in Model 2 results in only a slight decrement in the estimated net effect of religious attendance.[3]

The models displayed in Table 6.2 estimate the net effects of religious variables and covariates on the odds of reporting *very close* family relations. With regard to the estimated net effects of religious variables, these models are similar to those presented in Table 6.1. First, each increment in the ordinal measure of church participation is associated with an increase of nearly 20% in the odds of reporting *very close* family ties. Second, religious devotion again appears entirely unrelated to this subjective evaluation of the quality of family relationships. Third, even net of the effects of secular and religious covariates, the belief that the religious socialization of African American children is *very important* enhances the odds of high subjective family closeness by some 55%.

Again, all of these relationships withstand statistical controls for the potentially confounding effects of a range of covariates.

In Table 6.3, a parallel set of logistic regression models gauges the net effects of religious factors and covariates on yet a third dependent variable: high family satisfaction. As in the models presented in Tables 6.1 and 6.2, church attendance bears a modest positive relationship with family satisfaction, even net of other religious variables and a wide range of covariates. In addition, the estimated net effects of religious devotion on family satisfaction appear to be negligible. The belief, however, that it is *very important* for African American parents to take young people to church is associated with an increase of more than 85% in the odds of reporting high family satisfaction, even with the potentially confounding effects of church attendance held constant.

Estimated Net Effects of Additional Religious Variables

To specify further the multifaceted role of religious factors in African American family life, several additional religious items included in the NSBA were examined (analyses not shown). First, based on a denominational coding scheme used in previous studies with NSBA data (Ellison & Sherkat, 1990), a set of denominational dummy variables identifying the members of Baptist and Methodist (black mainline) groups, Conservative Protestant sects, predominantly white Protestant denominations, Catholics, and adherents of non-traditional and non-Christian religions were added to the full models in Tables 6.1 through 6.3. No significant collective variations were detected. Second, following previous research (Taylor & Chatters, 1988), dummy variables were used to identify the recipients of various types of informal assistance from church members: companionship and socioemotional support, information and advice, money, goods, and various kinds of services (e.g., transportation, help with child care). These dummy variables were added to the full models presented in Tables 6.1 through 6.3, and again no significant relationships surfaced. Although it is conceivable that informal support from coreligionists is really unrelated to the subjective quality of family life, it seems more likely that these NSBA items, which measure the diverse types of support rather than the quantity of support received, are inadequate to adjudicate this issue.

Finally, based on open-ended questions inquiring about the most important benefits of public or private religious involvement, a series of dummy variables were used to identify (a) individuals who emphasize the role of the church in moral guidance, (b) those who benefit primarily in more instrumental ways (e.g., via congregation-based family support), and (c) those who report other possible benefits, such as emotional well-being, existential certainty, or both (Ellison & Sherkat, 1995). When these dummy variables were added to the full models presented in Tables 6.1 through 6.3, no significant effects were observed. Again, however, it is not clear whether these null findings mean that individuals actually derive few subjective benefits from congregational programs, that they devalue church advice and directives regarding the family, or both, or whether the indicators available in the NSBA are insufficiently precise to resolve these issues.

Discussion

Why do frequent churchgoers and individuals with strong convictions regarding the religious socialization of young people enjoy a higher subjective quality of family life than other African Americans? On average, religious individuals may perform more admirably in family roles, may strive for and achieve greater family harmony and affective closeness, and may enjoy family life more than their less religious counterparts. Within religious congregations, traditional family models and values are frequently upheld as virtuous, and many black church communities make special efforts to provide positive feedback and reinforcement for individuals with strong family commitments. In addition, churchgoers may receive specific guidance concerning marital or intergenerational relations from clergy (e.g., via sermons and counseling), and through sharing and fellowship with church members. Furthermore, many congregations sustain programs designed to reduce the stressors confronting African American families and to help those families deal with family-related problems effectively.

It is also possible that various interpersonal processes within religious congregations help many African Americans to experience their family lives more positively, irrespective of objective circumstances. For instance, church communities may promote a sense of role clarity, developing broadly consensual understandings of what healthy families are like and what positive family role performance entails. Expressions of approval from coreligionists or clergy may help to convince an individual that he or she is (or can become) a "good" parent, a "good" spouse, and a "good" son or daughter. Additional reassurance on this score may come via informal comparisons with the family lives of other church members. Moreover, downward social comparisons may also occur, with churchgoers gaining feelings of affirmation or superiority by favorably comparing their family lives to those of their unchurched counterparts.

Most discussions of the religion-family connection emphasize the supportive functions of religious groups vis-à-vis families. Although many religious communities do support and nurture families through various formal and informal mechanisms, there is also a coercive dimension to the role of religious groups that merits more detailed investigation in the future. Religious institutions are institutions of social control, and may have the capacity to levy negative sanctions against deviant members. Persons who neglect family responsibilities, engage in negative lifestyles (e.g., idleness, infidelity/promiscuity, substance abuse, criminality), or both may bear the brunt of gossip, direct rebukes, and other forms of social pressure from other church members. Some may even confront formal expressions of disapproval from clergy and lay leaders. This threat of embarrassment and ostracism may deter some individuals from indulging in habits and behaviors that might undermine family harmony and stability.

Given the clear standards regarding respectable family lifestyles within religious communities, and the likely internalization of these standards by many members, some frequent churchgoers may be tempted to represent their family lives in inaccurately rosy terms due to social desirability motivations. Such biased responses would obviously taint the findings reported here. Therefore, to the extent possible, future survey instruments should include items designed to identify individuals with these motivations, to permit researchers to adjust for these possible sources of response bias (e.g., Crowne & Marlowe, 1964).

One likely consequence of attempts within church communities to regulate behavior and sanction deviance is *selection*—individuals who lack family commitment and who embrace libertine values and conduct may become estranged from congregational life, perhaps permanently. There is mounting evidence that significant numbers of young, urban African American males are abandoning organized religion for precisely these reasons, a pattern with potentially staggering long-term implications for both African American families and churches (Lincoln & Mamiya, 1990; Nelsen, 1988). Thus, the findings reported here may partly reflect the negative family lives and role performances of many nonreligious (or marginally religious) African Americans.

Although this study has demonstrated several nontrivial empirical relationships between aspects of religious involvement and the subjective quality of family life among African Americans, the precise mechanisms through which religious institutions and values may enhance family life remain elusive. In future research it would be desirable to have data on the religiosity of other family members (i.e., spouse, children). An established research literature demonstrates that spouses who share common denominational affiliations report happier marriages than those from more diverse theological traditions (Heaton

& Pratt, 1990; Ortega, Whitt, & Williams, 1988). This recurrent finding makes sense, because religiously similar spouses may (a) share basic assumptions about a wide range of lifestyle issues (e.g., child rearing, leisure activities, friendship choices), (b) harbor compatible views of marriage and similar levels of commitment to marital and familial roles, and (c) draw their associates from similar and relatively homogeneous social circles, and receive consistent feedback about familial and lifestyle matters from these network members. Although direct evidence on this point is thin, a similar logic may well extend to other family members, and the overall subjective quality of family life may be highest within families in which spouses and children attend the same church (or type of church) regularly. In other words, family members who pray together may not only stay together, but they may also find their relationships highly satisfying.

Future research should also collect and analyze data on the use of the various family support programs offered by religious congregations. Although much of the discussion of the religion-family connection among African Americans has centered on such programs, there is little concrete information on (a) what types of people use these various programs, (b) which programs are used most frequently, (c) which initiatives provide the greatest benefits for families, and (d) precisely how these programs might work to strengthen African American families. Such research would help to clarify the role of formal support activities in promoting the quality of family life. It might also aid churches in tailoring their programs to fit the needs of participants, and in allocating their limited financial and human resources more efficiently. Finally, although this study has focused exclusively on the relationships between religious involvement the subjective quality of family life, we need more information on other links between the institutions of religion and family among the African American population. There are sound theoretical reasons to anticipate that religious differences might well surface in cohabitation, courtship and marriage, fertility behavior, patterns of household organization, child rearing, and other areas. More sustained research is needed to clarify the extent and changing of the religion-family connection among multiple generations of African Americans.

Notes

1. Preliminary analyses also included indicators of region, urbanicity, and employment status, as well as a more detailed battery of dummy variables tapping marital status. Because these

additional covariates never emerged as significant predictors of subjective assessments of family life, they were dropped from the final models in the interest of parsimony.

2. A scale measuring the residential proximity of extended kin was included as a control in preliminary models. This variable is based on a series of NSBA items inquiring about the proportion of relatives living in the respondent's dwelling, neighborhood, city or town, county, state, and outside the state. Following Taylor (1986), this scale assigns higher scores to respondents with greater percentages of their relatives living nearby. This proximity variable, however, was unrelated to family role performance and family satisfaction, and was only a modest predictor of subjective family closeness. The subsequent decision to drop this variable from the final models presented here resulted in no meaningful change in the estimated net effects of religious factors in any of the models.

3. Although a thorough exploration of this issue lies beyond the scope of this chapter, I briefly considered several contingent hypotheses: (a) that the link between religion and family may be greater for females than for males; (b) that religion makes a greater difference in the family lives of younger African Americans with children than for others; and (c) that religion is more important for African Americans of lower socioeconomic status. Although the inclusion of cross-product terms in preliminary models revealed no support for these hypotheses, the possibility of subtler gender, age, and social class variations in these patterns merits further investigation.

7

Multiple Familial-Worker Role Strain and Psychological Well-Being

Moderating Effects of Coping Resources Among Black American Parents

RUBY L. BEALE

The work and family interface has become increasingly important in this changing society. The traditional perspective has been that one parent would stay home and provide care for the children and the other parent would work to provide the financial needs of the family. Historically, more black women than white women have worked outside of the home because their income has been needed for their families' economic survival. Men, however, (black or white) have generally been expected to be the primary financial provider for their families (Bowman, 1982). With the changing economic forecast that our society is changing from an industrial society to a technological and service industry, more jobs will require higher education and those who occupy service jobs will earn less income to support themselves and their families. Current trends suggest that more women and minorities are entering the workforce whether they are a part of a dual earner household or a single-parent household (Evans & Bartolome, 1984). It is expected that women and minorities will occupy more of the lower paying service jobs, which may require an increase in work hours and therefore disproportionately predispose them to economic, physical, and psychological strain. Along with the documented changes in parental role involvement for both men and women, there have been reports of role strain due to work and family role conflict and role overload of multiple role participation (Baruch & Barnett, 1986a; Crosby, 1984; Kando & Summers, 1971).

The general purpose of this study is to examine the operation of familial role strain and work role strain dimensions on psychological well-being. First, the study assesses effects of family role stain (FRS) and work role strain (WRS) indicators on family, job, and life satisfaction as measures of psychological well-being. Second, the impact of combined effects of family and work role strain on psychological well-being is measured. Finally, it examines the moderating effects of marital status, family closeness, occupational prestige, and religiosity as coping resources. Work and family role strain may combine additively, interactively, or both to adversely affect psychological well-being. Are there theoretical frameworks that predict potential problems with the changing trends? The spillover hypothesis states that stressors experienced in either the work or family domain can lead to stressors in the other domain (Champoux, 1978; Kando & Summers, 1971; Pitrkowski, 1978; Staines, 1980; Weitz, 1952). On the other hand the compensatory model suggests that people experiencing strain in one domain will find some solace or invest more energy and compensate in another domain (Champoux, 1978; Crosby, 1984; Evans & Bartolome, 1984).

A more inclusive social psychological approach, which incorporates both work and family domains, is conceptually rich but also more challenging to operationalize. Although still sparse, a growing theoretical and empirical literature on multiple role strain provides a coherent framework to guide future research (Baruch & Barnett, 1986a, 1986b; Campbell, Converse, & Rodgers, 1976; Crosby, 1984; Sieber, 1974). A pivotal article has investigated the multiple role strain concept (Evans & Bartolome, 1984) and suggests that if there are too many salient (important) roles that make excessive demands on an individual's time and energy, then role conflict and role overload are likely to result and in turn create role strain. Consistent with an open systems perspective, this work provides a framework to go beyond a narrow focus on either work or family roles as sources of strain to consider their joint effects on psychological well-being. Moreover, other researchers suggest that the feeling of internal strain caused by such external conflict and overload in salient roles such as work, family, or both can spill over into other areas of the individual's life and impinge on an individual's overall psychological well-being (Evans & Bartolome, 1984; Kahn, 1974; Kando & Summers, 1971; Sieber, 1974). Also, it is important to consider the multiple dimensions of work and family role strain to understand their psychological consequences (Baruch & Barnett, 1986a).

What are the effects of multiple role strains in family and work and how do people cope with these strains? This study will assess what the adverse effects of multiple role strain in family and work are on the overall psychological well-being of employed parents. Furthermore, the study will determine if personal and social coping resources moderate these adverse effects.

The existing literature would suggest that the multiple dimension of familial-related role strain will have an adverse effect on psychological well-being. There should be greater adverse effects on family satisfaction because it is a domain-specific measure, however, in line with the spillover hypothesis, family and life satisfaction should also be adversely affected. Therefore, the research questions for this study are the following:

> *H1.* What are the effects of family role strain and work role strain individually and collectively on the psychological well-being of black working parents?

Religiosity, family closeness, and marital status are viewed as coping resources. In addition, high occupational prestige is often associated with higher levels of psychological well-being. The second research question is as follows:

> *H2.* Do the coping resources of religiosity, family closeness, marital status, occupational prestige, or all of these moderate or buffer the negative adverse effects of FRS and WRS on the psychological well-being of working parents?

It is expected that family role strain (FRS) will have an adverse effect on psychological well-being. Work role strain (WRS) will also have an adverse effect on psychological well-being. The combination of FRS and WRS will have a particularly deleterious effect on the psychological well-being of black working parents. The personal and social coping resources of religiosity, family closeness, marital status, and occupational prestige will moderate the adverse effects of FRS and WRS on the psychological well-being of black working parents.

Method

Instrument

The instrument used is a questionnaire that was designed and implemented by the National Survey of Black Americans (NSBA) at the University of Michigan's Institute for Social Research. This survey is a nationally representative cross section of the adult black population living in the continental United States. Based on the census distribution of the black population, 76 primary areas were selected for inclusion. These sites were stratified according to racial composition and smaller geographic "cluster" areas within the sites were randomly chosen. Finally, within each selected black household, one person was randomly chosen to be interviewed. This sampling procedure resulted in 2,107 completed interviews, which represents a 68% response rate. The present study is based on a subsample of this national survey and includes only working parents who have children under 18 years of age living in the same household.

Sample

The respondents are 613 black working parents, of which 380 are mothers and 233 are fathers (18 years of age and older), who participated in National Survey of Black Americans. Of the respondents, 50% were between 18 and 34 years of age, 45% between 35 and 54 year of age, and 5% were 55 or older. About 27% had less than a high school education, 40% had a high school education, and 33% had some college or were college graduates. Fathers comprised 38% of black working parents and the remaining 62% of black working parents were mothers. Of the respondents, 64% were married (which included common-law or live-in partner) and 36% were unmarried (which included the divorced, separated, widowed, or never married); 71% worked 40 hours or more per week and 28% worked less than 40 hours per week.

Measures

There are four groups of variables for the dependent, independent, moderating, and control variables and most are on a 4-point Likert-type scale. The three dependent measures included in the study are job satisfaction, family satisfaction, and life satisfaction.

1. *Job satisfaction (JS).* All in all, how satisfied are you with your job?
2. *Family satisfaction (FS).* How satisfied are you with your family life, that is, the time you spend and the things you do with members of your family?
3. *Life satisfaction (LS).* In general, how satisfied are you with your life as a whole these days?

There are two clusters of independent measures: family role strain and work role strain. The five independent variables used to measure family role strain include the following:

1. *Meeting family demands (FD)*. Given the chances you have had, how well have you done in taking care of your family's wants and needs?
2. *Performance of parent role (PR)*. How well have you done at being a good (father or mother) to your children?
3. *Housework interference (HI)*. How much does housework keep you from doing other things you have to do?
4. *General role overload (GO)*. In general do you ever feel overworked because of all the things you have to do?
5. *Number of children (#C)*. How many children do you have?

The five independent variables used to measure work role strain are the following:

1. *Chances for promotion (CP)*. In the place where you work what are your chances of getting promoted?
2. *Skill use (SU)*. Do you feel that you have skills and abilities for a better job than the one you have now?
3. *Most important thing on job (MITJ)*. (Paraphrase of 2-part question.) Do you have the most important thing (to you) on the job?
4. *Occupational prestige (OP)*. (Paraphrase of 2-part question.) What is your job-occupational title?
5. *Pay*. What is your personal income?

The moderating variables used to measure the effects of coping resources are the following:

1. *Family closeness (FC)*. Would you say your family members are very close in their feelings to each other?
2. *Religious orientation (RO)*. A religious orientation index was used (Cunningham, 1984). It measures the extent of an individual's religiosity. Responses were dichotomized into two categories of low to moderately religious and very religious.
3. *Marital status (MS)*. Married included those who were legally married, common law, or had a live-in partner. Unmarried included those who were never married, divorced, separated, or widowed.
4. *Occupational prestige (OP)*. (Described under work role strain.)

The control variables were age, education, gender, hours worked per week, and marital status.

Results

Often the methodological thrust is to reduce data to some composite measures. Except for the religious orientation index, all of the items used in this study are single-item measures. The special interest of this study was in the unique contributions of the separate indicators. Literature suggests that each of the role strain indicators selected ought to show significant separate effects. Although there may be some overlap between indicators (e.g., meeting family demands and parent role performance), the preliminary analysis indicated that the items are related but distinct empirically. In addition, there were no violations of multicollinearity between the dependent measures.

The literature is replete with information and data on effects that age, education, gender, marital status, and number of hours worked per week have on well-being. This study's focus was to determine the separate and combined effects of family and work role on strain psychological well-being beyond the sociodemographic influences that are used as control variables. Also, moderator regressions are used to determine the moderating interaction effects that marital status, family closeness, religiosity, and occupational prestige may have between role strain and psychological well-being. Multiple regressions were done to examine the main effects, and moderator regressions were done to test for moderating effects on the research questions.

Regressions of the combined effects of family and work role strain indicators with and net of the controls are illustrated in Table 7.1. All of the regression models that include family and work role strain are statistically significant ($R^2 = .16, p < .001$ with controls and $R^2 = .09, p < .001$ net of controls; for family satisfaction: $R^2 = .31, p < .01$ with controls and $R^2 = .23, p < .001$ net of controls; for job satisfaction: $R^2 = .16, p < .001$ with controls and $R^2 = .08, p < .001$ net of controls). This provides support for *H1*—The combined effects of family and work role strain will have an adverse effect on the psychological well-being of working parents. After partialing out the effects of all of the other variables, those parents who did not feel they were meeting the demands of their families very well reported lower levels of family satisfaction ($r = -.12, p < .01$), job satisfaction ($r = -.16, p < .001$), and life satisfaction ($r = -.10, p < .05$). Those with low-prestige jobs reported higher levels of family satisfaction ($r = -.09, p < .05$) and life satisfaction ($r = -.16, p < .001$).

Older working parents reported higher levels of family satisfaction ($r = .09, p < .05$), job satisfaction ($r = .20, p < .001$), and life satisfaction ($r = .13, p < .01$). Black working parents who worked fewer hours per week reported higher levels of family satisfaction ($r = -.09, p < .05$) and life satisfaction ($r = -.11, p < .05$). Married working parents reported higher levels of life satisfaction ($r = -.17, p < .001$).

Table 7.1 Regressions of the Combined Effects of Family and Work Role Strain Indicators and Controls on the Psychological Well-Being of Black Working Parents

Predictors	Family Satisfaction			Job Satisfaction			Life Satisfaction		
	Partial	b	SE	Partial	b	SE	Partial	b	SE
Controls									
Age	.09	.006*	.030	.20	.016***	.004	.13	.010**	.004
Education	-.04	-.014	.016	-.05	-.016	.017	.04	.016	.017
Gender	-.05	-.112	.087	.05	.093	.091	.01	.078	.089
Weekly work hours	-.09	-.008*	.004	-.01	-.001	.004	-.11	-.009*	.004
Marital status	.01	.021	.073	-.04	-.072	.076	.17	.288***	.075
Family role strain									
Meet family demands	-.12	-.163**	.062	-.16	-.223***	.065	-.10	-.138*	.063
Perform parent role	-.14	-.217**	.073	-.04	-.065	.078	-.03	-.047	.076
Housework interferes	-.07	-.069	.045	-.07	-.069	.046	-.03	-.029	.046
General overload	-.09	-.134*	.067	-.11	-.168*	.069	-.12	-.183**	.069
Number of children	.02	.009	.024	.06	.035	.025	-.08	-.044	.025
Work role strain									
Chance for promotion	-.01	-.009	.029	-.21	-.142***	.030	-.06	-.039	.030
Skill utilization	-.04	-.079	.087	-.09	-.183*	.090	-.06	-.106	.089
Most important thing on job	-.05	-.088	.075	-.28	-.488***	.078	-.11	-.179*	.077
Occupational prestige	-.09	-.152*	.074	-.03	-.041	.077	-.16	-.269***	.076
Personal income	-.03	-.006	.010	-.02	-.004	.011	-.01	-.002	.010
R	.40			.56			.40		
R^2 for controls and family	.16***			.31***			.16***		
R^2 for work	.09***			.23***			.08***		
N	482			477			480		

*$p < .05$; **$p < .01$; ***$p < .001$.

Moderator Regression: Interaction Effects

Findings on the degree to which moderating variables buffer the adverse effects of role strain on psychological well-being are presented. In addition to partialing out the effects of other predictors, interaction effects provide insight into how the effects of role strain on psychological well-being might vary under conditions of high and low support. In line with the buffering hypotheses, it is expected that the adverse effects of role strain should be reduced under conditions of high support—married, high religiosity, very close families, and high occupational prestige jobs. Table 7.2 is a summary of the moderating effects of marital status, religiosity, family closeness, and occupational prestige on the role strain indicators and psychological well-being measures. It provides an overall view of what the interaction patterns are for the independent and buffering variables on the dependent variables.

Discussion

Some support was found for the hypothesis involving main effects for family and work role strain and buffering effects of the various coping resources. Wide differences emerged, however, in their relative effects on the specific role strain indicators, and the differences found within the family role strain indicators were particularly interesting. Significant interaction effects not only revealed the hypothesized buffering effects but other complex interaction patterns as well. For the most part, these research findings lend support for a spillover hypothesis, which states that the nature of one's experience in one sphere of life will spill over to other spheres and affect attitudes and behaviors (Champoux, 1978; Evans & Bartolome, 1984; Staines, 1980; Weitz, 1952).

As expected, the family role strain indicators do have a significant adverse effect on psychological well-being beyond the contribution of the sociodemographic control variables. Specifically, working parents who reported strain in meeting family demands and who experienced general role overload reported very low levels on all three measures of psychological well-being. Moreover, strain produced by performance problems in the parent role had an adverse effect on family satisfaction. Support for a spillover hypothesis is clear. Family role strain combined with work role strain intensifies the adverse effects on psychological well-being of working parents with and without the control variables. Although all three measures of psychological well-being were adversely affected, the deleterious effect on job satisfaction was almost twice as large as the negative effects on family and life satisfaction. This finding also

Table 7.2 Summary Table of the Moderating Effects of Marital Status, Religiosity, Family Closeness, and Occupational Prestige on the Relationship of Role Strain and Psychological Well-Being

	Marital Status			Religiosity			Family Closeness			Occupational Prestige		
						Satisfaction						
Predictors	Family	Job	Life	Family	Job	Life	Family	Job	Life	Family	Job	Life
Family role strain												
Meet family demands			.10[a]		.10[b]							
Perform parent role			.01/.05[a,b]	.05/.05[a]								
Housework interferes											.10[b]	
General overload						.05/.05[a,b]				.05		
Number of children						.10/.10[a]				.10		
Work role strain												
Chance for promotion	.10[a]			.10[a]					.10[a]	.05[a]		
Skill utilization										.05/.10[a]		
Most important thing on job	.10		.01/.05[a]	.10			.05/.10[a]		.05/.05[a]			
Occupational prestige								.05/.05[a]				
Personal income									.05/.01[a]			

NOTE: Numbers in each cell represent significance levels ($p < .05$) for interaction effects. Empty cells indicate that interaction effects were not significant. All other effects are from the separate family or work role strain models.
a. Represents the combined family-work role strain model interaction.
b. Buffering effect.

supports a spillover hypothesis and suggests family life variables should be taken into account when conducting research on work issues. Of the 10 role strain indicators used in the combined model, meeting family demands and general role overload were the only 2 role strain measures on which working parents reported very low levels on all 3 measures of psychological well-being. This finding suggests that strains in the family had a more onerous effect on psychological well-being than did strains directly related to work. Furthermore, for this population and the role strain items selected, family role strain seems to affect job satisfaction more than work role strain affects family satisfaction.

It is also interesting to note that some significant effects appeared in the control variables that were included in the role strain models. Age was the only control variable that was significantly related to all three measures of psychological well-being. Older working parents reported higher levels of family, job, and life satisfaction. This finding is in line with much of the existing literature that consistently shows that well-being tends to increase with age (Andrews & Withey, 1979; Campbell et al., 1976). Also consistent with existing literature is the finding that married people report higher levels of life satisfaction than the unmarried; and, those working parents who work fewer hours per week report higher levels of family and life satisfaction than those who worked 40 or more hours per week (Andrews & Withey, 1979; Campbell et al., 1976; Quinn, 1977; Staines, 1979; Veroff, Douvan, & Kulka, 1981b). Surprisingly, working parents with less education reported higher levels of family and job satisfaction. Parents with less education had lower, and perhaps more realistic, expectations of what they could achieve in the specific domains, and therefore did not internalize the stresses and strains related to family and work as adversely as the more educated parents, who may have had higher (and perhaps unrealistic) expectations.

Interaction Effects

Marital Status

Marital status did buffer the adverse effects of parent role strain on life satisfaction and moderated the negative effects of several other role strain indicators on family and life satisfaction. It provided no mediation, however, for the adverse effects of role strain on job satisfaction. Having a partner in the home operates as a social support in meeting family demands, and is particularly important to mediating the negative effects of role strain when performing and probably sharing parent role responsibilities (Bowman, 1982; Veroff et al., 1981b).

Religiosity

As a coping resource, high religiosity mediated some of the adverse effects of family work role strain on all three measures of psychological well-being. Religiosity buffered the negative effects on job dissatisfaction when working parents reported role strain in meeting family demands, and also buffered the negative effects of general role overload on life satisfaction. Perhaps not too surprisingly, high religiosity also moderated the negative effects of several role strain indicators on family satisfaction—low parent role performance, not having a good chance for promotion, and not having the most rewarding thing on the job.

Family Closeness

As expected, family closeness moderated some of the adverse effects of work role strain. Surprisingly, however, family closeness did not mediate any of the negative effects of familial role strain dimensions nor did it buffer any of the adverse effects of role strain on general psychological well-being. The negative psychological effects on life satisfaction related to not having a good chance for promotion, low occupational prestige, and not having the thing the worker felt was most important on the job, were moderated when working parents reported feeling very close to their families. Feeling very close to one's family also moderated the adverse effects of low occupational prestige on job satisfaction and of not having the most rewarding thing on the job on working parents' family satisfaction. These findings suggest that feelings of family cohesion are of more importance when dealing with strains in the work area than in the family. Again, this supports the need to include family variables when doing work-related research. It was somewhat perplexing that family closeness did not buffer or moderate any of the family role strain dimensions. Although there was no high multicollinearity between family closeness and the family role strain indicators, there could be some other methodological reasons for the lack of effect. Perhaps there is some suppression of interaction effects when family closeness is crossed with meeting family demands and parent role performance. Also, there could be strains within the close family relationships.

Occupational Prestige

Occupational prestige buffered the adverse effect of parent role strain on job satisfaction and moderated family and work role strain indicators on family satisfaction, but did not provide any mediation of the negative role strain effects on life satisfaction. When working parents had high occupational prestige, it buffered the adverse effects of not performing the parent role well on job satisfaction. This is in line with the findings of Barnett and Baruch (1981), Pietromonaco, Manis, and Frohardy-Lane (1984), and Sieber (1974). It appears that when working parents did not feel that they were performing the parent role well and had low occupational prestige they reported very low levels of psychological well-being. The higher occupational prestige working parents, however, reported relatively higher levels of job satisfaction despite feelings of inadequate parent role performance. Apparently, the good things associated with high occupational prestige are central to working parents and they are so invested in the job that parental strain does not significantly affect their psychological well-being. This is similar to the findings by Veroff et al. (1981b), which suggest that professional men and women's involvement with work may compete with family involvement as a focal concern and therefore these individuals are less overwhelmed by the inevitable conflicts in family life. Also, low occupational prestige mediated the adverse effects of housework interference, high number(s) of children, not having a good chance for promotion, and underuse of skills on the family satisfaction of working parents. This was an unexpected finding, but does give some support to the compensatory model, which states that dissatisfying conditions of lower-class occupations should lead to more satisfying expressive attainments of family life (Haavio, 1971). Indeed, in these research findings, low occupational prestige (parents in presumably less satisfying jobs and therefore less invested than parents in high prestige jobs) served as a buffer to the adverse effects of familial and worker role strain on family satisfaction.

Conclusion and Implications

The findings herein suggest that family and work role strain indicators separately and jointly have adverse effects on psychological well-being. The addition of family role strain indicators, however, seems to have a more deleterious effect on psychological well-being than does work role strain, as seen in the job specific domain. Furthermore, the findings suggest that personal and social coping resources can moderate some of the adverse effects on the psychological well-being of working parents. Findings reported in this study provide insight into a growing issue. Current trends show that whether it is because of economic, social, or personal reasons, working mothers' participation in the labor force is increasing (Quinn & Staines, 1979; Staines, 1980). Moreover, working fathers' involvement in family responsibilities is reportedly increasing (Bowman, 1982; Staines, 1980). Most people report that they want to work even if they have no economic need to do so (Kahn, 1974), and although the family constellation is more variant than the traditional family (more single-parent households), most people report wanting to have a family (Veroff et al., 1981b). Therefore, increasing numbers of individuals are likely to be fulfilling multiple role responsibilities in the very important areas of work and family and will also have to contend with the related stress, as well as the pleasure, that comes with these role fulfillments. There were no gender differences found in this study, and to the extent that the external stress of role overload and role conflict becomes internalized as role strain by working parents, it becomes critical to examine the perceptions of the experience for both men and women and important to investigate possible mediators of the stress and strain.

These results revealed support for the spillover hypothesis (Champoux, 1978; Weitz, 1952) and a compensatory model (Champoux, 1978; Staines, 1980) and suggest some implications for both policy and counseling approaches. There needs to be more sensitivity on the part of employers and work organizations to the well-being of employees as it relates to family issues. For high occupational prestige workers, it seems advisable for organizations to consider more flexible organizational structures and flexible work hours that would not affect an employee's professional advancement due to a perception of low commitment because of less time spent on the job. This would allow employees more time to address salient family concerns. Individuals themselves need to be very mindful of not only the kind of career they choose but also in selecting the appropriate organizational setting that allows them a more balanced (work and family) lifestyle with the least amount of conflict. For example, if an individual chooses to be a physician, he or she has several options for practicing medicine. He or she could decide to go into private practice, which generally requires not only an inordinate number of hours at work but also unusual, and at times unpredictable, work hours. Or, the physician could decide to work for a health maintenance organization (HMO) that has a more structured organizational setting and typically builds in (predictable) work hours for emergencies that are shared with other physicians on staff.

Finally, within the context of a stress adaptation perspective, the findings suggest that working parents experience stress from family and work strain that is partially offset by coping resources. This balance between role strain and coping resources affects working parents' psychological well-being. This is of particular importance to black working parents because they are more likely to be employed in lower paying jobs, to feel that they have skills that are not being used, and to be underemployed (Bowman, 1991). Future studies should also investigate organizational factors as buffers to stress. In addition, the model can be used for other measures of role strain, psychological well-being, and coping resources.

Future research should look at the family role strain and work role strain dimensions that were found to be significant for duplication and further exploration. Patterns that show complex interaction effects other than the buffering effect require more research to unravel the findings, address the many questions raised, and better understand what is going on in these relationships. Although overall there were no effects of gender found, interaction effects may operate. It would be interesting to see if there were any different patterns of results for mothers or fathers only. Furthermore, it would be intriguing to see if meeting family demands means the same thing to fathers and mothers. Perhaps, in the traditional sense, it still means providing primary financial support for fathers and primary socioemotional supports for mothers. More in-depth research and carefully worded questions could ferret out these and other relevant issues.

8

Informal Ties and Employment Among Black Americans

ROBERT JOSEPH TAYLOR
SHERRILL L. SELLERS

The importance of informal social support networks to African Americans has been well documented by historians (Guttman, 1976), developmental psychologists (Wilson, 1989), ethnographers (Aschenbrenner, 1975; Burton, 1992; Burton & Dilworth-Anderson, 1991; Stack, 1974), and survey researchers (e.g., McAdoo, 1980; Oliver, 1988; Taylor, 1986). Family (Taylor, 1986), friends (Taylor, Hardison, & Chatters, 1996), church members (Taylor & Chatters, 1988), and fictive kin (Chatters, Taylor, & Jayakody, 1994) have all been found to play a critical role in the informal social support networks of black Americans. Members of the informal support network have been found to play a crucial role in helping during an emergency (Taylor, Chatters, & Mays, 1988), providing assistance in dealing with a stressful life event (Chatters, Taylor, & Neighbors, 1988), and providing child care, financial and emotional assistance to single and married mothers (Jayakody, Chatters, & Taylor, 1993). Although in the past 10 years a significant amount of information has been learned about the informal support networks of black Americans, there are still a number of basic issues that have yet to be investigated. This chapter presents a preliminary investigation of the correlates of whether family and friends have assisted black Americans in finding a job.

Despite the growth of employment agencies and formal hiring procedures by employers, the role of family and friends in acquiring a job remains very strong. For instance, Corcoran, Datcher, and Duncan (1980b) found that 50% of the respondents in their study found their jobs through family and friends. Similarly, Granovetter (1974) found that 56% of respondents found their job through informal ties; Lin, Ensel, and Vaughn (1981) reported 59%, and Marsden and Hurlbert (1988) reported 64%. Various studies among Germans (see Wegener, 1991), Japanese, and English (see Granovetter, 1995) also indicate the importance of friends and relatives in finding jobs in other industrialized countries. The percentage of people in these other countries who find their jobs through informal ties, however, is lower than in the United States.

Research on the role of informal ties in acquiring a job began with the groundbreaking theory of Granovetter (1973, 1974) on the strength of "weak ties." According to this theory, rather than close friends and family, the most effective way to get a job is through a "weak tie." Granovetter suggests that individuals who have strong social ties are extremely similar to each other. Close friends and family may overlap too closely with the job seekers own knowledge, resources, and influence. Through weak social ties, however, individuals may be able to connect to persons with different characteristics. Consequently, the successful job seeker requires more distant contacts who have knowledge and influence beyond the domain of the job seeker. Research on the importance of weak ties in acquiring jobs and gaining status, however, has been inconclusive with some studies supporting the weak ties argument and others finding no support for this theory (see Wegener, 1991).

Several researchers have argued that work in this field should move beyond a weak versus strong tie dichotomy and consider other aspects of informal networks (Bridges & Villemez, 1986). Bridges and Villemez (1986) examined the influence of communal networks (i.e., relatives, neighbors, friends) versus work-related informal networks (i.e., coworkers, supervisors) on finding a job. They found that although the strong tie/weak tie dimension was important, factors such as ascribed characteristics and other social capital are as important in a person's success in the labor market. Carson's (1992) analysis among unemployed adults found that the length of time it took to become reemployed varied by whether respondents were members of isolated, restricted, or extended networks (as cited in Granovetter, 1995). Carson found that those respondents who had bigger and broader networks had a greater likelihood of being reemployed and had shorter time periods in between jobs. In addition, Morris (1984) differentiates among adults who are in collective, individualistic, and dispersed networks and finds significant differences in these networks in securing employment.

Much of the research that investigates the role of informal networks in finding a job has been conducted by sociologists, with the notable exception of Montgomery (1991), an economist (Granovetter, 1995, p. 148). To date, research in this field has not been undertaken by black family researchers. The present analysis focuses on the correlates of whether black Americans initially heard about their present job through a friend or family member. A full set of family, friendship, racial composition, and demographic variables are used as independent variables. This chapter differs from other research in this field in that it places more emphasis on the degree to which family and friends link black adults to jobs and places less emphasis on wage differentials in finding a job through informal as opposed to other means. This chapter contributes to this field by examining the role of family, friendship, and racial composition variables in using informal ties to find employment among a national sample of black adults. Several studies in this area do not include family or friendships variables (e.g., Corcoran, Datcher, & Duncan, 1980a, 1980b); few studies investigate the influence of racial composition variables or indirectly measure racial composition (e.g., Braddock & McPartland, 1987). In addition, to our knowledge, there are no studies that investigate these issues among a representative sample of black Americans.

Both family and job characteristics may influence the source of job information. Respondents who have larger families who reside in the same city as the respondent may receive more direct assistance in finding a job than respondents who have smaller families who are more geographically dispersed. Families who are subjectively closer to each other may be more willing to provide job information to other family members than families whose members are relatively estranged from each other. In the friendship domain, having a large number of friends may increase the number of network ties. For African Americans, having a white friend may increase the amount and quality of job information. Collectively, the family and friendship factors may extend the job seeker's knowledge of employment opportunities.

We are fortunate to have several indicators of racial composition in our data set. The present analysis includes measures of the racial composition of the respondent's neighborhood and the respondent's job. The racial composition of the neighborhood variable is a measure of racial segregation that is an important factor in research on the black underclass. This literature indicates that racial isolation in poor neighborhoods may impede employment opportunities (Bowman, 1991; Wilson, 1987). Bowman (1991) investigated the relationship between the racial composition of the neighborhood and occupational status.

He found that residing in an all-black environment or a racially balanced neighborhood (half black-half white) did not have any clear occupational status advantage or disadvantage. Black adults, however, who were the only blacks in all-white neighborhoods had higher status jobs than blacks who lived in racially balanced or all-black neighborhoods. It is important to note that only a few respondents in the National Survey of Black Americans (NSBA) sample resided in all-white neighborhoods. We believe respondents who have jobs and neighborhoods with a higher percentage of black workers/residents will have a greater tendency to use informal ties to acquire their job.

Method

Sample and Variables

The data for this analysis comes from the NSBA. The dependent variables investigated in this analysis address the degree to which family and friends helped respondents learn about and acquire their present jobs. The series of questions on these issues in the NSBA are based on a sequence of questions on job acquisition that are included in the 1978 Panel Study of Income Dynamics (see Corcoran et al., 1980a). The major dependent variable for this analysis is "How did you first hear about a job at the place that you're now working? Was it through a friend, a relative, a want ad, an employment agency, or what?" Other dependent variables investigated in this analysis are whether the family or friend worked at the present job ("Did they work there?") and whether respondents received help from family and friends in getting the job ("In addition to just telling you about the job, did they do anything to help you get it?").

The independent variables in this analysis include sets of family, friendship, racial composition, and demographic variables. The family variables consist of subjective family closeness and the proximity of relatives. Family closeness is measured by the question, "Would you say your family members are *very close* in their feelings to each other, *fairly close, not too close,* or *not close at all*?" Proximity of relatives was measured by asking respondents, "How many of your relatives, not in your immediate family, live in the following areas? Would you say *many, some, a few,* or *none*?" Using this same format, respondents were asked about the number of relatives who lived in the same household, in the same neighborhood, in the same city but not the same neighborhood, and in the same county but not the same city. Responses to the proximity of relatives questions were combined into a weighted index so that respondents who indicated having many relatives in the household would have a higher score than those who had many relatives in the neighborhood. Relatives in the household were weighted by a value of 4, relatives in the neighborhood by a value of 3, relatives in the city by a value of 2, and relatives in the county by a value of 1. In addition, responses to the four items—many, some, a few, or none—were assigned values of 4, 3, 2, and 1, respectively.

Two friendship variables are included in this analysis—size of the friendship network, and having a white friend. Size of the friendship network is measured by the question, "Think of the friends, not including relatives, that you feel free to talk with about your problems—would you say that you have *many, some, a few,* or *no friends* like that?" Having a white friend is measured by the question "Do you know any white person who you think of as a good friend—that is, someone to whom you can say what you really think?"

The racial composition variables include the racial composition of the present neighborhood and job. Neighborhood racial composition is measured by the question, "When you think about your present neighborhood, are mostly blacks or mostly whites there?" Job racial composition is measured by the question "When you think about your present job, are mostly blacks or mostly whites there?" Responses to the job and neighborhood racial composition question consist of the following categories—all blacks, mostly blacks, about half blacks, mostly whites, almost all whites.

A full set of demographic variables is used in this analysis including age, gender, education, income, occupational status, marital status, region, and urbanicity. Occupational status was coded into primary and secondary job sector categories based on theoretical criteria emerging from dual labor market paradigms (Bowman, 1991). The secondary sector includes lower-level unskilled labor, service, and operative jobs. The lower primary sector includes craft, clerical, and sales jobs. The upper primary sector consists of managerial, administrative, and professional jobs. These three major job categories differ with regard to pay, prestige, skill level, work conditions, stability, and advancement opportunities (Bowman, 1991).

Findings and Discussion

Informal Referral

Of the respondents, 6 out of 10 (61.2%) indicated that they found out about their present job from either friends or family members. A total of 43.9% of respondents found out about their jobs from friends, 17.3% from family, 10.9%

from an employment agency, 9.5% from a newspaper want ad, 2.1% from a school training program, 9.0% used direct action to find out about their job, and 7.2% used some other strategy. Table 8.1 presents the results of a series of logistic regression models that estimate the effects of family, friendship, racial composition, and demographic variables on the log odds of discovering a job through informal referrals of family or friends. The blocks of independent variables are considered separately in Models 1 through 5, whereas Model 6 estimates the joint effects of these factors.

Model 1 estimates the effects of the two family variables on the log odds of an informal referral. Family proximity has a significant positive association with the dependent variable, whereas subjective family closeness did not achieve significance. Respondents with larger and more proximate family networks had a higher likelihood of hearing about their job through an informal tie. Other research on the NSBA has shown that this proximity variable is an important correlate of several dimensions of family support networks (Taylor, 1988). Although family closeness did not achieve significance, it is a fairly consistent predictor of receiving assistance from family members (Taylor, 1988).

Neither of the two friendship variables (i.e., number of friends, having a white friend) were significantly associated with whether respondents found their jobs through family or friends (Model 2). The fact that the size of the friendship network did not achieve significance could be because this variable dealt with the number of friends with whom a respondent could discuss problems. This variable essentially measures the number of very strong friendship ties. A more general size of the friendship network variable would be a better indicator of the number of weak ties available to the respondent. It is interesting that having a close white friend was not associated with hearing about the job from an informal tie. Similar to the number of friends variable, the white friend variable may be a measure of a strong friendship tie; one that may be too close to that of the respondent. The close white friend may be of equal socioeconomic status and also lack access to higher occupational status positions. In addition, having a white friend does not necessarily imply that black adults are part of the white hiring network or that the white friend is able to assist in getting a job. Although this variable did not achieve significance in the present analysis, given the recent research on social isolation and neighborhood effects (e.g. Wilson, 1987), the white friend variable deserves serious attention in future research in this area.

Model 3 estimates the net effects of racial composition variables on whether respondents received assistance in finding their jobs from informal network members. The racial composition of the job was significantly associated with the dependent variable. Respondents whose job had a higher percentage of black workers were more likely to have found their job through informal referrals.

Table 8.1 *Logistic Regression Models of the Source of Job Information (Informal vs. Other)*

Independent Variable	Model 1 Family	Model 2 Friend	Model 3 Racial Composition	Model 4 Occupational Status	Model 5 Demographic	Model 6 Full
Family closeness	.152					.140
Family proximity	.031**					.030*
Number of friends		.089				.110
Have a white friend		-.188				-.083
Age					-.003	-.002
Gender					-.462***	-.455**
Education					-.078**	-.036
Income					.357***	-.061**
Region					.033	.049
Urban					-.010	.128
Marital status					-.065**	.382**
Racial composition						
Neighborhood			.102+			.015
Job			.230***			.163**
Occupational status						
Upper primary				-.734***		.673***
Lower primary				-.964***		-.667**
N	1,105	1,160	1,124	1,173	1,168	1,049
-2 Log Likelihood	1468.677	1546.268	1479.768	1519.333	1511.102	1311.523
Chi-square	10.192*	3.060	22.354**	48.227**	50.628*	94.062
df	2	2	2	2	7	15

+p < .10; *p < .05; **p < .01; **p < .001.

Based on research on the black underclass, we would expect that the racial composition of the neighborhood would be significantly associated with finding jobs through informal ties, but that was not the case.

The findings in Model 4 indicate that occupational status is significantly associated with whether black Americans found out about their present job through family and friends. Respondents who had jobs in the secondary sector were significantly more likely to have found out about their jobs through family or friends. This finding is consistent with the earlier work of Corcoran et al. (1980a, 1980b), who found that individuals who have higher occupational status jobs have a lower likelihood of finding their job through an informal tie. This finding is also consistent with the observations of Braddock and McPartland (1987) on employer job search procedures. They argue that employers typically do not spend much time or money in recruiting for lower-level jobs and use inexpensive job search methods such as informal referrals from current employees and "walk-in" applications.

Model 5 estimates the net effects of the demographic variables on the likelihood of an informal job referral. Gender, marital status, education, and family income were all significantly associated with finding out about the job through an informal tie. Men, married respondents, and respondents with lower levels of education and family income were more likely to have relied on an informal tie to find their job than their counterparts. The finding that men were more likely than women to find their job through informal ties is consistent with the work of Corcoran et al. (1980a, 1980b), but varies with the findings of Marx and Leicht (1992), who did not find a gender difference. This inconsistency could be due to the fact that both the present analysis and the work of Corcoran et al. (1980a, 1980b) are based on national samples, whereas the work of Marx and Leicht (1992) is based on a more limited sample of manufacturing plants in Indiana. Although there is little previous research on why black males are more likely to use informal ties, one possible explanation may center around differential labor market experiences of black men and women (Collins, 1989). Previous analysis of the NSBA (Bowman, 1991) found that black men had a higher likelihood of being unskilled laborers, operatives, and craft/kindred workers. Black women had a higher likelihood of being service workers and clerical workers. Consistent with these occupational differences, networks of job information may be divided along gender lines and may foster the use of one source by males and another source by females.

The marital status finding indicates that married blacks had a higher likelihood of finding their job through informal ties. Marital status differences are generally not investigated in research in this area. Work on black family support networks, however, indicates that married black adults have larger support networks than their unmarried counterparts (Taylor, 1988). Because married adults have the advantage of using both the husband and the wife's support network, they may have access to a larger number of individuals who can provide job information.

The findings of the negative education and income relationships with use of informal ties is consistent with the work of Corcoran et al. (1980a). Similar to the previous occupation finding, respondents who have low levels of education and income have a higher likelihood of finding their job through the use of an informal tie. The finding is also consistent with the aforementioned observations of Braddock and McPartland (1987) that employers rely on inexpensive search methods to fill lower-level jobs that require little education and pay meager wages.

Model 6 estimates the net effects of all the independent variables on the likelihood of hearing about the present job through an informal tie. The relationships are extremely consistent across all of the models. The only major difference is that whereas education was significant in Model 5, it fails to achieve significance in the full model. This finding is consistent with the previous work of Corcoran et al. (1980a), who found that for black men the negative association between education and finding a job through an informal tie became insignificant when occupation was controlled.

Additional analysis examined whether respondents initially heard about their job through a family member as opposed to a friend. The same set of independent variables were used in a series of logistic regressions (analysis not shown). The analysis of the full model indicates that age and the racial composition of the neighborhood were the only independent variables that were significantly associated with whether black Americans found out about their jobs through family as opposed to friends. Family proximity and occupational status bordered significance with the dependent variable. Older black adults were more likely to have initially heard about their job from a friend. This may be a function of maturation. Namely, as one ages network size increases. Furthermore, composition of the network may also diversify to include more nonkin. Respondents who resided in neighborhoods with a higher percentage of black respondents and those who had larger families who resided in the same city were more likely to have heard about their job from family members as opposed to friends. Respondents in upper primary jobs were less likely to have heard about their jobs from a family member. This finding is consistent with African American's position in the labor market. Because black Americans have a greater likelihood of having secondary jobs, their source of information about upper primary jobs will have a greater tendency of coming from weaker (friends) as opposed to stronger ties (family).

Influence Networks

Of the respondents, 4 out of 10 (42.8%) had a friend or family member who worked at their present job. One third of respondents (32.4%) had a friend or family member who, in addition to informing them about the job, also helped them get the job. Among the ways that respondents received help getting the job included providing a recommendation (8.5%), telling the employer about the respondent (9.4%), helping apply for the job (6.3%), and actually hiring the respondent (3.8%). Last, a series of logistic regressions were conducted on whether the family or friend who worked at the job also helped them get the job. Analyses were conducted using the family, friendship, racial composition, and demographic independent variables. Gender was the only independent variable that was significantly associated with the dependent variable. Men had a higher likelihood of receiving help in getting their job than women. This finding is consistent with previous theorizing about the differing occupational trajectories of black men and women (e.g., Collins, 1989).

Conclusion

The findings of this study indicate that most black Americans (6 of 10) find their jobs through informal sources. Although both family members and friends are important sources of job information, more people found out about their jobs from friends. Even though the use of informal ties is more frequent among respondents who have lower levels of occupational status, it is important to note that half (47.5%) of black adults who have upper primary jobs initially heard about their job through a family member or friend. The multivariate findings are generally consistent with previous work, especially the work of Corcoran et al. (1980a), who uses similar measures.

The findings that black men are more likely than black women to find out about their jobs through informal ties and receive help in getting their jobs are not consistent with research on black family support networks. Research using NSBA data and other data sets clearly indicate that in comparison to men, women have larger support networks and interact on a more frequent basis with their network members (Taylor, 1988). Collectively, these findings indicate that informal support networks clearly operate differently in providing job search assistance than in providing advice, companionship, or financial assistance.

The results of this analysis clearly indicate that family and friends play an important role in helping black Americans secure employment. Unfortunately, this heavy reliance on informal ties is not necessarily good. This is because black job seekers are primarily tied to social networks composed of other blacks, who, on average, are not as well-situated to find out about desirable job openings as members of the social networks used by white adults (Braddock & McPartland, 1987). The current workforce in most college-level jobs is predominantly white, so the informal networks of relatives and friends linked to these jobs will also be predominantly white (Braddock & McPartland, 1987). Because black Americans are excluded from the informal hiring networks of whites, they are excluded from quality positions because they have no contacts and never hear of these vacancies (Marx & Leicht, 1992).

This lack of access to higher status, better paying jobs by black Americans due to differences in social networks was found in a study by Korenman and Turner (as cited in Granovetter, 1995). They found that although black youths had higher educational attainment than white youths, they had jobs with wages that were 15% lower than whites. The lower wages of black youths were explained by the fact that jobs found through informal networks did not pay as well for black youths as white youths (Korenman & Turner, 1996; Granovetter, 1995).

Although this chapter has focused on informal ties and employment, it is important to note that a sole focus on job search procedures will not correct the current racial imbalance in wages, occupational status, and labor force participation. Employers committed to a diverse workforce must begin to actively recruit black workers and work to eliminate barriers to black labor force participation. In addition, policymakers should adopt a multistage strategy that includes recruitment, training and educational opportunities, and reduces barriers to unions and skilled positions (Marx & Leicht, 1992).

9

Families, Unemployment, and Well-Being

CLIFFORD L. BROMAN

In this chapter, we address the issue of how unemployment affects individuals and their families. Several studies have shown that unemployment has widespread negative effects. Communities suffer from unemployment as seen through increased racial tension, homelessness, and a decline in family stability (Bluestone & Harrison, 1982; Hakim, 1982; Jahoda, 1982). Families and individuals suffer as well. Unemployment has negative effects on mental and physical health. Greater mortality rates, increased heart attack risk, low birthweight offspring, chronic respiratory diseases, ulcers, alcoholism, depression, and suicide are some of the negative effects linked to unemployment (Cobb & Kasl, 1977; Dew, Bromet, & Schulberg, 1987; Gore, 1978; Hepworth, 1980; House, 1981; Kasl & Cobb, 1970; Kessler, House, & Turner, 1987; Kessler, Turner, & House, 1989; Linn, Sandifer, & Stein, 1985; Warr, 1987; Warr & Jackson, 1985). The negative effects of unemployment on the family of the unemployed individual are also clear. Liem and Liem (1988) reported that the distress of job loss affected both the job loser and his or her family. Broman, Hamilton, and Hoffman (1990) found that job loss caused an increase in family tension and stress. Other researchers have found associations between job loss and increased family stress (Perrucci, Perrucci, Targ, & Targ, 1988; Perrucci & Targ, 1988).

Recent research has shown that unemployment does not affect all workers equally. In fact, African Americans, who are already economically disadvantaged, are much more negatively affected by job loss. Blacks are more likely than whites to face prolonged unemployment after job loss (Kletzer, 1991). Unemployment has also been shown to provoke greater emotional distress for blacks than for whites (Hamilton, Broman, Hoffman, & Renner, 1990.) Although this is true, the Hamilton et al. (1990) article is one of the first to empirically document the increased vulnerability of African Americans to job loss for health outcomes.

The impact of unemployment on black families has also been little studied. The National Survey of Black Americans (NSBA) data are well suited to an exploration of the impact of unemployment on individuals and their families. In this chapter, we explore the link between unemployment and negative outcomes for families and individuals.

Method

In this investigation we will compare the unemployed to the currently employed. Because of the detailed information collected in the NSBA, we were able to ascertain whether respondents were currently employed, currently unemployed but looking for work, or engaged in other activities. Approximately two-thirds of respondents were either currently employed or currently unemployed but looking for a job. The unemployed category includes people who may have dropped out of the labor force because of being discouraged. Respondents were categorized by their current labor force status as either a homemaker (5.1%), disabled (8.6%), student (3.6%), retired (12.2%), employed (57.0%), or unemployed (13.6%). Because our comparisons will be between the employed and the unemployed, we exclude the homemakers, disabled, students, and retirees from our analysis. This results in a subsample of 1,486 NSBA respondents.

Measures

We use several measures of individual and family well-being in the analysis. A measure of contact with family is used, which is obtained from the question, "How often do you see, write, or talk on the telephone with family or relatives who do not live with you?" This measure is coded from 7 (*nearly everyday*) to 1 (*never*). A series of measures asked about problems in the past month, and three are used here. They ask whether the respondent has had problems over the past month with (a) your family or marriage, (b) your children (only for respondents with children living in the home), and (c) your "love life." Each was coded *yes-no*. A fifth measure is obtained from a question that asked "do you sometimes feel like you are not as good as a spouse as you would like to be." This is also coded *yes-no,* and the measure is referred to as "not good spouse" (this measure is obtained only for respondents who are currently married). The last three family measures are obtained from a series of questions that asked respondents "Given the chances you have had, how well have you done" (a) "in taking care of your family's wants and needs" (take care of family); (b) "being a good spouse" (good spouse); and (c) "being a good parent to your children" (good parent). The latter two items are obtained only for respondents who are currently married, and have minor children living in the home, respectively. The names with which these measures will be referred are in parentheses. Each measure was coded from *very well* (3) to *not too well* (2) or *not well at all* (1). Two measures of individual well-being are used. One is a measure of life satisfaction obtained from a question that asked, "How satisfied are you with life these days?" This measure is coded from *very satisfied* (4) to *very dissatisfied* (1). The second well-being measure is obtained from a question that asked, "How happy are you these days?" This measure is coded from *very happy* (3) to *not too happy* (1).

We use sociodemographic variables. Age and education are measured in years. Sex is a dummy variable where 1 = male. Family income refers to total annual family income and is measured in thousands. Marital status is a dummy variable where 1 = respondent is currently married, and parental status is coded as a dummy variable where 1 = respondent has minor children living in the household. Employment status is coded where 1 = unemployed, and 0 = employed.

Analysis will proceed as follows. We first investigate the impact of unemployment on families. We then examine the impact of unemployment on individual well-being.

Results

Table 9.1 presents descriptive data on the variables used in the study. We can see that 41% of the sample is male and about 43% are married. Approximately

20% are currently unemployed. This is an extremely high figure, consistent with the recessionary times in which these data were collected. The remainder of the table shows the percentage of respondents in the various categories of family variables. Of respondents, 40% sometimes feel that they are not good spouses. This strikes one as a very high percentage of people. Approximately 20% have experienced problems related to family and love life in the past month. A majority of respondents report at least weekly contact with their family members who do not live with them. Only slightly more than half of respondents report that they have done well in taking care of their family's want and needs, whereas the clear majority of respondents feel that they have done very well as a spouse and parent.

Table 9.2 shows how study variables are related to employment status. There are many instances of significant differences between the employed and the unemployed. The employed are almost twice as likely to be married as the unemployed, but they are less likely to be parents. The difference in feeling like not a good spouse is not significant. The unemployed are more likely to have problems in the past month than the employed. They are more likely to have family problems and problems with their love life. The unemployed are less likely to have frequent contact with their family. The other significant difference in this table is that the unemployed are less likely to feel they have taken care of their family than the employed. Overall, the unemployed have greater problems with family issues, and have less contact with family members who do not live with them.

Table 9.3 presents a correlation matrix for the variables used in this study. Many of the variables in the table are correlated with other variables only weakly. This is especially true of the relationship between employment status and other variables. The patterns we see in this table are similar to those shown in Table 9.2. Other variables that are significantly intercorrelated are experiencing problems—there are strong correlations between experiencing family and marital problems and experiencing other problems. Somewhat surprisingly, contact with family is almost unrelated to any other variable, except for two substantively interesting results. First, contact with family is negatively related to feeling that one has taken care of one's family. Although causality can not be disentangled, one can speculate that feeling like one has not taken care of one's family might lead one to avoid that family. The second interesting result is the total lack of relationship between unemployment and feeling like a good spouse or a good parent.

It is important that these relationships be examined with appropriate controls for sociodemographic factors. Tables 9.4 and 9.5 present multivariate

Table 9.1 *Descriptive Data on Study Variables*

Variable	Percentage	N
Male	41.2	1,486
Currently married	42.9	1,481
Parent	57.3	1,478
Employed	80.7	1,486
Who sometimes feel like not good spouse	40.0	637
With family or marital problems in past month	18.9	1,479
With child problems in past month	20.2	858
With "love life" problems in past month	21.4	1,479
Contact with family at least weekly	65.5	1,474
Saying "I have done very well" in taking care of family's wants and needs	56.0	1,454
Saying "I have done very well" in being a good spouse	70.5	633
Saying "I have done very well" in being a good parent	76.5	775

Table 9.2 *Percentage Differences Between Employed and Unemployed*

	Employed		Unemployed	
Variable	Percentage	N	Percentage	N
Currently married*	47.2	1,195	24.8	286
Parent*	55.5	1,191	64.8	287
Not good spouse	39.6	565	43.1	72
With family or marital problems*	17.7	1,194	24.2	285
With child problems	19.7	660	22.2	198
With "love life" problems*	19.5	1,194	29.4	285
Contact with family at least weekly*	66.7	1,190	60.2	284
Who have done "very well" in taking care of a families wants and needs*	57.3	1,175	50.5	279
Who have done "very well" in being a good spouse	70.4	560	71.2	73
Who have done "very well" in being a good parent	76.2	605	77.6	170

*Difference significant at $p < .05$.

Table 9.3 *Correlation Matrix*

Variable						*Correlation Coefficients*					
Married (1 = yes)	1.00										
Parent (1 = yes)	.19	1.00									
Not good spouse (1 = yes)	.09	.06	1.00								
Family or marital problems (1 = yes)	-.01	.14	.12	1.00							
Child problems (1 = yes)	.01	.11	.13	.22	1.00						
"Love life" problems (1 = yes)	-.23	.09	.11	.42	.16	1.00					
Contact with family	.00	.01	-.04	-.03	-.05	-.05	1.00				
Taking care of family	.09	.00	-.26	-.12	-.07	-.08	-.07	1.00			
Good spouse		-.09	-.39	-.19	-.08	-.17	.01	.42	1.00		
Good parent	-.06		-.24	-.05	-.07	-.04	-.02	.47	.52	1.00	
Unemployed (1 = yes)	-.18	.07	.02	.07	.03	.10	-.07	-.08	.00	.01	1.00

Table 9.4 *Logistic Regression of Family Variables on Unemployment and Controls*

Variable	Contact With Family	Take Care of Family	Good Spouse	Good Parent
Age	.00	.01**	.00	.00
Sex (1 = male)	−.61**	−.17**	−.03	−.08*
Education	.04**	.00	−.02**	−.02*
Family income	.03**	.00	.00	.00
Married (1 = yes)	−.02	.07*	—	.05
Parent (1 = yes)	−.04	.07*	−.03	—
Unemployed (1 = yes)	−.30**	−.09*	.01	.01
Constant	5.25	2.15	2.87	2.84
N	1,313	1,296	571	696
R^2	.06	.09	.03	.02

*$p < .05$; **$p < .01$.

Table 9.5 *Logistic Regression of Family Variables on Unemployment and Controls*

Variable	Not Good Spouse	Family or Marital Problems	Child Problems	"Love Life" Problems
Age	.02*	.04**	−.04**	.04**
Sex (1 = male)	−.07	.47**	.76**	.68**
Education	−.01	.05	.04	.02
Family income	−.01	−.02	−.26	.00
Married (1 = yes)	−6.51	−.12	−.07	1.12**
Parent (1 = yes)	−.05	−.35*	1.02**	−.20
Unemployed (1 = yes)	−.06	−.06	−.22	−.05
Constant	−6.41	.16	−3.39	.86
N	578	1,311	763	1,311
−2 Log Likelihood	15.79*	57.37**	44.69**	150.01**

*$p < .05$; **$p < .01$.

result is the total lack of relationship between unemployment and feeling like a good spouse or a good parent.

It is important that these relationships be examined with appropriate controls for sociodemographic factors. Tables 9.4 and 9.5 present multivariate analyses of family variables on control variables and unemployment. Table 9.4 presents multiple regression; results are presented for the variables that were continuous. Employment status is significantly associated with contact with family and taking care of family. Being unemployed is negatively related to having contact with family and taking care of family. Table 9.5 presents a logistic regression of family variables on controls and employment status. Significantly, employment status is unrelated to these family variables. The log odds of unemployment are not significant.

There are two instances in which unemployment has a significant effect on family factors in this study. We now turn to the impact of unemployment on individual well-being.

Table 9.6 presents results that consider impact of unemployment and family variables on well-being. An OLS regression of well-being on controls and employment status is performed and the results indicate that employment status is significantly related to well-being. The unemployed have significantly lower levels of well-being than the employed. This is consistent with the bulk of literature concerning this issue.

Further analysis was performed to assess the possible mediating effects of family factors on individual well-being. We tested a model that added the family factors that were significantly predicted by unemployment to controls and employment status. The results of this analysis are presented in Table 9.7.

Results in the table show that life satisfaction is significantly predicted by unemployment and taking care of family. The effects of these two factors are opposite on life satisfaction. Unemployment is related to decreased life satisfaction, whereas the more one feels that one has done a good job of taking care of family wants and needs, the greater is satisfaction with life. For happiness, results indicate that the relationship between unemployment and happiness is explained away when family factors are controlled for. Both family factors are positively related to happiness. Increased contact with family is related to increased happiness. Feeling like one has taken care of family wants and needs is related to increased happiness. In general, people derive satisfaction and well-being from feeling they have taken care of their family.

Table 9.6 *Logistic Regression of Well-Being Variables on Unemployment and Controls*

Variable	Life Satisfaction	Happiness
Age	.01**	.01**
Sex (1 = male)	.03	.00
Education	−.02*	.00
Family income	.00	.01
Married (1 = yes)	.14*	.14**
Parent (1 = yes)	.00	.02
Unemployed (1 = yes)	−.20**	−.12*
Constant	2.83	1.73
N	1,311	1,308
R^2	.06	.07

*p < .05; **p < .01.

Table 9.7 *Logistic Regression of Well-Being Variables on Unemployment, Family Variables, and Controls*

Variable	Life Satisfaction	Happiness
Age	.01**	.01**
Sex (1 = male)	.07	.06
Education	−.02*	−.01
Family income	.00	.01
Married (1 = yes)	.13**	.12**
Parent (1 = yes)	−.02	−.04
Unemployed (1 = yes)	−.17**	.08
Contact with family	.01	.03*
Take care of family	.19**	.22**
Constant	2.34	1.10
N	1,288	1,290
R^2	.08	.12

*p < .05; **p < .01.

Discussion

The results presented here have shown that unemployment is a significant factor to both families and individuals. The unemployed have been shown to have decreased contact with family who do not live with them, and to feel less that they have taken care of their family's wants and needs. The unemployed also have lower levels of satisfaction with life.

These basic results are consistent with the literature on unemployment. Unemployment is a stressor that hurts individuals and their families. Our task must now be to discover resources that may help individuals and families adapt to the stress and strain of unemployment. This is particularly important for the African American population, given the greater likelihood of experiencing unemployment, and having a harder time finding reemployment. This will continue to be an issue for black communities for some time, given the global economic restructuring that is underway. Retraining efforts for new jobs in the expanding service sector, as well as in other job areas is a priority. At the same time, increased human services needs can be expected to aid individuals and families in coping with the stress of unemployment.

10

Differences Among African American Single Mothers
Marital Status, Living Arrangements, and Family Support

RUKMALIE JAYAKODY
LINDA M. CHATTERS

Introduction

The dramatic increase in the number of single-parent families represents one of the major demographic changes occurring over the past few decades. Among African Americans, 55.6% of all families consist of a single parent, and 64% of all African American children live with only one parent, usually their mother (U.S. Bureau of the Census, 1992b). Single-parenthood itself, however, as well as the higher rate of single-parenthood among African Americans compared to whites, is not a recent development. Records from the 1900 census indicate that at the turn of the century the odds of living in a single-parent family were 3.6 times greater for African Americans than for whites (Morgan, McDaniel, Miller, & Preston, 1993). It was originally believed that the race difference was accounted for by the higher mortality rate among African Americans (Gordon & McLanahan, 1991). Recent research shows, however, that the mortality rate alone does not explain the difference (Morgan et al., 1993). Furthermore, information on household arrangements indicates that, at the turn of the century, African American single-mother families were much more likely to reside in extended arrangements than were white single mothers (Morgan et al., 1993). What has changed over the past 90 years is the magnitude of single parenthood. In 1900, single-parent families accounted for 22% of African American families (Morgan et al., 1993), whereas today black single-parent families (2.4 million) outnumber two-parent families (1.8 million) by a sizable margin (U.S. Bureau of the Census, 1992d).

Single-parent family structures are frequently accompanied by conditions of economic instability and high poverty rates. Of all major demographic groups, African American single-mothers and their children are the worst off economically. Of all poor black families, 73% are maintained by a single mother (U.S. Bureau of the Census, 1991c) and 53% of African American single-parent families fall below the official poverty line (U.S. Bureau of the Census, 1989b).

Given the high rates of single-mother families among African Americans, and the harsh economic and social conditions they encounter, black single-mother families have been the subject of considerable social science research and policy debate. Assistance from kin networks (i.e., family social support) has long been recognized as an important factor that may offset the economic and social disadvantages facing single mothers. Current policy debates focusing on program eligibility limits and reductions in benefits, will likely highlight the expanded role of family assistance in addressing the needs of single mothers and their children. It is important, however, to understand what is the nature, extent, and viability of kin resources for individual families and the factors that are associated with the provision of kin assistance. This chapter contributes to a broader understanding of the factors influencing family assistance to single mothers, as well as providing a clearer picture of the diversity of social circumstances that characterize this group.

Single-Parent Families

It is helpful to begin by clarifying terminology in this area of research. The term, *single mother,* has emerged as a commonly used phrase that actually refers to a range of complex living arrangements and circumstances. We use the term single mother to describe any situation in which a currently unmarried mother lives with her minor (under age 18) child(ren) and who is without a male partner (either a husband or a male cohabitor). Thus, single mothers could be divorced, separated, widowed, or never married mothers. Furthermore, this definition is appropriate regardless of the presence of other relatives or nonrelatives residing in the household. Although single-parent families also include father-only families, they are not the focus of the present discussion for several reasons. Single-father families are a rapidly growing family group in

America; however, they are still relatively rare, particularly among African Americans. Single fathers represent only 6% of African American single-parent families (U.S. Bureau of the Census, 1989a).[1] Concerns about the impact of marital status, living arrangements, and family support are valid considerations in relation to single-father families. Single-father families, however, do not face the same levels and forms of economic deprivations as do women who live alone with their children. We focus here on women because these issues are particularly salient for the economic and social status of this group of parents and children.

Inaccurate portrayals of single mothers and their children abound in both the academic literature and the popular media. Our understanding of single-mother families is limited by their common depiction as a relatively homogeneous group in which within-group variation is rarely recognized or documented. When within-group differences are acknowledged, single mothers are distinguished primarily on the basis of race or ethnicity. Certainly, recognizing differences in single-parent families by race and ethnicity is important. The investigation of other factors (e.g., marital status, age, living arrangements) that differentiate single-mother families (both within and across racial and ethnic groups), however, provides a more comprehensive understanding of the impact of these status characteristics on family form and functioning.

Marital Status Differences

African American single mothers are a diverse group with regard to marital status designations (i.e., never married, divorced-separated, and widowed). African Americans and whites differ substantially with respect to the prevalence of specific marital status categories within respective populations, as well as the dynamics of marital status transitions. For example, although divorce accounts for the largest proportion of single-mother families among whites (50%), among African Americans the profile is quite different. Of African American single mothers, 41% are never married mothers, 23% are divorced, 16% are separated, and 17% are widowed (U.S. Bureau of the Census, 1992e). Furthermore, the actual figures for nonmarital births may be underrepresented somewhat due to an undercount of the number of women who gave birth prior to marriage (i.e., never married mothers). A portion of these mothers will marry after giving birth, thereby exiting the never married category and entering the married category.

The marital status transitions of separation and divorce are experienced differently among African Americans and whites. For whites, the majority of

marital separations are followed rapidly by a legal divorce. Of separated couples, 63% formally terminate their marriage within a year of separating; 84%
divorce within two years. In contrast, only 28% of African Americans divorce
within the first year following marital disruption, and only 42% do so within
the second year (Sweet & Bumpass, 1987). As a consequence, among African
American women, spousal separation as a marital transition constitutes a
longer term circumstance than it does for white women (Cherlin, 1992).

Marital status differences among single mothers (i.e., never married, divorced, separated, widowed) are associated with significant variation in their
economic and social circumstances. On average, never married mothers have
fewer years of education than divorced mothers, tend to be economically
worse off, have lower levels of labor force participation, and are more likely to
receive welfare (Bane & Ellwood, 1984; Besharov & Quinn, 1987; Garfinkel
& McLanahan, 1986). Furthermore, social and economic circumstances associated with marital status also may have important implications for the amount
of support single mothers receive from family. Research examining marital
status distinctions in family assistance typically compares married mothers
with nonmarried mothers (aggregating never married, divorced-separated,
and widowed mothers into a single category). These findings indicate that nonmarried mothers are significantly more likely to receive assistance from their
families than married mothers (Allen, 1979; Angel & Tienda, 1982; Gibson,
1972; Hofferth, 1984; Hogan, Hao, & Parish, 1990; McAdoo, 1980; Tienda &
Glass, 1985). Other research compares never married mothers with previously
married mothers (aggregating divorced, separated, and widowed women).
Both dichotomies, however, do not allow for a systematic examination of the
marital status diversity that exists within the unmarried category (i.e., differen-
tiating between never married, divorced, separated, and widowed). Recent
findings (Jayakody, Chatters, & Taylor, 1993) of significant differences between (a) never married mothers and other marital statuses for financial assistance and (b) never married and widowed mothers for emotional assistance, indicate that marital status distinctions are meaningful.

Living Arrangement Differences

Although the term, single mother, is generally thought to be synonymous
with "female household head," there are important differences between these
two designations. The U.S. Bureau of the Census defines a *household* as

all persons who occupy a housing unit. The occupant might be a single family, an individual living alone, two or more families living together, or any group of related or unrelated persons who share living arrangements. (U.S. Bureau of the Census, 1992f, B-14)

That is, a household may contain one family, more than one family, or no family at all (an individual living alone or unrelated individuals living together). Consequently, a female household head includes women who live alone with their children, as well as women without children. In fact, a large proportion of female-headed households are comprised of elderly women with no minor children present. Furthermore, many single mothers do not live independently as distinct and separate family households. Nearly 25% of single mothers live as subfamilies within the household of a relative, usually their parents (Ellwood & Bane, 1984; Sweet & Bumpass, 1987). Other estimates indicate that close to 75% of never married mothers under the age of 24 coreside with relatives for at least 5 years following the birth of their child (Ellwood & Bane, 1984).

Racial differences in patterns of coresidence, subfamily, or extended family living indicate that African American families are much more likely than white families to enter such living situations (Angel & Tienda, 1982; Beck & Beck, 1989; Farley & Allen, 1987a; Hofferth, 1984; Sweet & Bumpass, 1987; Tienda & Angel, 1982). A number of scholars contend that extended family living is more common among African Americans because of explicit cultural norms that endorse these arrangements (Dilworth-Anderson, Burton, & Johnson, 1993; Sudarkasa, 1981), whereas others suggest the greater prevalence of coresidence is primarily motivated by economic considerations (Angel & Tienda, 1982; Jackson, 1973; Tienda & Angel, 1982). Extended living arrangements, however, are twice as common among African Americans as among white households (Farley & Allen, 1987a), even in analyses controlling for socioeconomic status. Furthermore, extended households are found among middle-class (McAdoo, 1978), as well as poor families (Stack, 1974).[2]

Coresidence patterns also vary on the basis of marital status. Never married mothers are generally more likely than other unmarried mothers to reside with kin (Parish, Hao, & Hogan, 1991) and divorced-separated mothers are more likely to coreside than are widowed mothers (U.S. Bureau of the Census, 1992a). In addition, age of both the mother and child appears to contribute to the relationship between marital status and coresidence. That is, never married mothers, because of their younger age (and their children's age), are more likely to coreside with family. In extended family living situations, never married and widowed mothers are more likely to reside with the mother's parents, followed by other relatives. Divorced mothers, in contrast, are more likely to live with nonrelatives, possibly reflecting higher rates of partner cohabitation among divorced women.

Living arrangements are related to both levels and types of support mothers receive from families. The living arrangements examined most often are (a) mother and child living alone versus (b) mother and child living with other family members and nonrelatives. Mother and child living with their families (compared to those living alone) tend to rely more on families for advice, support, food, clothing, child care, and other needs (Furstenberg & Crawford, 1978). Furthermore, previous research indicates that coresidence grants specific economic and social benefits in terms of housing assistance, economic aid, emotional support, and child care (Angel & Tienda, 1982; Cherlin, Chase-Lansdale, & Furstenberg, 1991; Furstenberg & Crawford, 1978; Furstenberg, Brooks-Gunn, & Morgan, 1987; Hogan et al., 1990; Jayakody et al., 1993; Kellam, Ensminger, & Turner, 1977; Tienda & Angel, 1982; Tienda & Glass, 1985). Shared resources in coresidential living and the child care that is provided by family members in the household, allow single mothers opportunities to continue or complete schooling or gain labor market experience. These benefits of coresidence, in turn, have direct economic consequences through higher wage rates and better employment prospects (Hill, 1990; Tienda & Glass, 1985).

Although coresidential living has a number of benefits, there are significant drawbacks as well. Conflicts with other family members may arise over child-rearing philosophies and parenting styles (Goetting, 1986; Stevens, 1988), and mothers may experience problems related to appropriate role allocation, expectations, and behaviors. Lack of privacy and difficulties related to crowding may present problems for all family members (Alwin, Converse, & Martin, 1985; Macpherson & Stewart, 1991). Furthermore, the benefits of extended family living may not accrue indefinitely. Evidence suggests that although relatively brief durations of coresidential living are helpful, longer periods may not be (Furstenberg et al., 1987; Hill, 1990). Long-term reliance on family resources may hinder economic independence by preventing the development of skills that are needed to live independently. In addition, an already precarious economic situation may be exacerbated when a family that is economically at risk (e.g., single mother with children) establishes coresidential arrangements with another at-risk family. Current profiles suggest that in households comprised of single mothers, their children, and a related single female, the related female is typically the single mother's own mother (i.e., maternal grandmother). In about 50% of these cases, both the single mother and her mother have children under 18 years of age present in the home (Winkler, 1993).

Households in which two single mothers with minor children "double up" are at particularly high risk economically and have the lowest economic status of all single-mother families (Winkler, 1993). Significantly, 73% of these household arrangements involve African American mothers (Winkler, 1993).

Although the advantages of coresidency are well documented, the benefits accruing from noncoresident kin should not be overlooked. In fact, exclusive attention to kin who reside within a given household restricts one's perspective on the extent and dynamics of family support (Chatters & Jayakody, 1995). A single-mother's support network often involves several kin who reside elsewhere, constituting functional extended kin groups that operate across separate households (Hogan et al., 1990; Stack, 1974). Several studies (Hogan et al., 1990; Taylor & Chatters, 1991a) indicate that kin residing outside the focal household often are an essential element in family support networks (Stack, 1974). In particular, ethnographic profiles of extended kinship relations that exist across households indicate that several separate nuclear families may reside in the same neighborhood and cooperate in daily tasks and responsibilities (Stack, 1974). Furthermore, in addition to noncoresident kin, fictive kin are often important sources of informal support and economic assistance (Chatters, Taylor, & Jayakody, 1994).

How Much Help Do Families Provide?

The present analysis examines mothers' perceptions of the extent of assistance they receive from their family. Whereas previous studies have examined whether or not help was received and types of assistance provided (Hogan et al., 1990; Jayakody et al., 1993; McAdoo, 1980), subjective assessments of the extent of support are not found in the literature. The present effort focuses on intragroup differences in examining the influence of marital status and living arrangements and other demographic factors on the amount of assistance single mothers (i.e., divorced-separated, never married, widowed) report receiving from their families. Although this analysis examines amount of family assistance independently of direct controls for need, proxies for need are present in a number of independent variables (i.e., poverty ratio, age, education). Along with a focus on unmarried mothers, the analysis includes married mothers, who serve as the reference group. The Discussion and Conclusion section places the present findings in the context of previous research and suggests future research avenues investigating substantive differences among African American single-mother families, and the impact these characteristics may have on the economic and social well-being of mothers and their children.

Data and Method

Inclusion criteria for this analysis are unmarried and married mothers who reside with at least one of their own minor children (17 years of age or younger) and who indicate that their family—including parents, grandparents, aunts, uncles, in-laws, and so on—has assisted them in some manner. The resulting sample consists of 501 mothers, of which 126 are divorced or separated, 68 are widowed, 100 are never married, and 207 are married mothers. Comparisons of this sample with data from the *Current Population Survey* for comparably defined persons (i.e., mothers with minor children) indicate that the study sample is representative of the larger population (see Jayakody et al., 1993 for further discussion).

Dependent and Independent Measures

The dependent variable assesses the amount of help mothers report receiving from their family. Following an initial item that identifies whether mothers receive assistance, the question asks specifically, "How much help are they (family) to you? Would you say *a great deal* of help, *a lot* of help, or *only a little* help?"

The independent variables included in the analysis are measures of various demographic characteristics and family factors. The demographic variables include marital status, age, education, and poverty ratio. Marital status is represented by four dichotomous variables, designating never married mothers, divorced-separated mothers, widowed mothers, and married mothers; married mothers represent the excluded category. Given the similarities in the marital transitions of divorce and separation for African American women (Cherlin, 1992), separated and divorced women are aggregated into one category in this analysis. Age of the mother is a continuous-level variable ranging from 18 to 55 years. Dichotomous variables represent the highest level of education completed by mothers and distinguish between mothers with (a) less than a high school education, (b) a high school degree, but no further schooling, and (c) more than a high school education (excluded category).

The poverty-ratio measure is an income-to-needs index that divides total family income (e.g., earnings, interests, dividends, government payments) by the total income needs of the household (adjusted for the age and sex of each household member). Values that range from 0 to .99 indicate that the family is below the official poverty line. Values of 1.00 and above indicate that the family is above the official government definition of poverty and the degree to which total household income exceeds the official definition of basic needs.

Compared to total family income, the poverty ratio is thought to be a more accurate indicator of hardship experience (Mayer & Jencks, 1989).

Prior research characterizes kinship networks along several structural and functional dimensions, such as frequency of contact, family satisfaction, and emotional closeness with family (Martin & Martin, 1978; Stack, 1974; Troll, 1971). These dimensions, in turn, predict family assistance among African Americans (Taylor & Chatters, 1991a). Family closeness is measured by a dichotomous variable that represents mothers who report feeling very close to their family (close = 1) and those who respond otherwise (close = 0). Similarly, family satisfaction indicates whether the mother reports being very satisfied with her family (satisfaction = 1) or not (satisfaction = 0). Family contact is measured with the following question: "How often do you see, write, or talk on the telephone with family or relatives who do not live with you? Would you say nearly everyday, at least once a week, a few times a month, a few times a year, or hardly ever?" This variable is included as an interval-level variable ranging from low to high. Living arrangement is a dichotomous variable indicating whether or not mother and children coreside with others. In the case of married mothers, the variable indicates whether or not her family (i.e., mother, father, and children) coresides with others. In either situation, coresidence is assigned a value of 1 if mother and child(ren) coreside with others and coresidence is assigned a value of 0 if mother and child(ren) live independently.

Method

As noted previously, there are three possible responses to the item assessing amount of assistance from family: (a) *only a little,* (b) *a lot,* or (c) *a great deal.* Although the three responses are ordered (i.e., exhibit a clear ranking among the categories), they do not form an interval scale and differences between adjacent intervals can not be treated as being equal (Liao, 1994). In addition, given there are only three responses, it would be inappropriate to treat this item as an interval-level variable, rendering ordinary least squares regression an inappropriate technique (DeMaris, 1995). A multinomial logit model could be used, but would not account for the ordinal nature of the dependent variable and would therefore fail to use all the available information (Liao, 1994).

An ordered probit model is used in this analysis to take full advantage of the natural order of the dependent variable (McKelvey & Zavoina, 1975). The ordered probit model assumes that there is a continuously distributed latent variable y^* that gives rise to the observed ordinal values ($y = 0$, *only a little* help received, $y = 1$, *a lot* of help received, and $y = 2$, *a great deal* of help received). A

Table 10.1 *Amount of Help From Family by Marital Status and Living Arrangements (in percentages)*

	A Little	A Lot	A Great Deal
Marital status			
Divorced/separated	29.4	26.2	44.4
Widowed	29.4	20.6	50.0
Never married	26.0	23.0	51.0
Married	21.3	26.1	52.7
Living arrangements			
Coresides	19.1	24.5	56.4
Lives alone	26.8	24.8	48.4

unique threshold parameter, μ, is estimated, which represents the threshold between receiving *a lot* of help and receiving *a great deal* of help from one's family. The threshold separating *only a little* help and *a lot* of help is normalized and therefore equal to zero. This analysis examines the net effects of the independent variables on the amount of assistance mothers report receiving from their families. Net effects express the relationship between an independent and dependent variable, controlling for the presence of other explanatory variables. For example, we would like to know if there is a net difference between mothers who coreside and mothers who live alone, after controlling for the fact that mothers who coreside are generally younger, poorer, and never married. Several steps are taken to facilitate the interpretation of coefficients from the ordered probit model. For categorical variables, we calculate the predicted probabilities of receiving *a great deal* of assistance, controlling for all other independent variables in the model at their mean. For continuous variables, the marginal effect of a unit increase in the independent variable on the probability of receiving *a great deal* of help is calculated, again controlling for all other independent variables. In addition, because the chapter focuses on the influence of marital status and living arrangements on the amount of support received, the predicted probabilities for each marital status and living arrangement group are graphically presented (see Greene, 1990 for a discussion of these calculations).

Results

Marital Status and Living Arrangements

Table 10.1 presents bivariate results for the relationships between marital status and living arrangements and amount of family assistance. Comparing levels of assistance across marital status groups, both divorced/separated and widowed mothers (29%) are more likely than married mothers (21%) to report that they receive *only a little* help from family. Reports of receiving *a lot* of help are least common among widowed mothers (21%) and most common among married and divorced-separated mothers (26%). Married mothers (53%) are the most likely to report receiving *a great deal* of help from family, whereas divorced-separated mothers are the least likely (44%).

Living arrangements bear a clear relationship to amount of family assistance. Mothers who co-reside with others are more likely than mothers living alone to report receiving *a great deal* of help from family (56% vs. 48%, respectively) and are less likely to report receiving *only a little* family assistance (19% vs. 27%, respectively). Differences by living arrangement for mothers who report receiving *a lot* of help from family are minor. Next, these relationships are examined in a multivariate context.

Table 10.2 presents the unstandardized beta coefficients and standard errors from the ordered probit model (columns 1 and 2). The third column presents the predicted probabilities of receiving *a great deal* of help from family ($y = 2$); probabilities for the omitted (i.e., comparison) categories (e.g., married = 0) are also presented. With regard to marital status differences, the probability of reporting *a great deal* of help from family is highest for married mothers (.53), compared to others. There is a significant difference in the level of family help reported by divorced-separated mothers and married mothers. Widowed and never married mothers also report receiving less help, but differences in family assistance for these groups, compared to married mothers, are not significant.

To illustrate the net effects of marital status on amount of family help, the predicted probabilities for each level of support (*only a little, $y = 0$; a lot, $y = 1$; a great deal, $y = 2$*) are calculated and graphed (Figure 10.1). Divorced-separated mothers have the highest probability of receiving *only a little* help, whereas married mothers have the lowest probability. Widowed and never married mothers demonstrate small differences in the probability of receiving *only a little* help from family, whereas both groups have a slightly lower probability of receiving *only a little* help compared to divorced-separated mothers.

Table 10.2 *Ordered Probit Coefficients for Amount of Help From Family*

	b	SE	prob (y = 2)
Constant	.892**	.334	
Marital status			
Divorced-separated	−.297*	.143	.42
Widowed	−.241	.157	.44
Never married	−.224	.161	.44
Married			.53
Education			
Less than high school	−.307*	.151	.43
High school graduate	−.263*	.131	.45
More than high school			.56
Poverty status	−.001	.001	−.0004
Age	−.010	.001	−.0030
Living arrangements			
Co-resides	.228*	.113	.49
Lives alone			.45
Family closeness			
Very close to family	.699***	.112	.59
Other			.32
Family satisfaction			
Very satisfied with family	.236*	.111	.53
Other			.43
Frequency of contact	.021	.044	.008
μ	.736		
Model χ^2	64.87		
df	11		

*$p < .05$; **$p < .01$; ***$p < .001$.

Married mothers also have the lowest probability of receiving *a lot* of help from family, although the difference between married mothers and all unmarried mothers is very small. In addition, there is very little difference between divorced-separated, widowed, and never married mothers in the probability of receiving *a lot* of help. Finally, married mothers have the highest probability of receiving *a great deal* of help; divorced-separated women have the lowest probability of receiving *a great deal* of help from their families.

Differences by living arrangement indicate that the probability of receiving *a great deal* of help from family is higher among mothers who coreside with others (.49) than for mothers who live alone (.45). The net effects of coresidence on amount of help from family is illustrated in Figure 10.2. Mothers who coreside are more likely than mothers living alone to report receiving *a great deal* of help from family, while being slightly less likely to report they receive *only a little* help. Differences between the two groups for the probability of receiving *a lot* of help from family are small.

Demographic and Family Factors

Mothers with a high school education or less have a significantly lower probability than mothers with educations beyond high school of receiving *a great deal* of help from family. The probability of receiving *a great deal of help* from family is highest for highly educated mothers (.56), whereas mothers with a high school education (.45) or less (.43) both have lower probabilities of receiving *a great deal* of assistance from family. Mothers reporting close emotional bonds to family are significantly more likely to receive more help than those who are less close to family. For mothers who are very close to their family (.59), the probability of receiving *a great deal* of assistance is nearly double that of mothers who are less close to their family (.32). Similarly, satisfaction with family life is significantly associated with receiving family assistance. Mothers who report being very satisfied with their family lives (.53) are more likely to receive greater amounts of assistance than mothers who report lower levels of family satisfaction (.43). Contrary to expectations, poverty status, age, and frequency of contact with family are unrelated to amount of family assistance.

Discussion and Conclusion

These findings highlight the role of demographic and family factors in understanding single mothers and the assistance they receive from family networks. Significant marital status and living arrangements findings, in particular, demonstrated that single-mother families are distinctive with respect to these factors and that they are consequential for family support. Overall, these

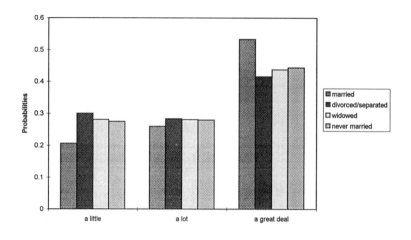

Figure 10.1. Predicted Probabilities for Family Assistance by Marital Status

analyses demonstrated a support advantage favoring mothers who (a) are married, (b) coreside with others, (c) have greater than a high school education, and (d) report emotionally close relations with kin and satisfaction with their families.

The marital status differences in this study are distinctive from other analyses in which nonmarried mothers are more likely than married mothers to receive assistance from family (Allen, 1979; Angel & Tienda, 1982; Gibson, 1972; Hofferth, 1984; Hogan, Hao, & Parish, 1990; McAdoo, 1980; Tienda & Glass, 1985). Earlier work, however, examined whether or not mothers received family support and involved contrasts of married mothers against nonmarried mothers in which never married, widowed, divorced, and separated mothers were aggregated into a single category. In addition to these differences, the current analysis examined subjective reports of the amount of help received. Single mothers may, in fact, receive extensive help from family. If, however, family assistance falls short of perceived need for aid, single mothers may report that they receive little assistance from kin (relative to their need requirements).

On the other hand, married mothers may require relatively lower levels of assistance from families. When family help is provided, and because it is adequate for their perceived support needs, married mothers may report that they receive considerable assistance from family. In some "objective" sense, then, the amount of family assistance to single mothers may, in reality, be equal to, or greater than, what married mothers receive. This issue may be resolved by

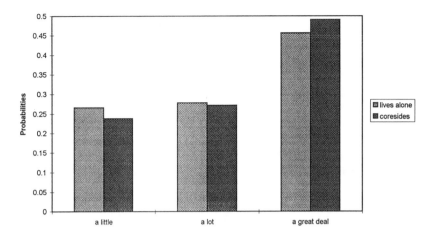

Figure 10.2. Predicted Probabilities for Family Assistance by Living Arrangements

incorporating measures that assess perceived need for family assistance, actual levels of support (i.e., discrete exchanges of money, time, or services), and felt adequacy of family support.

Married mothers may also report receiving more help from family than unmarried mothers because they have access to broader kin networks. In essence, married mothers have two family networks from which to draw support—their own as well as their husband's. These larger kin networks may provide married mothers with an expanded network of support resources that provide higher amounts of assistance overall. Divorced-separated and widowed mothers may also have access to (former) in-laws. The viability of support linkages to in-laws may be compromised, however, making these ties more restricted and fragile. As a consequence, unmarried mothers may be limited to their own (i.e., family of origin) kin networks for assistance. Furthermore, divorced-separated mothers may be particularly disadvantaged in terms of assistance from kin because the marital disruption may be viewed negatively by family. Divorce and separation could adversely influence affective relations (i.e., emotional closeness, family satisfaction) within families, which, in turn, could negatively influence levels of support from kin.

As anticipated, living arrangements were significantly associated with the amount of assistance that single mothers receive from their families. In general, mothers who coreside with others reported receiving more help than those who live alone. This finding is consistent with a number of previous studies reporting that coresident mothers have a higher likelihood of receiving support than mothers who live alone (Angel & Tienda, 1982; Furstenberg & Crawford, 1978; Hogan et al., 1990; Tienda & Angel, 1982). Proximate family can operate in two ways to facilitate support exchanges. First, by virtue of coresidency, mothers may receive more help because their support requirements are clearly identified and apparent to family members. Second, mothers who coreside have direct and ready access to individuals who are potential sources of assistance.

Turning to education differences, mothers with greater than a high school education were more likely than mothers with less education to receive more assistance from their families. Explanations for this finding may reflect the family's available resources and established patterns of assistance to the mother. It is possible that mothers who continue education beyond high school are able to do so precisely because they receive considerable help from their family. For young mothers who have had a premarital birth, support from family is regarded as crucial for continuing education (Furstenberg & Crawford, 1978). It may be the case that these findings reflect a more general pattern whereby, regardless of marital status, family assistance is instrumental in furthering the mother's education. The relationship between education and amount of family support, in effect, reflects established and continuing patterns of assistance to the mother.

Family closeness and satisfaction were significantly associated with level of family assistance. The direct causality of these relationships is open to question. That is, reported feelings of family closeness and satisfaction may prompt the provision of greater amounts of family assistance, as well as the possibility that family largess may engender in mothers positive sentiments regarding their family. It is likely, however, that in the ongoing processes of kin interactions and relationships, affective relations and supportive functions are reciprocally determined. In contrast, frequency of contact between mothers and their families was not significantly associated with amount of assistance. The absence of an effect for family contact, together with a significant effect for coresidency is somewhat puzzling. Taken together, the findings suggest that family contact, per se, is inconsequential for the amount of assistance mothers receive from kin. It may be the case, however, that whatever effect family contact exerts on amount of assistance is effectively delivered via the coresidency variable. In other words, coresident living arrangements effectively encompass contact with family (except in those instances where coresidents are nonkin). In analytic terms, family contact may fail to exert a significant effect on amount of family assistance because it is partially redundant with coresidency.

Far from being a homogeneous group, these findings verify that married and unmarried mothers are distinctive with respect to the amounts of aid they report receiving from family. Notable in this regard was the particular support advantage that married mothers possess and the possibility that divorced-separated mothers may be especially jeopardized. Several directions for future research are suggested by these findings. First, although in some instances differences between never married, divorced-separated, and widowed mothers were small, there was sufficient variability to warrant continued investigation of distinctions between these groups in family support relationships and related interpersonal phenomena. Although only suggestive, findings for divorced-separated mothers suggest that changes in the structural aspects of family networks (i.e., extensiveness) and affective relations with family (i.e., closeness and satisfaction) may have negative consequences for assistance levels from family. A comprehensive investigation of the impact of marital status on family support should employ a prospective design that permits monitoring marital status transitions and accompanying changes in other arenas. Failing that, however, the usefulness of cross-sectional data can be maximized by exploring possible differences existing within the category of unmarried mothers, fully employing the inherent variability within this group, and linking these differences in a meaningful manner to substantive concerns.

Consistent with other work on the benefits of coresident households (particularly for single mothers), coresident living arrangements were important for receiving aid from family. Coresidency may represent the most efficient means for identifying support needs and securing assistance. The liabilities and disadvantages (i.e., interpersonal conflict) of coresidency should, however, receive attention as well. Although coresident arrangements provide economic benefits for some families, among economically vulnerable families, coresidency represents a further strain on limited resources. The limits of coresidency are particularly apparent given the nation's continuing shortage of affordable low-income housing and the lack of housing that adequately accommodates larger than average family units. It is important to understand how and under what particular circumstances coresidency actually works to improve the economic and social circumstances of single mothers, their children, and the extended family.

In the current political climate, proposed strategies for welfare reform frequently focus on shifting government-based support to single mothers and their children back to the family support system. Although family support is an important factor contributing to the functioning of single-mother families, kin assistance should not be viewed as the primary support mechanism for single-mother families. This study found that between 44% to 51% of single-mother families report receiving a great deal of assistance from their families. Almost 50% of single-mother families, however, reported that they did not receive extensive assistance from kin. Furthermore, an increased reliance on kin support, caused by the removal of government-based aid and a shift to family resources, may deplete already scarce resources among families that are presently providing assistance. Family assistance can not be viewed as the solution to all the needs of single-mother families (e.g., housing, viable employment, education and job training, adequate and affordable child care), but instead should serve as a supplement to formal support strategies, such as Aid to Families With Dependent Children (AFDC) and other welfare programs. Research focusing on the economic and social circumstances of single-mother families can provide a better understanding of the nature and extent of support available from kin and the factors that operate to facilitate or hinder family assistance, as well as delineating the reasonable limits of these resources for individual families.

Notes

1. Because the census bureau did not accurately identify cohabiting couples prior to the 1990 census, this 6% is likely an overestimate. That is, a portion of this 6% includes unmarried couples with children. Among cohabiting couples, when the man is the father of the child he is classified as the father. The mother of the child, because she is not married to the father, is classified as an unrelated individual.

2. Although socioeconomic controls do not account for all the race differences, other differences between African Americans and whites (e.g., African Americans are more likely to be unmarried, more likely to be never married, and are more likely to be younger, and to have younger children) may explain higher rates of coresidence among this group.

11

Child Rearing, Social Support, and Perceptions of Parental Competence Among African American Mothers

CLEOPATRA HOWARD CALDWELL
LILAH RAYNOR KOSKI

The challenges of raising African American children to become competent, successful adults can seem daunting for some parents in a society that has a differential system of rewards and punishments based on race. Members of various cultural groups typically share some ideas about what is necessary to rear their children to succeed (Abell, Clawson, Washington, Best, & Vaughn, 1996; Bowman & Howard, 1985; Harrison, Wilson, Pine, Chan, & Buriel, 1990; Hurd, Moore, & Rogers, 1995; McLoyd, 1990; Ogbu, 1985; Spencer, 1990; Strom, Strom, Collinsworth, & Schmid, 1990). How well these ideals are imparted helps to shape a person's sense of competence as a parent. Because beliefs about one's proficiency in parenting may influence actual parenting behaviors (Belsky, 1984), it becomes important to identify factors that contribute to perceptions of parental competence to positively influence and enhance these perceptions if necessary.

Considerable research has been conducted on determinants of maternal parenting behaviors (Andersen & Telleen, 1992). Demographic characteristics associated with particular parenting styles and behaviors include maternal age, education (Kissman, 1989; Reis, 1989), ethnicity (Kelly, Power, & Wimbush, 1992; Kissman, 1989; McLoyd, 1990; Reis, 1989), employment (Cohn, Campbell, Matias, & Hopkins, 1986), and marital status (Belsky, 1984; Simons, Beaman, Conger, & Chao, 1993; Simons, Lorenz, Wu, & Conger, 1993). Personal attributes of mothers also have been found to influence maternal parenting behaviors. These include parenting attitudes and beliefs (Kissman, 1989; Reis, 1989), parenting satisfaction (Goetting, 1986), and maternal depressive symptomatology (Fleming, Klein, & Corter, 1992; Hammen, Burge, & Stansbury, 1990).

Factors that predict a sense of competence, especially among African American mothers, have not been as extensively investigated as factors that predict parenting behaviors. Nevertheless, we know that a sense of competence is influenced by both past experiences and current resources. Thus, an important resource to consider in developing a sense of parental mastery is the availability and use of social support. Social support has been defined as an interpersonal transaction involving (a) instrumental aid, (b) emotional support, (c) information, and (d) appraisal or self-evaluation (House, 1981). Social support may be formal or informal in nature. Within African American families, informal social support, especially from family members, is considered to be beneficial in a variety of situations (Billingsley, 1968, 1992; Chatters, Taylor, & Jackson, 1985; Hays & Mindel, 1973; McAdoo, 1980; Taylor, 1996; Taylor, Chatters, & Mays, 1988; Stack, 1974). An elaboration of the critical dimensions within supportive relationships, however, often is not incorporated in social support studies. These dimensions include the sources of support, types of support provided, amount and quality of support received (Kahn & Antonucci, 1980; Krause & Borawski-Clark, 1995; Levitt, Guacci, & Webber, 1991; Nath, Borkowski, Whitman, & Schellenbach, 1991; Taylor et al., 1988; Wan, Jaccard, & Ramey, 1996). Moreover, few studies have explored the relationship between diverse living arrangements and the provision of assistance (Hogan, Hao, & Parish, 1990; Jayakody, Chatters, & Taylor, 1993; McAdoo, 1980; Wilson, 1989).

In this chapter, we examine the effects of having child-rearing advice and informal social support from both relatives and friends on perceptions of parental competence among African American mothers living in an array of family configurations. Hunter (Chapter 15, this volume) has specified demographic characteristics of women who live in households of various family compositions. We use this information to further illuminate the influence of having child-rearing support on the perceptions of being a competent parent among diverse groups of African American mothers. Most investigations of social support examine the influence of instrumental (e.g., providing financial help), emotional (e.g., improving psychological well-being), or informational assistance provided by network members on a number of health and mental health outcomes (Abell et al., 1996; Krause & Borawski-Clark, 1995; Nath et al., 1991). By examining the influence of child-rearing social support and general support from family and friends on perceptions of parental competence, we extend this work to focus on the association between social support and maternal self-evaluations.

The concept of maternal competence has most often been used as a predictor of maternal behaviors rather than as an outcome variable. Consequently, limited literature is available on this concept other than for social support and mother-infant relationships. This study is concerned with a broader representation of mothers; therefore, this literature is not sufficient. Because an abundance of research exists on social support and parenting attitudes and behaviors, we rely on this literature to provide a framework for suggesting how specific characteristics may influence perceptions of maternal competence.

Social Support and Parenting Attitudes and Behaviors

Cumulative evidence suggests that for mothers, the availability of and satisfaction with the support received protects against the deleterious impact of negative life circumstances (Affleck, Tennen, Allen, & Gershman, 1986; Dunst, Vance, & Cooper, 1986; Jayakody et al., 1993). Affleck et al. (1986) found that mothers with a greater number of family members reported less need for emotional support from others. They concluded that these larger families were providing needed support. Furthermore, never married mothers living in close proximity to their families received financial assistance from family members more frequently than married mothers (Jayakody et al., 1993; Simons, Beaman, Conger, & Chao, 1993).

The importance of maternal support also has been demonstrated in studies showing that young mothers' responsivity to their infants was positively related to having social support (Nitz, Ketterlinus, & Brandt, 1995; Voight, Hans, & Bernstein, 1996), and mothers of infants with severe mental and physical conditions at birth had greater positive adaptation if they were satisfied with the social support they had received (Dunst & Trivette, 1986). Formal support for depressed mothers also has been found to increase the probability of optimal parenting behaviors; it did not, however, affect the mother's global mood state (Fleming et al., 1992). Other studies report no relationship between social support and mothers' responsivity, or involvement with their children (Crockenberg, 1986; Schilmoeller, Baranowski, & Higgins, 1991), whereas some have found that perceptions of maternal self-efficacy mediated maternal behaviors more than social support (Teti & Gelfand, 1991).

Social support as a moderator of parent behaviors and psychological well-being has been a common theme in a number of studies concerned with child development. The benefits of both formal (Fleming et al., 1992; Telleen, Herzog, & Kilbane, 1989) and informal support (Crockenberg, 1986; Dunst et al., 1986) have been analyzed. Data from these investigations, however, have resulted in inconsistent findings. Some studies indicate that social support interacts with demographic factors, such as education and income, to positively influence maternal behaviors (Crnic, Greenberg, & Slough, 1986; Koeske & Koeske, 1990; Simons, Beaman et al., 1993; Telleen et al., 1989). Other studies have found no direct or indirect effect of demographic and social support variables on parenting behaviors (Crockenberg, 1986; Kelley et al., 1992; Simons, et al., 1993).

Belsky (1984) developed a model of the determinants of parenting behaviors, which proposes that social support should have both a direct and an indirect influence on parenting behaviors. He asserts that the indirect influence of supportive relationships should operate through maternal personality factors. Previous research supports this position. For example, researchers have found that the relationship between social support and maternal competence may be moderated by maternal self-esteem. That is, mothers higher in self-esteem receive more social support and view themselves as better parents than mothers lower in self-esteem (Koeske & Koeske, 1990). Thus, social support and self-esteem may interact to influence perceptions of maternal competence.

Social Support and African American Families

Cultural differences in the availability and use of social support networks are evident. Historically, African Americans have been more likely than whites to rely on extended kin networks to provide material and emotional support (Billingsley, 1992; Hill, 1972; Hogan et al., 1990; McAdoo, 1980). Within the social networks of African Americans, family members have been the primary source of support (Billingsley, 1992; Chatters et al., 1985; Stack, 1974). Grandmothers in African American families have been instrumental in providing for the needs of various family members, especially young, unmarried mothers and their children (Brooks-Gunn & Chase-Lansdale, 1991; Burton, 1990; Burton & Bengtson, 1985; Chase-Lansdale, Brooks-Gunn, & Zamsky, 1994). They often provide a place to live, impart child development knowledge as well as assist with caregiving and household responsibilities (Colletta & Lee, 1983; Collins, 1981; Stevens, 1984; Wilson & Tolson, 1990). For elderly African Americans, their adult children were the helpers of preference rather than professionals or other external family sources of assistance (Taylor, 1986). In addition, family members continue to be a primary support resource for African American women, regardless of their marital status (Brown & Gary, 1985).

These findings highlight the importance of familial social support across the life course within African American families. Thus, we would expect that having social support specifically for child-rearing issues and having support from family members would increase the likelihood of African American mothers perceiving themselves as being competent parents. Findings on the influence of child-rearing supports from friends on maternal behaviors are not as prominent in the literature.

Summary and Expectations

Variations in findings regarding social support and maternal attitudes and behaviors may be explained by several factors including differences in samples and methods, and, especially, the use of widely different measures of social support (Nath et al., 1991). Moreover, perceptions of maternal competence as a construct has been used primarily in studies that focus on mother-infant relationships. Although maternal competence has been used as a predictor of maternal behaviors, our understanding of what contributes to this perception of competence is limited. The present study uses a national sample of African American mothers to explore the role of social support in predicting whether or not mothers of children of varying ages perceive themselves as being good parents. By using a representative sample, we are better able to determine correlates of maternal competence within a diverse group of African American mothers. We are also able to control for the influences of socioeconomic status, which is sometimes confounded with race in small, unrepresentative samples.

The specific hypotheses addressed in this study are the following: (a) having social support specifically for child-rearing problems will be positively associated with perceptions of maternal mastery among African American mothers; (b) family child-rearing support will be more influential than friendship support; (c) maternal age, maternal education, family income, and maternal self-esteem will be positively associated with the availability of child-rearing social support, as well as perceptions of maternal competence; (d) the relationship between social support and maternal mastery will be moderated by maternal self-esteem, with mothers who have high levels of self-esteem and social support perceiving themselves as more competent parents than those with lower self-esteem and less social support.

Method

Sample

Included in the study were 562 African American mothers. This sample is a subset of respondents from the National Survey of Black Americans (Jackson, 1991). We were interested in the perceptions of parental competence among mothers who, at the time, were involved in child-rearing activities. We, therefore, limited the sample to mothers between the ages of 18 and 45 who coreside with children 18 years or younger.

Measures

A series of questions were asked about family relationships and parental needs in the National Survey of Black Americans. Several items were used in the present study to provide information on issues that may be related to parental competence. The concept of maternal competence, the dependent variable for this study, was measured by a question that asked the respondent how well she had done at being a good mother. Response choices were on a 4-point Likert-type scale that ranged from *not very well* to *very well.* For purposes of analysis, we collapsed this variable to contrast mothers who saw themselves as very good mothers with all other mothers who saw themselves as less competent. A six-item index of self-esteem, based on Rosenberg's (1965) scale, was also administered to ascertain a measure of the mother's global self-perceptions. The internal consistency of this index was alpha = .65.

Because there are so many global social support measures in studies with varying results, we decided to use a simple measure of support for one specific need that may contribute to the formation of perceptions of maternal mastery. Consequently, we simply asked: "Is there anyone who you would talk to for help with problems with your children?" A dichotomized response of either "yes" or "no" was obtained for each respondent. We also included single-item family and friend support measures to determine how often the respondent saw, wrote, or talked on the telephone with family who did not live with them and with friends. Responses to these measures ranged from *never* (1) to *nearly everyday* (7). A measure of family cohesion was included as a means of characterizing the overall family climate. This question specifically asked the following: "Would you say your family members are very close in their feelings to each other, fairly close, not too close, or not close at all?" The 4-point Likert-type response scale was reversed to reflect those viewing their families as very close receiving the highest score.

The variety of family arrangements in which these mothers were living is reflected in a multilevel variable developed by Hunter (see Chapter 15, this volume) to elaborate household composition. For purposes of this chapter, four household types were included that allowed for mothers and children coresiding alone or with others. These household living arrangements are as follows:

1. Mothers and children living in nuclear family arrangements.
2. Single mothers and children households.
3. Married mothers living in extended family households.
4. Single mothers living in extended family households.

Demographic information for the study was obtained through conventional measures of age, education, income, and marital status. Respondents were also asked the number of living children they had as a way of controlling for the effects of being an experienced versus inexperienced mother.

Results

Sample characteristics of mothers in this study are shown in Table 11.1. As indicated earlier, the age range was limited to 18- to 45-year-old mothers. Most of these mothers (34%) were between the ages of 25 to 31, with a mean age of 31.4 years. Approximately one third (31%) had less than a high school education, whereas 44% were high school graduates, and 25% had some college-level training or more. Although many of the women (75%) had family incomes below $10,000, 18% had family incomes between $10,000 and $19,999. The remaining 7% were from families with incomes of $20,000 or more.

The overwhelming majority of mothers (76%) had been married at some time in their lives. Only 41% were married at the time of the study, however, with the never married mothers as the next largest group (24%). The number of children of each mother ranged from 1 to 11; the median number of children was 2. In terms of living arrangements, 47% of the sample lived in single, female-headed households, whereas 37% were a part of nuclear family

Table 11.1 *Sample Characteristics*

Variable	Percentage	N
Mother's age		
18 to 24	18.1	102
25 to 31	34.3	193
32 to 38	27.5	154
39 to 45	20.1	113
Mother's education		
< High school	31.2	175
High school	43.8	246
Some college	18.0	101
College +	7.0	39
Family income		
< $5,000	31.2	175
$5,000-$9,999	43.9	246
$10,000-$19,999	18.0	101
$20,000 +	6.9	39
Marital status		
Married	40.8	229
Divorced	16.0	90
Separated	14.8	83
Widowed	4.3	24
Never married	24.1	135
Number of children		
One	26.1	145
Two	29.3	163
Three	20.1	112
Four	12.1	67
Five +	12.4	69
Living arrangements		
Married with children	37.3	193
Single female headed	47.2	244
Multigeneration married	5.6	29
Single extended family	9.9	51

households. Approximately 6% and 10%, respectively, were married and re-sided in multigeneration families, or were single living with extended family members.

Proximity of helper is an important concept in network analysis with the assumption being that the closer in geographic distance and living arrangements, the more often help is provided. Technological advances in the communications field have made the physical distance between network members less important in the provision of certain types of assistance (Litwak & Kulis, 1987). Consequently, we decided to test for the effects of the various living arrangements of the mother on whether or not child-rearing support was available. At the bivariate level of analyses, we found that having child-rearing support was not dependent on where the mother lived. A number of demographic characteristics of the mothers, however, were associated with their living arrangements. Table 11.2 presents the results of the bivariate analyses.

Mothers between the ages of 25 and 31 were more likely than any other group to live in single, female-headed households, $X^2(9) = 18.39, p < .05$. In addition, mothers with less than a high school education were least likely to live in nuclear family arrangements, $X^2(9) = 18.61, p < .05$, whereas those with family incomes of \$20,000 or more were most likely to live in nuclear families. As expected, there was a clear pattern to the living arrangements of low-income mothers. Those who were in single, female-headed families and those who were single living with extended family members were at the lowest family income levels. Self-esteem, number of children, and maternal competence were not significantly associated with mothers' living arrangements.

Based on literature suggesting that having social support for a number of problems results in more positive outcomes (e.g., Crnic et al., 1986; Fleming et al., 1992; Koeske & Koeske, 1990), we examined the characteristics of mothers who had someone to give them advice about child-rearing problems and those who did not have such support. Again, demographic characteristics were associated with who received advice for child rearing. Younger mothers between the ages of 18 and 24 were more likely than any other age group to rely on members of their social network for child-rearing advice, $X^2(3) = 17.41, p < .001$. Mothers with less than a high school education reported that they did not have child-rearing advice more frequently than mothers with more education, $X^2(3) = 10.18, p < .05$. Furthermore, the mothers in our study with three or more children were most likely to report that they did not rely on others for child-rearing advice, $X^2(2) = 10.46, p < .01$. Family income was not associated with the receipt of child-rearing social support.

We assumed that perceptions of self as a mother would be influenced by a number of considerations. At the bivariate level, however, we found that the amount of education that the mother had obtained and self-esteem were the only predictors associated with her perceptions of herself as a mother. The educational data revealed a curvilinear relationship between maternal competence and mother's education. That is, mothers who had started but not completed college were least likely to see themselves as very competent parents, $X^2(3) = 9.06, p < .05$. Women in all other educational categories were much more likely to perceive themselves as being very good mothers.

Table 11.2 *Bivariate Analysis of Mothers' Living Arrangements by Selected Demographic Variables*

			Frequency of Family Living Arrangements				
Demographic Variable	Married Family	Female Headed	Married Multigenerational	Female Extended	$X^2(9)$	Cramer's Phi/V	N
Mother's age							
18 to 24	33.7	41.3	8.7	16.3	18.39*	.11	92
25 to 31	33.1	55.4	5.1	6.3			175
32 to 38	42.5	46.6	3.4	7.5			146
39 to 45	40.4	39.4	6.7	13.5			104
Mother's education							
< High school	27.3	52.1	8.5	12.1	18.61*	.11	165
High school	40.7	43.0	5.9	10.4			221
Some college	43.2	48.4	1.1	7.4			95
College +	48.6	45.7	2.9	2.9			35
Family income							
<$5,000	18.0	64.0	4.5	13.5	115.97***	.29	111
$5,000-$9,999	20.3	63.9	3.0	12.8			133
$10,000-$19,999	50.8	41.8	1.6	5.7			122
$20,000 +	70.7	8.7	12.0	8.7			92

*$p < .05$; **$p < .01$; ***$p < .001$.

Not surprisingly, mothers who were higher in self-esteem also saw themselves as being very competent mothers, $X^2(2) = 17.09$, $p < .001$. Although only approaching significance ($p < .07$), trends in the data suggested that mothers with more children were more likely to have said that they were very good mothers, whereas those with only one child were least likely to have indicated that they were at the highest maternal competence level.

Multivariate Analyses

Our primary concern has been to identify factors that predict a sense of parental mastery among a sample of African American mothers while focusing on the contributions of specific types of social support. Consequently, we developed multivariate models of relationships between demographic factors, personal characteristics of the sample, availability of social support, and level of maternal competence using logistic regression analysis. We used the analytic strategy of first testing direct relationships between the predictors and perceptions of maternal mastery. We then tested for interactions between social support for child-rearing advice and selected predictors based on previous findings regarding maternal behaviors. The results of these analyses are displayed in Table 11.3. We found no direct relationship between child-rearing social support and maternal competence when controlling for the influences of the other predictors.

Because our bivariate analysis indicated a curvilinear relationship between education and maternal competence, we included a categorical variable for education in our logistic regression model so that we could determine the influence of various educational levels on the dependent variable when compared with mothers who started but did not complete college. The multivariate findings indicated that mothers with less than a high school education were more likely to view themselves as very competent parents when compared with mothers with some college level training. In addition, living arrangement was also a significant predictor of perceptions of maternal competence. Mothers who lived with other family members were more likely to perceive themselves as being very competent when compared with single mothers who lived alone with their children. As expected, women with higher levels of self-esteem were more likely to indicate that they were very competent mothers.

The availability of helping resources measures were all significantly related to perceptions of maternal competence, except for child-rearing social support. Family cohesion and frequency of contact with friends were both positively associated with perceptions of maternal competence. That is, women

Table 11.3 *Logistic Regression of the Demographic, Personal, and Social Support Variables on Maternal Competence*

	Model 1[a]		Model 2[b]	
Predictors	b	SE	b	SE
Demographics				
Age	.016	.020	.014	.020
Education				
< High school	1.163**	.385	1.223**	.387
High school	.501	.306	.580	.310
Some college	.738	.569	.753	.579
Family income	−.139	.107	−.139	.108
Living arrangements	.586*	.287	.583*	.290
Personal characteristic				
Self-esteem	.129**	.049	−.038	.086
Social support				
Child-rearing advice	−.293	.275	−5.604**	2.209
Family contact	−.224*	.113	−.207+	.113
Family cohesion	.334*	.161	.343*	.163
Friend contact	.191*	.085	.212**	.086
Self-Esteem Child-Rearing Advice	—	—	.258*	.106
Constant	−2.757	1.365	.459	1.976

NOTE: Living arrangements: 0 = living alone, 1 = living with others; child-rearing social support: 0 = no advice, 1 = have advice. Having some college education is the reference category for educational level.
a. $G^2 = 437.663$, $df = 11$, $p < .001$.
b. $G^2 = 433.705$, $df = 12$, $p < .000$.
+$p < .10$; *$p < .05$; **$p < .01$; ***$p < .001$.

from close-knit families, as well as those who had frequent contact with friends, were more likely than those who did not to perceive themselves as being very competent mothers. Contrary to our expectations, mothers who had frequent contact with nonresidential family members were less likely to see themselves as very competent parents.

We tested for an interaction effect between child-rearing social support and maternal age, education, and self-esteem because the literature review suggested that maternal behaviors could be moderated by factors such as demographics, social support, and self-esteem. The results of the interaction models revealed that only self-esteem and child-rearing social support produced a significant interaction. This model is presented in the second column of Table 11.3. Because it was difficult to interpret the meaning of the interaction, we ran a three-way contingency table analysis for guidance. These analyses showed a trend in the data that suggested that mothers who were low in self-esteem with no one to provide child-rearing advice were more likely to perceive themselves as very competent when compared to mothers low in self-esteem who did have child-rearing advice, $X^2(1) = 2.82$, $p < .09$. Thus, the relationship between child-rearing social support and maternal competence could be moderated by level of self-esteem.

Discussion

This chapter has identified several factors associated with the formation of perceptions of parental competence among a national sample of African American mothers. Our main interest, the influence of having social support for child-rearing, proved to have a complex relationship with perceptions of maternal competence. Although there was no direct relationship between having child-rearing advice and perceptions of maternal competence, we found an interaction between child-rearing social support and self-esteem. Our findings indicated that having child-rearing social support may not influence perceptions of maternal competence for women higher in self-esteem. Mothers low in self-esteem with people available to give child-rearing advice were least likely to see themselves as very good mothers. Perhaps receiving such advice, especially unsolicited advice, is perceived as criticism by mothers who lack self confidence. This finding provides partial support for Belsky's (1984) model, which indicated that social support for parenting may operate through the mother's personality—in this case, maternal self-esteem. The impact of this support, however, was negative.

Like Mercer and Ferketich (1995), we also found that self-esteem had a direct influence on maternal competence. Mothers higher in self-esteem viewed themselves as very competent more often than did mothers lower in self-esteem. Numerous other studies have found a positive relationship between self-esteem and a variety of maternal behaviors such as parental satisfaction, seeking family health care, and child rearing (Dunst et al., 1986; Koeske & Koeske, 1990). In an examination of variations in mothers' self-esteem in daily life, Wells (1988) found that self-esteem was a multifaceted phenomenon that changes over contexts, even though global self-esteem remained relatively stable over time. Collectively, these findings support the position that mothers who generally feel good about themselves are also confident about their parenting abilities.

Living arrangement is another important predictor of maternal competence. Single mothers who were head of households were less likely to perceive themselves as very competent when compared with mothers living with other family members. The presence of husbands, extended family members, or both in the household seems to heighten these mothers' sense of competence, which suggests that child-rearing social support may be influenced by proximity of helper. Previous research has indicated that social support is more available to African American single mothers than to married mothers who live in close proximity to family members (Jayakody et al., 1993; Wilson & Tolson, 1990); although husbands have been identified as a prominent part of support systems for married mothers living with their husbands (Belsky, 1984; Frank et al., 1986; Kitson & Morgan, 1990).

Mothers who live with others may be in a better position to engage in shared child-rearing responsibilities, which in turn, may bolster their perceptions of their parenting capabilities. Teti and Gelfand (1991) found that married mothers or mothers living with partners had higher maternal competence scores than those who did not. Other studies have found that living in multiple adult households, especially the presence of the mother's mother, can be stressful with regard to specific child-rearing activities (Richardson, Barbour, & Bubenzer, 1991; Wilson, 1986). Our findings seem to suggest that child-rearing stress may be more situation specific and it does not interfere with a mother's overall sense of parental accomplishment. The quality and effectiveness of support received, however, as well as need for support must be considered before family stress factors can be fully understood.

Because age and family income were not associated with maternal competence at the multivariate level of analyses, we could not simply assume that mothers who lived alone with their children were younger or poorer than mothers living with others. Thus, being younger or less secure financially did not seem to be plausible explanations for diminished perceptions of maternal competence. It could be that single mothers who live alone feel less competent because it is more difficult for them to admit that they are having problems with their children. In addition, asking for assistance requires tremendous effort that these mothers may not be willing to expend. Mothers living with family members, on the other hand, may have less difficulty asking for assistance because problems may be obvious to others in the household and advice may be more freely provided. Given our data, we are not able to test these propositions; however, living arrangement appears to be a contributing factor in the formation of perceptions of maternal competence.

Mothers from close-knit families and those who had regular contact with friends were also more likely to see themselves as very competent. Surprisingly, mothers who had regular contact with nonresidential family members were less likely to see themselves as very competent parents. Although somewhat contradictory, these findings stress the multidimensional nature of social support, with both family and friendship networks being important components. They also demonstrate that social support can be both positive and negative regarding maternal self-evaluations, especially within family relationships.

The dual valence of our social support finding is similar to those in Wilson's (1986) study of three-generation African American families and Richardson et al.'s (1991) study of adolescent mothers. Both studies found that relatives can be extremely helpful, yet they can sometimes interfere—especially in the child-rearing process. Frequent contact with relatives may lead to unsolicited and unwanted child-rearing advice, assistance, or criticism, which in turn may negatively influence perceptions of maternal competence. The quality and costs involved in the giving and receiving of support from family members may be more important in the formulation of maternal mastery than mere frequency of contact with family members.

Finally, our results indicated that mothers who had not completed college perceived themselves as less competent than mothers who had not completed high school. Because both groups had not received a degree, it was interesting that mothers who were high school drop-outs were more confident as parents. It could be that the inability to achieve the desired educational goal may have contributed to a general sense of failure for college drop-out mothers, whereas obtaining a high school degree may not have been the most salient goal for mothers who did not complete high school. Thus, their global sense of competence was not affected.

We were not able to test this idea in the present study; however, research on educational expectations and high school drop-out rates for adolescent mothers (Furstenberg, Brooks-Gunn, & Morgan, 1987) would suggest that educational goals vary and could affect maternal behaviors.

Conclusions and Implications

The results of this study underscore the importance of viewing the availability of maternal social support from a multidimensional perspective. For some mothers, appraising their child-rearing competencies depends on the appropriateness of responses received from specific members of their social networks. Although the social support literature indicates that extended kin networks are typically a source of assistance for African Americans in general, our results suggest that there are some African American mothers (those low in self-esteem) who may feel more competent without child-rearing social support.

Mothers living with other family members, on the other hand, seem to benefit most from having someone to provide child-rearing advice. Furthermore, frequent contact with friends seems to encourage parental competence.

Intervention programs designed to improve maternal capabilities should involve members of the mothers' existing social networks who provide child-rearing advice for those who would benefit from such support. Cumulative evidence suggests that program participants are favorable toward involving selected network members in their intervention experiences. Crockenberg (1986) found that 76% of the mothers in her study reported that they thought it would be helpful to have members of their informal support network participate in their professional sessions. Programs including members of the social network could enhance the continuity of desired parenting behaviors in the home through positive feedback without interference. The ability to sustain positive outcomes would also be improved with the involvement of appropriate network members. The greatest challenge, however, is to determine who appropriate network members are based on both maternal characteristics and perceived needs.

In this study, we found that level of educational attainment, self-esteem, living arrangements, and having child-rearing social support under certain conditions can influence a mother's perception of herself as a good parent. Future research should specify under what conditions child-rearing social support could be helpful or harmful for mothers in various living arrangements or with specific personal characteristics. More systematic examination is needed of the nature and cost of support provided by members of a mother's social network and how this support is received by the mother. A longitudinal design would be useful for determining the most effective forms of social support necessary to increase a mother's sense of parental competence at various developmental stages for both mothers and their children because social support is expected to vary across the life course (Kahn & Antonucci, 1980).

12

Strategies of Racial Socialization Among Black Parents
Mainstream, Minority, and Cultural Messages

MICHAEL C. THORNTON

This society makes the socialization of children the primary responsibility of families. For parents, the general goal of the socialization process is to make children familiar with statuses, social roles, and prescribed behavior. In addition, part of this process should be to prepare them to recognize their position within the larger social structure. For black parents this process occurs within a wider social environment that is frequently incompatible with realizing a positive group identity. In this milieu, black parents must act as a buffer between their offspring and society (Peters & Massey, 1983). They become a filter of societal information and a primary interpreter of the social structure for their children.

It is within the family context that the individual first becomes aware of and begins to grapple with the significance of racism and discrimination (Alejandro-Wright, 1985). The intrafamilial socialization of group and personal identity has ample bearing on personal functioning in a society that cultivates negative conceptions of racial minorities, whether through direct interaction, the media, or institutional barriers (Allen & Hatchett, 1986). Despite its importance to issues of identity development, however, there is little systematic evidence regarding how black families buffer and insulate their children and foster a functional group and personal identity. Similarly, coping strategies derived from this identity and nurtured in familial contexts have only recently received theoretical and empirical attention (Bowman & Howard, 1985; Jackson, McCullough, & Gurin, 1988; Peters, 1985; Spencer, 1985; Thornton, Chatters, Taylor, & Allen, 1990). Furthermore, researchers exploring the buffer provided by families focus on the parent-child (i.e., minor child) relationship (Jackson et al., 1988; Milner, 1983; Peters & Massey, 1983; Slaughter, 1981). With this focus, the influence of social location (e.g., socioeconomic status) and attitudes on parental perceptions of the social system are ignored (Bronfenbrenner, 1986). How these perceptions relate to the socialization process will presumably differ for parents of diverse class backgrounds. How structural and other variables intercede in the socialization process is the focus of this chapter.

Racial Socialization

The process of explicit racial socialization is a distinctive child-rearing activity that black parents engage in to prepare their children for life in America. Black families at all income levels believe that racial identity has an important impact on the amount of protection black parents can provide their children. Even those with good incomes believe they cannot protect family members completely from irrational restrictions, insults, and degradation due to racial machinations (Renne, 1970). Parents who explicitly inculcate race into socialization processes do so because they perceive they are raising not an American, but a black or African American, whose situation and experience is distinct from that of other American children (Peters, 1985). Anticipating that they will encounter a hostile environment that will attack blackness as a matter of course, these parents believe it is necessary to teach their children to be comfortable with what others will assail (Daniel, 1975; Harrison, 1985). Given this experience, not surprisingly the environment in which the racial socialization process occurs is complex and stressful. To have friends, parents recognize that their children must be accepted in black communities; survival is contingent on acceptance in white communities. Many parents also realize that this preparation also means their offspring will be burdened by needing to outperform whites to be recognized (Peters & Massey, 1983). Because of the constant exposure to overt or concealed racism, this phenomenon has been described as living under mundane extreme environmental stress (Peters & Massey, 1983; Pierce, 1975).

How parents encounter this environment of real or potential racial discrimination and prejudice has rarely been examined. For example, Peters and Massey (1983) explored the process of how being black affected the way parents viewed their children. For 2 years, 30 children were observed and their parents interviewed once a month. The sample consisted of 30 two-parent working and middle-class families. The authors describe several strategies parents chose in preparing their children for life. The parents saw experience with racism as unavoidable. Such encounters could be devastating and destructive if the child was unprepared to recognize or develop techniques and strategies for coping with these certainties. To help fortify them for this experience, parents equipped their children with survival tools. For them, survival meant being able to cope. Not surprisingly, the foundation to coping was to give their children love and a sense of security, and to help them obtain a good education. To better enable them to cope, children were also taught that white society would try to push them around, and that whites did not play fair or by the rules. To counteract these predictable trends, they needed to develop a tough skin and high levels of tolerance. Finally, it was important that their children develop self-pride and self-respect, and to develop both in such a way as to not use them obsessively or as crutches (Peters, 1985).

The literature is much less clear about the association between type of socialization message and sociodemographic factors. Certain factors have been identified consistently. Conveying racial messages to children is related to the gender, marital status, and education of the parents (Bowman & Howard, 1985; Thornton et al., 1990). Mothers more often than fathers socialize children to racial issues, a trend in part related to the greater responsibilities mothers generally have for this sort of task (Lamb & Lamb, 1976). Never married parents were less likely than their married counterparts, as were more educated than less educated parents, to instill the importance of race in their children (Thornton et al., 1990). Why marriage and education are associated with socialization is unclear.

Emerging works highlight a major limitation of existing ideas of socialization and its relationship to group identification and consciousness; in the simplistic either-or perspective, a person identifies or does not identity, feels pride in or rejects the group. With few exceptions, the empirical literature has not dealt with the valence of feelings toward the group. Rarely does one feel all good or all bad about one's own group. Furthermore, identity is usually aimed at subgroups within the racial group, such as other poor or elite blacks, and not at blacks as a racial group (Thornton et al., 1994). The process usually involves identification with some aspects of the group and attempting to dissociate oneself from others (Jackson et al., 1988). Relationships with the group, however, have rarely been appreciated for their complexities.

The complexity of the socialization process and its relationships to identity has been identified conceptually by Boykin and Toms (1985). They argue that blacks must simultaneously negotiate through three distinctive realms of experience to acquire a racial consciousness-identity (Cole, 1970; Jones, 1979). They call this process the triple quandary—containing what they call mainstream, minority, and cultural experiences. Participation in mainstream American culture characterizes blacks of all walks of life. This is reflected in the similarity in parenting values of working- and middle-class black mothers (Radin & Kamii, 1965), and in the agreement with avenues of legitimate success of all parents, regardless of racial heritage (Simmons, 1979). Black parents still strive for and teach their children those things that are American.

Parents with the mainstream perspective see their primary role as that of teaching life skills. Conveying the importance of personal qualities such as confidence, ambition, and respect is more meaningful to them than messages regarding race. Thus, these parents transcend racial issues, focusing instead on human values (Spencer, 1983) and socializing race-neutral children. This strategy appears to highlight what researchers describe as personal self-esteem, a reference to a comprehensive feeling about the self (Porter & Washington, 1993).

The minority experience involves ways of responding to racially and economically problematic life circumstances. Highlighting the minority experience is associated with preparing children for an oppressive environment (Richardson, 1981; Tatum, 1987). For parents with this view, being black means that their children must prepare for a nonsupportive world by building self-respect and pride, and learning how to survive and cope with prejudice. To build a foundation to enable one to cope with the dilemmas of being black, for these parents, points to the need to grasp the importance of a good education and to understand that fair play will not be reciprocated by whites (Peters, 1985).

Thus, adaptive reactions, coping styles, and adjustment techniques are part of the social negotiating reality for blacks. These ways depend on the orientation to and meanings black families ascribe to exigencies of oppression and racism. Boykin and Toms (1985) identify several strategies involved in this orientation. Families can take an active or passive role in confronting racism. Does one acquiesce or actively confront such circumstances? Does one orient oneself toward participating in mainstream institutions, tying one's fate to mainstream avenues or prescriptions for appropriate/successful attainment (what they call system engagement)? Or, in contrast, do these parents seek to function orthogonally to active engagement and operate separately from such avenues (termed system disengagement)? These strategies are related to blaming the system or person and seeking to maintain the status quo or changing it.

The final strategy of preparing ones' children to be black in America is what Boykin and Toms (1985) call black cultural expressions. They argue that the core character of these expressions is linked to a traditional West African cultural ethos. Evidence of behavioral practices consistent with West African traditions abounds and is witnessed within black family life (Nobles, 1978). According to the authors, this influence exists even if proponents cannot articulate their origins. They are manifest through a tacit cultural conditioning process, one that parents are generally unaware of. Nevertheless, not all such disclosures are so subtle. A more obvious artifact of this African link may be seen in parents recounting historical events in their family's life or speaking of famous black/African historical figures (Spencer, 1983; Tatum, 1987).

Boykin and Toms (1985) suggest that although a range of socialization experiences exist across all three types, some parts of all will be found in every family. They might be represented in one family by the extent to which mainstream goals and values are promoted or embraced. They may be seen in the extent to which black cultural socialization goals have been overtly articulated. The orientation pattern and display of responses used to cope with oppressed minority status may also be seen in the same family.

As far as I know, only one study using national data has examined the utility of this model. Thornton et al. (1990) found several components comparable to the Boykin and Toms (1985) paradigm. Most parents mentioned socialization goals that conformed to the theme of the mainstream experience. These responses highlighted achievement and hard work (e.g., "You must work hard to get a good education") or moral virtues. The second most popular socialization approach conformed to the theme of the minority experience. The parents choosing this strategy acknowledged the presence of racial restrictions (e.g., "blacks don't have the opportunities that whites have") or emphasized a general recognition of one's race (e.g., "accept your color"). Other responses provided information helpful to developing appropriate psychological coping styles and outlooks regarding minority status. The least popular approach involved parents who pointed to the importance of overtly socializing black cultural experience. The messages conveyed reflect an emphasis on black heritage, history, and traditions (e.g., "I taught what happened in the past about how people coped").

In this chapter I explore in greater detail the paradigm of socialization messages originally identified in Boykin and Toms (1985) and further explored in

Thornton et al. (1990). I examine the relationship between what parents choose as important socialization messages and a set of independent variables. Besides most of the sociodemographic variables examined in the previous works, I include a set of contact and attitudinal measures. Among the contact variables are measures of the racial composition of the neighborhood the respondent lived in at the time of the survey, and a question about whether they had white friends. Attitude measures include the level of support the respondent gave to a number of negative and positive stereotypes of other blacks, a measure of relative closeness to black Africans and white Americans, and the respondents' perceptions about how whites feel about blacks.

This chapter adds to the literature by highlighting the role of social factors in the socialization process, and by doing so with analysis on a nationally representative data set (the National Survey of Black Americans). It also delineates for the first time how these and other factors are associated with the three dimensions of racial socialization identified by Boykin and Toms (1985).

The Measures

Dependent Variables

The dependent variable of racial socialization messages assessed whether respondents racially socialized their children and, if so, delineated the content of these messages. The dummy variable consists of parents who said they did nothing to explicitly socialize their children to racial issues. To uncover whether they prepared their children in this way, parents were asked, "In raising your children, have you done or told them things to help them know what it is to be black?" If they responded "yes," they were asked, "What are the most important things you've done or told them?" Preliminary responses to this item (pretest data) were used to develop a detailed coding scheme. Subsequent elaborations and changes in the code structure were carefully monitored, documented, and incorporated during production coding phases. Individual categories within the code structure represent discrete information and are mutually exclusive of each another. Based on these criteria, there are three themes identified as the most important racial messages conveyed to black children:

1. *Mainstream experience.* These parents highlight achievement and hard work (e.g., "you must work hard to get a good education"), moral virtues ("be honest and fair"), and the importance of good citizenship ("be a good citizen"). They also emphasize the fundamental equality of blacks and whites (e.g., "recognize

all races as equal"), and the maintenance of a positive self-image (e.g., "you are as good as anyone else," "take pride in your self").

2. *Minority experience.* Parents here underscore and acknowledge the presence of racial restrictions ("blacks don't have opportunities that whites have"), or highlight a general recognition of one's race (e.g., "accept your color," "realize you're black"). They also provide coping styles and perspectives regarding minority status.

3. *Black cultural experience.* Racial pride (e.g., "be proud of being black") and discussions of black heritage and historical traditions ("taught what happened in the past and how people coped") are special issues for parents in this group.

Independent Variables

A full complement of sociodemographic factors (i.e., age, gender, marital status, education, income to needs ratio, region, and urbanicity) were used as independent variables for the analysis. Age is a chronological measure. For education, 0 to 11 years of education is the dummy variable, as is the South for the regional measure, and urban for urbanicity. Male is the excluded category for the gender variable. The income-to-needs ratio (i.e., poverty rate) is a poverty index calculated by dividing the total family income (earnings, interest, dividends, government payments, and so forth) by the total income needs of the household (adjusted for age and sex of each member). Values ranging from 0 to .99 mean that total reported household income is less than the total annual needs of the household, revealing that the household is below the official poverty line. Values of 1 and above manifest the degree to which total household income exceeds the official definition of basic needs. This calculation replicates a measure in the Panel Study of Income Dynamics (Morgan, 1991), which is based on the low cost of the food plan developed by Orshansky (1965). Mayer and Jencks (1989) report the income-to-needs ratio to be more predictive of hardship experience than the total family income.

Sets of attitudinal and contact measures were also included as independent variables in the analysis. The former assesses how much credence respondents gave to positive and negative stereotypes about blacks, how close respondents felt to Africans versus white Americans, and how much support black adults feel whites give to black efforts at progress. Dpositive, Mednegative, and Lownegative are indexes developed from responses to the question, "Many different words have been used to describe black people in general. Some of these words describe good points and some of these words describe bad points. How true do you think each of these words is in describing most black people?" Seven questions measured the extent to which respondents believed in first positive and then negative stereotypes applied to blacks. Support for positive stereotypes was measured by questions with the following format: "How true do you think it is that most black people keep trying?" Other questions asked how true they believed it was that most black people love their families, are hardworking, do for others, are proud of themselves, are honest, and are strong. Dpositive is an index of the positive variables, ranging from 1 to 4, from not believing the positive views to believing in them very strongly. Holding negative views was measured by questions such as the following: "How true do you think it is that most black people are ashamed of themselves." Other questions were asked about how true was it that most blacks are lazy, neglect their families, are lying or trifling, give up easily, are weak, and are selfish. Responses were coded 1 = *not true at all* to 4 = *very true*. Mednegative is an index of those who responded *somewhat true* to the negative stereotypes and Lownegative are those who responded *a little true*. The excluded category is Highnegative, responses of those who believed very strongly in these negative perceptions of blacks.

Another attitudinal measure involved a question about the parents' relative identification with America and Africa. They were asked: "Who do you feel closer to—black people in Africa or white people in America?" Responses were coded 1 = *blacks in Africa*, 2 = *whites in America*, 3 = *neither*, or 4 = *both*. Blacks in Africa is the excluded category. The final attitudinal measure assessed respondent perceptions of how supportive whites were toward black progress. The question asked: "On the whole, do you think that most white people want to see blacks get a better break, or do they want to keep blacks down or don't they care one way or the other?" Responses were coded 1 = *blacks get a better break*, 2 = *keep blacks down*, or 3 = *whites don't care*. The dummy variable here is "keeps blacks down."

The contact variables used for the analysis examined how interaction with whites influenced the choice of socialization message. Respondents were asked if they had white friends: "Do you know any white person who you think of as a good friend—that is, someone to whom you can say what you really think?" The excluded category was not having a white friend. Included in the analysis also was a variable representing the racial composition of the respondent's neighborhood. Respondents were asked, "When you think of the places where you have lived, gone to school, or worked—were mostly blacks or mostly whites there? How about your present neighborhood?" Responses were coded from 1 = *almost all white* to 5 = *all black*.

Table 12.1 Step-Wise Logit Regressions of Determinants of Racial Socialization Messages (SE)

Variable	Mainstream Model 1 b	SE	Mainstream Model 2 b	SE	Minority Model 1 b	SE	Minority Model 2 b	SE	Culture Model 1 b	SE	Culture Model 2 b	SE
Age	.027	.005***	.027	.005***	.007	.006	.008	.006	-.008	.006	-.009	.006
Female	.345	.128**	.390	.130**	.346	.172*	.353	.176*	.326	.154*	.324	.157*
Marital status												
Divorced-separated	-.141	.143	-.147	.145	-.071	.184	-.058	.187	-.042	.169	-.008	.171
Widow	-.373	.206+	-.400	.209+	-.198	.266	-.204	.269	.011	.250	-.045	.254
Never married	-.804	.226***	-.811	.228***	-1.89	.478***	-1.86	.480***	-.647	.255*	-.646	.258*
Rural	-.079	.162	-.095	.165	-.546	.224*	-.568	.227*	-.153	.194	-.150	.196
Region												
North Central	.220	.155	.252	.158	-.158	.202	-.160	.206	-.207	.190	-.212	.194
Northeast	.258	.170	.275	.174	-.174	.225	-.146	.230	.260	.194	.270	.199
West	.040	.266	.005	.272	-.918	.448*	-.941	.452	.066	.307	.083	.314
Poverty	.000	.000	.000	.000	.000	.000	.000	.000	-.000	.000	-.000	.000
Education												
High school graduate	.272	.150+	.303	.153*	-.436	.206	-.448	.210*	-.376	.180*	-.327	.183+
Some college	.487	.185**	.502	.189**	-.009	.237	-.031	.243	.061	.211	.064	.217
College graduate	.322	.235	.303	.242	-.186	.307	-.328	.315	.271	.258	.294	.267
Stereotype response												
DPositive	.218	.126+			-.082	.167			.411	.148***		
Mednegative	-.044	.146			.126	.192			.061	.173		
Lownegative	-.050	.150			.056	.202			-.009	.179		
Have white friends	.401	.126**			.174	.167			.152	.150		
Neighborhood composition	.029	.060			.021	.081			-.069	.069		
Closer to:												
Whites	-.325	.150*			-.142	.198			-.140	.175		
Neither	-.054	.209			.034	.271			-.638	.284*		
Both	-.299	.226			-.852	.373*			-.513	.295+		
Whites	.168	.138			-.528	.189**			.010	.167		
Don't care												
Want blacks to get a break	-.015	.159			-.381	.210+			.367	.183*		
Intercept	-1.99	.296***	-2.45	.417***	-1.83	.378***	-1.72	.545**	-1.03	.340**	-1.03	.479*
Chi-square	98.88***				71.88***				50.85***			

NOTE: Several of the predictors are represented by dummy variables: gender (0 = male), marital status (0 = married), region (0 = South), urbanicity (0 = urban), education (0 = 0-11), urbanicity (0 = high negative), mednegative (0 = high negative), close to whites/neither/both (0 = closer to Africans), and whites don't care/want blacks to get break (0 = want to keep blacks down).
+p < .10; *p < .05; **p < .01; ***p < .001.

Results

Table 12.1 presents the results of the logit analyses of the determinants of three dimensions of racial socialization messages among black parents. The first step in the analysis was to incorporate the sociodemographic variables into the model (Model 1). These were followed with the addition of attitudinal and contact variables (Model 2). In Model 1, age, sex, marital status, and education were associated with socializing children to mainstream perspectives. Adding the second set of variables strengthened the association between the sociodemographic factors and choosing the mainstream strategy. Older and female parents were more likely than were their younger and male counterparts to highlight mainstream messages. Alternatively, parents who have never married were less likely to racially socialize their children when compared to married parents. Finally, mainstream parents were more likely to be high school graduates and to have attended some college than not to have graduated from high school.

One attitudinal and one contact variable was related to mainstream views. Parents who used this strategy to racially socialize their children were more likely to have a white friend than were those who did nothing to prepare their children in this way. Being close to certain whites, however, did not signify a general bond with whites. These parents were more likely to feel close to Africans than they were to whites, which means, of course, that in contrast parents who thought race was not an important part of the socialization process felt more of an affinity with whites than with Africans.

Like the patterns found for those of the mainstream views, Model 1 indicates that mothers and married parents were most likely to highlight minority socialization patterns. Education, although related to both dimensions, differed in its effect on choosing minority strategies. In addition, for this group urbanicity and region were important influences. When the contact and attitudinal variables were added for Model 2, the first set of factors retain their significance. Parents who lived in urban areas (vs. rural) and those who did not graduate from high school (vs. those who did) were more likely to teach their children about racial restrictions. Those from the West (vs. the South) were less likely to do so. Reflecting the marginality at the core of this strategy, these parents were less likely to feel close to whites and to Africans. Interestingly, they also were more likely to believe that whites want them to get a better break.

As was true for the previous strategies, parents who highlighted the cultural view of socialization were more likely female and married (vs. male and never married). Education is a significant influence in Model 1, but loses significance when the attitudinal and contact variables were added to the equation. In Model 1, parents with less than a high school education were more likely than high school graduates to advocate including culture in socialization. Unique to this group of parents, holding positive stereotypes is an important determinant in choice of strategy. Those feeling very positive about blacks were most likely to socialize their children explicitly to black culture. Parents here also were least likely to choose the category of feeling close to neither Africans nor whites, but were most likely to believe that whites want them to get a better break.

Discussion

Parents have available to them any number of racial socialization strategies. The choices are part of a multidimensional process that mirrors important streams and perceptions of the black experience in the United States. Expanding on work by Boykin and Toms (1985), in this chapter I explored the determinants of choosing between the types of strategies identified by black parents. Although not examined directly here, one third of the parents report they do not convey racial messages in the socialization process (Bowman & Howard, 1985; Thornton et al., 1990). Many of them are ill equipped to instill a positive identity in their children. This failing may be due to their accepting the negative images of blacks perpetuated by society, or to their failing to realize the importance of race in the process. Other parents choose not to speak of racial issues because they do not want their children to feel bitter, resentful, or prejudiced against others (Lewis, 1955). Ogbu (1983) describes this group of parents as populations at risk and their children as manifesting problems of racial dissonance. Our analysis indicates that the parents in this category are typically young, fathers, never married, and poorly educated.

The three remaining socialization messages described here fit into what the wider literature reports as personal self-esteem and group self-esteem. The focus of the mainstream socialization experience highlights personal self-esteem. The minority and cultural experiences fit into the general literature of group identity.

Personal Self-Esteem

Most parents were likely to inculcate in their children the mainstream experience. Although they do not deny the role race plays in their children's lives, typically they see racial issues as secondary to broader issues of personal growth. These parents argue that the way to prepare their children to function as a black person in America is to bring them up as human beings, as Americans and all that the term implies. Parents who gravitate toward socializing this view appear on the surface to be the most assimilated into American society, for they are among the better educated and have white friends.

Although they have white friends, these parents feel closer to blacks in Africa than they do to whites in America. Thus, highlighting personal self-esteem rather than explicit racial identity is not associated with a special rapport with whites, as a lack of explicit concern with racial issues might imply. That relations with individual whites are not necessarily related to feelings about them as a group has also been found in one other study (Jackson et al., 1991). That they tend to distance themselves from whites generally and focus on qualities that are esteemed in "American" culture suggests that these parents identify with America and not whites per se.

Although apparently these parents do not feel close to whites, their feelings toward other blacks remains in question. That those in this category are more likely than those who do nothing to socialize their children to hold positive stereotypes about blacks (even if marginally significant) suggests that parents stressing this approach also feel close to black Americans. Because income is not important in this picture, something other than social class may be at play. Perhaps even among this group of the most successful black Americans (at least in terms of educational level), race plays a more important role in explaining racial attitudes than does class. The realization that race remains significant across class strata within black communities is a trend supported by emerging work (e.g., Allen, Thornton, & Watkins, 1992). If this is the case, we can better understand that even among these so-called assimilated parents racial group membership remains an important part of their worldview, even if not ostensibly in terms of socialization messages.

Certain sociodemographic factors influence these patterns. Older parents are more likely than younger to advocate mainstream views. In the present context, this age relationship may be related to a different political socialization among earlier than later generations of parents. Older parents grew up at a time when the ideas of good citizenship, self-image, and achievement were more strongly emphasized; these ideas are implicit in this socialization dimension. Older parents grew up at a time when the bond with other blacks was vital to personal and group survival. Yet, a collective focus also signified a mutual reliance to uphold behavior that would reflect positively on the community and enhance individual and group advancement (Smith & Thornton, 1993). That we found that these parents were also more likely to be the educational backbone of black communities (high school graduates and those with some college education) may also be related to stressing success and mainstream values.

That single parents are less likely than married parents, and that mothers rather than fathers are more likely to socialize their children are relationships found for all three sets of messages. That these are important determinants reflects functional realities of their respective lives (Thornton et al., 1990). Single parents provide less supervision than married parents (Dornbusch et al., 1985) and often reduce the time involved in child rearing because of the excessive demands of employment and housekeeping (McLanahan, 1985). Mothers have more responsibility for children and tend to specialize in intellectual and emotional aspects of socialization (Lamb & Lamb, 1976).

Group Self-Esteem

In contrast to parents of the mainstream perspective of socialization, those who highlight the minority or cultural experience would seem on the surface to be more ambiguous about their place in American society. Given their stress on barriers in the larger society, it is not unexpected that parents who stress the minority experience are detached from other groups. They have no special rapport with Africans, and they are least likely to feel close to Africans and whites. They do have, however, definite opinions about whites. Whites are seen as unsupportive of black efforts to gain equality, for they do not want them to get a better break in life. This perception, of course, provides the broader context of what their children must prepare for. This is an attitude absent among parents who advocate the other strategies.

The sociodemographic variables predictive of minority socializers give us some clue about why these parents choose this approach. They are among the most affected by racial restrictions. Besides the factors found for all groups (gender and marital status), poor education (0 to 11th grade), urban residence, and region were associated with stressing minority socialization. The poorly educated and urban residents are among the most dispossessed Americans. Why living in the West (vs. the South) is negatively related to adhering to minority socialization is unclear. In contrast to the South, the West is noted for racial diversity and more relaxed racial attitudes. These qualities may suggest a more racially tolerant environment. Thus, in contrast to those from the South, black parents living in the West might feel less need to socialize their children to the idea of racial restraints. Our earlier study (Thornton et al., 1990) is, as far as I know, the only other one to consider regional variations on socialization patterns. In it we found that parents in the Northeast are more likely to racially socialize their children. The difference in results between the two works may be related to adding additional variables to the present work not included in the earlier research.

Parents stressing black culture make special efforts to teach children about their heritage and historical traditions. Traditionally, discussions of black culture have assumed the link is to African roots, presumably in part because there is no real African American culture. Therefore I assumed that these parents would feel a special bond with Africa and Africans. On closer inspection, however, I found little affinity to Africans (or to whites). Apparently these parents highlight black American heritage in the socialization process.

In contrast to the parents choosing the minority strategy, those accenting the culture approach seem more optimistic about various aspects of their lives. That cultural socialization is a tactic that attracts parents who hold many positive stereotypes about other blacks is perhaps not surprising. One would expect that positive aspects of one's heritage would be highlighted. What is puzzling is that these parents are also more likely to trust that whites support black efforts to better themselves. Perhaps many of the parents who strive to teach their children about black culture also believe in black efforts of self-determination. Self-determination often means that blacks' efforts for progress come out of black communities, usually meaning without outside (i.e., white) assistance. This is a stand promoted by a number of so-called black nationalist groups and has received support from much of the white community, but particularly white conservatives.

Surprisingly, holding negative stereotypes about blacks is unrelated to the choice of socialization strategy. Perhaps those who fail to include race as part of the socialization process do so in part to distance themselves from blacks because they feel negative about blackness. Subsequent analysis examining parents who do not socialize their children for racial issues might help clarify this. That those who do not socialize may indeed have more doubt about their ties to other blacks suggests something about their self-esteem. This potential association should be explored in further analysis.

Conclusion

This study is among the first to examine sociodemographic, contact, and attitudinal effects on specific socialization strategies. Most black parents feel it is important to prepare their children for life as a black in America. But how parents do this, and what strategy they choose to do it with, is affected by several factors, but most consistently sex and marital status. Future research needs to focus on more multivariate and causal models underlying the present patterns of findings. We need a clearer understanding of the role gender plays in this process. What function do networks of community-based child care play in the socialization process (Collins, 1991)? Does the presence of extended families perhaps compensate for single parents not socializing their children?

There is also need to rethink the cultural dimension to the Boykin and Toms (1985) model. They suggest that this component relates to attitudes and feelings from Africa. They assert that many of these attitudes are subtle and are, of course, hardly measurable by the survey research methods used in this study. Nevertheless, the emphasis of the parents examined in the present study intimates that the more overt cultural ties lie with Afro-American and not African culture. Although they may indeed be influenced subtly by their African heritage, the present results suggest that a cultural component to black life has important domestic links as well. We need a clearer understanding of both the subtle and overt influences of the international and domestic connection in the socialization process.

Although this study is exploratory, the consistent relationship found between single parenthood and the likelihood that parents will not socialize their children to any of the socialization dimensions examined here has important implications for future work and social policy. Single-parent households are among the fastest growing segments of black communities, and among the most dispossessed. An important outcome of successful racial socialization strategies is children with a positive group self-esteem. Children produced in single-family structures are handicapped by poverty but also by a basic ignorance of who they are as people and how they fit into the structures of this society. Given these demographic developments, there is an urgent need to better understand how social factors relate to socialization patterns and how these in turn influence personal but also group self-esteem among black Americans.

13

Instrumental and Expressive Family Roles Among African American Fathers

PHILLIP J. BOWMAN
TYRONE A. FORMAN

During the final quarter of the 20th century, fathers' roles within American families have received increasing attention among researchers, professional practitioners, and policymakers (Biller, 1993; Berman & Pedersen, 1987; Bronstein & Cowan, 1988; Cosby, 1986; Furstenberg & Harris, 1992, 1993; Harris, 1995; Lamb & Sagi, 1983; Levant & Kelly, 1989; Lewis & O'Brien, 1987; Parke, 1981). In particular, the 1980s and 1990s have been filled with growing debate about the role of father absence in the erosion of family values, the growth in unwed teen parenting, the decline of marriage, and the feminization of family poverty. Such debate operates within a context in which few

AUTHORS' NOTE: The authors would like to thank Amanda E. Lewis for helpful comments on an earlier version of this chapter.

participants have a clear understanding of the nature, antecedents, and conse-quences of father role involvement within diverse race, ethnic, and cultural groups in the United States (Billingsley, 1992; Bowman, 1993; Crano & Aronoff, 1978). In this chapter, we focus on both the nature and context of fa-ther role involvement among a nationally representative sample of African American fathers.

In general, parental roles consist of the following five interrelated functions, responsibilities, or expectations: (a) an economic provider role to insure the material well-being of children; (b) a caregiver role to provide child nurtur-ance, socioemotional well-being, and socialization; (c) a homemaker role to maintain an orderly and healthy home environment; (d) a security role to pro-tect children and the home from external threats; and (e) an interface role to guide and advocate for children with others in the community and society. Tra-ditional studies on African American fathers have depicted them as essentially irresponsible in their performance of such roles. Much of the evidence sup-porting the claim of African American fathers' irresponsibility is drawn from trend data that shows their increasing physical absence from the household (Anderson, 1989; Evans & Whitfield, 1988; Gordon, Gordon, & Nembhard, 1994; Harris, 1995). Between 1970 and 1980, the overall number of father-absent households more than doubled. As we approach the 21st century, two out of three African American families with children are without a father pres-ent. Another source of evidence for the irresponsibility claim derives from the family provider role problems confronting many African American fa-thers—one example being the low levels of child support received by unmar-ried mothers of their children (McAdoo, 1984; Mincy, 1994a, 1994b).

The unprecedented wave of industrial-plant shutdowns and corporate relo-cations during the 1970s, 1980s, and 1990s has had an adverse impact on thou-sands of poor, working-class, and middle-class families (Bluestone, 1983; Newman, 1988; Rubin, 1994; Wilson, 1987, 1996). Increasing numbers of dis-placed and dislocated workers once employed in high-paying industrial jobs face either chronic joblessness or permanent underemployment in low-paying jobs. Demographic data suggest that, at least partially as a result of these labor market changes, fathers within all race and ethnic groups in the United States face growing risk for provider role difficulties and subsequent absence from their children's household (e.g., Blankenhorn, 1995; Farley & Allen, 1987a; Lerman, 1993; Wilkie, 1991; Wilson, 1987). African American fathers, how-ever, are at particularly alarming risks because of their overrepresentation in low-skilled manufacturing jobs, which continue to be eliminated by postin-dustrial automation and global macroeconomic restructuring (Bluestone, 1983; Bowman, 1988, 1989, 1991a, 1991b, 1993, 1995a, 1995b; Collins,

1986; Darity & Myers, 1995; Johnson & Oliver, 1991, 1992; Kletzer, 1991; McAdoo, 1984; Wilson, 1987). In short, the increasing difficulty faced by African American fathers in fulfilling primary or coprovider roles reflects their growing joblessness and economic obsolescence within expanding sectors of a postindustrial labor market.

To be sure, African American fathers have long confronted difficulty as primary family providers due in large part to historically shifting patterns of racial discrimination (Billingsley, 1992; Bowman, 1991a, 1991b, 1993; Frazier, 1939; Staples, 1982; Wilkinson & Taylor, 1977; Wilson, 1978). During earlier historical periods, their higher risks for provider role difficulties stemmed from chattel slavery or underemployment in low-wage sectors of dual agricultural and industrial labor markets. This historical problem of underemployment is being increasingly exacerbated by alarming rates of chronic joblessness. As we approach the 21st century, rapid industrial job displacement has combined with urban-suburban "resegregation" and the failure of urban public schools to prepare students for a "postindustrial information age" to further escalate chronic joblessness and provider role difficulties among African American fathers (Bowman, 1988, 1995a, 1995b; Cross, 1984; Wilson, 1996).

As the salient employment problems among African American fathers shift from low-skilled work to chronic joblessness, there have been corresponding increases in marital and family problems related to provider role difficulty—unwed teen pregnancies, mother-headed households, and the feminization of family poverty (Billingsley, 1992; Bowman, 1995b; Darity & Myers, 1995; McAdoo, 1988b; Staples & Johnson, 1993; Tucker & Mitchell-Kernan, 1995a; Wilson, 1987). Figure 13.1 provides a framework for considering how growing postindustrial economic obsolescence among African American fathers may influence their family provider role, have an adverse impact on marriage, and contribute to persistent family poverty and related psychosocial difficulties (Bowman, 1988). The basic idea here is that the destabilizing influence of postindustrial job displacement on African American communities is mediated primarily by family stability or strain among fathers, mothers, and children. Frequently, family economic provider role difficulties are initially experienced by jobless African American fathers, then by unmarried mothers, and finally by children in poverty (Billingsley, 1992; Bowman, 1988, 1993; Liebow, 1967; Marsiglio, 1995b; McLoyd, 1989; Sampson, 1987).

Decline of Marriage

During earlier periods in the 20th century, African American men were more likely to be employed and young African American women were more

Table 13.1 *The Relationship of Parental Status to Instrumental and Expressive Family Role Orientations*

Family Role Orientations	Parental Status		T Test
	Fathers	Mothers	
Instrumental			
1. Personal income	12.05	6.11	15.78**
2. Monetary stress	1.19	1.70	−6.13**
3. Perceived income inadequacy	2.00	2.23	−4.18**
4. Parental role strain	1.29	1.18	4.55**
5. Primary role strain	1.47	1.38	3.25**
6. Coprovider attitude	2.78	3.07	−7.24**
Expressive			
7. Father-child stress	.34	.78	−5.45**
8. Marital-family stress	.41	.65	−3.57**
9. Co-childcare attitude	3.24	3.39	−4.10**
10. Housework involvement	1.87	2.66	−23.58**
11. Religious socialization	3.72	3.79	−2.63**
12. Racial socialization	2.10	2.14	−.78

$+p$ .10; $*p$ .05; $**p$ .01.

likely to get married than whites. Similarly, Wilkie (1991) found that not only was there steady decline between 1960 and 1988 in the labor force participation rate and income of African American men, but there was also a substantial decline in their marriage rates. Male joblessness and related provider role difficulty may be the pivotal factor in the precipitous decline in marriage rates among African Americans, which has dropped from 95% to 70% in recent years (Hampton, 1979; Manning & Smock, 1995; Ross & Sawhill, 1975; Testa, Astone, Krogh, & Neckerman, 1993; Tucker & Taylor, 1987; Tucker & Mitchell-Kernan, 1995a; Wilson, 1987). The decline in marriage rates among African American men, which covaries with their growing jobless rates, is currently more pronounced than among either white or Latino men (Wilkie, 1991). Despite this decline, a recent *Newsweek* poll reported that 88% of single African American adults still want to get married. Hence, it appears that growing postindustrial joblessness among African American men may help to explain this discrepancy between persistent family values for marriage on the one hand and the conflicting decline in actual marriage rates on the other.

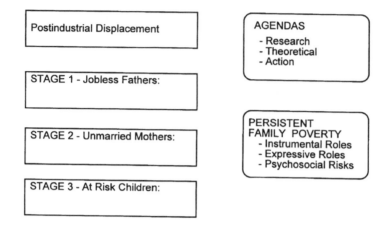

Figure 13.1. Postindustrial Displacement and Familial Consequences

As Jaynes and Williams (1989, p. 512) note "men with no earnings are not good prospects as husbands and fathers." Increased joblessness among African American fathers has rendered them less desirable as mates, less willing to take on the responsibility of marriage, and less able to provide economic support to unwed mothers as in earlier years. A major consequence of the dramatic decline in marriage rates among African Americans has been the increased numbers of children growing up in single parent households that are in poverty.

Growth of Persistent Family Poverty

As illustrated in Figure 13.1, postindustrial displacement of unskilled jobs has created provider role difficulties that create a ripple affect within the African American family—from jobless fathers, to unmarried mothers, to children in poverty (Bowman, 1988; Jaynes & Williams, 1989). After declining from 1939 to 1973, African American family poverty rates began to escalate, especially in northern and western urban areas, which were hardest hit by postindustrial job displacement. Between 1970 and 1985, poverty among African American families increased dramatically along with the number of unmarried mothers and jobless fathers. By 1985, 44% of African American children lived in poor households compared to only 16% of white children. A full 75% of these African American children in poverty lived in female-headed households in which their fathers were absent (compared to only 42% for whites). By March 1995, *Current Population Survey* data revealed two-parent households accounted for only 12.9% of all African American families with children in poverty whereas single-parent households represented a full 87.1% (U.S. Bureau of the Census, 1996f).[2]

One of the most critical findings in research on race and poverty has been that African American families not only have a higher rate of poverty, but also remain in poverty for longer periods than white families (Adams, Duncan, & Rodgers, 1988; Duncan & Rodgers, 1988; Gottschalk, Mclanahan, & Sandefur, 1994; Jaynes & Williams, 1989). Slaughter (1988) and others suggest that single-parent status may be strongly associated with persistent poverty among African American families because they more often need two incomes to adequately provide for children. In addition to being an unmarried mother, the lack of income support from noncustodial fathers who are increasingly jobless contributes to the persistent nature of African American poverty (e.g., McAdoo, 1984; Mincy & Sorenson, 1994). Unmarried African American mothers are less often eligible for child support, less often receive awards even when they are eligible, and receive smaller amounts when child support is provided. For example, during 1981 only 16% of African American single mothers received child support payments from noncustodial fathers (U.S Bureau of the Census, 1983). Over the past 10 years, however, there has been considerable improvement in this percentage; by 1991, the portion had increased to 43% of African American single mothers who received some type of child support payment from noncustodial fathers, 16% more than white single mothers (U.S. Bureau of the Census, 1995a). Hopefully, this figure will increase even more if the new welfare reform begins to promote the employability of the many noncustodial African American fathers—fathers who face disproportionate joblessness, which has not been adequately addressed under past family support policies (Mincy, 1994a, 1995b; Wilson, 1987, 1996).

Psychosocial Development Issues

In his recent study, Wilson (1996) not only linked African American male joblessness to persistent family poverty but also found that discouraging race and class barriers to meaningful jobs and responsible family roles have devastating psychosocial consequences within inner-city neighborhoods. Risks for psychosocial distress among African American fathers may increase systematically as their economic provider role difficulties erode the quality of family life among mothers and children (Bowman, 1989, 1992, 1993, 1996a; Hood,

1986). Familial stress among jobless African American males may also contribute to the alarming incidence and prevalence of the psychosocial problems they face especially within isolated inner-city ecologies. Hence, joblessness combined with related family provider role difficulties may be major contributing factors to their growing risks for violence, drug abuse, and stress-related illness at various stages of the adult life cycle (Bowman, 1989; Gary, 1981; Gary & Leashore, 1982; Heckler, 1985; Sampson, 1987; Staples, 1982; Wilson, 1987, 1996). Although not directly life threatening, chronic joblessness can be especially devastating to fathers when it threatens their valued goal strivings within the family or other major social roles. For example, several studies have found job loss to be especially devastating if it precipitates chronic provider role difficulties within the family context (Cohn, 1978; Pearlin, Lieberman, Menaghan, & Mullan, 1981). Moreover, provider role difficulties may mediate the relationship often found between family poverty or other socioeconomic inequalities and emotional distress (Eron & Peterson, 1982; Kessler, Price, & Wortman, 1985).

Despite the growing risk and widespread consequences, we still know very little about how instrumental and expressive family roles differ among fathers from distinct age groups. Research on African American fathers has either ignored life span development or focused on teenage fathers or a particular adult age group, rather than systematically addressing life cycle issues (e.g., Bowman, 1989; McAdoo & McAdoo, 1994). Therefore, the present study will explore instrumental and expressive family role experiences of African American fathers during different stages of the adult life course. Indeed, African American fathers may experience instrumental and expressive role difficulties quite differently if they are young, middle aged, or older. Guided by an adult development framework, studies on fathers from different age groups can explore critical life cycle issues that have been largely ignored in past research.

We can extrapolate some of the critical life cycle issues from the growing literature on adult development (e.g., Baltes, Reese, & Lipsitt, 1980; Bozett, 1985; Hughes & Noppe, 1985; Lemme, 1995). Erikson (1966, 1968, 1980) and other life span researchers suggest that fathers of all race-ethnic groups generally move through three sequential stages during the adult life cycle: early adulthood, middle adulthood, and old age. During each adult period, African American fathers' success in instrumental and expressive family roles may depend on resolving salient conflicts and mastering related developmental tasks in the face of discouraging barriers. Bowman (1989) formulated a life cycle model that specifies how discouraging race-class barriers may threaten cherished instrumental and expressive family goals in stage-specific ways as African American fathers proceed through adulthood. In psychosocial terms, such discouraging family role barriers may challenge a sense of identity, intimacy, generativity, or integrity as African American fathers mature from adolescence to early, middle, and later adulthood. A recent study by Bowman & Sanders (in press) clearly shows that both salient family provider role barriers and modes of coping operate in distinct ways among young, midlife, and older African American fathers. Such age differences raise some important questions about developmental as well as cohort and period changes in the instrumental and expressive family roles of African American fathers in postindustrial America.

National Findings

Guided by the foregoing literature, national data presented in the following section address several critical questions regarding the experiences of African American fathers within instrumental and expressive family roles. For both family domains, the focus is on a range of family role orientations including role perceptions, beliefs, attitudes, and behavior. Twelve specific dependent variables are investigated, which include measures of six instrumental and six expressive role orientations. The six instrumental role measures include personal income, monetary stress, perceived income inadequacy, paternal role strain, primary provider role strain, and coprovider role attitude. The six expressive role measures include father-child stress, marital-family stress, religious socialization, racial socialization, co-involved child care attitude, and housework involvement.

This chapter addresses six major questions: (a) Do African American fathers and mothers differ in their instrumental and expressive role orientations? (b) Are African American fathers' instrumental family role difficulties linked to their involvement in expressive family roles? (c) How does joblessness among African American fathers differentiate various instrumental or expressive role orientations? (d) Are African American husband-fathers consistently more engaged in both instrumental and expressive family roles than their unmarried counterparts? (e) Are African American fathers faced with extreme family poverty less engaged in various instrumental and expressive family roles? (f) Do instrumental and expressive family role experiences appear to shift as African American fathers mature from early, to middle, and to later adulthood?

To explore these questions, findings are presented in the next section from the National Survey of Black Americans (NSBA). Approximately one third (28%) of the respondents in the national sample of 2,107 were fathers. These

582 African American fathers represent a fairly heterogeneous national cross section. A majority of these fathers resided in the South (52.7%), another 16.9% lived in the Northeast, 23.6% in the north central section of the United States, and 6.9% in the West. In terms of education, 46.8% of the fathers had no high school diploma, 25.6% were high school graduates, 18.4% had some college classes, and only 9.1% had a college degree. Despite their modest education, these African American fathers were not concentrated in poverty. About one in five of the fathers lived in poverty households, with the remaining 80.6% living above the poverty line. This diverse group of fathers were also fairly equally distributed across the adult life span with 32.4% between the ages of 18 and 34, another 37% between 35 and 54, and 30.6% were 55 years of age or older.

Fathers' Versus Mothers' Family Role Orientations

Do African American fathers and mothers differ in their instrumental and expressive family role orientations? As shown in Table 13.1, African American fathers differ from mothers on almost every instrumental and expressive role orientation investigated. With respect to instrumental roles, fathers clearly had higher personal income, less monetary stress, and worried less about family income inadequacy than mothers. Personal income was measured as a continuous variable with the median of their self-reported income category. Monetary stress was measured by the following question, "Over the past month or so have you had money problems—how much did that upset you?" (scale ranging from 0 = *no problem* to 4 = *a great deal*). Perceived income inadequacy was measured by the question, "How much do you worry that your income will not meet your family's expenses and bills?" (scale from 1 = *not at all* to 4 = *a great deal*).

African American fathers, despite a higher personal income, perceived significantly greater difficulty than mothers as primary providers and providers for their children. As suggested earlier, a stronger investment among fathers in the family provider role may help to explain their greater level of strain as both primary providers and fathers despite higher income. Primary provider strain was measured by asking, "Given the chances you have had, how well have you done in taking care of your family's wants and needs?" (scale from 1 = *not well at all* to 4 = *very well*). Similarly, parental (paternal and maternal) role strain was measured by the item "How well have you done at being a good father or mother to your children?" (scale from 1 = *not well at all* to 4 = *very well*). More intense self-identification as primary providers may also explain why fathers' coprovider attitude was less egalitarian than among mothers who more often agreed that "both men and women should have jobs to support the family" (scale range from 1 = *strongly disagree* to 4 = *strongly agree*).

When we turn to expressive roles, African American mothers were consistently higher on all except one of these more child- and home-related family orientations. Mothers were significantly higher than fathers in parent-child stress, marital-family stress, co-involved child care attitude, housework involvement, and religious socialization. Parent-child stress was measured by asking, "Over the past month or so have you had problems with your children—how much did that upset you?" (scale ranging from 0 = *no problems* to 4 = *a great deal*). Similarly, the marital-family stress item asked, "Over the past month or so have you had family or marriage problems—how much did that upset you?" (scale ranging from 0 = *no problems* to 4 = *a great deal*). The co-involved child care attitude measure asked, "Both men and women should share equally in child care and housework" (scale range from 1 = *strongly disagree* to 4 = *strongly agree*). Housework involvement was measured by asking "Who does most of the cooking, cleaning, and laundry in your household?" (1 = *someone else*, 2 = *respondent and someone else,* and 3 = *respondent*). Religious socialization was measured by asking the following question, "How important is it for African American parents to send or take their children to religious services?" (scale from 1 = *not important at all* to 4 = *very important*).

The racial socialization question was the only expressive family role measure in which fathers reported equal levels of involvement as mothers: "In raising your children, have you done or told them things to help them know what it is to be Black?" and "Are there any (other) things you've done or told your children to help them know how to get along with white people?" (1 = *transmitted nothing about "being Black" or "getting along with whites,"* 2 = *transmitted something about "being Black" or "getting along with whites,"* and 3 = *transmitted something about both "being Black" and "getting along with whites"*).

Links Between Instrumental and Expressive Family Role Orientations

Do African American fathers' difficulties in the instrumental family provider role appear to impede their involvement in more expressive family roles? Findings in Table 13.2 show clear support for the notion that fathers' success or failure as instrumental family providers may differentiate their expressive role involvement. As expected, fathers' family provider role difficulties are related to their expressive role problems with both mothers and children. Fathers who experienced instrumental stress over money and primary provider difficulty were also confronted with greater stress in marital-family relationships.

Table 13.2 *Correlations of Instrumental and Expressive Family Role Orientation Variables*

Family Role Orientations	Instrumental						Expressive					
	1	2	3	4	5	6	7	8	9	10	11	12
Instrumental												
1. Personal income	1.000											
2. Monetary stress	-.091*	1.000										
3. Perceived income inadequacy	-.131**	.507**	1.000									
4. Parental role strain	-.043	.117**	.061	1.000								
5. Primary role strain	-.103*	.204**	.203**	.445**	1.000							
6. Co provider attitude	-.068	.111**	.074+	.006	-.031	1.000						
Expressive												
7. Father-child stress	.039	.039	.139**	.131**	.031	-.021	1.000					
8. Marital-family stress	-.001	.203**	.254**	.134**	.139**	.028	.220**	.1000				
9. Co childcare attitude	-.135**	.048	.012	-.033	.101*	.227**	.005	.003	1.000			
10. Housework involvement	-.038	-.001	-.025	.031	-.014	.024	-.034	.015	.065	1.000		
11. Religious socialization	-.070	-.096*	-.046	-.142**	-.248	-.098*	-.021	-.072+	.068	.004	1.000	
12. Racial socialization	.101*	-.064	-.006	-.162**	-.182	-.057	.004	-.099	.061	-.016	.096*	.1000

NOTE: *N*s range from 401 to 579.
+*p* ≤ .10; *p* ≤ .05; **p* ≤ .01.

226

Monetary stress was not only linked to increased marital-family stress, but also less engagement in religious socialization of children. The instrumental worry about inadequate family income and paternal role difficulty was also associated with elevated distress in father-child relationships. Paternal role strain, or perceptions of difficulty in providing for children, was also linked to less engagement in religious as well as racial socialization of children. Similarly, low personal income among fathers was linked to less involvement in racial socialization, but greater support for father co-involvement in child care. Coprovider-oriented fathers who support sharing the breadwinner role with mothers also supported the co-involved child care belief that "both men and women should share equally in child care and housework." Such liberal coprovider attitudes among African American fathers, which tended to increase with their monetary stress, were also slightly associated with a weaker commitment to religious socialization.

Table 13.2 also reveals greater internal consistency among the instrumental than the expressive family role variables when we examine intercorrelations within each of the two domains. Not surprisingly, personal income, monetary stress, perceived income inadequacy, paternal role strain, and primary provider strain were significantly correlated. In contrast, the expressive family role orientation variables were much less interrelated within this national sample of African American fathers with three exceptions. First, father-child stress was most strongly linked to marital-family stress. Second, fathers' level of marital-family distress was associated with less support for religious socialization. Finally, a significant correlation was found between fathers' support for religious socialization and race-related socialization of children.

Labor Market Status and Fathers' Family Role Orientations

How does joblessness among African American fathers differentiate their instrumental and expressive role orientations? As shown in Table 13.3, joblessness was measured in this study by a labor market status variable that contrasts both official and hidden unemployment from three sectors of employment—secondary sector, lower primary sector, and upper primary sector. Building on the earlier work of Bowman (1991a; 1991b), this dual labor market classification scheme distinguishes between the officially unemployed who are still actively seeking work and the hidden unemployed who are interested in working but not actively searching (because of discouragement and other reactions to labor market barriers). African American fathers faced with these two types of joblessness are then distinguished from those with employment in the low-skilled secondary sector, moderately skilled lower primary

Table 13.3 *The Relationship of Labor Market Status to Instrumental and Expressive Family Role Orientations.*

			Work Status			
Family Role Orientations	*Upper Primary Sector*	*Lower Primary Sector*	*Secondary Sector*	*Officially Unemployed*	*Hidden Unemployed*	*F Ratio*
Instrumental						
1. Personal income	11.92	15.20	18.74	10.57	6.62	21.05**
2. Monetary stress	1.15	1.13	1.06	2.23	1.53	6.07***
3. Perceived income inadequacy	2.01	1.85	1.96	2.53	2.21	3.70**
4. Parental role strain	1.31	1.26	1.35	1.43	1.26	1.07
5. Primary role strain	1.52	1.44	1.41	1.72	1.56	2.22+
6. Co provider attitude	2.79	2.82	2.65	2.91	2.83	.85
Expressive						
7. Father-child stress	.40	.39	.27	.56	.25	.63
8. Marital-family stress	.47	.38	.56	.45	.21	.94
9. Co childcare attitude	3.26	3.23	3.09	3.24	3.34	1.00
10. Housework involvement	1.81	1.82	1.83	1.91	2.33	5.86**
11. Religious socialization	3.79	3.65	3.64	3.58	3.71	1.81
12. Racial socialization	2.03	2.07	2.22	1.69	2.36	.489**

$+p \leq .10$; $*p \leq .05$; $**p \leq .01$.

228

sector, and high-skilled upper primary sector. Hence, each father's past or present occupational status was recoded to reflect one of the five labor market sectors: (a) upper primary, (b) lower primary, (c) secondary, (d) officially unemployed, and (e) hidden unemployed.

In general, joblessness appears to increase risks for instrumental role difficulties but not necessarily expressive role difficulties. As expected, jobless African American fathers among both the officially and hidden unemployed had the lowest personal income, highest monetary stress, and worried most about their inadequate family income. The links between the two types of joblessness and expressive family role orientations, however, appear more complex. The hidden unemployed fathers may be most involved in housework involvement because they are neither working nor involved in active job search (e.g. Bowman, 1991b). Moreover, Bowman (1991b) found that hidden unemployed fathers were older, which may explain why they had been more involved than the officially unemployed in their children's race-related socialization. More surprising, fathers with unskilled secondary jobs had higher incomes than either the jobless or those in more highly skilled primary jobs. These fathers with unskilled secondary jobs not only had the highest income, but also experienced the least monetary stress and worried least about family economic subsistence. Although joblessness was linked to provider role difficulties, it had no significant direct relationships to expressive role difficulties—with father-child stress, marital-family stress, attitudes toward egalitarian child care, or religious socialization.

Marital Status and Fathers' Family Role Orientations

Are unmarried African American fathers consistently less successful in their instrumental and expressive family roles than their married husband-fathers? Marital status was coded into three categories: married (e.g., legal and common law marriage), formerly married (e.g., divorced, widowed, and separated), and never married. As revealed in Table 13.4, presently married fathers clearly had the highest personal income and least difficulty in instrumental family roles. As expected, never married fathers were consistently the most economically marginal with significantly less personal income, highest monetary stress, greatest difficulty in their efforts to be good fathers, and greatest strain in their efforts to be primary family providers. In the face of such provider role difficulties, it is not surprising that never married fathers more often endorsed positive coprovider attitudes about sharing the family economic responsibilities with mothers. There was no significant difference between married and unmarried fathers in their perception that their income was insufficient to meet their family's expenses and bills.

Never married fathers, who faced more instrumental role difficulties, were also significantly less involved in expressive family roles on two of our five indicators. Never married fathers were significantly less involved than the formerly married in housework as well as race-related socialization. Presently married fathers, although less involved in housework, were most engaged in race-related socialization of their children. Surprisingly, fathers' marital status had no relationship to any of the other expressive role orientations—father-child stress, marital-family stress, co-involved child care attitude, or religious socialization.

Poverty Status and Fathers' Family Role Orientations

Are African American fathers who are faced with extreme family poverty less engaged in instrumental and expressive family roles? To address this question, findings on the relationship of family poverty status to instrumental and expressive family role orientations among African American fathers is presented in Table 13.5. Because family size obviously affects the level of family need, family poverty status was measured by the income-to-needs ratio, which provides a more meaningful assessment of economic status than does mere family income. Furthermore, past research has found that the income-to-needs ratio is more predictive of hardship experiences than total family income (e.g., Mayer & Jencks 1989; Morgan, 1991). The income-to-needs ratio is a poverty index that divides total family income (earnings, interest, dividends, government payments, and so forth) by the total family income needs of the household. This measure takes into consideration the size of the household as well as the age and gender of each member in the household. Values from 0 to .99 indicate that households are below the official poverty line or that the total household income is less than the total annual needs of the household. Values above 1.00 indicate the degree to which the total household income exceeds the official definition of basic needs (e.g., above poverty). This calculation replicates the Panel Study of Income Dynamics (Morgan, 1991) measure, which is based on the low-cost food plan developed by Orshansky (1965).

In Table 13.5, we classify African American fathers into three family poverty categories: extreme, moderate, and above poverty based on the income-to-needs ratio. This distinction was created by coding values ranging from 0 to .5 into *extreme poverty,* values ranging from .51 to .99 into *moderate poverty,* and values higher than 1.00 into *above poverty.* As expected, fathers within extreme poverty households had significantly less personal income to contribute,

Table 13.4 *The Relationship of Marital Status to Instrumental and Expressive Family Role Orientations*

Family Role Orientations	Marital Status			
	Married	*Formerly Married*	*Never Married*	*F Ratio*
Instrumental				
1. Personal income	13.47	10.09	7.65	14.76**
2. Monetary stress	1.11	1.18	1.78	4.80**
3. Perceived income inadequacy	2.03	1.91	2.04	.73
4. Parental role strain	1.25	1.31	1.55	7.74**
5. Primary role strain	1.45	1.45	1.74	5.14**
6. Co provider attitude	2.71	2.84	3.08	5.38**
Expressive				
7. Father-child stress	.35	.37	.26	.19
8. Marital-family stress	.37	.46	.50	.55
9. Co childcare attitude	3.22	3.22	3.39	1.16
10. Housework involvement	1.53	2.65	1.96	182.31**
11. Religious socialization	3.72	3.76	3.59	1.45
12. Racial socialization	2.19	2.14	1.42	21.23**

+$p \leq .10$; *$p \leq .05$; **$p \leq .01$.

231

and worried most that their income was inadequate to meet their families expenses and bills. Regardless of family poverty status, however, the African American fathers experienced similar levels of difficulty in the other instrumental family roles—monetary stress, paternal role strain, and primary provider strain. Moreover, fathers facing extreme, moderate, and above poverty status tend to be similar in their coprovider beliefs that both women and men should have jobs to support the family.

Among this sample of African American fathers, poverty status appeared to have even less direct links to expressive than instrumental family roles. As shown in Table 13.5, poverty status had a modest relationship to only one of the six indicators of expressive family role orientations. Surprisingly, fathers below rather than above the poverty line were the strongest in their beliefs that parents should take their children to church services. Poverty status had no significant relationship to the other five expressive role orientations—father-child stress, marital-family stress, co-involved child care attitudes, housework involvement, or race-related socialization.

Adult Life Cycle and Fathers' Family Role Orientations

Do the family role experiences of African American fathers differ across major stages in the adult life cycle—early, middle, and older adulthood? Adult life cycle stage was measured by coding each respondent into one of three conventional age categories to correspond to early (18 to 34 years old), middle (35 to 54 years old), and older (those 55 and older) adulthood. With some exceptions, findings in Table 13.6 suggest that both instrumental and expressive family role difficulties tend to systematically decline as African American fathers grow older—from younger, to middle aged, to older adults. Despite the lowest personal income, older African American fathers experienced less provider role difficulties than fathers in the middle or young adult years. Older fathers consistently reported the least monetary stress, worry about income inadequacy, paternal role difficulty, and primary provider strain. Even with the highest personal income, midlife fathers worried even more than younger fathers about their family's income, which supports Erikson's (1980) notion that the middle years may intensify such generative familial role concerns. Most striking, younger fathers experienced the greatest monetary stress, primary provider difficulties, and shared with midlife fathers the highest paternal strain with doubts about their personal efficacy as good fathers for their children. There were no significant differences across fathers in the three age groups in their positive coprovider beliefs that fathers and mothers both need jobs to support the family.

Table 13.5 *The Relationship of Poverty Status to Instrumental and Expressive Family Role Orientations*

Family Role Orientations	Poverty Status			F Ratio
	Extreme Poverty	Moderate Poverty	Above Poverty	
Instrumental				
1. Personal income	2.17	4.07	14.19	82.12**
2. Monetary stress	1.28	1.44	1.15	1.41**
3. Perceived income inadequacy	2.24	2.22	1.94	3.02*
4. Parental role strain	1.38	1.24	1.30	.80
5. Primary role strain	1.48	1.61	1.45	2.46+
6. Co provider attitude	3.00	2.80	2.76	1.24
Expressive				
7. Father-child stress	.25	.30	.35	.14
8. Marital-family stress	.21	.34	.43	.78
9. Co childcare attitude	3.38	3.24	3.23	.53
10. Housework involvement	1.97	1.84	1.87	.27
11. Religious socialization	3.76	3.88	3.69	3.61*
12. Racial socialization	2.21	2.05	2.11	.45

+$p \leq .10$; *$p \leq .05$; **$p \leq .01$.

233

Table 13.6 *The Relationship of Life Cycle Stage to Instrumental and Expressive Family Role Orientations*

	Life Cycle Stages			
Family Role Orientations	*Early Adulthood*	*Middle Adulthood*	*Late Adulthood*	*F Ratio*
Instrumental				
1. Personal income	12.56	14.37	8.54	21.25**
2. Monetary stress	1.62	1.14	.80	14.66**
3. Perceived income inadequacy	2.09	2.14	1.73	7.99**
4. Parental role strain	1.35	1.32	1.20	3.82*
5. Primary role strain	1.68	1.45	1.29	18.74**
6. Co provider attitude	2.82	2.78	2.73	.62
Expressive				
7. Father-child stress	.19	.61	.20	7.78**
8. Marital-family stress	.56	.50	.14	7.83**
9. Co childcare attitude	3.26	3.25	3.20	.33
10. Housework involvement	1.81	1.86	1.95	1.69
11. Religious socialization	3.56	3.74	3.86	11.32**
12. Racial socialization	1.77	2.19	2.35	25.97**

$+p \leq .10$; $*p \leq .05$; $**p \leq .01$.

With the exception of father-child stress, findings in Table 13.6 also revealed that expressive as well as instrumental family role difficulties appeared to decline as African American fathers matured from younger, to midlife, to older adults. These findings suggest that instrumental provider role experiences may spill over into expressive roles in age specific ways. First, among older fathers, relative freedom from provider role difficulties was consistent with their lower levels of marital-family and father-child stress. These older fathers also reported the greatest involvement in both religious and race-related socialization. Among midlife fathers, anxiety about family income appeared to spill over into higher father-child stress. In greatest contrast to older fathers, the younger fathers were least oriented toward either religious or race-related socialization. There were no significant differences across fathers in the three age groups on either their attitudes about fathers and mothers sharing child care or their actual housework involvement.

These age differences provide insight into potential adult developmental changes in the instrumental and expressive family role experiences of African American fathers. We believe, however, that such cross-sectional findings on age differences raise some important questions concerning life cycle, period, and cohort. By using only cross-sectional data, we run the risk of confounding age effects with influences due to cohort and period while trying to better understand life cycle changes. First, do the observed age differences refer to a developmental process, that is, are African American fathers' instrumental and expressive role difficulties declining systematically as they move through the three distinct stages of the adult life cycle? Or are the age differences we observed cohort or period related, that is, due to shared generation or postindustrial experiences?

To be sure, these complex questions about life cycle changes in family role difficulties are well beyond the scope of this chapter. Preliminary analysis of NSBA longitudinal data on selected family role orientations among African American fathers, however, can provide a foundation for addressing such issues more systematically. As shown in Figure 13.2, the panel data reveal a very clear pattern of increased difficulty on two of the six family role orientations over the four waves of data collection—1979-1980, 1987-1988, 1988-1989 and 1992. African American fathers' primary provider strain and paternal role doubts about being a good father to their children increased substantially between 1979-1980 and 1988 before leveling off during the last two periods of data collection. Whereas the cross-sectional data showed decreasing family role difficulty with increased age, the panel data revealed that early difficulty in these two instrumental family roles became much worse over the 12-year

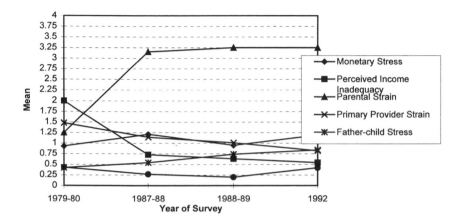

Figure 13.2. Changes in Select Instrumental and Expressive Family Role
Orientations, 1979-1992

span of data collection. Despite several periodic shifts, longitudinal data on the
other four items reveal a general pattern of stability or chronicity in instrumental and expressive family role difficulties among African American fathers
over the 12 years. Fathers' instrumental family role problems of monetary
stress and anxiety about family finances also rose between 1979-1980 and
1988 but not as sharply as the other two instrumental items. There was a slight
decline in these two instrumental items between the second and third data
collection periods (1987-1988 and 1988-1989). Expressive father-child
stress showed a slight upward trend in the direction of greater difficulty over
the four data collection periods. In contrast, expressive marital-family stress
declined slightly over the first three waves of data collection before a slight increase in 1992. As discussed in the final section, understanding such longitudinal findings requires a more careful consideration of complex age, cohort, and
period issues.

Summary and Implications

This chapter focused on the importance of African American fathers' involvement in family roles as economic providers as well as nurturers and socialization agents for their children as we approach the 21st century (e.g.,
Billingsley, 1992; Bowman, 1993; McAdoo & McAdoo, 1994). Our national

findings provide a basis to better understand the nature, context, and implications of both instrumental and expressive family role experiences among African American fathers (Bowman, 1988, 1989, 1993; Gary, 1981; Pearlin, 1983). These findings can also help to bridge theory, research, and policy to better address the growing crisis facing African American fathers and families within postindustrial America. In general, the findings support the importance of six major issues confronting African American fathers within the contemporary family context: (a) the gender complexities in instrumental and expressive family role orientations; (b) the critical interconnections between family provider role difficulties and more expressive role involvement; (c) the erosive impact of escalating male joblessness on instrumental and expressive family role difficulties; (d) how the continuing decline in marriage rates may influence such family role problems; (e) how extreme family poverty may further exacerbate such family role difficulties; and (f) how such family role experiences might differ among young, midlife, and older fathers.

Future research on African American fathers should further clarify the apparent coherence among instrumental aspects of their family roles and the rather complex multidimensional nature of the father-child, egalitarian child care, housework, and socialization aspects of their more expressive family roles. The following discussion of major findings points to the importance of increasing family role flexibility among African American fathers, uncoupling their instrumental and expressive roles and several related postindustrial ecological challenges as emerging agenda items.

Increasing the Flexibility of Family Roles

Findings showing that fathers had clear personal income advantages over mothers, but still perceived greater difficulty as primary providers and as providers for their children are consistent with the substantial literature on the especially strong value that fathers stake in the traditional breadwinner role (Allen & Doherty, 1996; Bowman, 1993, 1996a; Cazenave, 1981; Cohen, 1987, 1988; Liebow, 1967; Marsiglio, 1995b; Marsiglio & Scanzoni, 1990; Pearlin, 1983; Staples & Johnson, 1993; Thompson & Walker, 1989). Hence, these and other findings suggest that the traditional psychosocial investment of fathers in instrumental provider roles and mothers in expressive child care roles remain a defining feature of contemporary African American family life (e.g., Biller, 1993; Gould, 1976; McAdoo, 1993; Merton, 1968). Therefore, the salience of the primary breadwinner role among African American fathers remains a central issue, despite the fact that economic necessity has long required them to share the breadwinner role with mothers (Billingsley, 1992; Bowman, 1993;

Bowser, 1991; Forman, 1995; Gary, 1981; Hill, 1971; Jaynes & Williams, 1989; McAdoo, 1988b; Mincy & Sorenson, 1994; Staples & Johnson, 1993).

An increase in family role flexibility among African Americans is a major agenda item for the future given the growing barriers that African American fathers face in postindustrial America as primary providers, coproviders, or even secondary providers for their children (Allen & Farley, 1985; Bowman, 1989; Forman, 1994, 1995; Green, 1982; Taylor, Leashore, & Toliver, 1988). The argument that additional flexibility is needed in African American family role orientations is also supported by findings in this study that fathers were still less enthusiastic than mothers about coprovider role arrangements (e.g., Billingsley, 1968, 1992; Hill, 1971). To promote greater flexibility in traditional provider roles within African American families, corresponding changes are needed in the disposition of many fathers to more expressive co-involved child care attitudes and housework involvement, both of which were lower among fathers than mothers in this national sample.

The traditional gender bifurcation in the allocation of instrumental-expressive family roles becomes even more obsolete and maladaptive with unprecedented increases in coprovider role arrangements among African American fathers and mothers (Bowman, 1991a; Dechter & Smock, 1994; Farley & Allen, 1987a; Ross & Sawhill, 1995; Wilkie, 1991). The need to increase flexibility in traditional expressive roles within African American families is also supported by our findings that mothers were consistently higher than fathers in marital-family stress, parent-child stress, and religious socialization. Hence, a strong tradition of flexible family roles among African Americans has apparently not yet produced egalitarian orientations among African American fathers toward either the provider role or expressive roles such as child care or housework. Existing changes in both instrumental and expressive roles within African American families appear especially adaptive for the postindustrial era as increasing numbers of fathers face joblessness while mothers increasingly work for pay (Bowman, 1988, 1991a, 1991b; Jaynes & Williams, 1989).

In both the short and long run, increased egalitarian family roles may also help to reduce rather intense psychosocial conflicts facing African American fathers and mothers within families (Billingsley, 1992; Bowman, 1992, 1996a; Cazenave, 1981; 1984; Liebow, 1967). For example, intrafamilial conflicts may intensify as African American fathers' growing difficulties in the traditional breadwinner role threaten their masculine identity, and working mothers face growing role overload as economic providers who also assume traditional expressive role responsibilities within the family, what Hochschild (1989) labeled the "second shift." Family role flexibility, despite its virtues for promoting child and family well-being, may prove very challenging for

African American fathers, mothers, and other advocates. Not only would changes be necessary in the traditional socialization of African American males (see Allen, 1981, 1985), but socially structured changes would also be necessary in their role set of significant others—for example, mothers, children, grandmothers, extended family, community and society—who often reinforce and sanction traditional breadwinner role expectations.

Uncoupling Instrumental and Expressive Roles

Normative uncoupling of instrumental and expressive family roles among African American fathers could significantly help to increase the flexibility of family roles. Findings that fathers' economic provider role difficulties are often coupled with stressful expressive transactions with children and mothers are consistent with past studies (Allen, 1981; Bowman, 1993; Cazenave, 1979; Liebow, 1967; Mack, 1978; McAdoo, 1988a; McAdoo & McAdoo, 1994; Staples & Johnson, 1993; Willie & Greenblatt, 1978). For example, objective joblessness among African American fathers may combine with subjective reactions to related provider role difficulties such as family income anxiety, self-blame, and low paternal self-efficacy to elevate their risks for father-child stress or other expressive role problems (Bowman, 1992; 1996a). Moreover, African American fathers' low paternal self-efficacy beliefs about not being able to be good fathers were linked to lower commitments to both religious and racial socialization of children. These findings support the notion that African American fathers' opportunities for and inclinations toward expressive father-children relationships may too often depend on success as economic providers.

Studies that have emphasized the pivotal role of father-mother relationships as mediators of father-child transactions are also consistent with our findings (e.g., Liebow, 1967; McAdoo & McAdoo, 1994; McLoyd, 1989). Fathers who experienced recent stress over money were not only confronted with greater marital-family stress, but were also less engaged in religious socialization of children. The significant bivariate relationship between marital-family stress and father-child stress provides further support for the mediating role of mothers in father-child relationships. Such findings suggest that father-mother relationships represent a pivotal focal point in uncoupling instrumental and expressive family roles and in promoting more nurturing father-child relationships among economically marginal African American fathers. It is instructive to note that low-income African American fathers were more supportive of sharing provider role responsibilities such as child care and housework. Despite expressive father-child difficulties, these low-income fathers' greater inclination toward egalitarian family roles suggests a particular receptivity toward flexibility within their families.

Postindustrial Ecological Challenges

Theoretical, research, and action agendas to address the growing crisis facing African American fathers must also focus directly on their growing joblessness and its erosive impact on both instrumental and expressive family roles in a rapidly changing postindustrial context. Within this postindustrial context, dislocated African American fathers face interlinking social ecological constraints characterized by an alarming growth in chronic joblessness and corresponding increases in the number who never marry, who live in concentrated inner-city poverty, and who confront age-specific psychosocial barriers.

Our findings suggest that joblessness among African American fathers elevates risks for difficulties within instrumental roles much more directly than within expressive roles. In line with past studies, both officially and hidden unemployed fathers faced greater risks than those employed in three aspects of family instrumental role functioning—low income, monetary stress, and anxiety about family subsistence (e.g., Bowman, 1991b; Hill, 1971). This is the first study, however, to explore the relationship, which appears to be particularly complex, between the two types of joblessness and expressive family role orientations. The fact that the hidden unemployed tend to be older, quasi-retired, and spend less time in job search than the officially unemployed helps to explain why such fathers were most heavily involved in housework (e.g., Bowman, 1991b; Gibson, 1991). The tendency for hidden unemployed fathers to be older may also explain why they were more likely than those officially unemployed to report past involvement in race-related socialization with their children.

Future research must further explore why joblessness did not have significant direct relationships with other expressive role experiences such as father-child stress, marital-family stress, attitudes toward egalitarian child care, or religious socialization. Perhaps the impact of joblessness on expressive role outcomes may be indirectly mediated through instrumental provider role difficulties and buffered by protective resources within African American communities. Links found in this study between provider role difficulties and both joblessness and expressive role problems are consistent with a mediating or intervening model. That is, joblessness may cause instrumental provider role difficulties, which, in turn, result in expressive role problems. Findings showing joblessness to be more strongly linked to instrumental rather than expressive role stress may also reflect the efficacy of indigenous cultural resources such as cohesive extended families, spiritual beliefs, and ethnic coping orientations. As suggested by Bowman (1993), such protective cultural resources may buffer "joblessness-expressive role stress" relationships but not more objective "joblessness-provider role stress" relationships.

The findings on joblessness and labor market status also have important theoretical and policy implications related to sectoral stratification among African American fathers. Hill (1993, p. 41) points out that, "more attention should be given to examining the impact of sectoral stratification on the functioning of African American families." Moreover, McAdoo (1988b) and others have noted the importance of studies on the role of such socioeconomic factors in the functioning of African American fathers in family roles. One of the most widely discussed socioeconomic measures of sectoral stratification has been dual labor market status (Bowman, 1991a, 1991b; Hill, 1993). Dual labor market models provide a basis for future researchers and policymakers to look beyond individual socioeconomic status—income and education—to consider more fully labor market, structural, and ecological aspects of inequalities facing African American fathers and mothers in the postindustrial era.

Dual labor market paradigms consider the ways in which historical and sectoral cleavages create distinct subgroups of workers whose work conditions, socioeconomic circumstances, and opportunity structures are quite divergent (Bowman, 1991a; Edwards, 1979; Piore, 1975; Ryan, 1981). Each subgroup of workers not only differ in education and skills, but also sociopolitical interests related to differential tracking into primary sector jobs "with a future" and more unstable secondary jobs that are relatively "dead end" (Edwards, 1943; Montaga, 1977). Dual labor market paradigms emerged as a critique of mainstream stratification theories, most notably human capital theory from economics and status attainment theory, which is its variant in sociology (Bowman, 1991a; Hodson, 1983; Kallenberg, 1983; Kallenberg & Sorenson, 1979). Dual labor market paradigms are based on a critique of these mainstream models that focus too narrowly on the individual and fail to fully acknowledge how opportunities among individuals from subordinate groups facing structural inequalities are often constrained by systematic institutional barriers (Kallenberg, 1983; Kallenberg & Sorenson, 1979).

The current study of African American fathers extended theoretical criteria emerging from traditional dual labor market research, which placed working respondents into either secondary or primary sector job categories (Averitt, 1968; Edwards, 1943, 1979; Montaga, 1977; Piore, 1975). Building on Bowman (1991b) and others, the primary sector was further broken down to better clarify trends among upwardly mobile African American workers who have gained greater access into the lower rather than upper primary tier of the postindustrial labor market. A rather surprising finding was that fathers with jobs in the secondary sector of the labor market had higher personal incomes than those in the upper or lower primary sector, which demanded more education and skills. Although seemingly a contradictory finding, Hill (1993) notes that equating white collar jobs with middle-class status is quite problematic because many African American white-collar workers do not have middle-income earnings. Furthermore, he found that a large proportion of African American operatives (e.g., secondary sector) have higher earnings than the upwardly mobile in white-collar jobs (e.g., especially the lower primary sector). According to Hill, movement of African Americans from the secondary to primary sector jobs is too often associated with downward rather than upward mobility in terms of income. This may also help to explain why fathers with unskilled secondary jobs not only had the highest income, but also experienced less monetary stress and worried less about family economic subsistence than those in higher level primary sector jobs.

The provider role advantages among African American fathers in the unskilled manufacturing sector also highlight the profound implications of the rapid postindustrial displacement of such high-paying secondary jobs, which will continue well into the 21st century (Bowman, 1988, 1989, 1993, 1995a, 1995b; Darity & Myers, 1995; McAdoo, 1984; Wilson, 1987). As deindustrialization continues, African American fathers still remain overrepresented in such vulnerable but high-paying secondary jobs—those being eliminated by strategic postindustrial transformations including automation, corporate relocation, and global macroeconomic restructuring (Bowman, 1988, 1991a, 1991b; Collins, 1986). As Wilson (1996) and others have noted, African American fathers who have relied on these unskilled industrial jobs for decades remain at great risk for economic obsolescence as they become structurally dislocated from expanding unskilled service as well as more skilled sectors of the postindustrial labor market. This makes public policy agendas that address the unique pattern of structural joblessness and related discouragement among African American fathers a critical feature of the growing urban underclass debate (Auletta, 1982; Bowman, 1984, 1988, 1995a, 1995b; Cross, 1984; Glasgow, 1980; Wilson, 1978, 1987, 1996).

Findings on marital status also support a growing literature that links economic provider role difficulties with the decline in marriage among African American fathers (Allen & Farley, 1986; Billingsley, 1992; Bowman, 1993, 1995b; Darity & Myers, 1995; Farley & Allen, 1987a; Jaynes & Williams, 1989; Staples & Johnson, 1993; Tucker & Mitchell-Kernan, 1995a; Wilson, 1987). Indeed, whereas presently married fathers had the least difficulty within family roles, never married fathers were the most economically marginal and experienced greater difficulty in several expressive family roles. Future research, however, should also explore why presently married fathers were at equal risk as the never married for several other expressive role difficulties. Perhaps, among the presently married, the intimate day-to-day interaction with mothers and children placed them at as much risk for pressing father-child stress and marital-family stress as the never married who are less intimately involved. Moreover, presently married fathers are more often employed, which may reinforce conservative family role orientations and restrict their egalitarian co-involved child care attitudes (e.g., Bowman, 1993). Commitment to the religious socialization of children may be a core cultural value that is retained among African American fathers regardless of marital status.

Among the never married fathers, a hopeful finding was their strong coprovider attitudes about sharing family economic responsibilities with mothers. Unfortunately, however, such support for more flexible family roles may not be sufficient to offset the marriageability issues facing growing numbers of unmarried African American fathers who find themselves without jobs during the final quarter of the 20th century (e.g., Bowman, 1988, 1995a; Tucker & Mitchell-Kernan, 1995a; Wilson, 1987). Responsive policy agendas to address such marriageability issues may be the most effective strategy to address the alarming crisis of unwed teen mothers, female-headed households, and chronic poverty among African American families. Indeed, more father-focused policy agendas may be the only viable long-run strategy to render larger numbers of African American fathers more desirable as mates, more willing to take on the responsibility of marriage, and more able to provide economic support to mothers whether they are married, never married, separated, or divorced.

Our national findings that fathers within extreme poverty households had significantly less personal income to contribute is consistent with several studies (e.g., McAdoo, 1984; Mincy & Sorenson, 1994). These studies suggest that family poverty among African Americans is not only associated with female-headed households, but also the lack of income and child support from noncustodial fathers who are increasingly jobless. The fact that fathers in extreme poverty worried most about their family income not meeting their expenses and bills suggests provider role difficulties carry heavy psychosocial burdens in the context of chronic poverty (e.g., Bowman, 1988, 1992; Liebow, 1967). Similar to results on joblessness, however, the surprising findings that extreme poverty had little direct impact on other indicators of instrumental and expressive role stress suggest that greater attention needs to be placed on the operation of protective factors in future research on family roles among African American fathers.

Protective cultural resources among African American fathers such as the flexibility of family roles, cohesive multigenerational kinship bonds, para-kin friendships, racial consciousness, and strong spiritual beliefs may help to buffer the potentially devastating impact of extreme poverty on their family role functioning (Billingsley, 1992; Bowman, 1989, 1992, 1993, 1996a; Gary, 1981; Hill, 1971; Liebow, 1967). This may help to explain why African American fathers facing extreme poverty were no more likely than those above poverty to suffer from monetary stress, paternal role strain, and primary provider strain. Similarly, fathers in extreme poverty were no more likely than their more affluent counterparts to experience expressive role problems such as father-child stress, or marital-family stress. Moreover, regardless of poverty status, African American fathers were similar in their inclinations toward sharing the economic provider role, child care responsibilities, and housework. African American fathers facing family poverty were also equally involved in race-related socialization with their children and even stronger than those above the poverty line in their religious socialization beliefs that parents should take their children to church services.

With the decline in formal resources due to contemporary welfare reform, a consideration of protective cultural resources available to at-risk African American fathers may provide more options as we seek ways to offset the potentially devastating impact of concentrated urban poverty. Within the contemporary urban context, a social ecological approach that is more culturally responsive may help to better clarify both risk and protective factors that differentiate instrumental and expressive family role functioning among African American fathers (Allen, 1985; Billingsley, 1992; Bowman, 1988, 1993; Cazenave, 1984; Forman & Bowman, 1996; Honig & Mayne, 1982; Kelley & Colburn, 1995; Ray & McLoyd, 1986; Taylor et al., 1988). Related father-focused agendas need to consider ways to better mobilize African American cultural resources in the struggle against chronic family poverty, which continues to be linked to growing male joblessness, associated with a decline in marriage, and concentrated within inner-city neighborhoods, which are segregated by both race and class (e.g., Bowman, 1988; Duncan & Rodgers, 1988; Farley & Allen, 1987a; Jaynes & Williams, 1989; Wilson, 1987, 1996).

Findings that younger, middle-aged, and older African American fathers often differed in instrumental and expressive family role experiences support both the theoretical and policy relevance of critical adult life cycle issues (Bowman, 1989, 1996a; Bowman & Forman, 1995). Andrew Billingsley argued as early as 1968 that a developmental perspective is critical to understanding African American family functioning. More recently, the emerging literature on fathers has begun to give systematic attention to the relationship between life cycle stage and paternal role functioning (Bozett, 1985; Daniels & Weingarten, 1988; De Luccie & Davis, 1991; Gooden, 1989; Snarey & Pleck, 1988). Although suggestive, these life cycle studies on predominantly white middle-class fathers have limited generalizability for understanding paternal role functioning among African American fathers.

The specific finding that African American fathers' instrumental and expressive family role difficulties declined systematically when we compared younger, middle-aged, and older fathers has several important theoretical implications (e.g., Bowman, 1989; Bowman & Forman, 1995; Bowman & Sanders, in press; Erikson, 1966, 1968, 1980; Hawkins & Dollahite, 1997). In developmental terms, these findings provide hopeful signs that instrumental problems among African American fathers such as monetary stress, income inadequacy, primary provider strain, and paternal role strain may decline naturally as fathers move through the adult life course. A similar developmental pattern is apparent in the expressive roles in which fathers experienced less marital-family stress and reported greater involvement in both religious and race-related socialization in each successive age group. In normative psychosocial developmental terms, young fathers may temporarily experience transitional family role difficulties as they enter the labor market and struggle for self-reliance. Hence, such early transitional difficulty may be naturally reduced as fathers gain greater control over work and family challenges during the generative middle adult years and reduced even further as they disengage from generative familial and civic pressures during old age.

Some unique stage-specific psychosocial developmental patterns are also suggested in the data on older, middle-aged, and young African American fathers (e.g., Bowman, 1989; Erikson, 1980; Hawkins & Dollahite, 1997). Given their extremely low income, older fathers' relative freedom from distress in instrumental and expressive family roles may reflect age-specific psychosocial coping; they may successfully maintain psychosocial integrity through selective and self-protective appraisals of painful familial role difficulties, which occurred earlier in their lives. In contrast, despite having the highest income, midlife fathers may be most anxious about family finances because of pressing generative family demands including teenage children. This interpretation is consistent with other findings that only among midlife fathers is worry over family finances accompanied by higher father-child stress. Among younger fathers, multiple provider role difficulties may become major obstacles in their psychosocial strivings to establish a stable intimate relationship and expressive family roles. Monetary stress and primary provider role strain both appear to be risk factors in young fathers' efforts to establish loving family relationships and avoid isolation. Marital-family stress as well as self-efficacy doubts about being a good father appear as psychosocial risks among both young and midlife fathers but not among older fathers when children are less dependent.

As noted earlier, the foregoing life cycle developmental inferences from cross-sectional data must be made with caution because of alternative cohort or period interpretations. Older fathers may not experience less instrumental and expressive family role difficulties because of adult development, but due to cohort or period effects. For example, being socialized during the Depression era may make the older cohort of fathers more adaptive in the face of extreme economic hardship. Similarly, the extreme difficulty among young fathers in provider and expressive family roles may not be transitional but reflect more persistent postindustrial period effects; their joblessness could become permanent, unlike older fathers who were able to establish themselves in jobs and the family provider role more easily during earlier agricultural and industrial eras. More rigorous multivariate analysis of existing NSBA longitudinal data on selected instrumental and family role orientations can help to further unravel such life cycle, period, and cohort issues (e.g., Bowman & Forman, 1995).

The change and stability in instrumental and expressive role experiences among African American fathers across the four data collection waves between 1979-1992 present a rather complex picture. The precipitous increase from 1979-1988 in African American fathers' primary provider role strain and self doubts about being a good father to their children may reflect erosive events during this early postindustrial period rather than developmental change. For example, all four instrumental role items to varying degrees but more so than the expressive role items seemed to be adversely affected by this period effect. Within this period, a clear decline in the status of African American children has been linked to drastic cutbacks during the 1980-1988 Reagan years and growth in joblessness that reached a higher level during the early 1980s than any period since the Great Depression (e.g., Billingsley, 1992; Bowman, Jackson, Hatchett, & Gurin, 1982; Farley & Allen, 1987a; Jaynes & Williams, 1989; Wilson, 1987, 1996). Future studies should explore why these adverse economic events of the 1980s appear to have especially devastating effects on African American fathers' difficulties in the traditional family provider role. Apparently, African American families were more successful in finding ways to manage household financial problems, family stress, and expressive father-child problems than fathers' provider role frustrations.

To be sure, future NSBA studies on African American fathers should use both the longitudinal data and more strategic multivariate analysis to further unravel critical period, cohort, and life cycle effects on their instrumental and expressive family roles. Such studies along with others suggested in this discussion section would help provide further insight into important parameters of a more comprehensive social ecological approach. As indicated throughout this chapter, a more integrative ecological approach is essential to future research and policy that systematically considers the critical sources of difficulty as well as resiliency among African American fathers (Allen, 1985; Billingsley, 1968, 1992; Bowman, 1988, 1989, 1991a, 1991b; Forman, 1994; Smith & Graham, 1995). The manner in which shifting postindustrial challenges influence instrumental and expressive family role experiences of African American fathers at each stage of the adult life cycle will have far-reaching consequences well into the 21st century. Indeed, effectively addressing this escalating "family crisis" may be pivotal to any viable agenda to reverse pressing problems of race and class such as welfare dependency, chronic poverty, family instability, inner-city schools, drugs, violence, crime, and delinquency, which increasingly erode the quality of urban life for all Americans. Like the solution for any "family problem," denial is the greatest impediment and a better understanding is a necessary condition for effective intervention.

Notes

1. Here we define responsible fatherhood as fathers who are involved in their children's life either by being reliable economic providers, being meaningfully involved in the socialization of their children, or both. Note that our definition enables these role obligations to be performed by either custodial or noncustodial fathers. We believe that such a definition is important given the rise of single-parent households and relevant research that suggests that father absence should not be equated with noninvolvement by fathers (see Danziger & Radin, 1990; Earl & Lohmann, 1978; Miller, 1994; Stack, 1974; Stier & Tienda, 1993).

2. African American single-mother households represent 82.2% of all African American families with children in poverty, single-father households represent 4.9%.

14

Family Roles and Family Satisfaction Among Black Men

ROBERT JOSEPH TAYLOR
WALDO E. JOHNSON, JR.

The past 10 years have seen an increase in research concerning the lives of black men, which coincides with the general development of research on the family roles of men. Although this research is relatively recent, it indicates that men differ substantially in their attitudes and behaviors regarding marriage and parenthood. This work reflects the changes taking place in how American men define and participate in principal family roles (i.e., husband and father). Increasingly, men of all ages are finding fulfillment in roles in which they nurture and support their children, wives, relatives, and friends. Men are becoming centrally involved in roles and behaviors that were customarily ascribed to women in earlier decades.

One explanation for the shift in men's investments of time and effort in families suggests that it reflects greater psychological involvement in family life. Pleck and Lang (1978) found that men's self-rated psychological involvement with marriage and family was greater than with work. Of the men in that study, 94% rated events in marriage and family life as the most important things that had happened to them; this compares to 55% of men who rated events associated with their jobs as most important. A growing body of evidence suggests that men who value parenthood are more involved with child care and find parenthood to be more satisfying (Lamb, Pleck, & Levine, 1986; Owen, Chase-Lansdale, & Lamb, 1982). Furthermore, increased participation of fathers in child care also seems to be associated with reports of greater satisfaction in nurturing children and developing a better understanding of their children (Russell, 1982).

Despite important changes in the family roles that are assumed by men, society's views about the roles of men in family life are often paradoxical. Conflicts and ambiguities surrounding appropriate family roles for men reflect a state of transition and change as we attempt to define what is normative and desirable. Furstenberg (1988) was one of the first family scholars to recognize this paradox in his work on *Good Dads-Bad Dads: Two Faces of Fatherhood.* One end of the continuum idealizes fatherhood and characterizes men as involved, caring, and responsive to their wives and children. The other end of the continuum characterizes men as uninvolved husbands and fathers who ignore their spousal and parental obligations.

Conventional portrayals of African American men as husbands and fathers, in large part, reflect the negative side of fatherhood. Among researchers and the general public alike, black males are stereotypically perceived as residents of poor inner-city neighborhoods, hypermasculine, financially irresponsible, and uninvolved in their children's lives (Marsiglio, 1995a, p. 5). Unfortunately, the majority of social science research focuses on black men in relation to various social problems such as adolescent fatherhood (e.g., Marsiglio, 1987; Sullivan, 1985), out of wedlock paternity (e.g., Christmon, 1990), child support enforcement (e.g., Johnson, in press), and street corner men (e.g., Anderson, 1978). Furthermore, research on black men is predominated by a focus on young men or young fathers, reflecting concerns over the issues of teenage parenting and mother-only families. By virtue of the restricted scope of research on black men, these efforts reflect and reinforce media depictions of black men as street corner criminals who are absent fathers and marginal participants in extended family networks (Cazenave, 1979; Gary, 1981). Such characterizations fail to take into account the broad diversity of family, spousal, and parental roles that African American men perform (Hunter & Davis, 1992).

Scholarship on black men has not followed the example and direction of Gary's (1981) classic work on African American men. His edited volume addressed social problems (e.g., adolescent fathers, incarceration, and substance abuse), as well as normative life issues (e.g., coping strategies, support systems, father-child interactions) as they affected black men. Following in the tradition of Gary's work, a body of literature is slowly developing on black men that moves beyond characterizations of black men as either victims (e.g., an endangered species) or offenders (e.g., deadbeat dads). Notable examples of this work are evident in the programmatic research of Franklin (e.g., 1985) on masculinity, of Bowman (e.g., 1990) on the provider role, and in the development of two new research journals on black men (i.e., *Journal of African American Males, Challenge: A Journal of Research on African American Men*). Collectively, these research efforts have an explicit interest in the investigation of basic normative issues and processes that affect black men, their roles within families, and black men's contributions to family development.

The Provider Role

A major research topic concerning black men examines their perceptions of personal adequacy in providing for the material well-being of their families. Interest in this area developed because of the historic labor market restrictions facing black men and the negative impact of economic marginality on family life. An early study among middle-income black fathers (Cazenave, 1979), found that the role of economic provider was the most often cited familial role, as well as the most salient aspect of masculine identity. Respondents felt that higher levels of income and occupational status equipped them to be better providers for their families than their own fathers had been (whose own labor market experiences were characterized by low income, low status, and irregular employment).

A number of studies addressing the issue of provider role have used National Survey of Black Americans (NSBA) data. Taylor, Leashore, and Toliver (1988) found that age and personal income were both positively associated with assessments of provider role performance. Older respondents and those with higher personal incomes were more likely than their counterparts to perceive themselves as being good providers for their families. The relationship between personal income and provider role performance demonstrates the importance of economic stability in influencing perceptions of familial role performance.

Bowman's program of research involves the development of a conceptual framework for understanding the antecedents and consequences of provider role perceptions (1989, 1995), as well as empirical articles (1985, 1990) concerning the significance of provider role performance for the family lives of black men. Bowman's (1985) analysis of married black men found that provider role strain had a negative impact on level of life happiness. Informal coping resources functioned to enhance life happiness, but they were unable to compensate for the more extreme negative effects of provider role strain. Both religiosity and familial cohesion were important coping resources, religiosity being the more influential of the two.

In a later study, Bowman (1990) examined the impact of provider role strain and cultural resources on family satisfaction among black husband-fathers. Those who indicated that they did not perform well in the husband, father, or provider roles reported significantly lower levels of satisfaction with their families. Evidence in support of a buffering hypothesis indicated that among black husband-fathers whose families had high levels of family affection, there was no relationship between performance in the father and husband roles and family satisfaction. Among those whose families had low levels of family affection, however, there were strong relationships between performance in the husband and father roles and family satisfaction.

The Spousal Role

Although only a few studies examine the correlates of father role performance, there is a growing literature on declining rates of marriage among African Americans (Tucker & Mitchell-Kernan, 1995a). This work indicates that black adults tend to marry later than whites and are more likely to be separated, divorced, or widowed. As a consequence, blacks are much less likely to be married and have marriages of shorter duration than their white counterparts.

One of the primary theories addressing the delay in marriage suggests that black couples decline marriage if the male partner experiences difficulties in providing for the future family (i.e., provider role theory). In essence, higher rates of unemployment and underemployment and low levels of income among black men constitute impediments to marriage (Darity & Myers, 1986/1987; Kiecolt & Fosset, Chapter 3, this volume; Tucker & Taylor, 1989; Wilson, 1987). Chadiha's (1992) qualitative study of marriage and family formation among black couples is an explicit test of the provider role theory. Her findings indicated that although various factors influenced a couple's decision to marry, the most important factor was the husband's ability to find a job and generate a viable income for the family.

Hatchett, Veroff, and Douvan (1995) found that black men's anxiety about providing for the financial needs of their families also contributes to marital instability. Black husbands who indicated a significant degree of worry about providing for their families, also experienced extensive marital difficulties.

Overall, it appears that income and labor market worries felt by many black men discourage entering marriage and, once married, may have a negative impact on marital quality that impedes long-term commitment.

The Parental Role

Research on black men within parental roles is dominated by work focusing on adolescent fathers and out-of-wedlock paternity. Work on these issues reveals increasing complexity and sophistication, providing valuable information about black men in these family circumstances. Little research has been conducted, however, on black fathers more generally. The programmatic research of the late John McAdoo (e.g., 1981, 1986, 1988) investigated differences among black fathers with respect to the socialization patterns and practices they employ in raising children. As reaction to previous research that focused on extremely poor or socially vulnerable black families, McAdoo explicitly chose to study a sample of middle-income black fathers. His work indicated that black fathers were actively involved in the socialization of their children, displaying warm and loving patterns of interaction with their children. McAdoo argued that the black fathers in his study did not appear to be different in their child-rearing attitudes from middle-income fathers of other ethnic groups.

One of the consequences of declining rates of marriage, coupled with high rates of divorce and separation and mother-only families, is that black men are increasingly less likely to live with their biological children. Less than one third of black children live with both parents and, it has been projected (Bumpass, 1984) that, 9 out of 10 black children are likely to spend some portion of their childhood in single-parent households. A large proportion of fathers who do not reside with their children have little to no contact with their minor children and father-child contact declines appreciably over time (Marsiglio, 1995a). Mott's (1990) longitudinal analysis, however, indicates that traditional definitions of residential status may underestimate the extent to which black fathers (both biological and surrogate) play critical roles in their children's development.

Satisfaction With Family Life

Research on the subjective well-being of African Americans, including work on adjustment, morale, life satisfaction, and happiness (Chatters, 1988a), has grown substantially over the past few years. It is generally agreed that subjective well-being is an overarching construct characterized by a focus on subjective experiences, the explicit incorporation of positive measures, and use of an overall assessment of life or particular domains of life (Chatters, 1988a, p. 237). An emerging body of research focuses on the correlates of subjective well-being among black adults generally (see Broman, Chapter 9, this volume; Ellison, 1990 and Chapter 6, this volume; Levin, Chatters, & Taylor, 1995; Thomas & Holmes, 1992), older black adults (Chatters, 1988a, 1988b; Chatters & Ellison, in press), and other subgroups of black Americans (see Beale, Chapter 7, this volume; Keith, Chapter 5, this volume).

In addition to research on social participation (i.e., family and friendship) correlates of subjective well-being (see Ellison, 1990), work also focuses on perceptions of satisfaction with family as a separate area of well-being. This literature is representative of a body of subjective well-being research that examines well-being within individual domains of life. Within this "bottom-up" approach, overall well-being is defined as an aggregate of satisfactions across life domains (e.g., marriage, family, housing, job, neighborhood). Investigations of domain satisfactions suggest that they differ from general life satisfaction with respect to significant predictors (Broman, 1991). In some sense, the effects of domain-specific factors (e.g., family roles and stresses) on general life satisfaction are thought to be mediated via domain satisfactions (e.g., family satisfaction).

Broman's (1988a) examination of family satisfaction among African Americans indicated that older age, being married, and parenting a minor child were associated with higher ratings of family satisfaction. Furthermore, persons who were divorced had significantly lower levels of family satisfaction. In another study, Broman (1991) found that black men and women had equally high levels of family satisfaction. Black men who reported that they performed the majority of the household chores, however, had lower levels of family satisfaction. An analysis of family satisfaction among three-generation black families (i.e., grandparent, child, and grandchild) found that black Americans generally express high levels of satisfaction with their family lives (Taylor, Chatters, & Jackson, 1993). Members of the grandparent generation expressed the highest levels of family satisfaction, with 8 of 10 indicating that they are very satisfied with their lives. Members of the grandparent generation displayed the highest levels of satisfaction followed by the parent and the child generation.

A few tentative conclusions about family satisfaction can be drawn from these studies. Older age and being married appear to be important determinants of positive ratings of family life. Persons who are divorced may be from other groups in terms of lowered family satisfaction perceptions. Certain aspects of family roles may function to bolster (i.e., parental status) or hinder (i.e., household responsibilities) family satisfaction. With the notable exception of work by Bowman (1985, 1990), little research examines indicators of subjective well-being or family satisfaction specifically among black men. The present chapter hopes to contribute to a broader understanding of black men within the context of family life by examining demographic and other correlates of family satisfaction and perceptions of spousal and parental roles.

Method

Sample Description

The NSBA sample comprised a total of 797 black men. A more detailed description of the black male sample in the National Survey of Black Americans can be found in Taylor et al. (1988).

Dependent and Independent Variables

This analysis examines three dependent variables: (a) perceptions of the spousal role, (b) perceptions of the parental role, and (c) overall satisfaction with family life. Perception of adequacy in the spousal role was measured by the question, "Given the chances that you had, how well have you done at being a good husband to your wife? Do you think that you have done *very well, fairly well, not too well,* or *not well at all*?" This question was asked only of respondents who were currently married. Perception of adequacy in the parental role was measured by the question, "Given the chances that you have had, how well have you done at being a good father to your children? Do you think that you have done *very well, fairly well, not too well,* or *not well at all*?" Perception of performance in the parental role was asked only of respondents who were currently parents. Satisfaction with family life was measured by the question, "How satisfied are you with your family life, that is, the time you spend and the things you do with members of your family? Would you say that you are *very satisfied, somewhat satisfied, somewhat dissatisfied,* or *very dissatisfied*?"

Demographic factors used as independent variables include age, marital status, education, poverty status, urbanicity, number of children, and region. Employment and occupational status are incorporated into a summary variable labeled working status. This variable consists of the following five categories:

primary sector (i.e., white collar), secondary sector (i.e., blue collar), officially unemployed (i.e., actively searching for a job), hidden unemployed (i.e., interested in working but not actively seeking employment), and not in the labor force (e.g., retirees, students, and physically disabled). In addition, three separate variables assess whether in the past month respondents experienced (a) a problem in their family or marriage, (b) a problem with their children, or (c) a problem on the job.

Analysis Strategy

Each of the dependent variables is ordinal level and possesses a fairly skewed distribution. As a consequence, multiple regression is not an appropriate multivariate statistical technique to use for data of this type. Logistic regression, however, can be used with a dichotomous dependent variable and either continuous or nominal scaled independent variables. For spousal and parental role perceptions, the dependent variables contrast respondents who report doing *very well* in the relevant role, against those who report *fairly well, not too well,* or *not well at all* (aggregated across the three response categories). For family satisfaction, the dependent variable contrasts respondents who report being *very satisfied* with their family life, against those who report being *somewhat satisfied, somewhat dissatisfied,* and *very dissatisfied* (aggregated across the three response categories).

Results

Three of four respondents (72.4%) indicate that they perform *very well* in the spouse role, 26.4% indicate *fairly well,* and 1.2% indicate *not too well.* Table 14.1 (Model 1) presents the results of the logistic regression for (married) black men's perceptions of the spouse role. Education and having had a family-marriage problem within the month prior to the interview are significantly related to perceptions of performance in the spouse role. Black men with more years of formal education are less likely to indicate that they performed *very well* in the spouse role, compared to their counterparts. In addition, respondents who experienced a problem involving family or marriage in the past month were less likely to indicate that they performed *very well* in the husband role.

Three quarters of black men who are parents indicate that they perform *very well* in the parental role, 23.3% report *fairly well,* 2.4% *not too well,* and 0.3% indicate *not well at all.* Logistic regression results for black men's perceptions of their performance in the parental role are presented in Table 14.1 (Model 2).

Table 14.1 *Logistic Regressions of the Correlates of the Perceptions of the Husband Role, Father Role, and Satisfaction With Family Life*

	Husband Role	Father Role	Family Satisfaction
	b	*b*	*b*
Age	−.001	.006	.023**
Marital status			
Divorced		−.099	−.714*
Separated		−.521	−.292
Widowed		−.733	−.807*
Never married		−.602	−.077
Poverty	−.327	−.057	−.034
Education	−.123**	.000	−.023
Work status			
Secondary sector	−.467	.047	.283
Officially unemployed	−.907	−.269	.111
Hidden unemployed	.592	.705	.431
Not in labor force	.601	.810	.376
Region			
Northeast	−.117	−.013	−.633**
North Central	−.209	.078	.029
West	−.610	.313	−.256
Urban	−.221	−.113	.111
Number of children	−.031	.046	.043
Family problem	−1.062**	−.687*	−.743**
Child problem	.134	−.790*	−.876*
Constant	3.064	.981	−.416
Chi-square	40.830	42.838	86.440
N	388	535	730

*p < .05; **p < .01.

Black men who indicate that they had a family-marriage problem, and those who report a problem with their children are less likely than their counterparts to indicate that they have performed *very well* in the parental role.

Half of the sample (53.9%) report that they are *very satisfied* with their family lives, one third of respondents (33.7%) indicate that are *somewhat satisfied,*

10.3% report being *somewhat dissatisfied,* and 2.0% indicate that they are *very dissatisfied* with their family lives. Age, marital status, region, family-marriage problems, and problems with children are all significantly associated with whether respondents indicate they are *very satisfied* with their family life (Table 14.1, Model 3). In general, older respondents are more likely than younger respondents to report being satisfied with their family life. With regard to marital status, divorced and widowed men are less likely than married respondents to indicate that they are *very satisfied* with their family life. Regional differences indicate that black men who reside in the Northeast have a lower likelihood of reporting that they are *very satisfied* with their family life than black men who reside in the South. In addition, black men who experience problems with their family or marriage and those who had problems with their children are less likely to indicate that they are *very satisfied* with their family lives.

Discussion

The present findings indicate that, on the whole, African American husbands and fathers rate their performance in spousal and parental roles favorably and report being very satisfied with their family life. These general findings corroborate earlier research regarding the significance that black men ascribe to the competent execution of familial roles (Bowman, 1985, 1990; Cazenave, 1979: McAdoo, 1981). Like men in general, black men report that performing well in both husband and father roles is an important component of their lives. Before discussing these findings in detail, it is important to consider these reports in light of social desirability and other factors that may have an impact on perceptions of spouse and family role performance.

Nearly all of respondents indicated that they performed either *very well* or *fairly well* in marital and parental roles. By any standard, this is a surprisingly high level of performance in these roles. Conventional wisdom and social science research (Hochschild, 1989) indicate a substantial discrepancy between men's actual participation in household and child care and their *perceptions* of their contributions in these areas. Studies of time use suggest that men characteristically overestimate the amount of time they devote to housework and child care. Given this prior research assessing actual behaviors, it is important to consider explanations for the high levels of perceived husband and father role performance.

Two general interpretations are possible. Respondents may be aware of the high social approval associated with competency in spousal and parental roles and their responses reflect a desire to provide a socially acceptable response. Alternatively, because we have no information as to respondents' own normative expectations for performance in these roles, it could be that assessments of role performance do correspond to their actual behaviors and expectations. Small discrepancies between expected and actual behaviors could result in more positive perceptions of role performance, whereas larger differences could result in negative assessments of role adequacy.

In a related manner, it is possible that respondents' assessments of their performance in these roles reflect specific social comparison processes to others (real or imagined) who are performing less adequately in these roles (i.e., downward comparisons). Downward comparison processes may inflate self-perceptions, whereas upward comparisons to self (ideal) or others who excel in these roles may diminish perceptions of husband and parental role performance. This issue can not be resolved in the present study because of the lack of data on social desirability factors and specific information on normative expectations and actual time use and activities (i.e., child care). Information such as this, however, is clearly critical for understanding behavioral role expectations and the processes by which black men evaluate their role adequacy.

Indicators of family stress (i.e., family-marriage problem, problem with children) were the most consistent correlates of family role performance and family satisfaction. Black men who indicated they had experienced a family or marriage problem in the past month were less likely to report that they performed well in husband and father roles, as well as indicating lower levels of family satisfaction. Similarly, fathers who reported having a problem with their children in the past month had less positive appraisals of their performance in the father role and lower levels of family satisfaction. These findings correspond to research indicating that stress in various areas of life have a negative impact on overall evaluations of life quality (Chatters, 1988b; Tran, Wright, & Chatters, 1991). In particular, stress is thought to affect well-being by virtue of its role in eroding positive self-conceptions and self-worth. In the present study, problems with family-marriage and children may erode one's sense of competency in these roles. Family factors also make important contributions to life quality. Marital happiness and good affective relations with family are related to higher overall perceptions of well-being (Ellison, 1990; Thomas & Holmes, 1992). Although not tested as a causal sequence, conflicts involving one's family-marriage and children could depress positive perceptions of role performance, which, in turn, lower general feelings of family satisfaction. Taken together, the findings indicate that judgments as to spousal and paternal role adequacy and family satisfaction are responsive to reported conflicts in these areas.

Contrary to expectations, however, socioeconomic status indicators had limited effects on perceptions of husband role performance and were unrelated to performance in the father role. The thrust of previous research suggested that the tenuous occupational position of black men, coupled with high rates of poverty experienced by this group would result in more negative evaluations of husband and father role performance. Our results, however, did not support these expectations. In fact, findings for education indicated that men with higher levels of education were less likely to indicate that they performed well as a husband. Men with higher levels of education are likely married to women of comparable educational backgrounds. Highly educated couples are likely to be exposed to circumstances and situations that acknowledge and possibly en-dorse modifications in spousal roles and expectations. The inverse education effect might suggest that highly educated men are unsuccessful in meeting their own expectations for their performance as a husband.

The distinction between various aspects of marriage and family life (i.e., marriage formation, provider role perceptions, role performance) are signifi-cant. Although the literature suggests that economic factors are important for marriage and family formation and general provider role perceptions, they do not appear to be a major factor for perceptions of actual family role perform-ance. For many black men who have endured years of economic hardship, in-adequate income has been an ongoing feature of their labor market experi-ences. As such, it is likely that perceptions of being a good father and husband are not determined by income, working status, or other structural issues over which black men may feel that they exert little direct control.

Several demographic factors exhibited significant relationships with family satisfaction. Consistent with Broman's work (1988a) and analysis of three-generation family data (Taylor et al., 1993), age was positively associated with family satisfaction, indicating that older men had higher levels of satisfaction with family life than their younger counterparts. These findings corroborate a body of gerontological findings indicating that older adults, compared to younger persons, consistently endorse attitudes and sentiments that reflect family solidarity and cohesion (e.g., familial affection) (Bengtson, Burton & Managen, 1985; Taylor et al., 1993).

With respect to marital status differences, widowers were less likely than married men to indicate that they were satisfied with their family life. Troll et al. (1979) argue that widowers experience particular difficulty in making the emotional and social adjustment to the loss of spouse. Daily functioning in the area of household maintenance (e.g., meal preparation, house cleaning, laun-dry) are especially demanding for widowed men. In the areas of personal rela-tionships and networks, widowers exhibit poorer social adaptability and curtailed interaction with children (Antonucci, 1985). Consequently, the emotional and social losses suffered by widowed men may significantly impact their perceptions of and satisfaction with family life. This analysis also found that divorced men reported significantly lower levels of family satisfaction than their married counterparts. The process of marital dissolution and the stigmatized status of divorce may result in emotional estrangement from one's own family network and from in-laws (Furstenberg, 1981), as well as decreases in satisfaction with family life.

The divorce finding is consistent with work by Broman (1988a) indicating lower family satisfaction among the divorced and with related research on the informal support networks of elderly blacks. In comparison to older black adults who were married, divorced respondents (a) reported lower levels of subjective family closeness (Taylor & Chatters, 1991a); (b) were less likely to have informal networks comprised of immediate family members (Chatters, Taylor, & Jackson, 1985); and (c) were more likely to rely on distant relatives, friends, and neighbors (Chatters et al., 1985). Taken together, the findings suggest that the consequences of divorce are far ranging and affect the emotional climate of family relationships, as well as the extent to which families constitute support resources.

In the majority of research on families, regional differences are rarely addressed. One of the advantages of the NSBA data is the ability to examine regional differences in family phenomena. Previous research using NSBA has reported significant regional differences in various family factors (Chatters & Taylor, 1993; Chatters et al., 1985, 1986; Taylor, 1985; Taylor & Chatters, 1991a; Taylor, Hardison, & Chatters, 1996), whereas in other studies, differences by region were insignificant (Chatters, Taylor, & Neighbors, 1989; Taylor, 1986). In the present analysis, southerners indicated higher levels of satisfaction with family life than men residing in the Northeast. In contrast, Broman (1988a) found no significant regional differences in level of family satisfaction. This might be accounted for by the aggregation of Northeast and North Central regions into a single category (i.e., North, South, West), the use of the entire NSBA sample (i.e., both women and men), or both.

Other related work on family issues indicates that in comparison to respondents who resided in the Northeast, (a) older black southerners receive support from extended families more frequently and (b) black Southern adults are more likely to use family members (Taylor et al., 1996). Collectively, the findings indicate that southerners (particularly older adults) have a family support advantage in comparison to persons residing in other regions. Explicit, regionally based cultural values among black Americans may promote affective and functional aspects of family relationships in the South. This is an area in which much more research is needed among black Americans in general and discrete subgroups of the black population.

Taken together, these results indicate that husband and father role perceptions and family satisfaction, along with provider role assessments, reflect related family issues that are of concern to black men. This and other studies suggest, however, that despite their similarities, they are distinctive and determined by different factors. Specifically, the present findings indicate that perceptions of family satisfaction are influenced to a greater extent by demographic factors (i.e., age, marital status, region), whereas performance in family roles is determined largely by factors that characterize the quality of family relationships (i.e., family problems). The significant education effect for perceptions of the husband role suggests that black men with more years of education are not as content with their performance in this family role. This could result from escalating expectations for the changing nature of the marital relationship, personal aspirations for change that black men themselves possess, or both.

As indicated in prior research, the prominence given to the provider role (Cazenave, 1979) and socioeconomic factors as determinants of these role perceptions (Taylor et al., 1988), suggest that this aspect of family roles may be unique in its ability to define notions of masculinity and influence perceptions of well-being among black men (Bowman, 1985, 1990). In contrast, the present findings indicate that aspects of family roles that are specifically tied to the quality of relationships are more important influences on black men's assessments of their performance in these spheres. Future research efforts should investigate the ways in which male identity, husband and father role performance, and qualitative aspects of family life converge (e.g., Bowman, 1990). Such efforts would further an understanding of the diversity of family role behaviors among African American men, help to monitor changes in normative attitudes regarding appropriate role performance, and clarify misconceptions and myths regarding black men as husbands and fathers.

15

Living Arrangements of African American Adults

Variations by Age, Gender, and Family Status

ANDREA G. HUNTER

African Americans are more likely to be unmarried, live in single-parent and extended family households, and to live alone during their elder years than are nonblacks (Beck & Beck, 1984; Richards, White, & Tsui, 1987). African American living arrangements are also diverse and household boundaries malleable; as a result; black adults are likely to be members of a variety of family and nonfamily households as they age (Beck & Beck, 1984; Richards et al., 1987; Slesinger, 1980). Although several studies document the fluidity of African American households and the diversity of family patterns, focus on the prevalence of female-headed households and children's lives has tended to obscure the complexities of residential patterns across adulthood and gender. This chapter examines variations in the living arrangements of African American adults by age, gender, and family status.

The Life Course, Family Trajectories, and Living Arrangements

Families are shaped by an intersection of individual lives that collectively form, reconfigure, and extend family lineages through marriages, births, death, martial dissolution, and fictive family ties (Aldous, 1990; Elder 1978, 1991; Hareven, 1977; Stack, 1974). Kinship positions and family responsibilities expand and contract as individuals move through varied marital and family careers across the life span. Family developmental and life course perspectives suggest that household formation, evolution, and dissolution are driven by this dynamic process (Aldous, 1990; Elder, 1991). Indeed, living arrangements are fluid, and vary across age, gender, and family status (e.g., marital status, custodial parent) (Chevan & Sutton, 1985; Slesinger, 1980; Richards et al., 1987).

Age, the Life Course, and the Intergenerational Family Life Cycle

Age locates people temporally in individual time (e.g., early adulthood, midlife), family time (i.e., sequencing and timing of family events), and historical time (e.g., cohort, era) (Elder, 1978; Hareven, 1977; Riley, 1986). Elder (1978, p.21) describes the life course as pathways through the age-differentiated life span structured by patterns in the timing, spacing, duration, and order of social roles and events. Central tendencies in living arrangements by age reflect normative patterns in the timing of family events (e.g., child-bearing, child launching), and the family life cycle (Aldous, 1990; Hareven, 1987). Differences in the timing and sequencing of family events and social roles in a population, as well as "skipping" conventional family statuses (e.g., remaining never married and childless), create variations within birth cohorts (Elder, 1991).

Rapp, Ross, and Bridenthal (1979, p. 176) write: "because people accept the meaningfulness of families, they enter into relations of production, reproduction, and consumption with one another. They marry, beget children, work to support dependents, accumulate, transmit, and inherit cultural and material resources." Within the individual life course, family trajectories are forged by the sequence of family transitions and events (Elder, 1985). The family life cycle broadly refers to the sequencing of developmental tasks linked to family formation, reproduction, and child rearing (Aldous, 1990). Furthermore, it is assumed that individuals will live through a variety of patterns of family structure, household organization, and familial relationships that are linked to the developmental course of families as collective units (Hareven, 1987). Although the family developmental perspective is criticized for its emphasis on unidirectional stages and the "traditional" nuclear family (Aldous, 1990), the family life cycle is a useful framework in the study of living arrangements because with whom one lives is closely linked to family events (e.g., marriage, divorce, childbearing) and age-graded social norms (e.g., adult children leaving home). A focus exclusively on the nuclear family and the parent-child dyad, however, overlooks the intergenerational family context in which individuals, families, and households are embedded.

The intergenerational family life cycle, a product of overlapping life course and family trajectories, highlights the continuity in family systems and accommodates normative and nonnormative family transitions (e.g., early childbearing) and family events (e.g, nonmarital childbearing) that may occur within multigeneration family lineages. Off-time transitions and nonnormative sequencing of family events add to the complexities of family relationships and fuel variations in family trajectories and living arrangements within family lineages (Burton, 1990; Burton & Bengston, 1985; Hunter & Ensminger, 1992). Extending the family life cycle beyond the nuclear family and parent-child dyad is particularly important in the study of African American families because of the centrality of extended family relationships (Dressler, Hoeppner, & Pitts, 1985; Elder, 1985; Martin & Martin, 1978; Jackson, Jarakody, & Antonucci, 1996). In addition, African Americans are more likely than white Americans to exit married-couple nuclear households and to move in and out of households with extended kin and friends (Bianchi, 1981; Richards et al., 1987).

Race, Gender, and Family Trajectories

Across race and ethnicity, the type of households individuals are likely to move into and where they move from varies by gender (Chevan & Sutton, 1985; Richards et al., 1987). Changes in African American marriage and family formation since 1960 (e.g., unmarried childbearing, divorce, and separation) have widened the gender gap in living arrangements and are fostering distinctively gendered family trajectories among African Americans (Farley & Allen, 1987b; Walker, 1988). African American women are more likely to spend a significant proportion of their adulthood in alternative family living arrangements (i.e., single-parent, extended-family households) than are men (Beck & Beck, 1984; Richards et al.,1987). During old age, African American women are also more likely to live alone (U.S. Bureau of the Census, 1991d). Although men are more likely than women to currently live in married-couple nuclear households, nonmarital childbearing and divorce increases the likelihood that men will live apart from their children (Furstenberg & Harris, 1992; Marsiglio, 1995b; U.S. Bureau of the Census, 1991d).

Historically in African American family studies, the rate of female-headed households has driven the discussion on gender differences in family structure and living arrangements (Frazier, 1939; McDaniel, 1990; Staples & Mirande, 1980). This is increasingly problematic because one of the byproducts of the decline in married-couple nuclear family households is greater diversity in family patterns and household composition (Chevan & Sutton, 1985; Hunter & Ensminger, 1992; Kellam, Adams, Brown, & Ensminger, 1982; Richards et al., 1987; Slesinger, 1980). Furthermore, an emphasis on the rate of female-headed households oversimplifies (e.g., female headed, male absent) the divergent family trajectories of African American men and women. For example, although African American men occupy a variety of overlapping family roles (e.g., father, son, uncle) and their living arrangements are diverse, men's residence in a variety of family living arrangements are seldom explored (see, for exception, Beck & Beck, 1984; Hawkins & Eggebeen, 1990). Similarly, African American women's living arrangements outside of reproduction, marriage, and child rearing are frequently overlooked.

Examining African American Living Arrangements

Living arrangements at any one point in time reflect a stop-over in a journey across marital and family careers. This chapter highlights normative patterns in African American living arrangements by age, as well as variations within age groups that reflect diverse life course and family trajectories. In addition, as noted, changes in African American family demography during the past three decades have different implications for the lives of men and women. In the wake of the increase in female-headed households, a central question is: what are the emergent patterns in African American living arrangements by gender across adulthood?

This study is based on the total sample ($N = 2,107$) from the National Survey of Black Americans (NSBA). NSBA sampled households and adults within households. This sampling approach allows us to examine the distribution of household types and variations within households. It is important to note that using both household (e.g., household type) and individual data (e.g., age, gender, family status) highlights the connections between age, the intergenerational family life cycle, and household composition. We can also examine household types from vantage points (e.g., adult men in female-headed house-

Table 15.1 *Distribution of Household Types*

	Percentage	*N*
Nonfamily households	23.2	491
Married-couple/nuclear	37.6	795
Single-parent/nuclear	19.9	421
Married-couple/extended	7.7	162
Single-head/extended	9.8	207
Cohabitating family	1.8	37

holds), which may otherwise be obscured. Although cross-sectional data does not allow an examination of individual lives or household trajectories over time, we do have a snapshot of people's lives that reflects marital and family trajectories (Hareven, 1987).

Overview of Household Types

Table 15.1 shows the distribution of household types in the total sample. Household type is determined by the household head(s) and household members' relationship to them. There are two major categories: (a) nonfamily and (b) family households. Nonfamily households include respondents living alone or with unrelated adults. Family household is defined as the coresidence of two or more persons related by blood, marriage, or adoption and may also include nonrelatives. Family households include four major types: (a) married-couple nuclear households are headed by a married couple with or without offspring; (b) single-parent nuclear households are headed by a single parent with offspring present (minor, adult, or both); (c) extended family households are headed by either a married couple or a single person and include extended kin (i.e., relatives who are not members of the nuclear family of the household head[s]); and (d) cohabiting family households are headed by a cohabiting couple with offspring present.

Most households (76.8%) were family-based. Nuclear family households headed by a married couple were the modal household type (37.6%) and nearly 20% were nuclear family households headed by a single parent. Extended family households (married couple and single heads) were almost as common as nuclear single-parent households. Almost 18% of households included

Table 15.2 *Household Income by Household Type*

	Nonfamily		Nuclear Married Couple		Nuclear Single Parent		Extended Married Couple		Extended Single Person		Cohabiting Family	
	%	N	%	N	%	N	%	N	%	N	%	N
Under $4,000	49.6	115	6.8	24	28.1	89	17.1	13	29.5	39	20	4
$4,000-$9,999	29.7	69	25.4	89	43.2	137	25	19	37.9	50	25	5
$10,000-$14,999	12.1	28	17.4	61	14.5	46	9.2	7	11.4	15	20	4
$15,000-$24,999	7.3	17	27.1	95	11.4	36	27.6	21	11.4	15	20	4
$25,000-$29,999	.4	1	12.3	43	1.6	5	9.2	7	3	4	10	2
$30,000 +	.9	2	11.1	39	1.3	4	11.8	9	6.8	9	5	1
Model χ^2	355.86											

NOTE: $p < .01$.

extended kin, 9.8% of extended family households were headed by a single person, and 7.7% were headed by a married couple. Less than 2% of households were headed by a cohabiting couple with children. Although family households were most common, a substantial minority (23.2%) were nonfamily households.

As shown in Table 15.2, household income varied significantly by household type, $X^2(25, 2,107) = 355.86$, $p < .01$. Nonfamily, single-parent nuclear, and single-headed extended households had the lowest yearly earnings. Of nonfamily households, 49.6% had earnings below $4,000, as did 28.1% of nuclear single-parent households, and 29.5% of extended single-headed households. Households headed by a married couple, with or without extended kin, were the most affluent. Over two thirds of all households with earnings $25,000 and above were headed by a married couple.

Living Arrangements: Variations by Age, Gender, and Family Status

With whom people lived varied significantly by age, $X^2(5, 2,107) = 163.16$, $p < .001$; gender, $X^2(20, 2,107) = 323.95$, $p < .001$); family status (i.e., marital status), $X^2(20, 2,107) = 1789.37$, $p < .001$); and parental status (i.e., has own children), $X^2(5, 2,107) = 175.82$, $p < .001$. The following section highlights the

Table 15.3 *Women's Living Arrangements by Age*

	18 to 24		25 to 34		35 to 49		50 to 64		65+	
	%	N	%	N	%	N	%	N	%	N
Nonfamily households	10.5	20	7.5	25	9.3	29	33.6	85	55.3	12
Married-couple/nuclear	31.4	60	31.3	146	37.5	117	29.6	75	17.8	39
Single-parent/nuclear	27.2	53	43.6	146	33.3	104	15	38	7.8	17
Married-couple/extended	7.9	15	7.2	24	8.7	27	7.1	19	6.8	15
Single-head/extended	18.3	35	8.4	28	9.3	29	14.2	36	11.9	26
Cohabiting family	4.2	8	2.1	7	1.9	6	0.4	1	0.5	1
Total	100	191	100	335	100	312	100	253	100	219

diversity within household types and links age, gender, and family status to observed patterns in living arrangements. Tables 15.3 and 15.4 show the distribution of living arrangements within age group by gender.

Nonfamily Households

Adults who lived in nonfamily living arrangements varied in their marital history and parental status across the life span. Young adults living alone were recently launched from their family home, most were never married and without children. During middle age, living alone was increasingly a consequence of divorce and separation, especially for men. For women, who were largely never married and childless, residence in nonfamily households reflected an alternative family trajectory. From late midlife to late adulthood, marital dissolution and widowhood coupled with the end of child rearing left significant proportions of men and women living alone. The latter pattern was particularly pronounced for elderly women.

Early Adulthood

Under age 25, patterns of residence in nonfamily households were similar across gender. Most young adults were never married and did not have children. During the prime childbearing and rearing years, ages 25 to 34, nonfamily living arrangements began to diverge by gender and marital history. In

Table 15.4 *Men's Living Arrangements by Age*

	18 to 24		25 to 34		35 to 49		50 to 64		65+	
	%	N	%	N	%	N	%	N	%	N
Nonfamily households	16.9	22	21.1	43	26.9	50	33.8	51	34.1	43
Married-couple/nuclear	30.8	40	58.3	199	59.1	110	46.2	70	45.2	57
Single-parent/nuclear	20.8	27	6.4	13	6.5	12	4.0	6	3.2	4
Married-couple/extended	8.5	11	2.9	6	4.8	9	12.6	19	14.3	4
Single-head/extended	18.5	24	7.8	16	2.2	4	3.3	5	3.2	4
Cohabiting family	4.6	6	3.4	7	0.5	1	—	—	—	—
Total	100	130	100	204	100	186	100	151	100	126

this age range, 21.1% of men and 7.5% of women lived in nonfamily households. Men and women's marital histories and parental status also varied. Although never married men continue to be the most frequent residents in nonfamily households, men were more likely than women to have had a marriage dissolve. All of the men whose marriages dissolved were fathers and 31.7% of never married men were parents. None of the never or formerly married women who lived in nonfamily households were parents.

From the mid-20s to mid-30s, women not living with family members had delayed childbearing and most were never married. In contrast, men in nonfamily households show three major patterns: (a) never married without children, (b) never married parents, and (c) fathers from dissolved marriages. This is not surprising given the likelihood of mother custody in the case of nonmarital childbearing, divorce, and separation. These patterns do illustrate, however, that during early adulthood men and women living in nonfamily households have very different marital and childbearing histories.

Middle to Late Adulthood

At midlife, ages 35 to 49, gender differences in the likelihood of residence in nonfamily living arrangements remained. As women age, however, they were as likely to be formerly married as men. Approximately 70% of respondents living in nonfamily households at midlife have had marriages end via divorce or separation. Although the numbers are small, there was an emerging trend of higher levels of widowhood among women and never married status among men. In terms of parental status, almost all (97%) of the formerly married men were fathers and one quarter of never married men had children. Middle-aged women living in nonfamily households were more likely to be childless than their male counterparts. Middle-aged women, however, were more likely to be parents than younger women who lived in nonfamily households.

Beginning in late midlife, ages 50 to 64, women were more likely than men to live in nonfamily households. Due to gender differences in mortality, men in these households were more likely to have had marriages dissolve due to separation or divorce (68.9%) than were women, who were almost equally likely to be widowed (50%) as divorced or separated (42.8%). During the elder years, ages 65 and over, the gap between men and women's residence in nonfamily households widens. In our study, 43.2% of women and 20.6% of men lived in households without family members. Over one half of elderly women (55.3%) and about one third of men lived alone. The majority of elderly men (58%) and women (80.9%) not living with family members were widows.

Nuclear Married-Couple Households

Across the family life cycle, nuclear married-couple households vary in age configuration (Aldous, 1990; Hill & Mattessich, 1979). As is suggested by the family developmental perspective, there was substantial variation in nuclear married-couple households as respondents aged. In addition, because of the lower rates of marriage and remarriage among African American women, residence in nuclear married-couple households varied by gender as well. In the NSBA sample, 49.7% of male respondents lived in nuclear married-couple household compared to 30% for women.

Early Adulthood

In early adulthood, ages 18 to 24, men and women were equally likely to live in nuclear married-couple households. About 30% of young adult respondents lived in this household type; however, there were two types of patterns found: (a) young adults living in their parents' household and (b) young married couples. These patterns reflect different points in the family life cycle (i.e., the launching of adult children and early family formation) and vary by gender. Over one half of young men (57.5%) living in nuclear married-couple households were never married and living with their parents. In contrast, about two thirds of young adult women who lived in nuclear married-couple households were married with children. Women and men who lived with their parents were most often never married and did not have children. A significant minority of young adult respondents, however, 27.7% of men and 16% of women, had children who did not live with them.

Men and women's residence in nuclear married-couple households also diverged in the 25 to 34 age group. This is primarily due to the movement of men into nuclear married-couple households. Almost 6 out of 10 men (58.3%) lived in nuclear married-couple households. The majority of these men were married (93.3%) and heading households. The percentage of women, ages 25 to 34, who lived in nuclear married-couple households did not differ from the under 25 age group. Women may not be entering into nuclear families as married heads at the same rate as men. Alternatively, women who married earlier may be beginning to exit marriages, thereby offsetting any increase in nuclear married-couple formation among women who are 25 to 34 years old.

Middle to Late Adulthood

Middle-aged women, ages 35 to 49, were more likely (37.5%) to live in married-couple nuclear households than women in all other age groups. Middle-aged men were as likely as younger men (ages 25 to 34) to live in married-couple nuclear households, perhaps reflecting men's continued advantage in the marriage market. The patterns for women may be a cohort effect, age effect, or both. Women born between 1930-1944 have lower divorce rates than post-World War II birth cohorts and the rate of widowhood is higher for women born prior to 1930 (Epenshade, 1987; Walker, 1988). Alternatively, some women who exit marriages under age 35 may reenter marital relationships in middle age. At 50 years and older, the percentage of men and women who live in married-couple households declines.

During middle age there are also shifts in the family life cycle. Among married-couple household heads aged 35 to 49, 77.5% were rearing children under 18 and about 30% had adult offspring living with them. Among older respondents aged 50 to 64, approximately 26.5% lived with minor children and 24% lived with adult offspring. Only about 8% of the respondents over 65 lived in nuclear married-couple households with offspring.

Nuclear Single-Parent Households

Residence in single-parent nuclear family households varied dramatically by gender, both in prevalence and type. Twenty-seven percent of women and less than 8% of men lived in nuclear single-parent households. For women, single parenthood was an alternative family form. The peaks and valleys in the likelihood of women's residence in nuclear single-parent households varied by age and reflected shifts associated with the family life cycle. Men tended to live in nuclear single-parent households most frequently during early adulthood, primarily as the adult offspring of female heads of households. Men typically transition out of nuclear single-parent households during early adulthood.

Early Adulthood

During early adulthood, ages 18 to 24, 20.8% of young adult men and 27.2% of women lived in single-parent nuclear households. Gender differences in percentage of men and women living in these households were smallest during this period. The position of men and women in nuclear single-parent households, however, was quite different. Most men were never married and few were parents. Most women were never married, but, 70% were parents. Among the few women who were formerly married, all were parents. Thus, for most young adult women, residence in nuclear single-parent households represented a transition to nonmarital parenthood and independent households—whereas young adult men in these households continued to live with a parent, primarily their mothers.

The likelihood of men living in nuclear single-parent households dropped considerably after age 24. Among the few men aged 25 to 34 who lived in nuclear single-parent households, most were never married (61.5%) and two thirds were parents (formerly married and never married). Although all of the formerly married men in single-parent nuclear households had children, none appeared to be the custodial parent. Hence, most men who lived in nuclear single-parent households in this age group appear to be living with their family of origin, as did younger men. For women, single parenthood was an alternative family trajectory. Nuclear single-parent households was the modal family type (43.6%) for women aged 25 to 34. The majority of the women were formerly married women with children and 30% were never married mothers. These patterns represent two distinct pathways to nuclear single-parent households for women in this age group.

Middle to Late Adulthood

During midlife, ages 35 to 49, about one third of women lived in single-parent nuclear households but few middle-aged men lived in this type of household. Most middle-aged adults living in nuclear single-parent households were separated or divorced. Most respondents were still rearing children—85% lived in households with children under 18, and about 31% had adult children living with them. After the primary child rearing years, ages 50 and older, the percentage of women living in nuclear single-parent households continues to decline. This trend is likely a function of adult children leaving home. Among respondents aged 50 to 64 who continued to live in nuclear single-parent households, two thirds lived with adult children and over one half (54.5%) were raising minor offspring. During late adulthood, ages 65 and over, few men or women lived in nuclear single-parent households. Among those who did, about 31% appeared to be under the care of their adult children. A few older respondents were rearing children under 18.

Extended Family Households: Married Couples and Single Heads

Extended family households tend to be child rearing households, that is, households with minor children. During young and late adulthood, respondents were more likely to live with extended kin across gender and extended family type. At just under 8%, men and women were equally likely to reside in extended family households headed by a married couple. Women (11.8%) were about twice as likely as men (6.6%) to live in extended family households headed by a single person. There were also significant variations in the marital and childbearing trajectories of respondents living in extended family households by type of headship.

Married-Couple Headed: Young to Late Adulthood

Of young women, ages 24 and under, 69% who lived in extended married-couple households were never married mothers. This suggests that unmarried parenthood is a frequent source of family extension in households headed by married couples. From middle age to preretirement years, ages 35 to 64, respondents living in extended family households were more likely to be household heads and appeared to be taking others in. Most married household heads (90.1%) were taking in children and relatively few included older relatives. It appears that extended family households tend to form by extending "downward." This is consistent with other studies of extended living arrangements among black adults (Beck & Beck, 1984, 1989) and children (Hofferth, 1985; Hunter & Ensminger, 1992).

Single-Person Headed: Young to Late Adulthood

Single-headed extended households include two family types: (a) single-person heads, without a spouse or offspring present, and relatives, and (b) single parents with offspring and other relatives. Single-headed extended family households include a variety of generational configurations and reflect different types of extended family formation. Like extended married-couple households, the percentage of extended single-headed households with children under age 18 remains high regardless of the age of the respondent. Only in households with an elderly respondent, ages 65 and older, do less than one half of the households include minor children. It is noteworthy, however, that 43% of elderly respondents who live in extended family households shared a residence with children under age 18.

Single-headed extended households also appear to provide alternative family living arrangements for never married and formerly married men and women. Young adult men and women most frequently lived in these households. As was found in other family household types, some young adults in single-headed extended households continue to live with a parent. Many were also parents themselves, 42.8% were never married mothers, and 30% were never married fathers. Interestingly, never married men who lived in these households were more likely to be fathers than never married young adult men living elsewhere. It is unclear whether more of these men were custodial parents or at least shared a residence with their children. Young never married women, ages 18 to 24, were less likely to be parents in extended single-person headed households than were young women in extended married-couple households. Perhaps for young adult women without children, living with other adult kin (e.g., cousins, siblings, aunts) may be a step toward an independent living arrangement after leaving their parental home.

Many of the men and women who lived in extended single-headed households during early adulthood and midlife did not follow conventional marital and family patterns. Most men and women under age 35 were never married. Of never married women, 72% were parents, the same rate as formerly married women. Over one half (54.4%) of the men were never married parents. Until age 35, men and women lived in extended single-headed households at similar rates with the percentage of never marrieds remaining high. After age 35, this living arrangement began to diverge by gender and marital status. There was a decrease in the percentage of men in these households during midlife and an increase in the percentage of formerly married women.

Cohabiting Families: Young to Late Adulthood

Less than 2% of respondents lived in a cohabiting family household. The prevalence of this living arrangement did not vary by gender, but, residence in cohabiting family households occurred most frequently among adults under age 35. Most young adults, age 24 and under, who lived in cohabiting households were never married. Of cohabiting women, 43.8% and 50% of men had their own children. Among cohabitants, ages 26 to 34, 90% were never married parents. Although this is a small group, they had the highest rates of never married parenthood of any age group. After age 25, there was a decline in the percentage of respondents living in cohabiting family households. As cohabitants age they were more likely to have been married.

Summary and Conclusions

The living arrangements of African American adults varied by age, gender, and family status. Although household types were diverse, the majority of respondents lived with family members. Where respondents lived also had implications for their economic well-being. Nonfamily, nuclear single parent, and single-headed extended households were more likely to cluster at the lowest income levels. Although cross-sectional data does not allow us to look at changes over time or to disentangle effects due to age, cohort, and period (Riley, 1986), the variations in living arrangements reported are suggestive of the diverse pathways to any given household destination. In addition, these findings illustrate the importance of considering age, the intergenerational family life cycle, and individual family trajectories (e.g., marriage, divorce, never married childbearing) in cross-sectional studies of family structure and living arrangements.

Longitudinal studies of household trajectories and individual living arrangements document well the intricacies and complexity of change (e.g., Chevan & Sutton, 1985; Richards et al., 1987; White & Tsui, 1986). Living arrangements reflect shifting family roles and responsibilities across the family life cycle and life span (e.g., childbearing and rearing, launching of offspring) (Hareven, 1987; Hill & Mattessich, 1979; Elder, 1991). In addition, the constraints and opportunities that give rise to specific family and nonfamily living arrangements are broadly shaped by economic resources and opportunities (Bianchi, 1981; Darity & Myers, 1984), the parameters of the extended kin group (e.g., composition, proximity) (Martin & Martin, 1978; Shimikin, Shimikin, & Frate, 1978), demographic characteristics of a population (e.g., age structure, sex ratio) (Guttentag & Secord, 1983; South & Lloyd, 1992; Tucker & Taylor, 1987), and the cultural framework through which people evaluate their circumstances (Angel & Tienda, 1982; Burton, 1990; Elder, 1978; Levine, 1977; Stack & Burton, 1993). This study explored only the product of these processes. As we attempt to understand the complexities of African American families, understanding what factors influence with whom people live and under what conditions is an important area of inquiry.

16

Husbands, Wives, Family, and Friends
Sources of Stress, Sources of Support

HAROLD W. NEIGHBORS

Introduction and Overview

Estimating the magnitude of mental health needs and the degree to which these needs are being met was one of the many goals of the National Survey of Black Americans (NSBA). Following in the tradition of the classic study of the public's willingness to turn to professional help for assistance with life problems, *Americans View Their Mental Health* (Gurin, Veroff, & Feld, 1960), the NSBA took a nondiagnostic, problem-focused approach to the study of mental health needs (Neighbors & Jackson, 1996b, pp. 1-13). Rather than impose professional, psychiatric perspectives of distress on survey respondents, the need for professional mental health services was examined from the ethno-cultural perspective of black community residents. Respondents were asked to define a personally upsetting incident and to list the various sources of help they consulted to cope with this serious personal problem. Over the years, cumulative results from the NSBA have highlighted the tremendous impact these lay conceptualizations of distress have on where African Americans turn for help (Neighbors, 1985, 1991; Neighbors & Howard, 1987; Neighbors & Taylor, 1985). Such findings have convinced us of the need to focus more directly on differential problem definition.

277

In fact, the NSBA data on help seeking behavior raises the more basic question of what we actually mean when we speak of "having a problem." The word "problem" certainly has negative connotations. Problems are sources of distress—things to be avoided or obstacles to be overcome. They interrupt the normal flow of life and, when chronic and severe, can cause unhappiness and even depression. Perhaps no type of problem is as upsetting as conflict with members of one's immediate social support network. The need to belong or to feel part of a community is essential for personal well-being (Chatters & Taylor, 1990, pp. 84-85; Schwab & Schwab, 1978, pp. 158-178; Weissman, Myers, & Ross, 1986, p. 5). This position is further supported by the fact that almost 90% of respondents in the NSBA reported seeking help from family and friends when confronted with a serious personal problem (Neighbors & Jackson, 1984). Yet, surprisingly, the NSBA data also show that the most frequently mentioned types of personal problems were those that occurred as a result of interpersonal difficulties within the informal social network (Neighbors, 1996). This chapter uses data from the NSBA to explore the paradox that the people we rely on for help during times of crisis may be the very same people who at other times tend to initiate those crises.

The Importance of Family and Friends

No other aspect of black survival has been more written about than the role of African American families (Taylor, Chatters, Tucker, & Lewis, 1990; Taylor, Tucker, Chatters, & Jayakody, Chapter 2, this volume). Black families are seen as the first line of defense against racism and are a primary mechanism for upward social mobility (Davis, 1981, p. 130; McAdoo, 1981, p. 156). In short, black extended families and their conceptual offshoot, social support, are fundamental to the well-being of African Americans. Previous analyses of the NSBA data clearly document that African American extended families are an excellent source of support (Jackson, 1991). More than 90% of the NSBA respondents said they feel very or fairly close to other family members. In terms of frequency of contact, it appears that black family members "stay in touch" with each other on a regular basis. When asked how often they saw, wrote, or talked on the phone with family and relatives, 66% said nearly every day or at least once per week. Only 6% said as little as a few times per year, and a mere 2% said they never contacted relatives. Female-headed households with children and people living alone reported the highest levels of contact with relatives (Hatchet, Cochran, & Jackson, 1991, pp. 68-69). Other NSBA results reveal how often family members help each other out. For example, 42% of

NSBA respondents indicated that they received help from family and relatives either very often or fairly often—only 29% reported never receiving help.

The NSBA also investigated how African American families cope in the face of adversity. One manner in which the NSBA did this was to ascertain whether people experiencing serious personal difficulties were receiving help for their problems and where that help came from. Previous analyses have documented the extensive use of the informal support network, including family members and relatives, during times of crisis (Neighbors, Jackson, Bowman, & Gurin, 1983). Chatters, Taylor, and Neighbors (1989) found that when faced with a serious personal problem, people were more likely to call on other family members than nonkin. Interestingly, whereas men were more likely to request help from other male family members, particularly brothers, and women in crisis were more apt to seek the assistance of sisters, there were no gender differences in the use of mothers as helpers (Taylor, Hardison, & Chatters, 1996, p. 135). The importance of informal helpers is also evidenced by the fact that although a little less than half (48.7%) of those with a serious personal problem sought some form of professional help, 87% obtained help with such problems from family, friends, and neighbors (Neighbors & Jackson, 1984).

Neighbors (1986) reported that economic problems were a major source of stress, particularly for low-income respondents. Neighbors & LaVeist (1989) explored the process of coping with economic problems and found that other family members were the main source of help during economically stressful situations. Results indicated that the vast majority (89%) of people experiencing economic difficulties contacted at least one member of their informal network whereas less than half (46%) sought some form of professional help. When informal and professional help were taken together, it was found that only 6% of those with economic problems received no outside help at all. More important, 21% of those who sought help for financial stress were able to translate help seeking into the actual receipt of financial aid, most of that coming from the family and other relatives—only 3% received money from professional sources. The authors found that those who were successful in obtaining financial assistance during an economic crisis displayed significantly lower levels of psychological distress than those who were unsuccessful in obtaining material aid from their informal support networks.

Although we know that being able to successfully obtain help during tough times is crucial for survival and advancement, it can also be a source of strain, especially among those providing assistance (Bengtson, Rosenthal, & Burton, 1996, pp. 262-263). Thus, although black families have been a tremendous resource in the survival and progress of African Americans, the necessity of relying so heavily on kin relations can stretch scarce resources beyond acceptable limits, thereby causing a new and different set of crises that must be dealt with. In fact, it has been argued that repeated requests for informal help for problems and needs that are burdensome "may severely tax support providers and actually diminish potential resources for assistance" (Chatters & Taylor, 1990, p. 89). Similarly, Hatchet, Cochran, and Jackson (1991) point out that "although extended households may be supportive in terms of providing the possibility of multiple earners, help with household tasks and child care, and socioemotional support, they can also be stressful because of dependency of very young or very old relatives and possible personal conflict" (Hatchett et al., 1991, pp. 80-81). The fact that many African Americans are confronted with serious family difficulties is also confirmed by NSBA data on the prevalence of personal problems. Of the NSBA sample, 63% reported that they had experienced a problem that had interfered with social functioning—and almost half of them (47%) felt that the problem had driven them to the point of a nervous breakdown. More important, when we look specifically at how the NSBA respondents defined these problems, the vast majority (41%) stated that they were stressed as a result of interpersonal difficulties. Interpersonal problems within this context refer to the inability to resolve some important situation or "get along" with a family member or some close acquaintance within the immediate social support network. Given the finding that 87% sought help from informal helpers, it was surprising to discover that members of those same informal networks were also the most frequently mentioned source of problems.

The nature of what we mean when we refer to interpersonal problems within the context of the NSBA is complex and needs further investigation. This is clearly indicated by results reported by Washington (1996) in her examination of the use of police as a social service resource for African Americans. Washington found that most respondents (93%), in addition to consulting police, sought assistance from members of their informal networks. When the exact sources of informal help were explored, it was clear that respondents limited their requests for informal help almost exclusively to other family members. These results raised questions about the contextual meaning of personal problems, because over three fourths of those seeking the assistance of police did so as a result of interpersonal difficulties. Interestingly, Washington discovered that most of the interpersonal problems were confrontations that women were having with boyfriends or husbands. These results raise negative connotations with respect to the types of social situations categorized as "interpersonal problems" within the NSBA. Such results, although certainly provocative, must be considered with caution due to the very small number of NSBA respondents who actually did seek help from the police. This further underlines the necessity of proceeding with a more comprehensive analysis of the meaning of interpersonal problems in the NSBA.

In summary, a number of prior publications using data from the NSBA have raised the possibility that family members who provide social support during times of crisis are also the very same persons who, at other times, are sources of stress. Thus, the purpose of this chapter is to conduct an in-depth exploration of the meaning of those stressful problems previously categorized more generally as interpersonal problems (Neighbors, 1991). We do not have enough detailed information about the nature of interpersonal problems as defined in the NSBA. We need to know more about where people turn for help when informal helpers are causing difficulties. We do not know how many of these interpersonal problems have to do with conflict between spouses. Neither do we know how many involve family more broadly defined. In fact, we do not really know if these are problems in the negative sense implied by Washington's (1996) results. It is important to ask whether it is always the case that interpersonal problems are difficulties in the sense that a friend or family member is doing something upsetting or disturbing to the respondent. The topic addressed in this chapter should add substantially to our knowledge of how families and social support operate during crisis situations.

Method

The Sample

All analyses presented here were performed on the National Survey of Black Americans Panel Study. All results were weighted to reflect the original 2,107 NSBA cross-section respondents. For a more detailed description of the Panel Study, the reader is referred to Jackson and Wolford (1992). The analyses revealed remarkable consistency across the data collections. Therefore, to save space, only findings from the NSBA cross section are presented.

The Measures

To address issues relevant to how differential problem definitions affect help-seeking behavior, each respondent who had experienced a problem was probed to describe the details of the problem in their own words. This question was designed to ascertain how the person conceptualized the nature of the distress experienced. It represents the specific locus to which the respondents attributed the causes of their distress. Responses were categorized into five problem categories: (a) physical health problems, (b) interpersonal difficulties, (c) emotional adjustment problems, (d) death of a loved one, and (e) economic difficulties. All prior analyses have focused on this five-category variable. The present analysis redefines the general interpersonal problems (Category 2 above) as described here.

Problem Type

All types of previously coded interpersonal difficulties had been "lumped" together, thereby sacrificing some of the richness and diversity of what is actually meant by interpersonal problems. So, for example, problems related to spouses, family (parents, children, and relatives) as well as friends, neighbors, and coworkers were all categorized together. This chapter "breaks apart" these gross categories to explore the variability and heterogeneity of what has been previously referred to as interpersonal problems (Neighbors, 1996).

To conduct a more in-depth exploration of the meaning of previously coded "interpersonal" problems, it was necessary to perform a detailed inspection of the original responses at the individual respondent level. This process entailed an item-by-item inspection of the code book definitions used to define the problem type variable. This process was performed by the author and a research assistant who carefully compared the recoding process. In doing this initial exploration, we discovered a number of personal problems that had previously been coded into other, noninterpersonal problems categories, such as economic, death, or financial. Thus, even though these problem descriptions may have mentioned money (to use an economic example), they also had as much to do with interpersonal dynamics as they did with financial concerns. Therefore, any code previously defined as "nonresidential financial matters that happened to respondent's spouse" for example, was recoded to interpersonal for the analyses reported here. Similarly, many problems previously coded as health concerns (e.g., "physical illness of respondent's parents" or "violence-crime—respondent's child as victim") were also coded interpersonal.

Help Seeking

The ability to describe variability in problems, needs, and help seeking among African Americans is a major strength of the NSBA. Investigating black help seeking in this manner provides a much more complete understanding of the various forces influencing how African Americans use informal helpers to deal with life problems. In this chapter, both informal and formal help seeking will be explored in relation to the new definition of interpersonal problems.

Table 16.1 *Distribution of Types of Serious Problem as Defined by National Survey of Black Americans Respondents*

Type of Problem	N	Percentage
Interpersonal		
Marital	244	20.6
Family	304	25.7
Other-general	113	9.5
Subtotal	661	55.8
Noninterpersonal		
Financial	329	27.8
Physical health	116	9.8
Mental health	79	6.6
Subtotal	524	44.2

Results

Table 16.1 shows the distribution of interpersonal problems as well as those coded as "noninterpersonal" for the purposes of this analysis chapter. The distribution indicates that interpersonal problems are indeed very prevalent. More than half (56%) of the personal problems mentioned by respondents are interpersonal in nature. Within the interpersonal problem category, Table 16.1 reveals that about 1 in 5 (21%) are marital problems and 1 in 4 (26%) are family problems. Another way to look at this is to say that the vast majority of interpersonal problems are kin-related. In fact, 83% (548 of 661) of the interpersonal problems involve the nuclear family, extended family (e.g., spouse, parent, child, sibling, and relatives), or both in some way. Even more interesting is the fact that almost half (45%) of the kin-related interpersonal problems are marital problems. Very few (10%) of the interpersonal problems involve situations with friends and acquaintances. A little more than 44% of the personal problems are due to noninterpersonal issues, the majority of which have to do with financial (28%) concerns. Given the chapter's focus, the remaining tables collapse across the financial, physical, and mental health problems (labeled as noninterpersonal) to highlight variations in the subcategories of interpersonal problems.

Table 16.2 shows how gender, marital status, and family income are related to a dichotomous definition of serious problems into interpersonal and noninterpersonal. Whereas Table 16.2 does not reveal dramatic differences in the

Table 16.2 *Relationship of Gender, Marital Status, and Family Income to Type of Personal Problems (interpersonal vs. noninterpersonal)*

	Interpersonal (%)	Noninterpersonal (%)	N	X^2
Gender				29.5***
Male	44.7	55.3	394	
Female	61.3	38.7	791	
Marital status				15.7***
Married	55.8	44.2	464	
Nonmarried	61.3	38.7	462	
Never married	45.9	54.1	259	
Family income				8.9**
< $10,000	52.2	47.8	517	
$10,000 +	61.4	38.6	528	

$*p < .05; **p < .01; ***p < .001.$

distribution of interpersonal problems, all three demographic variables are significantly related to the prevalence of the dichotomous interpersonal problem variable. Women are much more likely than men to mention some type of interpersonal problem as causing them significant distress. Specifically, 61% of women but only 45% of men mentioned an interpersonal problem. With respect to marital status, the highest rate of interpersonal difficulties is reported among the previously married (61%), which is significantly different from the lower prevalence (46%) among the never married group. Finally, upper income respondents are more likely than those making less than $10,000 to report interpersonal problems.

In exploring the specific nature of the kinds of interpersonal problems mentioned, it became evident that there were actually two types of interpersonal problems that caused people a significant amount of distress. One type was related to stressful situations or crises that happened to the significant other of the respondent, for example, "my spouse had a heart attack," or "my aunt died." These types of problems were labeled as interpersonal problems showing concern. The second type of interpersonal problem involved matters describing difficulties between the respondent and the significant other. For example, people with these types of problems made statements such as "I was getting a divorce from my husband," or "I can't get along with my boss at work," or "my kids were driving me crazy." Such problems were coded as mentioning issues of conflict. After coding responses to differentiate interpersonal problems of conflict from interpersonal problems of concern, Table 16.3

Table 16.3 *Distribution of Interpersonal Problems of Conflict, Interpersonal Problems of Concern, and Noninterpersonal Problems*

Type of Personal Problem	N	Percentage
Interpersonal-conflict	429	36.2
Interpersonal-concern	232	19.6
Noninterpersonal	524	44.2

shows that over one third (36%) of the interpersonal problems show conflict whereas 20% of the interpersonal problems are problems of concern. Table 16.4 explores the conflict-concern dimension by the same demographic variables explored in Table 16.2. Women are slightly more likely than men to report interpersonal problems of conflict as well as interpersonal problems of concern. As was shown in Table 16.2, men are much more likely than women to focus on noninterpersonal problems. No dramatic differences in the distribution of problems of conflict and concern are revealed with respect to marital status. Respondents making $10,000 or more are much more likely to have mentioned interpersonal problems of both conflict and concern, again reflecting the fact that noninterpersonal problems of a financial nature are likely to be more salient among lower income people.

Table 16.4 shows the distribution of conflict and concern within the specific types (i.e., marital, family, other) of interpersonal problems. Table 16.5 shows that people with marital problems are much more likely to characterize those problems as involving conflict than as problems of concern. Specifically, 17% of the problems with spouses are categorized as involving conflict whereas only 4% of the marital problems had to do with concern issues. Among people reporting problems in the family problems area, concern and conflict were equally split; 13% of the interpersonal problems had to do with family conflict and 13% dealt with problems of family concern. Finally, nonmarriage, nonfamilial interpersonal problems of a general nature, although relatively low in prevalence, show that conflict problems are higher than problems of concern, 7% and 3% respectively.

Demographic differences in the prevalence of the specific types of interpersonal problems taking issues of conflict and concern into account are explored in Table 16.6. Table 16.6 shows a higher prevalence of all types of interpersonal problems (except conflict problems labeled "other") among women than men. In general, however, the differences between men and women are not

Table 16.4 *Relationship of Demographics to Interpersonal Problems Showing Conflict, Concern, and Noninterpersonal Problems*

	Conflict (%)	Concern (%)	Noninterpersonal	N	X^2
Gender					32.1[a]
Male	31.2	13.3	55.3	394	
Female	38.7	22.6	38.7	791	
Marital status					20.3
Married	35.6	20.3	44.2	464	
Nonmarried	38.3	22.9	38.7	462	
Never married	33.6	12.4	54.1	259	
Family income					13.1
< $10,000	31.7	20.5	47.8	517	
$10,000 +	42.2	19.1	38.6	528	

a. All relationships were significant at $p < .001$.

Table 16.5 *Distribution of Conflict and Concern Problems and Specific Type of Problem*

Type of Problem	N	Percentage
Marital Problems		
Conflict	195	16.5
Concern	49	4.1
Family Problems		
Conflict	152	12.8
Concern	152	12.8
Marital Problems		
Conflict	82	6.9
Concern	31	2.6
Noninterpersonal	524	44.2

dramatic with respect to marital problems, either of conflict or concern. The major gender difference revealed by Table 16.6 is that women appear to be more likely than men to mention family problems, especially those involving conflict. Specifically, 14% of women as opposed to 10% of men mentioned family conflict problems. Similarly, 15% of the women compared to 8% of the men mentioned family concern problems as causing distress. In general, marital conflict problems were the most frequently mentioned type of interpersonal

Table 16.6 Relationship of Gender, Marital Status and Family Income to Serious Personal Problems showing both Conflict/Concern and Problem Type

	Interpersonal Problems showing Conflict			Interpersonal Problems showing Concern			Non-IP	N	X^2
	Marital	Family	Other	Marital	Family	Other			
Gender									41.5*
Male	13.7	9.6	7.9	3.0	7.9	2.5	55.3	394	
Female	17.8	14.4	6.4	4.7	15.3	2.7	38.7	791	
Marital Status									249.6*
Married	17.0	15.1	3.4	4.3	14.4	1.5	44.2	464	
Not Married	25.1	10.6	2.6	6.3	13.6	3.0	38.7	462	
Never Married	0.0	12.7	20.8	0.0	8.5	3.9	54.1	259	
Family Income									32.2*
<$10,000	13.0	12.8	6.0	4.8	12.4	3.3	47.8	517	
$10,000 +	20.6	12.7	8.9	4.0	13.3	1.9	38.6	528	

*$p < .001$.

287

problem for both women (18%) and men (14%). The other consistent trend is the higher involvement of women in family-related problems of both concern and conflict, which is more than offset by male overrepresentation on the non-interpersonal problem category. The analysis also explored gender differences controlling for marital status and very similar male-female patterns emerged (tables available from the author).

Table 16.6 also shows the relationships of marital status and family income to the detailed breakdown of interpersonal and noninterpersonal problems. With the exception of the fact that those who have never been married do not, of course, report any marital difficulties, no dramatic or noticeable differences in marital status stand out in Table 16.6. There is some indication that the never married group has a higher prevalence of nonfamily (other) interpersonal problems of conflict. Finally, Table 16.6 reveals that when looking at family income, the initial pattern of a higher prevalence of interpersonal problems among the higher income group (indicated in Table 16.2) remains. In general, however, the detailed distribution of the various types of interpersonal problems are surprisingly equal across the two income groups. The only exception to this trend is the higher prevalence of marital conflict problems (21% compared to 13%) among those making $10,000 or more.

The use of family and friends in response to interpersonal problems is quite high. The percentage using family ranges from a low of 64% for other types of interpersonal problems to 78% for family concerns to 86% for general conflict. The same pattern holds for the use of friends. Here, percentages range from 58% for general concern to 74% for marital conflict to 74% for family conflict. In short, personal problems with family or friends, either conflict or concern, do not differentiate whether the respondent turns to the informal network for help. All types of problems are taken to the informal network in roughly equal percentages. Overall, respondents who do seek professional help are most likely to seek it from their physicians (35%) and ministers (30%).[1] There is very low use of mental health resources, with only 7% going to a community mental health center and 15% going to a psychiatrist or psychologist. About 20% went to either the hospital or the medical clinic. Results with respect to the use of professional help are not striking, except that people are much less likely to seek formal rather than informal help for interpersonal problems. Of the professional sources, the role of the doctor and minister is highlighted. People do not seem to discriminate the types of problems taken to these two help sources.

Discussion

By the very nature of the questions used in the NSBA, this chapter presents a selective view of African American problems. Specifically, we asked people to dip into their bag of troubles and think only about those that were the most serious. It is important to put these findings into context, because the meaning of interpersonal problems for the typical African American depends on the situation and the nature of the difficulty (McKenry & Price, 1994). It is important to note that not all situations identified as problems were the result of disagreements or family discord. Many of these problems were stressful because of a sense of concern for the pain and suffering experienced by a member of the informal network. A substantial number of these serious personal problems had to do with the strain associated with the help and support offered by the respondent to another family member.

The overall conclusion supported by the data reported here is a more positive impression of informal help and support for interpersonal difficulties among African Americans than was originally expected given the "problem-focused" orientation of the NSBA approach to mental health need assessment. Despite the fact that personal relationships can at times be troubling, the findings on help seeking clearly show that informal helpers are there when they are needed, much more so than professional services.

McAdoo (1981) highlighted the "inherent reciprocity" of social networks that requires families to keep resources fluid and open to those considered to be members of the extended family network. This helped to ensure that the positive aspects outweighed the negative aspects of involvement within the kin network (McAdoo, 1981, p. 163). This contrasts somewhat with the picture of informal exchanges in "the Flats" painted by Stack (1974) and others (Bowman, 1996) who have shown that the struggle to obtain adequate financial resources is a significant stressor for many African American families. Stack found that attempts to ameliorate economic deprivation can occasionally disrupt the stability of black male-female bonds. Family members will sometimes work against the formation and maintenance of relationships if that relationship causes a drain on the economic resources of the extended network (see Stack, 1974, p. 112). "People in the Flats recognize that one cannot simultaneously meet kin expectations and the expectations of a spouse. Although cooperating kinsmen continually attempt to draw new people into their personal networks, they fear the loss of a central, resourceful member in the network" (Stack, 1974, pp. 113-114). Stack concludes that there can be strong conflicts between kin-based domestic units and lasting ties between husbands and wives in that a relationship with an unproductive man dilutes the resources of the kin network. Network participants try to break up the relationship to maximize their potential resources and the services they expect to exchange.

Despite the fact that many interpersonal difficulties were problems of concern, it deserves noting that when interpersonal problems were due to conflict, they were disproportionately found to be related to issues of marriage. This was true among the currently married as well as the previously married. Consistent with the high divorce rate and marital disruptions that affect all ethnic groups, but especially African American families, these findings raise some cause for concern. Many have speculated that the inability of some black husbands to assume the role of primary provider for the family might contribute to marital instability (Hatchet et al., 1991, p. 103; Tucker & Taylor, 1989). That is, unstable economic conditions may place undue stress on families as black married women attempt to find ways to be supportive of their husbands' feelings of discouragement in a society that emphasizes the married man's responsibility to be the "good-provider/bread-winner," while, at the same time, inhibiting the black male's ability to achieve that status (Bowman, 1992, pp. 138, 148-149; Tucker & Mitchell-Kernan, 1995a, pp. 167-168, 350). Hatchet et al. (1991) questioned the value African Americans place on the institution of marriage. These authors reported that 50% of respondents in the NSBA disagreed with the statement, "There are so few good marriages that I don't know if I want to get married." Similarly, more than 40% felt they were unsure about marrying because "there were so few good marriages" (see Hatchet et al., 1991, p. 100). Interestingly, there were no male-female differences in these attitudes. Married and never married respondents, both male and female, were more likely to hold a positive view of marriage. Thus, although Hatchet et al. (1991) conclude that the NSBA findings indicate that marriage is still valued among many African Americans, Tucker and Mitchell-Kernan (1995a, p. 100) state that whereas blacks still prefer marriage (particularly black men), they are increasingly accepting of remaining single.

The findings on marital conflict problems also raise questions about the relationship of marital status to emotional well-being. Brown (1996) explored marital status in relation to psychological distress using data from the NSBA. She concluded that although being married is better than being separated or divorced, being married is not necessarily better than having never married (p. 92). Brown speculated that this finding could be due to gender differences in what men and women derive from marriage. Even more interesting (and provocative), Brown found that even though previously married women evidenced the highest levels of psychological distress, separated and divorced black women preferred their current marital status to being married. Divorced and separated men, on the other hand, would rather have remained married.

These issues convinced us that the marital problem data deserved a closer inspection of the specifics surrounding gender differences in conflict and concern. The vast majority of women who evidenced a marital conflict problem (74%), talked about "having trouble" (e.g., quarreling, arguing, fighting, and not being able to get along in the marriage). This compared to 48% of the men, who, along with having trouble were also likely to mention "marital separation" (19%) and the specifics of actually going through a divorce (26%). Men and women looked more similar in the specifics of marital concern problems. Here, half of the men as well as half of the women volunteered that it was the death of their spouse that was most upsetting. Another one third of the men and 30% of the women mentioned a health problem of the spouse. Women were more likely than men to mention an unwanted pregnancy (19% vs. 8%) as the source of their concern. Interestingly, when gender differences in specific family conflict problems were explored, women were much more likely than men to mention child rearing (38% compared to 8%) as a source of conflict.

Conclusions

In summary, these results from a nationally representative sample of adult African Americans paint a realistic picture of African American informal networks. Informal social support is a "double-edged sword." Black social networks have and will continue to provide the kind of support crucial for successful adaptation to the stressful situations that characterize the lives of most African Americans. At the same time, it is clear that the provision of such support does, at times, take its toll on members of the network. Bengtson et al. (1996) commented on the paradox that families evidence, over time, both solidarity and conflict, noting that we actually "know very little about the tenuous balance between them" (p. 269).

It is a testament to the centrally important and highly valued role of the family that, when asked to think back over the many problems faced during their lives, so many of the respondents mentioned interpersonal difficulties as being their most significant stressful event. This demonstrates the salience of family issues for African Americans. It is true that we are upset most when things go wrong in those life domains we value most highly. The findings reported in this chapter support the conclusion that although black family dynamics can precipitate problematic encounters, kin-based networks are highly valued and, as such, remain the "first line of defense" when individuals need help in dealing with the inevitable challenges of family life.

Appendix: What Did Black Couples Say?

1. One man put it this way: "When my wife was home, she was extremely rebellious, disrespectful; she loved to hurt extremely and deeply; she'd find your weakness." (M, 2,004)

2. Another man said, "Me and my wife—when we was talking about divorcing." (M, 1,996)

3. "I was married to a hypochondriac, a self-centered, psychosomatic mate, which made life unbearable, always creating problems. I can go on the rest of the night but I won't. I made money too fast. I took her out of Montgomery Ward and put her in Nan Duskin. She didn't know how to act." (M, 1,767)

4. "It was personal. It was a delicate problem between filing for divorce, certain people felt I should and certain people felt I shouldn't. I was going batty and didn't know what to do." (F, 0958)

5. "It was about me going back to school. My child was about 9 months old and I wanted to go back to school and my husband didn't want me to go back to school." (F, 0927)

6. "I was trying to save my marriage." (F, 1,364)

7. "My husband—he had a drinking problem." (F, 1,264)

8. "My husband's ex-girlfriend; it involves another child." (F, 0399)

9. "My love life—he was just messin' up." (F, 0300)

10. "Marriage . . . I don't care to discuss it in any detail." (M, 0045)

11. "About marriage." (M, 0006)

12. "I was married then. Lack of communication between myself and my wife. I don't know if I was about to have a nervous breakdown or a suicide. If it hadn't been a divorce it would have been one of the two." (M, 0021)

Note

1. The placement of ministers within the professional category is somewhat arbitrary because the minister is someone who is sometimes viewed as part of the informal network. On the other hand, although not equivalent to a health care provider, some ministers are trained in pastoral counseling and are clearly different from the typical family member or friend.

17

Changes Over Time in Support Network Involvement Among Black Americans

ROBERT JOSEPH TAYLOR
LINDA M. CHATTERS
JAMES S. JACKSON

A long tradition of theory and research in the social sciences has documented the critical position and functions of supportive networks for the well-being of black Americans. These supportive networks, organized within family, friendship, church, and neighborhood settings, exert diverse and far-reaching influences on individuals, families, and communities. Although the most widely investigated support networks are those organized within the family, church, friend, and neighborhood networks are receiving increasing attention in the literature. These informal networks provide a variety of assistance including the provision of instrumental or material assistance (e.g., food, money, transportation, running errands), cognitive aid (e.g., advice, counseling), and emotional support (e.g., visiting, companionship). Among the many functions of support, assistance from network members is useful for coping with serious health problems (Chatters, Taylor, & Neighbors, 1989) and in buffering the negative impact of psychological distress (Brown & Gary, 1985; Thomas, Milburn, Brown, & Gary, 1988). Informal network members are also critical links to referrals for jobs (Taylor & Sellers, Chapter 8, this volume) and professional social service providers (Taylor, Neighbors, & Broman, 1989). Given the diversity in types of assistance, face-to-face interaction and proximity of family members are not strict prerequisites for receiving support.

Black Families in Transition

Black families have experienced considerable demographic change in the past 40 years including increases in the rates of nonmarital births, female-headed households, and childhood poverty. A number of scholars argue that these demographic changes have a negative impact on black family life and are potentially detrimental to the functioning of the supportive networks existing within black families. Ultimately, it is suggested that these changes undermine and threaten the viability of black families. Clearly, the challenges facing today's black families are considerable. Demographic events and transitions of the types experienced recently can be expected to have significant impacts on the structure and functioning of families. We suggest, however, that when black families are seen in historical perspective, their experiences in America have been characterized by numerous and repeated encounters with social, economic, and political circumstances that constituted serious threats to their individual and collective well-being. Over the course of their history in the United States, black families have endured the experience of slavery; existed under Jim Crow laws and share-cropping agricultural systems; experienced political and social disenfranchisement, geographic migration, and urbanization; and chronic economic and social hardship. Repeatedly, black families and their support networks have overcome various threats to their existence and well-being.

This discussion is not meant to diminish the real significance and urgency of the present issues facing black families. We argue, however, that there is a need for continued research on how black families respond and adapt to change and challenges. Furthermore, we need data that systematically assesses the operation of family networks, as well as the impact of family events, transitions, and change on supportive networks and relationships. Information of this sort can assist our understanding of how black families address the internal difficulties and challenges that they and their individual members confront.

Black Family Support Networks

The publication of the Moynihan Report (1965) and the ensuing period of research and debate, marks the beginning of contemporary research addressing the support networks of black families. As previous critiques have made clear (Billingsley, 1992; Dilworth-Anderson, Burton, & Johnson, 1993; Staples & Johnson, 1993), the Moynihan Report was an important benchmark in the study of black families. Following the Moynihan Report, a series of books and articles were published that rebutted Moynihan's arguments regarding the structure and operation of black families, critiqued the reification of a particular ideal of what constitutes a family, and decried the lack of appreciation of social and economic context. Several of the most notable works during this period were Andrew Billingsley's (1968) *Black Families in White America,* Robert Hill's (1972) *The Strength of Black Families,* and Carol Stack's (1974) book, *All Our Kin.* This group of studies took as their point of departure an attempt to understand black families as social organizations possessing a distinctive structure and function, that exist within a particular set of social and economic circumstances, and are in contact and interaction with other important institutions in their immediate and broader environment. Notably, this work also made it clear that black families maintain a set of cultural values and perspectives that are uniquely grounded in the historical and contemporary experiences of black Americans in this country. Finally, these efforts underscored the point that given important differences in the social location and circumstances of black Americans (e.g., income, education, region, urbanicity), there exists a multiplicity of ways in which black families define and organize themselves.

This broader perspective on black families introduced the notion that, although black families are clearly affected by broader social forces, they are capable of adapting to new and oftentimes adverse situations and circumstances. These important developments saw a shift from a "social problems" perspective on black families (i.e., the identification of black families with the problems they encounter), to one in which black families were viewed as social organizations that adapt to challenge and change, within the context of both internal and external demands, resources, and opportunities.

Ethnographic approaches conducted during this period recognized the importance of informal support networks for the social and economic viability of black families. This body of research identified specific functional characteristics of informal support networks (i.e., elastic household boundaries, lifelong bonds to three-generational households, elaborate exchange networks), that reflected adaptive responses to socioeconomic conditions of chronic poverty and unemployment (Stack, 1972, 1974). Furthermore, due to the persistence of adverse economic conditions, extended family forms (in addition to their cultural significance for blacks) were viewed as the most enduring and viable family configuration for persons of lower-class status. Collectively, this body of work indicated that blacks used extended family arrangements to pool limited resources, mitigate economic deprivation, and, consequently, create more viable economic units. Extended family members participated in support networks characterized by shared responsibility for child care, joint household cooperation in domestic tasks (i.e., meal preparation, grocery shopping), financial assistance, and the provision of care for aging parents and grandparents.

These early ethnographic studies provided important information on the support networks of black Americans. A major limitation of this work, however, was its lack of generalizability to the broader population. These studies tended to focus on low-income, and to a lesser extent, urban blacks. Furthermore, sampling strategies relied on "snowball" techniques, whereby selected respondents provided names of other potential respondents. As a consequence, study samples were biased in favor of the active members of an identified support network. Individuals who were socially isolated or estranged from their family and friends were typically not included as sample members in the majority of ethnographic studies. As a result, these studies tended to overemphasize the helping behaviors of network members who were heavily involved with their support systems, while underemphasizing the relationships of those who were less involved.

The nature of study samples employed in previous ethnographic research is not a trivial matter, particularly when examining trends in the status of black family support networks. As described previously, studies that are based on the sample generation techniques used in ethnographic research of the early seventies (i.e., snowball techniques) would tend to characterize the support networks of black families as being proximal, cohesive, dense, and responsive to their members. In contrast, more recent survey data employing systematic sampling procedures reveal a slightly different picture of black support networks. Based on these differences, several researchers have concluded that the support networks of black families are less viable now than in the past (e.g., Hogan, Eggebeen, & Clogg, 1993). Clearly, these data reflect very different sampling frames, research strategies, and study objectives. Consequently, it would be incorrect to assume comparability of information from ethnographic and survey approaches or to conclude that these "trends" are evidence of deterioration in black family support networks over time.

Survey Approaches

The past 15 years has seen a substantial increase in survey-based research focusing on the support networks (both kin and nonkin) of black Americans. Some of this work involves small nonprobability samples of particular groups (e.g., Burton & Bengtson, 1985; Stevens, 1984, 1988), whereas other efforts use area-based probability samples (Brown & Gary, 1985; Dressler, 1985). The majority of studies on this topic employing multivariate analysis techniques are derived from the National Survey of Black Americans (NSBA) data set. Research in the area of family assistance has examined support networks among a variety of subgroups of the black population including older adults (Taylor, 1985; Taylor & Chatters, 1991a), women (Coleman, Antonucci, Adelmann, & Crohan, 1987), single and married mothers (Jayakody, Chatters, & Taylor, 1993), adult children (Chatters & Taylor, 1993), and three-generation families (Taylor, Chatters, & Jackson, 1993). Collectively, this research demonstrates that variables such as kin proximity, subjective closeness, and frequency of kinship interaction are especially important predictors of assistance from family. Furthermore, these supportive relationships make important contributions to the physical and emotional well-being of black Americans and family support networks vary significantly with respect to sociodemographic factors (i.e., within-group heterogeneity).

Church Support

Recent work (Taylor & Chatters, 1986a, 1986b, 1988) documents the importance of religious communities as sources of assistance to black Americans. Black Americans frequently affiliate with a church at an early age and develop life-long associations with them. As a result, churches are integrally involved with a number of important life events and transitions such as marriage, the birth of children, personal illness, and losses of significant others. A number of studies identify church involvement variables (e.g., frequency of attendance, perceived importance of church attendance and religion, church membership) as important determinants of support from church members (Taylor & Chatters, 1986a, 1988). These findings are congruent with research on informal support networks more generally and suggest that support from church members is often viewed as a reward for one's past record of participation in church activities and contributions to the broader church community. Taylor and Chatters (1986a) found that church members provided several types of assistance to elderly black adults. Frequency of church attendance, as a form of public commitment, was important for both receiving assistance and the amount of aid provided to older persons. In analyses focusing on adults of all ages, sociodemographic and religious involvement factors (i.e., church attendance, church membership, subjective religiosity, and religious affiliation) were associated with support from church members (Taylor & Chatters, 1988). Overall, two out of three respondents indicated that church members provided some level of support to them. The emergence of network involvement variables as predictors of church support is congruent with other work indicating that assistance is linked to participation and integration in the social network.

Friendship Support

In recent years, nonkin associations or friendships have received increased attention as sources of support to individuals. In contrast to family relationships, which are socially defined and regulated, friendships embody more latitude with respect to the initiation, maintenance, and termination of personal relationships. On the whole, very little research focuses on friendship networks among black Americans. One body of work examined the kinship and friendship interaction patterns of urban blacks (Feagin, 1968; Martineau, 1977; Meadow, 1962). This research, developed largely in reaction to the claims that migration and urbanization had destroyed the social networks of black Americans, documented that urban blacks had frequent contact and involvement with friends. For example, Meadow (1962) reported that 43% of respondents visited with friends at least three times a week; Martineau (1977) found that 40% of respondents interacted with friends three times a week and 75% interacted with friends at least once a week. Among African Americans, family and friends perform distinctive functions in the social network. Family members tend to provide material aid to a greater extent, whereas friends address largely emotional and affiliative concerns (Taylor & Chatters, 1986b). A number of studies, however, demonstrate that friends are important in providing direct and primary support. Using data from two national probability samples, Gibson (1982) found that blacks at middle and late life used friends and neighbors to cope with psychological distress. McAdoo's work examining the support networks of black adults (1978) and black mothers (1980), in particular, confirms that friendships are important sources of assistance. Although kin generally played a more dominant support role, 20% of blacks and 25% of mothers indicated that friends provided more support than did family. Studies focusing on types of support (both given and received) indicate that respondents are more likely to exchange emotional support with friends and financial assistance with family. Recent work indicates that friends and nonkin associates are integral components of the helping networks of black adults (Taylor, Hardison, & Chatters, 1996) and older persons (Chatters, Taylor, & Jackson, 1985, 1986). Furthermore, nonkin are especially prominent in the networks of persons who are not married, who are childless, seldom interact with family members, and who describe their family relations as emotionally distant.

Multiple Sources of Support

Recognizing that individuals can receive assistance from a variety of sources, Taylor and Chatters (1986b) explored the roles of family, friends, and church members in providing assistance to older adults. They found that 80% of elderly blacks received assistance from friends, 60% received help from church members, and over half received support from family. Only a small minority of respondents were "socially isolated" in that they had no best or close friend nor support from family or church members. Focusing on type of support received, family, friends, and church members tended to provide specific types of assistance. Family members were more likely to provide either total support (i.e., would do anything, everything for me) or instrumental assistance (i.e., goods and services, financial help, and transportation), whereas companionship was provided by friends. Finally, church members provided assistance in the form of advice and encouragement, help during sickness, and prayer. The present study contributes to this literature by providing a descriptive analysis of changes in network involvement over time using data from the NSBA Panel Study. In addition to a focus on family networks, we also examine church members and friendship networks.

Method

Data

The data for this analysis are from the NSBA Panel Study. The original respondents of the NSBA (1979-1980) were reinterviewed three additional times in 1987-1988, 1988-1989, and 1992. A telephone follow-up method was used because the cost of locating the original 2,107 respondents and conducting face-to-face interviews was prohibitive. Tracking began in August 1987, and continued through the completion of interviewing in September 1988. Approximately 57% (1,210) of the original NSBA respondents were located and an interview was attempted. Of the remaining original NSBA sample, approximately 7% were thought to be deceased; another 34% either had no telephone, their whereabouts were unknown to relatives, or both; while only 2% refused involvement at the initial tracking stage. Out of 1,210 respondents, 82% (951) participated in a second interview, while only 6.4% (77) refused an interview. The remainder of the Wave 2 sample were either hospitalized or otherwise physically or cognitively unable to participate during the specified field period. The Wave 3 data collection (interviewing begun in 1988 and completed in March 1989), attempted interviews on all 951 respondents who were located and interviewed in 1987-1988. A total of 83.4% of this group agreed to be reinterviewed (793) and only 6.1% (58) refused. Approximately 11 (1.2%) were deceased, 49 (4.2%) were physically or mentally unable to participate in an interview, and a total of 40 (4.2%) respondents were lost to follow up.

Overall, the results of the tracking and interviewing procedures were highly successful in locating original NSBA respondents. After an 8-year period, only 34% of all 2,107 original respondents were lost to tracking; the remaining 66% were located and accounted for. Once found, respondents were extremely cooperative, with an average of 83% participating over two waves of reinterviewing. Finally, a fourth wave of data was collected in 1992. Of the 779 respondents recontacted, 659 were interviewed, representing a response rate of 84%. With regard to response rates, it is important to point out that the NSBA was designed as a study of noninstitutionalized African American adults. As such, tracking information and procedures did not provide for the exclusion from the sampling frame those original respondents who might have entered an institutional setting (e.g., Armed Services, nursing home) following the Wave 1 data collection. As a result, response rates for subsequent waves of interviewing are likely underestimated.

Sample attrition and its impact on the composition of the panel is always a major concern in conducting prospective research. The NSBA, because it was not originally planned as a panel study, has a considerable time lag between Waves 1 and 2 (8 years). To assess the impact of respondent attrition on sample composition, respondents in Wave 1 were compared to persons who subsequently became nonrespondents at Waves 2 and 4. NSBA respondents who participated in multiple waves of data collection are more likely to own their own homes, be employed, be women, have more years of education, and to be slightly older. These differences are largely consistent with other panel studies in which renters, men, and younger respondents have higher rates of nonparticipation in later waves of data collection (O'Muircheartaigh, 1989). These noted changes in sample characteristics with subsequent waves of NSBA data should always be kept in mind when interpreting and generalizing the findings reported here.

The present analysis examines change, over time, in selected characteristics of the family, friend, and church support networks of black Americans. For the purposes of this study, the relevant comparisons involve Waves 1 and 2 and Waves 1 and 4 from the Panel Study of the NSBA. The selection of these data collection points was based on the wish to obtain fairly sizable time lags between Waves of the Panel (8 years between Waves 1 and 2, 12 years between Waves 1 and 4). Furthermore, it was reasoned that the demographic trends and family transitions that are significant for family structure and function (e.g., divorce, nonmarital births) occur over extended periods of time. It is unlikely that their effects would be identified within or isolated to relatively brief time periods. This analysis focuses broadly on the extent to which NSBA respondents are involved with family, friend, and church support networks over time. In addition to an interest in change in network involvement, the analysis also assesses the degree to which support network involvement remains stable over time.

Measures

Two independent (i.e., gender, age) and seven dependent variables (i.e., family interaction, family support, family closeness, family satisfaction, friendship interaction, presence of a best friend, church support) are examined. Family interaction is measured by the question, "How often do you see, write, or talk on the telephone with family or relatives who do not live with you? Would you say nearly everyday, at least once a week, a few times a month, at least once a month, a few times a year, or hardly ever?" Support from family is measured by the question, "How often do people in your family—including children, grandparents, aunts, uncles, in-laws, and so on—help you out? Would you say very often, fairly often, not too often, or never?" Subjective family closeness is measured by the question, "Would you say your family members are very close in their feelings to each other, fairly close, not too close, or not close at all?" Satisfaction with family life is measured by this item, "How satisfied are you with your family life, that is, the time you spend and the things you do with members of your family? Would you say that you are very satisfied, somewhat satisfied, somewhat dissatisfied, or very dissatisfied?" Friendship interaction is measured by the question, "How often do you see, write, or talk on the telephone with your friends? Would you say nearly everyday, at least once a week, a few times a month, at least once a month, a few times a year, hardly ever, or never?" Presence of a best friend is measured by the question, "Not counting your husband/wife/partner, do you have a best friend?" Finally, church support is measured with the question, "How often do people in your church or place of worship help you out? Would you say often, sometimes, hardly ever, or never?"

Several of the dependent variables were recoded prior to data analysis. A portion of respondents, when asked how often they received assistance from their church members or family members, volunteered that they never needed assistance from those groups. In Wave 1 of the NSBA, 17.9% of the respondents volunteered that they never needed help from church members (Taylor & Chatters, 1988) and 9.7% volunteered that they never needed help from family (Taylor, 1986). Previous analysis indicated that respondents who volunteer that they never need assistance are conceptually and empirically distinct from both persons who receive some level of assistance and those who report that they do not receive any help at all (Taylor, 1990; Taylor & Chatters, 1988). Consequently, respondents who volunteer that they never needed help from family and church are excluded from the analysis.

For the purposes of this descriptive analysis of change in support network involvement, we aggregated across response categories of the dependent variables in a manner consistent with the primary research questions. With respect to family and church support, the response format reflects whether or not respondents receive help from these groups (did not receive help, received help). With regard to family and friendship interaction, we are interested in whether respondents report fairly frequent (i.e., a few times a month or more) contact with family and friends or whether their level of contact is fairly infrequent (i.e., once a month or less). For family closeness, the comparisons involve respondents who feel that their families are close (i.e., very close or fairly close) versus not close (i.e., not too close or not close at all) in their feelings toward one another. Respondents who report being satisfied (i.e., very satisfied or somewhat satisfied) with their family lives are contrasted with those who are dissatisfied (i.e., somewhat dissatisfied or very dissatisfied).

Results

The data presented here report on patterns of respondent involvement in family, church, and friend support networks across Waves 1 and 2, and Waves 1 and 4. Type of change is reflected along two separate dimensions. First, respondents could indicate whether or not they were involved in these support networks (e.g., received help or not, close to family or not). Second, responses could reflect either change or stability in network involvement across time. For example, a response pattern indicating initial dissatisfaction with family life, subsequently followed by satisfaction, would reflect an increase in network involvement. Similarly, a decrease in network involvement could occur over time (from frequent to infrequent family contact). Stability in network involvement would occur when there was no reported change across time (i.e., from 1980 to 1987 or 1980 to 1992) in level of involvement. Consequently, network involvement across time is described with respect to four distinct categories: (a) an increase in network involvement (i.e., increase), (b) stable involvement in networks (i.e., stable-involved), (c) stable noninvolvement in networks (i.e., stable-noninvolved), or (d) a decrease in network involvement (i.e., decrease), across time.

Table 17.1 presents data on respondents' involvement in family, church, and friend support networks between the years 1980 and 1987 (Waves 1 and 2) for the total sample, by gender and age. As indicated, over half of the respondents (55.3%) report receiving help from church members in both 1980 and 1987 (i.e., stable-involved). In contrast, one out of five respondents (17.9%) did not receive assistance from church members in both 1980 and 1987 (i.e., stable-noninvolved). Roughly 11% received assistance from church members in 1980, but not in 1987 (i.e., decrease). On the other hand, 15.2% of respondents report an increase in support from church members from Waves 1 to 2 over this 8-year period.

With regard to family contact, over 75% of respondents indicate that they interact with their family members at least a few times a month in both Waves 1 and 2 (i.e., stable-involved). Only 5.2% of respondents report infrequent contact with their family members during Waves 1 and 2 (i.e., stable-noninvolved). One out of 10 respondents (9.4%) indicate that interaction with family members increased between 1979-1980 and 1987, whereas 8.1% indicate that interaction with family members decreased during this period (from fairly frequent contact in 1980 to infrequent contact in 1987). Finally, although roughly half of the sample report that they had a best friend at both Waves 1 and 2, a fairly substantial percentage of respondents initially report a best friend in Wave 1, but not in Wave 2 (approximately 20%).

Overall between 1980 and 1987, support network involvement is relatively stable for the majority of the sample. The majority of respondents are fairly well integrated in their family, friend, and church support networks across both data points. The percentages of respondents reporting network involvement that is stable-involved range from 55.3% for church support to 88.7% for family closeness. Relatively smaller percentages of respondents are not well integrated in their networks at either time point (i.e., percentages reporting stable-noninvolved range from 1.3% for family closeness to 17.9% for church support). Decreases in network involvement across time are observed across all of the support variables. They are offset, however, by comparable

Table 17.1 Change from 1980 to 1987 (Waves 1 to 2) in Support Network Involvement by Gender and Age

Change From 1980 to 1987	Received Church Help	Family Interaction	Received Family Help	Family Closeness	Family Satisfaction	Friendship Interaction	Having Best Friend
Total							
Increase (%)	15.2	9.4	9.4	4.4	7.7	10.4	11.7
Stable-involved (%)	55.3	77.2	78.7	88.7	77.9	74.6	56.7
Stable-noninvolved (%)	17.9	5.2	4.2	1.8	3.5	4.8	12.4
Decrease (%)	11.6	8.1	7.8	5.1	10.8	10.1	19.3
N	637	923	745	913	906	910	909
Men							
Increase (%)	16.0	10.5	9.1	4.3	10.3	12.0	13.7
Stable-involved (%)	52.4	68.8	76.6	90.5	76.7	65.7	54.2
Stable-noninvolved (%)	21.2	8.9	5.2	1.3	3.3	8.0	10.7
Decrease (%)	10.4	11.8	9.1	3.9	9.6	14.3	21.4
N	212	304	231	304	301	300	299
Women							
Increase (%)	14.8	8.9	9.5	4.4	6.4	9.7	10.7
Stable-involved (%)	56.7	81.4	79.6	87.8	78.5	79.0	57.9
Stable-noninvolved (%)	16.2	3.4	3.7	2.0	3.6	3.3	13.3
Decrease (%)	12.2	6.3	7.2	5.7	11.4	8.0	18.2
N	425	619	514	609	605	610	610

Table 17.1 (continued)

Change From 1980 to 1987	Received Church Help	Family Interaction	Received Family Help	Family Closeness	Family Satisfaction	Friendship Interaction	Having Best Friend
17 to 34 years							
Increase (%)	18.8	10.6	4.4	5.9	9.0	10.5	10.7
Stable-involved (%)	56.3	77.0	90.3	87.9	67.9	75.1	65.0
Stable-noninvolved (%)	14.0	4.8	0.3	2.5	6.5	5.9	9.0
Decrease (%)	11.0	7.6	5.0	3.7	16.6	8.5	15.3
N	272	357	319	355	355	353	354
35 to 54 years							
Increase (%)	11.7	8.1	10.6	2.0	9.2	12.5	12.0
Stable-involved (%)	55.2	78.5	75.2	89.6	80.8	71.5	57.6
Stable-noninvolved (%)	21.5	4.9	4.7	1.4	2.1	3.2	11.1
Decrease (%)	11.7	8.4	9.5	6.9	8.0	12.8	19.3
N	223	344	274	346	338	344	342
55 to 102 years							
Increase (%)	14.1	9.5	17.8	5.7	3.3	7.0	12.7
Stable-involved (%)	53.5	75.7	60.5	88.7	90.1	78.9	41.3
Stable-noninvolved (%)	19.7	6.3	11.2	0.9	0.9	5.6	20.2
Decrease (%)	12.7	8.6	10.5	4.7	5.6	8.5	25.8
N	142	222	152	212	213	213	213

percentages of respondents indicating increases in level of network involvement.

In addition to these overall trends, several important variations are evident in Table 17.1. Although church members are integral members of support networks, respondents are more likely to report assistance from family members. Only a few gender and age differences in support network involvement are noted. Women have higher levels of contact with both family members and friends than do men. Differences by age group indicate that age is negatively associated with having a best friend at both Waves 1 and 2. Respondents 17 to 34 years of age (a) have a greater likelihood of having a best friend from Wave 1 to Wave 2, (b) are less likely to be without a best friend at both time points (i.e., stable-noninvolved) and, (c) are less likely to experience a loss of a best friend (i.e., decrease). Conversely, respondents aged 55 to 102 years are the least likely of the three age groups to have a best friend at both Waves 1 and 2 and are the most likely to be without a best friend at both time points and to report that they no longer have a best friend at Wave 2.

Two other factors are notable with respect to age of respondent. There is a negative age gradient for reports of consistently receiving help (i.e., stable-involved) from family at Waves 1 and 2. That is, the percentage of respondents reporting help from families at Waves 1 and 2 is 90.3% among persons 17 to 34 years, 75.2% for persons 35 to 54 years, and 60.5% for those 55 years and older. In contrast, respondents reporting consistently high levels of satisfaction with their family lives from Wave 1 to Wave 2 (i.e., stable-involved) demonstrates a positive age gradient (i.e., 67.9% among young persons, 80.8% for middle-aged persons, and 90.1% for the oldest respondents).

Table 17.2 presents a similar analysis of change in support network involvement, focused on the time period of 1979-1980 to 1992 (Waves 1 and 4). The trends identified earlier in Table 17.1 are evident here as well. The overwhelming majority of respondents indicate that they are involved with their networks both at Waves 1 and 4. There is some indication of decreases in network involvement from Wave 1 to Wave 4, but these are offset by comparable increases in network involvement for particular variables. Very small percentages of respondents are not involved with family, church, and friend support networks across both Waves 1 and 4 (i.e., stable-noninvolved). Gender differences indicating women's higher level of contact with family and friends are noted. With respect to age differences, an identical pattern of findings for family support is found involving comparisons across Waves 1 and 4 (negative age gradient), whereby older age is related to less consistent family support across Waves 1 and 4. Similarly, reports of satisfaction with family across Waves 1 and 4 show the identical positive age gradient observed earlier.

The next step in the analysis examines the possible influences that panel attrition may have on the results. Table 17.3 compares level of network involvement for respondents in Waves 2 and 4, with nonrespondents at Waves 2 and 4. Using data derived from the Wave 1 survey, network involvement information for persons who are identified as respondents in later waves, are compared with information from those who became nonrespondents in subsequent waves of the study. Table 17.3 indicates that there are significant differences in network involvement for respondents and nonrespondents. Persons who were respondents across subsequent waves of the study, demonstrate consistently higher levels of involvement in support networks than do persons who eventually become nonrespondents. These differences, although notable, are not particularly large; none of them exceed 10 percentage points. As described earlier, nonresponse to subsequent data collections could result from death, relocation to an institutional setting, respondent refusals, as well as failure to relocate respondents following moves.

As part of the recontact procedures, all respondents in Wave 1 were asked to provide the names of two family members or friends (i.e., recontact persons) with whom they maintain regular contact. This information is used to track respondents in the event that they move from their current residence. The noted differences in network involvement factors between respondents and nonrespondents are consistent with the methods used to relocate original respondents for follow-up interviewing. In this analysis, persons identified as nonrespondents are characterized as having more tenuous ties to family, friend, and church networks. This profile of marginal network involvement likely contributes to difficulties in sample follow-up and recontact. In other words, respondents with initially lower levels of social network integration would be less likely than others to maintain contact with identified recontact persons and more likely to be lost to tracking and follow-up procedures.

Discussion

Overall, these findings indicate that family, church, and friend network involvement among black Americans is consistent and viable. Despite important changes in black family structure that have occurred over the past 30 years, black adults are well integrated within important social networks. The majority of respondents reported support network involvement across all waves of the NSBA Panel Survey, whereas only a small group of respondents reported low levels of involvement with family and friend networks in Wave 1 and later waves of the NSBA. Respondents' involvement in church-based support networks

Table 17.2 Change From 1980 to 1992 (Waves 1 to 4) in Network Involvement by Gender and Age

Change From 1980 to 1992	Received Church Help	Family Interaction	Received Family Help	Family Closeness	Family Satisfaction	Friendship Interaction	Having Best Friend
Total
Increase (%)	15.7	10.4	8.5	3.4	8.2	11.0	13.9
Stable-involved (%)	54.5	81.3	75.9	91.2	80.9	73.9	64.7
Stable-noninvolved (%)	15.0	3.3	4.7	1.7	1.6	3.1	8.7
Decrease (%)	14.8	5.0	10.8	3.6	9.4	12.0	12.8
N	479	642	553	639	638	635	635
Men
Increase (%)	18.1	11.8	8.2	4.9	10.8	14.0	15.1
Stable-involved (%)	50.0	75.4	74.1	90.6	78.8	63.0	62.8
Stable-noninvolved (%)	18.8	5.4	6.5	1.0	1.5	6.0	8.0
Decrease (%)	13.1	7.4	11.2	3.4	8.9	17.0	14.1
N	160	203	170	203	203	200	199
Women
Increase (%)	14.4	9.8	8.6	2.8	6.9	9.7	13.3
Stable-involved (%)	56.7	84.1	76.8	91.5	81.8	78.9	65.6
Stable-noninvolved (%)	13.2	2.3	3.9	2.1	1.6	1.8	8.9
Decrease (%)	15.7	3.9	10.7	3.7	9.7	9.7	12.2
N	319	439	383	436	435	435	436

Table 17.2 (continued)

Change From 1980 to 1992	Received Church Help	Family Interaction	Received Family Help	Family Closeness	Family Satisfaction	Friendship Interaction	Having Best Friend
17 to 34 years							
Increase (%)	17.4	11.3	3.9	4.9	10.6	12.2	13.5
Stable-involved (%)	57.9	83.1	89.0	91.4	72.8	72.8	69.7
Stable-noninvolved (%)	11.8	2.4	0.9	1.6	2.4	3.3	6.6
Decrease (%)	12.8	3.2	6.1	2.0	14.2	11.8	10.2
N	195	248	228	245	246	246	244
35 to 54 years							
Increase (%)	15.0	9.5	10.5	1.9	8.4	11.1	12.3
Stable-involved (%)	49.7	82.1	71.7	93.2	81.0	73.6	67.4
Stable-noninvolved (%)	16.6	3.1	4.1	1.5	1.5	3.4	9.2
Decrease (%)	18.7	5.3	13.7	3.4	9.1	11.9	11.1
N	187	262	219	264	263	261	261
55 to 102 years							
Increase (%)	13.4	10.6	14.2	3.8	3.1	8.6	17.7
Stable-involved (%)	56.7	76.5	56.6	86.9	96.1	76.6	50.0
Stable-noninvolved (%)	18.6	5.3	14.2	2.3	0.0	2.3	11.5
Decrease (%)	11.3	7.6	15.1	6.9	0.8	12.5	20.8
N	97	132	106	130	129	128	130

was not as widespread, although fully half of all respondents reported consistent use of these networks over time. Finally, relatively small decreases in network involvement were noted across waves of data collection for network involvement factors. These decreases, however, were offset by comparable increases in involvement with family, friend, and church networks.

Although the findings indicate generally high levels of involvement in family and friendship networks, there were important variations. Initial assessments of network involvement indicated that respondents were more likely to volunteer that they did not need support from church members, compared to support from family members (18% vs. 10% for Wave 1 respondents, respectively). Although these individuals were excluded from subsequent analyses, they provide some sense of the preference given kin relations. The analysis of network involvement revealed that respondents were much more likely to report assistance from family members than from church members. Furthermore, although there was an increase in the numbers of respondents reporting assistance from church members over time, it should be noted that there were also decreases in support across waves of data collection. These patterns of findings demonstrate that although church members provide an important source of assistance to individuals, families remain the most enduring source of support. Church-based support networks possess many of the attributes of family associations (e.g., long-term associations, reciprocal exchanges) and many individuals and families may be members of the same church for several generations. Events such as marital transitions (e.g., divorce, separation) and moves, however, may disrupt social relationships within the church and require that individuals establish membership in churches new to them (Taylor & Chatters, 1988). Furthermore, family relationships (as opposed to church associations) are more closely governed by explicit normative rules for familial interaction, assistance exchanges, and filial obligations. Despite the important supportive functions played by church-based networks for particular groups of individuals, they appear to be similar to other nonkin groups in that these relationships are generally not as durable as family bonds.

The only major gender differences observed in these data were that women had higher levels of family and friendship interaction than did men. Compared to men, women maintained more frequent contact with family and friends across time. Furthermore, the percentages of women reporting decreases in the amount of contact with these groups over time was smaller than for men. These findings are consistent with other research among both black (Hatchett & Jackson, 1993; Taylor & Chatters, 1991a) and white adults indicating higher levels of kin and nonkin interaction among women. Taken together, these studies reinforce the portrayal of women as the "kin keepers" of families (Stack &

Table 17.3 Comparisons of Network Involvement for Respondents and Nonrespondents: Waves 2 and 4 of National Survey of Black Americans Panel Study

Type of Change	Received Church Help	Family Interaction	Received Family Help	Family Closeness	Family Satisfaction	Friendship Interaction	Having Best Friend
Wave 2 (1987)							
Respondents (%)	66.7	85.2	85.3	94.0	89.0	84.6	75.4
Nonrespondents (%)	58.3	77.5	79.3	88.4	88.3	76.2	69.2
Differences (%)	8.4	7.7	6.0	5.6	0.7	8.4	6.2
Wave 4 (1992)							
Respondents (%)	68.7	86.2	86.4	94.7	90.4	85.4	77.2
Nonrespondents (%)	59.0	78.5	80.0	89.2	87.8	77.5	69.6
Differences (%)	9.7	7.7	6.4	5.5	2.6	7.9	7.6

NOTE: All differences are statistically different from zero at the .01 level except for family satisfaction.

Burton, 1993), to whom fall the responsibilities of maintaining and facilitating interaction within families and wider social groups.

These data indicated relatively large decreases over time in the percentage of respondents who reported that they had a best friend, particularly with respect to age differences. Persons 55 years and older were more likely than other age groups to report having lost a best friend between Waves 1 and 2 and Waves 1 and 4. In fact, the pattern of results suggested the presence of a negative age gradient, such that age was associated with a decreased likelihood of having a best friend over time. These findings are likely attributable, in part, to higher rates of mortality among older adults. The data also reveal several other interesting patterns of network involvement that are associated with age. Comparisons involving both Waves 1 and 2 and Waves 1 and 4 revealed that two factors, family assistance and family satisfaction, were associated with age group membership. For family assistance, the percentages of respondents reporting consistent levels of support across time decreased with age. The reverse pattern was found in connection with family satisfaction; that is, the percentages of respondents reporting consistently high levels of satisfaction with their family lives across time increased with age.

Similar age differences have been reported in cross-sectional data of family support and satisfaction. In several studies, age-associated declines in family and church support are noted (Taylor, 1986; Taylor & Chatters, 1988; Taylor et al., 1993). These changes were offset, however, to some extent, by the presence of an adult child who appeared to facilitate assistance to older parents (Taylor, 1986; Taylor & Chatters, 1988; Taylor et al., 1993). Furthermore, age differences in the affective dimensions of family life, indicate that older age is associated with the expression of positive family sentiments. This pattern is thought to reflect the notion of the "generational stake" (Bengtson, 1973; Bengtson, Burton, & Mangen, 1985; Bengtson & Cutler, 1976; Bengtson & Kuypers, 1971), whereby older persons tend to invest in and value the emotional aspects of family life to a greater degree than do younger persons. In interpreting these age findings, it could be argued that the noted attrition of persons already marginal with respect to network involvement, could have affected the sample in such a way that those who had viable family support linkages and who expressed greater family satisfaction were retained (i.e., constituting a larger proportion of the samples in subsequent Waves). In contrast, those whose ties to family were more tenuous, as evidenced by their initial lower levels of network involvement, were lost to follow up. Indeed, comparisons of family satisfaction changes between 1980 and 1987 with those occurring between 1980 and 1992, reveals that a higher percentage of the sample endorsed this sentiment across Waves 1 and 4 (across all age groups).

Slightly greater numbers of respondents reported receiving family support in the shorter term (1980-1987) than the longer term comparison (1980-1992). In both cases, however, these differences were not large enough to suggest that these sample attrition influences were substantial. Furthermore, if this were the case, we might expect that other network involvement factors would show a similar pattern of findings, and they do not. Of particular note, the other family affection factor, family closeness, failed to exhibit the positive age gradient noted for family satisfaction.

Taken as a whole, these data suggest that examining the network involvement of black Americans across time and within selected subgroups, reveals important patterns of continuity and change for a fairly diverse group of behaviors and attitudes. Gender comparisons indicated that women and men were distinctive with respect to their level of contact with family networks, whereas age differences suggested that network involvement among older persons may be compromised with respect to the absence of close confidants and lower levels of family support. In contrast, however, older persons were more likely to indicate that they derived satisfaction from their families.

Despite a long tradition of research on family and social networks of black Americans, this work comprised an assortment of individual studies, conducted on diverse samples, and pursued divergent aims and objectives. As a consequence, findings from these investigations have not always been comparable or easily reconciled. Together with the tendency to ignore the heterogeneity inherent within the black population, these combined problems limited progress toward the systematic investigation of fundamental questions and issues regarding black family structure and function. In considering the direction that future research should pursue, this discussion will explore the strengths and limits of both ethnographic and survey methodologies and ways that these approaches might be used to better inform our perspectives on network involvement and support exchanges within black families.

A particular difficulty in black family research is that the methods and specialized procedures employed by survey research and ethnographic studies often impede the task of integration of research findings (Chatters & Jayakody, 1995). Clearly, representative surveys conducted within samples of respondents of sufficient size to permit generalizations to the underlying population have an advantage with regards to sample coverage and generalizability of findings. Survey research methods have been effectively employed to provide a sense of the broad outlines of family and social phenomena. Furthermore, survey research efforts have been instrumental in developing an understanding of the fundamental diversity that exists within the black population with respect to family structures, behaviors, and attitudes.

Ethnographic methodologies, on the other hand, possess several unique strengths that are indispensable for understanding black family phenomena. For example, ethnographic methods are useful for providing an understanding of the nuances of reciprocal exchanges (e.g., types, duration and time frame, normative expectations) and support transfers involving respondent groups that are not represented in traditional surveys (e.g., street corner men, Anderson, 1978; Liebow, 1967). For these and other intricate forms of family behavior, ethnographic methods provide a unique window into a very personal and complex world. The subtlety of these types of phenomena can not be captured using traditional survey approaches. Furthermore, traditional survey research approaches that are based on a household sample, are inappropriate for examining support exchanges that occur across (involving two or more households) or outside of household boundaries (Chatters & Jayakody, 1995).

Comparisons of ethnographic and survey research methods are especially challenging with respect to the conceptualization and definition of family support transfers. For example, survey research approaches to studying family support frequently examine monetary aid exclusively and employ restrictive operational definitions of assistance that are based on arbitrary dollar amounts. Monetary exchanges meeting these thresholds (e.g., $100 or $200) are defined as a support transfer, whereas exchanges that involve dollar amounts below the threshold level fail to qualify as a family support transfer. As a consequence, reports of monetary transfers are biased in favor of groups with greater financial resources (Chatters & Jayakody, 1995, p. 107). Furthermore, because these approaches focus attention on limited types of support transfers (e.g., specified monetary exchanges), other categories of assistance transfers within families (e.g., goods and services) are unaccounted for, resulting in an underestimation of the full range of supportive behaviors occurring within families.

In contrast, ethnographic approaches often assess separate domains of family support including affective dimensions and goods and services, as well as monetary exchanges. Ethnographic and survey research methods, however, can be successfully allied. An example focusing on family support transfers suggests that capitalizing on the ethnographic method's careful attention to conceptualization issues and operational definitions of family factors can advance an understanding of race differences in family support.

Studies of financial transfers within families often employ income controls to determine whether race differences in family support are independent of family income level. These findings suggest that, controlling for income level, black families are less likely than white families to participate in intrafamily monetary transfers (Hogan et al., 1993). Careful interpretation of these findings, however, should pay particular attention to the conceptualization and operational definitions of family financial resources. The typical means used to determine a family's financial resources are to inquire about family income, assessing earned income from paid employment and income transfers for a given time period (e.g., during the past year). The construct of family wealth, in contrast, which assesses a family's total assets (i.e., savings, investments, home ownership, and property) minus all debts, is employed much less frequently as a measure of financial resources. Several have argued, however, that family wealth provides a more accurate accounting of a family's available resources and their economic well-being (Oliver & Shapiro, 1989). Furthermore, black families not only have lower levels of wealth than do whites, but racial discrepancies in family wealth are much larger than those for family income. Family wealth, being the more sensitive indicator of available resources, is preferable over family income as a measure of financial resources and in gaining a better appreciation of family support transfers.

As this discussion indicates, interpretations of race differences in intrafamily monetary transfers should take into account clear disparities in the distribution of important financial resources (i.e., income and wealth) across black and white families. The issue of family financial resources, seen within a broader economic context, helps us to appreciate the tenuous financial status of black families generally, as well as those who are relatively recent arrivals to the middle class. The new black middle class, although appearing comparable to their white counterparts with respect to income levels, has yet to amass significant durable assets that can be passed down to successive family generations and thus remains vulnerable to downturns in the economy. Broader conceptualizations of family financial resources should incorporate the construct of family wealth, in addition to available family income. Finally, this discussion focuses attention on the ways that specific operational definitions of intrafamily transfers (both monetary and nonmonetary) may not reflect the realities and circumstances of black families. Given this situation, differences in intrafamily support exchanges across discrete groups within the population may be misinterpreted and the range of supportive behaviors may not be fully appreciated (see Chatters & Jayakody, 1995 for a discussion of these issues).

These and other differences in ethnographic and survey approaches to issues of family support make comparisons across these literatures problematic. Both approaches, however, possess unique and important strengths that are useful for studying black families. The task of future research is to always remain cognizant of these important differences between survey and ethnographic studies in the specific problems they examine and in the approaches they adopt. This is particularly critical when speculations about trends over time in the supportive behaviors of black families are based on a collection of disparate studies representing divergent objectives and methodological approaches (i.e., Hogan et al., 1993, p. 1450). Despite the intuitive appeal of such speculations, it is impossible to reconcile studies that are fundamentally distinct with respect to samples, problem conceptualization, and methods.

Finally, future research examining the supportive behaviors of black family and other social networks should explore ways to capitalize on the unique features of survey and ethnographic approaches (e.g., kin maps, life history calendars). These strategies would reflect a synthesis of qualitative and quantitative approaches, involving adaptations of existing procedures, the incorporation of techniques novel to each approach, or both. The creative use and adaptation of ethnographic and survey methodologies could be used to investigate a wide range of support behaviors occurring within family and nonfamily settings and in a variety of household contexts (Chatters & Jayakody, 1995; Chatters, Taylor, & Jayakody, 1994).

References

Abell, E., Clawson, M., Washington, W. N., Best, K. K., & Vaughn, B. E. (1996). Parenting values, attitudes, behaviors, and goals of African American mothers from a low-income population in relation to social and societal contexts. *Journal of Family Issues, 17,* 593-613.

Abrahamse, A., Morrison, P., & Waite, L. (1988). Teenagers willing to consider single parenthood: Who is at greatest risk? *Family Planning Perspectives, 20,* 59-64.

Adams, T. K., Duncan, G. J., & Rodgers, W. L. (1988). In F. R. Harris & R. W. Wilkins (Eds.), *Quiet riots: Race and poverty in the United States* (pp. 78-99). New York: Pantheon.

Adelmann, P. K. (1996). *Gender differences in housework characteristics and satisfaction.* Unpublished manuscript, Northwestern University, Evanston, IL.

Affleck, G., Tennen, H., Allen, D. A., & Gershman, K. (1986). Perceived social support and maternal adaptation during the transition from hospital to home care of high-risk infants. *Infant Mental Health Journal, 7*(1), 6-18.

Ahmeduzzaman, M., & Roopnarine, J. L. (1992). Sociodemographic factors, functioning style, social support, and fathers' involvement with preschoolers in African American families. *Journal of Marriage and the Family, 54*(4), 699-707.

Ahn, N. (1994). Teenage childbearing and high school completion: Accounting for individual heterogeneity. *Family Planning Perspectives, 26,* 17-21.

Alan Guttmacher Institute. (1992). Facts in brief: Abortion in the United States. New York: Author.

Alan Guttmacher Institute. (1993). Facts in brief: Teenage sexual and reproductive behavior. New York: Author.

Albrecht, C., Fossett, M. A., Cready, C. M., & Kiecolt, K. J. (1995). *Mate availability, women's marriage prevalence, and husbands' education.* Unpublished manuscript.

Aldous, J. (1990). Family development and the life course: Two perspectives on family change. *Journal of Marriage and the Family, 52,* 571-583.

317

Aldrich, J. H., & Nelson, F. D. (1984). *Linear probability, logit, and probit models.* Beverly Hills, CA: Sage.

Alejandro-Wright, M. (1985). The child's conception of racial classification: A social-cognitive developmental model. In M. Spencer, G. Brookins, & W. Allen (Eds.) *Beginnings: The social and affective development of black children* (pp. 185-200). Hillsdale, NJ: Lawrence Erlbaum.

Allen, R., & Hatchett, S. (1986). The media and social reality effects: Self and system orientations of blacks. *Communications Research, 13*(1), 97-13.

Allen, R., Thornton, M. C., & Watkins, S. (1992). An African American racial belief system and social structural relationships: A test of invariance. *National Journal of Sociology, 6,* 157-186.

Allen, W. D., & Doherty, W. J. (1996). The responsibilities of fatherhood as perceived by African American teenage fathers. *Families in Society, 77,* 142-155.

Allen, W. D., & Connor, M. (1997). An African American perspective on generative fathering. In A. J. Hawkins & D. C. Dollahite (Eds.), *Generative fathering: Beyond deficit perspectives* (pp. 52-70). Thousand Oaks, CA: Sage.

Allen, W. R. (1978). The search for applicable theories of black family life. *Journal of Marriage and the Family, 40*(1), 117-131.

Allen, W. R. (1979). Class, culture, and family organization: The effects of class and race on family structure in urban America. *Journal of Comparative Family Studies, 10*(3), 301-313.

Allen, W. R. (1981). Moms, dads, and boys: Race and sex differences in socialization of male children. In L. Gray (Ed.), *Black men* (pp. 99-114). Newbury Park, CA: Sage.

Allen, W. R. (1985). Race, income, and family dynamics: A study of adolescent male socialization. In M. B. Spencer, G. K. Brookins, & W. R. Allen (Eds.), *Beginnings: The social and affective development of Black children* (pp. 273-292). Hillsdale, NJ: Lawrence Erlbaum.

Allen, W. R. (1995). African American family life in societal context: Crisis and hope. *Sociological Forum, 10*(4), 569-592.

Allen, W. R., & Farley, R. (1985). The shifting social and economic tides of black America, 1950-1980. *Annual Review of Sociology, 12,* 277-306.

Alwin, D. F., Converse, P. E., & Martin, S. S. (1985). Living arrangements and social integration. *Journal of Marriage and the Family, 47,* 319-334.

American Humane Association. (1988). Highlights of child welfare and abuse reporting: 1986. Denver, CO.

Andersen, P. A., & Telleen, S. L. (1992). The relationship between social support and maternal behaviors and attitudes: A meta-analytic review. *American Journal of Community Psychology, 20,* 753-774.

Anderson, E. (1989). Sex codes and family life among poor inner-city youth. *Annals of the American Academy of Political and Social Science, 501,* 59-78.

Anderson, E. (1978). *A place on the corner.* Chicago: University of Chicago Press.

Andrews, F., & Withey, S. (1976). *Social indicators of well-being: Americans' perceptions of life quality.* New York: Plenum.

Andrews, F., & Withey, S. (1979). *Social indicators of well-being.* New York: Plenum.

Angel, R., & Tienda, M. (1982). Determinants of extended household structure: Cultural pattern or economic model? *American Journal of Sociology, 87,* 1360-1383.

Anthony, E., & Cohler, B. (1987). *The invulnerable child.* New York: Guilford.

Antonucci, T. C. (1985). Personal characteristics, social support, and social behavior. In E. Shanas & R. H. Binstock (Eds.), *Handbook of aging and the social sciences* (2nd ed., pp. 94-128). New York: Van Nostrand.

Antonucci, T. C., & Jackson, J. S. (1990). The role of reciprocity in social support. In I. G. Sarason, B. R. Sarason, & G. R. Pierce (Eds.), *Social support: An interactive view* (pp. 173-198). New York: John Wiley.

Aschenbrenner, J. (1975). *Lifelines: Black families in Chicago.* New York: Holt, Rinehart & Winston.

Auletta, K. (1982). *The underclass.* New York: Vintage.

Austin, R. L. (1992). Race, female headship, and delinquency: A longitudinal analysis. *Justice Quarterly, 9,* 585-607.

Averitt, R. T. (1968). *The dual economy.* New York: Norton.

Axinn, W. G., & Thornton, A. (1992). The relationship between cohabitation and divorce: Selectivity or causal influence. *Demography, 29,* 357-374.

Bachrach, C. L., Stolley, K. S., & London, K. A. (1992). Relinquishment of premarital births: Evidence from national survey data. *Family Planning Perspectives, 24*(1), 27-48.

Ball, R., & Robbins, L. (1986). Marital status and life satisfaction among black Americans. *Journal of Marriage and the Family, 48,* 389-394.

Baltes, P. B., Reese, H., & Lipsitt, L. (1980). Life-span developmental psychology. *Annual Review of Psychology, 31,* 65-110.

Bane, M. J., & Ellwood, D. T. (1984). *Single mothers and their living arrangements* (Working Paper). Cambridge, MA: Harvard University.

Barnett, R. C., & Baruch, G. K. (1985). Women's involvement in multiple roles, role strain, and psychological distress. *Journal of Personality and Social Psychology, 49,* 135-145.

Baruch, G. K., & Barnett, R. C. (1981). Fathers' participation in the care of their preschool children. *Sex Roles, 7,* 1043-1055.

Baruch, G. K., & Barnett, R. C. (1986a). Consequences of father's participation in family work: Parent role strain and well-being. *Journal of Personality and Social Psychology, 51,* 983-992.

Baruch, G. K., & Barnett, R. C. (1986b). Role quality and psychological well-being. In F. J. Crosby (Ed.), *Spouse, parent, worker: On gender and multiple roles* (pp. 63-73). New Haven, CT: Yale University Press.

Beck, R. W., & Beck, S. H. (1989). The incidence of extended households among middle-aged black and white women: Estimates from a 5-year panel study. *Journal of Family Issues 10,* 147-168.

Beck, S. H., & Beck, R. W. (1984). The formation of extended family household during middle age. *Journal of Marriage and the Family, 46,* 277-287.

Becker, G. S. (1973). A theory of marriage: Part I. *Journal of Political Economy, 81,* 813-846.

Becker, G. S. (1981). *A treatise on the family.* Cambridge, MA: Harvard University Press.

Bell, C. C., & Jenkins, E. J. (1991). Traumatic stress and children. *Journal of Health Care for the Poor and Underserved, 2,* 175-188.

Belsky, J. (1984). The determinants of parenting: A process model. *Child Development, 55,* 83-96.

Bengtson, V. L. (1975). Generation and family effects in value socialization. *American Sociological Review, 40,* 358-371.

Bengtson, V. L., & Cutler, N. (1976). Generations and intergenerational relations: Perspectives on age groups and social change. In R. H. Binstock & E. Shanas (Eds.), *Handbook of aging and the social sciences* (2nd ed., pp. 130-159). New York: Van Nostrand Reinhold.

Bengtson, V. L., & Kuypers, J. A. (1971). Generational differences and the developmental stake. *Aging and Human Development, 2,* 249-260.

Bengtson, V. L., Burton, L., & Mangen, D. J. (1985). Generations, cohorts, and relations between age groups. In R. H. Binstock & E. Shanas (Eds.), *Handbook of aging and the social sciences* (2nd ed., pp. 304-338). New York: Van Nostrand Reinhold.

Bengtson, V. L., Rosenthal, C., & Burton, L. (1996). Paradoxes in families and aging. In R. H. Binstock & L. K. George (Eds.), *Handbook of aging and the social sciences* (pp. 253-282). New York: Academic Press.

Bennett, N. E., Bloom, D. E., & Craig, P. H. (1989). The divergence of black and white marriage patterns. *American Journal of Sociology, 95,* 692-722.

Berman, P. W., & Pedersen, F. A. (Eds.). (1987). *Men's transitions to parenthood.* Hillsdale, NJ: Lawrence Erlbaum.

Bernard, J. (1981). The good-provider role: Its rise and fall. *American Psychologist, 36*(1), 1-12.

Besharov, D. J., & Quinn, A. J. (1987). Not all female-headed families are created equal. *Public Interest, 89,* 48-56.

Bianchi, S. M. (1981). *Household composition and racial inequality.* Camden, NJ: Rutgers University Press.

Bianchi, S. M. (1995). Changing economic roles of women and men. In R. Farley (Ed.), *State of the union, America in the 1990s. Vol. 1: Economic trends* (pp.107-154). New York: Russell Sage.

Biller, H. (1993). *Fathers and families: Paternal factors in child development.* Westport, CT: Auburn House.

Billingsley, A. (1968). *Black families in white America.* Englewood Cliffs, NJ: Prentice Hall.

Billingsley, A. (1992). *Climbing Jacob's ladder: The enduring legacy of African American families.* New York: Simon & Schuster.

Billy, J. O. G., Tanfer, K., Grady, W. R., & Klepinger, D. H. (1993). The sexual behavior of men in the United States. *Family Planning Perspectives, 25*(2), 52-60.

Blankenhorn, D. (1995). *Fatherless America: Confronting our most urgent social problem.* New York: Basic Books.

Blee, K. M., & Tickamyer, A. R. (1995). Racial differences in men's attitudes about women's gender roles. *Journal of Marriage and the Family, 57*(February), 21-30.

Bluestone, B. (1983). Deindustrialization and unemployment in America. *Review of Black Political Economy, 12*(3), 27-42.

Bluestone, B., & Harrison, B. (1982). *The deindustrialization of America: Plant closing, community abandonment and the dismantling of basic industry.* New York: Basic Books.

Blumstein, P., & Kollock, P. (1988). Personal relationships. *Annual Review of Sociology, 14,* 467-490.

Bowman, P. (1982, November). Black fathers and the provider role strain, informal coping resources, and life happiness. Paper presented at the National Black Empirical Conference, Hampton, VA.

Bowman, P. (1991). Work life. In J. S. Jackson (Ed.), *Life in black America* (pp. 124-155). Newbury Park, CA: Sage.

Bowman, P. J. (1984). A discouragement-centered approach to studying unemployment among black youth: Hopelessness, attributions, and psychological distress. *International Journal of Mental Health, 13*(1-2), 68-91.

Bowman, P. J. (1985). Black fathers and the provider role: Role strain, informal coping resources, and life happiness. In A. W. Boykin (Ed.), *Empirical research in black psychology* (pp. 9-19). Rockville, MD: National Institute of Mental Health.

Bowman, P. J. (1988). Postindustrial displacement and family role strains: Challenges to the black family. In P. Voydanoff & L. Majka (Eds.), *Families and economic distress* (pp. 75-101). Newbury Park, CA: Sage.

Bowman, P. J. (1989). Research perspectives on black men: Role strain and adaptation across the adult life cycle. In R. L. Jones (Ed.), *Black adult development and aging* (pp. 117-150). Berkeley, CA: Cobbs & Henry.

Bowman, P. J. (1990). Coping with provider role strain: Adaptive cultural resources among black husband-fathers. *Journal of Black Psychology, 16*(2), 1-21.

Bowman, P. J. (1991a). Work life. In J. S. Jackson (Ed.), *Life in black America* (pp. 124-155). Newbury Park, CA: Sage.

Bowman, P. J. (1991b). Joblessness. In J. S. Jackson (Ed.), *Life in black America* (pp. 156-178). Newbury Park, CA: Sage.

Bowman, P. J. (1992). Coping with provider role strain: Adaptive cultural resources among black husband-fathers. In A. K. H. Burlew, W. C. Banks, H. P. McAdoo, & D. Azibo (Eds.), *African American psychology: Theory, research, and practice* (pp. 135-154). Newbury Park, CA: Sage.

Bowman, P. J. (1993). The impact of economic marginality on African American husbands and fathers. In H. McAdoo (Ed.), *Family ethnicity* (pp. 120-137). Newbury Park, CA: Sage.

Bowman, P. J. (1995a). Marginalization of black men and the underclass debate. In M. B. Tucker & C. Mitchell-Kernan (Eds.), *The decline in marriage among African Americans* (pp. 309-321). New York: Russell Sage.

Bowman, P. J. (1995b). Education and responsible fatherhood among African Americans: Socialization, mobilization, and allocation challenges. In V. Gadsen & W. Trent (Eds.), *Transitions in the life course of African American fathers* (pp. 13-22). Philadelphia, PA: National Center on Fathers and Families.

Bowman, P. J. (1995c). Commentary. In M. B. Tucker & C. Mitchell-Kernan (Eds.), *The decline in marriage among African Americans: Causes, consequences, and policy implications* (pp. 309-322). New York: Russell Sage.

Bowman, P. J. (1996a). Naturally occurring psychological expectancies: Theory and measurement among African Americans. In R. L. Jones (Ed.), *Handbook of test and measures for Black populations* (pp. 553-578). Berkeley, CA: Cobbs & Henry.

Bowman, P. J. (In press). Toward a cognitive adaptation theory of role strain: Implications of research on black male providers. In R. L. Jones (Ed.). *Advances in black psychology*. Vol. 2. Berkeley: University of California Press.

Bowman, P. J., & Forman, T. A. (1995, March). *Life cycle issues among African American fathers: Theoretical, research, and social policy issues.* Paper presented at the 61st Biennial Meeting of the Society for Research in Child Development, Indianapolis.

Bowman, P. J., & Howard, C. S. (1985). Race-related socialization, motivation, and academic achievement: A study of black youth in three- generation families. *Journal of the American Academy of Child Psychiatry, 24*(2), 134-141.

Bowman, P. J., Jackson, J., Hatchett, S., & Gurin, G. (1982). Joblessness and discouragement among black Americans. *Economic Outlook USA, 9*(4), 85-88.

Bowman, P. J., & Sanders, R. (in press). Unmarried African American fathers: A comparative life span analysis. *Journal of Comparative Family Studies.*

Bowser, B. (Ed.). (1991). *Black male adolescents: Parenting and education in community context.* Lanham, MD: University Press of America.

Boykin, A. W., & Toms, F. (1985). Black child socialization: A conceptual framework. In H. McAdoo & J. McAdoo (Eds.), *Black children* (pp. 33-51). Beverly Hills, CA: Sage.

Bozett, F. W. (1985). Male development and fathering throughout the life cycle. *American Behavioral Scientist, 29*(1), 41-54.

Braddock, J., & McPartland, J. (1987). How minorities continue to be excluded from equal employment opportunities: Research on labor market and institutional barriers. *Journal of Social Issues, 43*(1), 5-39.

Bridges, W., & Villemez, W. (1986). Informal hiring and income in the labor market. *American Sociological Review, 51,* 574-582.

Broman, C. (1988a). Satisfaction among blacks: The significance of marriage and parenthood. *Journal of Marriage and the Family, 50*(1), 45-51.

Broman, C. (1988b). Household work and family life satisfaction of blacks. *Journal of Marriage and the Family, 50,* 743-748.

Broman, C. L. (1991). Gender, work-family roles, and psychological well-being of blacks. *Journal of Marriage and the Family, 53,* 509-520.

Broman, C. L., Hamilton, V. L., & Hoffman, W. S. (1990). Unemployment and its effect on families: Evidence from a plant closing study. *American Journal of Community Psychology 18,* 643-659.

Bronfenbrenner, U. (1986). Ecology of the family as a context for human development: Research perspectives. *Developmental Psychology, 22*(6), 723-742.

Bronstein, P., & Cowan, C. P. (Eds.). (1988). *Fatherhood today: Men's changing role in the family*. New York: John Wiley.

Brooks-Gunn, J., & Chase-Lansdale, P. L. (1991). Children having children: Effects of the family system. *Pediatric Annals, 20,* 467-481.

Brown, D. (1996). Marital status and mental health. In H. W. Neighbors & J. S. Jackson (Eds.), *Mental health in black America* (pp. 77-94). Thousand Oaks, CA: Sage.

Brown, D. R., & Gary, L. E. (1985). Social support network differentials among married and non-married black females. *Psychology of Women Quarterly, 9,* 229-241.

Brown, D. R., & Gary, L. E. (1987). Stressful life events, social support networks, and physical and mental health of urban black adults. *Journal of Human Stress, 13,* 165-174.

Bumpass, L. L. (1984). Children and marital disruption: A replication and update. *Demography, 21*(3), 71-81.

Bumpass, L. L. (1990). What is happening to the family? Interactions between demographic and institutional change. *Demography, 17*(4), 39-56.

Bumpass, L. L., & Raley, R. K. (1995). Redefining single-parent families: Cohabitation and changing family reality. *Demography, 32*(1), 97-109.

Bumpass, L. L., & Sweet, J. A. (1989). National estimates of cohabitation. *Demography, 26,* 615-625.

Bumpass, L. L., Raley, R. K., & Sweet, J. A. (1995). The changing character of stepfamilies: Implications of cohabitation and nonmarital childbearing. *Demography, 32,* 425-436.

Bumpass, L. L., Sweet, J. A., & Cherlin, A. (1991). The role of cohabitation in declining rates of marriage. *Journal of Marriage and the Family, 53,* 913-927.

Burton, L. M. (1990). Teenage childbearing as an alternative life-course strategy in multigeneration black families. *Human Nature, 1*(2), 123-143.

Burton, L. M. (1992). Black grandparents rearing children of drug-addicted parents: Stressors, outcomes, and social service needs. *The Gerontologist, 32,* 744-751.

Burton, L. M., & Bengtson, V. L. (1985). Black grandmothers: Issues of timing and continuity of roles. In V. L. Bengston & J. F. Robertson (Eds.), *Grandparenthood: Research and policy* (pp. 61-77). Beverly Hills, CA: Sage.

Burton, L. M., & Dilworth-Anderson, P. (1991). The intergenerational family roles of aged black Americans. *Marriage and Family Review, 16,* 311-330.

Caldwell, C. H., Greene, A. D., & Billingsley, A. (1992). The black church as a family support system: Instrumental and expressive functions. *National Journal of Sociology, 6*(1), 21-40.

Campbell, A. (1981). *The sense of well-being in America: Recent patterns and trends.* New York: McGraw-Hill.

Campbell, A., Converse, P. E., & Rodgers, W. (1976). *The quality of American life: Perceptions, evaluations, and satisfactions.* New York: Russell Sage.

Cancian, F. (1985). Gender politics: Love and power in the private and public spheres. In A. Rossi (Ed.), *Gender and the life course* (pp. 253-262). Hawthorne, NY: Aldine.

Carson, E. (1992). *Social networks in the labor market: Job acquisition by retrenched workers in south Australia.* Unpublished doctoral dissertation, Flinders University of South Australia.

Cates, W., Jr., & Stone, K. M. (1992). Family planning, sexually transmitted diseases, and contraceptive choice: A literature update—Part 1. *Family Planning Perspectives, 24*(3), 75-84.

Cazenave, N. (1979). Middle-income black fathers: An analysis of the provider role. *Family Coordinator, 28*(4), 583-593.

Cazenave, N. (1981). Black men in America: The quest for "manhood." In H. McAdoo (Ed.), *Black families* (pp. 176-185). Beverly Hills, CA: Sage.

Cazenave, N. (1984). Race, socioeconomic status, and age: The social context of American masculinity. *Sex Roles, 11,* 639-656.

Chadiha, L. A. (1992). Black husband's economic problems and resiliency during the transition to marriage. *Families in Society: Journal of Contemporary Human Services, 73,* 542-552.

Champoux, J. E. (1978). Perceptions of work and nonwork: A reexamination of the compensatory and spillover models. *Sociology of Work and Occupations, 5,* 402-422.

Chase-Lansdale, P. L., Brooks-Gunn, J., & Zamsky, E. S. (1994). Young African American multigenerational families in poverty: Quality of mothering and grandmothering. *Child Development, 65,* 373-393.

Chatters, L. M. (1988a). Subjective well-being among older black adults: Past trends and current perspectives. In J. S. Jackson (Ed.), *The black American elderly: Research on physical and psychosocial health* (pp. 237-258). New York: Springer.

Chatters, L. M. (1988b). Subjective well-being evaluations among older black Americans. *Psychology and Aging, 3,* 184-190.

Chatters, L. M. (1991). Physical health. In J. S. Jackson (Ed.), *Life in black America* (pp. 199-220). Newbury Park, CA: Sage.

Chatters, L. M., & Ellison, C. G. (in press). Subjective well-being among African American elderly: Recent developments in theory and research. In J. S. Jackson (Ed.,) *African American elderly.* New York: Springer.

Chatters, L. M., & Jayakody, R. (1995). Intergenerational support within African American families: Concepts and methods. In V. Bengtson, K. W. Schie, & L. M. Burton (Eds.), *Adult intergenerational relations: Effects of social change* (pp. 97-118). New York: Springer.

Chatters, L. M., & Taylor, R. J. (1990). Social integration. In Z. Havel, E. A. McKinney, & M. Williams (Eds.), *Black aged: Understanding diversity and service needs* (pp. 82-99) Newbury Park, CA: Sage.

Chatters, L. M., & Taylor, R. J. (1993). Intergenerational support: The provision of assistance to parents by adult children. In J. S. Jackson, L. M. Chatters, & R. J. Taylor (Eds.), *Aging in black America* (pp. 69-83). Newbury Park, CA: Sage.

Chatters, L. M., Taylor, R. J., & Jackson, J. S. (1985). Size and composition of the informal helper networks of elderly blacks. *Journal of Gerontology, 40,* 605-614.

Chatters, L. M., Taylor, R. J., & Jackson, J. S. (1986). Aged blacks' choice for an informal helper network. *Journal of Gerontology, 41*(1), 94-100.

Chatters, L. M., Taylor, R. J., & Jayakody, R. (1994). Fictive kinship relations in black extended families. *Journal of Comparative Family Studies, 25,* 297-312.

Chatters, L. M., Taylor, R. J., & Neighbors, H. W. (1989). Size of the informal health network mobilized in response to serious personal problems. *Journal of Marriage and the Family, 51,* 667-676.

Chaves, M., & Higgins, L. H. (1992). Comparing the community involvement of black and white congregations. *Journal for the Scientific Study of Religion, 31,* 425-440.

Cherlin, A. J. (1992). *Marriage, divorce, remarriage* (2nd ed.). Cambridge, MA: Harvard University Press.

Cherlin, A. J., Chase-Landsdale, P. L., & Furstenberg, F. F. (1991). Longitudinal studies of effects of divorce on children in Great Britain and the United States. *Science, 5011,* 1386-1389.

Chevan, A., & Sutton, G. H. (1985). Race and sex differentials in the life course. In G. H. Elder (Ed.), *Life course dynamics* (pp. 282-301). Ithaca, NY: Cornell University Press.

Children's Defense Fund. (1992). *The state of America's Children.* Washington, DC: Author.

Chiriboga, D. A. (1977). Life event weighting systems: A comparative analysis. *Journal of Psychosomatic Research, 21,* 415-422.

Christmon, K. (1990). Parental responsibility of African American unwed adolescent fathers. *Adolescence, 25,* 645-653.

Churchill, J. C. (1946). Your chances of getting married. *Good Housekeeping, 123,* 38, 313-319.

Cobb, S., & Kasl, S. V. (1977). *Termination: The consequences of job loss.* Cincinnati, OH: Department of Health, Education, and Welfare (NIOSH).

Cohen, S., & Wills, T. (1985). Stress, social support, and the buffering process. *Psychological Bulletin, 98,* 310-357.

Cohen, T. F. (1987). Remaking men: Men's experiences becoming and being husbands and fathers and their implication for reconceptualizing men's lives. *Journal of Family Issues, 8*(1), 57-77.

Cohen, T. F. (1988). Gender, work, and family: The impact and meaning of work in men's family roles. *Family Perspective, 22,* 293-308.

Cohn, J. F., Campbell, S. B., Matias, R., & Hopkins, J. (1986). Face-to-face interactions of postpartum depressed and nondepressed mother-infant pairs at 2 months. *Developmental Psychology, 26*(1), 15-23.

Cohn, R. M. (1978). The effects of employment status change on self-attitudes. *Social Psychology, 41*(2), 81-93.

Cole, J. (1970). Black culture: Negro, black, and nigger. *Black Scholar, 1,* 40-43.

Coleman, L. M., Antonucci, T. C., Adelmann, P. K., & Crohan, S. E. (1987). Social roles in the lives of middle-aged and older black women. *Journal of Marriage and the Family, 49*(4), 761-771.

Colletta, N. D., & Lee, D. (1983). The impact of support for black adolescent mothers. *Journal of Family Issues, 4,* 127-143.

Collins, P. (1991). *Black feminist thought.* New York: Routledge & Kegan Paul.

Collins, P. H. (1981). The meaning of motherhood in black culture. In K. G. Scott, T. Field, & E. G. Robertson (Eds.), *Teenage parents and their offspring.* New York: Grune & Stratton.

Collins, P. H. (1986). The Afro-American work/family nexus. *Western Journal of Black Studies, 10,* 148-158.

Cooper-Lewter, N. C., & Mitchell, H. H. (1986). *Soul theology: The heart of American black culture.* San Francisco: Harper & Row.

Corcoran, M., Datcher, L., & Duncan, G. (1980a). Information and influence networks in labor markets. In G. Duncan & J. Morgan (Eds.), *Five thousand American families: Patterns of economic progress* (Vol. 8, pp. 1-37). Ann Arbor, MI: Institute for Social Research.

Corcoran, M., Datcher, L., & Duncan, G. (1980b). Most workers find jobs through word of mouth. *Monthly Labor Review, August,* 33-35.

Cornwall, M. (1987). The social bases of religion: A study of the factors influencing religious beliefs and commitment. *Review of Religious Research, 29,* 44-56.

Cosby, B. (1986). *Fatherhood.* New York: Dolphin/Doubleday.

Cox, O. C. (1940). Sex ratio and marital status among Negroes. *American Sociological Review, 5,* 937-947.

Crano, W. D., & Aronoff, J. (1978). A cross-cultural study of expressive and instrumental role complementarity in the family. *American Sociological Review, 43,* 463-471.

Crnic, K. A., Greenberg, M. T., & Slough, N. M. (1986). Early stress and social support influences on mothers' and high-risk infants' functioning in late infancy. *Infant Mental Health Journal, 7*(1), 19-33.

Crockenberg, S. B. (1986). Professional support for adolescent mothers: Who gives it, how adolescent mothers evaluate it, what they would prefer. *Infant Mental Health Journal, 7*(1), 49-58.

Crosby, F. (1984). Job satisfaction and domestic life. In M. D. Lee & R. N. Kanungo (Eds.), *Management of work and personal life* (pp. 41-60). New York: Praeger.

Cross, T. L. (1984). *The black power imperative: Racial inequality and the politics of nonviolence.* New York: Faulkner.

Crowne, D. P., & Marlowe, D. (1964). *The approval motive: Studies in evaluative dependence.* New York: John Wiley.

Cunningham, B. (1984). *Religious orientation as a coping resource.* Unpublished doctoral dissertation, University of Michigan.

Daniel, J. (1975). A definition of fatherhood as expressed by black fathers (Doctoral Dissertation, University of Pittsburgh, 1975). *Dissertation Abstracts International, 36,* 2090A.

Daniels, P., & Weingarten, K. (1988). The fatherhood click: The timing of parenthood in men's lives. In P. Bronstein & C. P. Cowan (Eds.), *Fatherhood today: Men's changing role in the family* (pp. 36-52). New York: John Wiley.

Danziger, S. H., Sandefur, G. D., & Weinberg, D. H. (Eds.). (1994). *Confronting poverty: Prescriptions for change.* New York: Russell Sage.

Danziger, S. K., & Danziger, S. D. (1993). Child poverty and public policy: Toward a comprehensive antipoverty agenda. *Daedalus, 122*(1), 57-83.

Danziger, S. K., & Nichols-Casebolt, A. (1988). Teen parents and child support: Eligibility, participation, and payment. *Journal of Social Service Research, 11*(2/3), 1-20.

Danziger, S. K., & Radin, N. (1990). Absent does not equal uninvolved: Predictors of fathering in teen mother families. *Journal of Marriage and the Family, 52,* 636-642.

Darity, W., & Myers, S. L. (1984). Does welfare dependency cause female headship? The case of the black family. *Journal of Marriage and the Family, 46,* 765-779.

Darity, W., & Myers, S. (1986/1987). Public policy trends and the fate of the black family. *Humboldt Journal of Social Relations, 14,* 134-164.

Darity, W., & Myers, S. (1995). Family structure and the marginalization of black men: Policy implications. In M. B. Tucker & C. Mitchell-Kernan (Eds.), *The decline in marriage among African Americans: Causes, consequences, and policy implications* (pp. 263-308). New York: Russell Sage.

Davis, F. G. (1981). Economics and mobility: A theoretical rationale for urban black family well-being. In H. P. McAdoo (Ed.), *Black families* (pp. 127-138). Newbury Park, CA: Sage.

Davis, K. (1941). Intermarriage in caste societies. *American Anthropologist, 43,* 376-395.

De Luccie, M. F., & Davis, A. J. (1991). Do men's adult life concerns affect their fathering orientations? *Journal of Psychology, 125*(2), 175-188.

Dechter, A., & Smock, P. J. (1994). *The fading breadwinner role and the economic implications for young couples* (IRP Discussion Paper No. 1051-94). Madison: University of Wisconsin, Institute for Research on Poverty.

DeMaris, A. (1995). A tutorial in logistic regression. *Journal of Marriage and the Family, 57,* 956-968.

Dew, M. A., Bromet, E. J., & Schulberg, H. C. (1987). A comparative analyses of two community stressors' long-term mental health effects. *American Journal of Community Psychology 15,* 167-184.

Dilworth-Anderson, P., Burton, L. M., & Johnson, L. B. (1993). Reframing theories for understanding race, ethnicity, and families. In P. G. Boss, W, J Doherty, R. LaRossa, W. R. Schumm, & S. K. Steinmetz (Eds.), *Sourcebook of family theories and methods: A contextual approach* (pp. 627-645) New York: Plenum.

Dilworth-Anderson, P., & McAdoo, H. P. (1988). The study of ethnic minority families: Implications for practitioners and policymakers. *Family Relations, 37,* 265-267.

Dornbusch, S., Carlsmith, J., Bushwall, S., Ritter, P., Leiderman, H., Hastorf, A. & Gross, R. (1985). Single parents, extended households, and the control of adolescents. *Child Development, 56,* 326-341.

Dressler, W. (1985). Extended family relationships, social support, and mental health in a Southern black community. *Journal of Health and Social Behavior, 26*(1), 39-48.

Dressler, W., Hoeppner, S. H., & Pitts, B. J. (1985). Household structure in a Southern black community. *American Anthropologist, 87,* 853-862.

Du Bois, W. E. B. (1898). The study of the Negro problem. *Annals of the American Academy of Political and Social Science, 1,* 1-23.

Duck, S., & Gilmore, R. (1981). *Personal relationships. Vol. 1: Studying personal relationships.* New York: Academic Press.

Duncan, G. J., & Hoffman, S. D. (1990). Welfare receipt and subsequent dependence among black adolescent mothers. *Family Planning Perspectives, 22*(1), 16-20.

Duncan, G. J., & Rodgers, W. (1988). Longitudinal aspects of childhood poverty. *Journal of Marriage and the Family, 50,* 1007-1021.

Dunst, C. J., & Trivette, C. M. (1986). Looking beyond the parent-child dyad for the determinants of maternal styles of interaction. *Infant Mental Health Journal, 7*(1), 69-80.

Dunst, C. J., Vance, S. D., & Cooper, C. S. (1986). A social systems perspective of adolescent pregnancy: Determinants of parent and parent-child behavior. *Infant Mental Health Journal, 7*(1), 34-48.

Earl, L., & Lohmann, N. (1978). Absent fathers and black male children. *Social Work, 23*(5), 413-415.

Edwards, A. M. (1943). *Comparative occupational statistics for the United States, 1870-1940.* Washington, DC: Government Printing Office.

Edwards, R. (1979). *Contested terrain: The transformation of the workplace in the 20th century.* New York: Basic Books.

Eggebeen, D. J., & Lichter, D. T. (1991). Race, family structure, and changing poverty among American children. *American Sociological Review, 56,* 801-817.

Eggebeen, D. J., Snyder, A. R., & Manning, W. D. (1996). Children in single-father families in demographic perspectives. *Journal of Family Issues, 17,* 441-465.

Elder, G. H. (1978). Family history and the life course. In T. Hareven (Ed.), *Transitions* (pp. 17-64). New York: Academic Press.

Elder, G. H. (1985). Household, kinship, and the life course: Perspectives on black families and children. In M. Spencer, G. Brookins, & W. Allen (Eds.), *Beginnings: The social and affective development of black children* (pp. 29-43). Hillsdale, NJ: Lawrence Erlbaum.

Elder, G. H. (1991). Family transitions, cycles, and social change. In P. A. Cowan & M. E. Hetherington (Eds.) *Family transitions* (pp. 31-57). Hillsdale, NJ: Lawrence Erlbaum.

Ellison, C. G. (1990). Family ties, friendships, and subjective well-being among black Americans. *Journal of Marriage and the Family, 52,* 298-310.

Ellison, C. G. (1991). Identification and separatism: Religious involvement and racial orientations among black Americans. *Sociological Quarterly, 32,* 477-494.

Ellison, C. G. (1993). Religious involvement and self-perception among black Americans. *Social Forces, 71,* 1027-1055.

Ellison, C. G., & Sherkat, D. E. (1990). Patterns of religious mobility among black Americans. *Sociological Quarterly 31,* 551-568.

Ellison, C. G., & Sherkat, D. E. (1995). The "semi-involuntary institution" revisited: Regional variations in church participation among black Americans. *Social Forces, 73,* 1415-1437.

Ellwood, D. T. (1988). *Poor support.* New York: Basic Books.

Ellwood, D. T., & Bane, M. J. (1984). *The impact of AFDC on family structure and living arrangements* (Working Paper). Cambridge, MA: Harvard University.

Eng, E., Hatch, J., & Callan, A. (1985). Institutionalizing social support through the church and into the community. *Health Education Quarterly, 12*(1), 81-92.

England, P., & Farkas, G. (1986). *Households, employment, and gender: A social, economic, and demographic view.* New York: Aldine.

Ensminger, M. E., Kellam, S., & Rubin, B. (1983). School and family origins of delinquency: Comparisons by sex. In K. Teilmann Van Dusen & S. Dednick (Eds.), *Prospective studies of crime and delinquency* (pp. 73-97). Boston: Kluwer Nijhoff.

Epenshade, T. J. (1985). Marriage trends in America: Estimates, implications, and underlying causes. *Population and Development Review, 11,* 193-245.

Epenshade, T. J. (1987). Marital careers of American women: A cohort life table analysis. In J. Bongaarts, T. Burch, & K. Wachter (Eds.), *Family demography: Methods and their applications* (pp. 150-167). New York: Oxford University Press.

Ericksen, J. A., Yancey, W. L., & Ericksen, E. P. (1979). The division of family roles. *The Journal of Marriage and the Family, 41,* 301-313.

Erikson, E. H. (1968). *Identity, youth, and crisis.* New York: Norton.

Erikson, E. H. (1966). The concept of identity in race relations. In T. Parsons & K. B. Clark (Eds.), *The Negro American* (pp. 227-253). Boston, MA: Beacon.

Erikson, E. H. (1980). *Identity and the life cycle.* New York: Norton.

Eron, L. D., & Peterson, R. A. (1982). Abnormal behavior: Social approaches. *Annual Review of Psychology, 33,* 231-264.

Evans, B., & Whitfield, J. (1988). The status of black males in America: A database search. *American Psychologist, 43,* 401-402.

Evans, P., & Bartolome, F. (1984). The changing pictures of the relationship between career and family. *Journal of Occupational Behavior, 5*(1), 9-21.

Fagan, J. (1996). A preliminary study of low-income African American fathers' play interactions with their preschool-age children. *Journal of Black Psychology, 22*(1), 7-19.

Farley, R., & Allen, W. (1987a). *The color line and the quality of life in America.* New York: Russell Sage.

Farley, R., & Allen, W. R. (1987b). *Blacks and whites: Narrowing the gap?* Cambridge, MA: Harvard University Press.

Farley, R., & Bianchi, S. (1987). *The growing racial difference in marriage and family patterns* (Research report No. 87-107). Ann Arbor: University of Michigan, Population Studies Center.

Feagin, J. (1968). The kinship ties of Negro urbanites. *Social Science Quarterly, 69,* 600-665.

Filene, P. G. (1987). The secrets of men's history. In H. Brod (Ed.), *The making of masculinities* (pp. 103-119). Boston, MA: Allen & Unwin.

Fleming, A. S., Klein, E., & Corter, C. (1992). The effects of a social support group on depression, maternal attitudes and behavior in new mothers. *Journal of Child Psychology and Psychiatry and Allied Disciplines, 33,* 685-698.

Forman, T. A. (1994). *Black family poverty, children, and social policy: The role of black fathers.* Unpublished manuscript, Northwestern University, Program in Human Development and Social Policy, Evanston, IL.

Forman, T. A. (1995). *A comparison of black and white fathers: Provider role strain, social support, and family life quality.* Unpublished manuscript, University of Michigan, Department of Sociology, Ann Arbor.

Forman, T. A., & Bowman, P. J. (1996, November). *African American fathers' family roles across the life course.* Paper presented at the annual meeting of the National Council on Family Relations, Kansas City, MO.

Forrest, J. D., & Singh, S. (1990). The sexual and reproductive behavior of American women, 1982-1988. *Family Planning Perspectives, 22,* 206-214.

Fossett, M. A., & Kiecolt, K. J. (1990). Mate availability, family formation, and family structure among black Americans in nonmetropolitan Louisiana 1970-1980. *Rural Sociology, 55,* 305-327.

Fossett, M. A., & Kiecolt, K. J. (1991). A methodological review of the sex ratio: Alternatives for comparative research. *Journal of Marriage and the Family, 53,* 941-957.

Fossett, M. A., & Kiecolt, K. J. (1993). Mate availability and family structure among African Americans in U.S. metropolitan areas. *Journal of Marriage and the Family, 55,* 288-302.

Frank, S., Hole, C. B., Jacobson, S., Justkowski, R., & Huyck, M. (1986). Psychological predictors of parents' sense of confidence and control and self- versus child-focused gratifications. *Developmental Psychology, 22,* 348-355.

Franklin, C. W. (1985). The black male urban barber shop: A sex-role socialization setting. *Sex Roles, 12,* 965-979.

Frazier, E. F. (1939). *The Negro family in the United States.* Chicago: University of Chicago Press.

Frazier, E. F. (1974). *The Negro church in America.* New York: Schocken. (Original work published in 1964).

Freiden, A. (1974). The U.S. marriage market. In T. W. Schultz (Ed.), *Economics of the family* (pp. 352-371). Chicago: University of Chicago Press.

Furstenberg, F. F. (1976). *Unplanned parenthood: The social consequences of teenage childbearing.* New York: Free Press.

Furstenberg, F. F. (1981). Remarriage and intergenerational relations. In R. Fogel, E. Hatfield, S. Kiesler, & E. Shanas (Eds.), *Aging: Stability and change in the family* (pp. 115-142). New York: Academic Press.

Furstenberg, F. F. (1988). Good dads-bad dads: Two faces of fatherhood. In A. J. Cherlin (Ed.), *The changing American family and public policy* (pp. 193-218). Washington, DC: Urban Institute Press.

Furstenberg, F. F. (1991). As the pendulum swings: Teenage childbearing and social concern. *Family Relations, 40*(2), 127-138.

Furstenberg, F. F. (1992). Teenage childbearing and cultural rationality: A thesis in search of evidence. *Family Relations, 41,* 239-243.

Furstenberg, F. F., & Crawford, A. G. (1978). Family support: Helping teenage mothers to cope. *Family Planning Perspectives, 10*(6), 322-333.

Furstenberg, F. F., & Harris, K. (1992). The disappearing American father?: Divorce and the waning significance of biological parenthood. In S. J. South & S. E. Tolnay (Eds.), *The changing American family: Sociological and demographic perspectives* (pp. 197-223). Boulder, CO: Westview.

Furstenberg, F. F., & Harris, K. (1993). When and why fathers matter: Impacts of father involvement on the children of adolescent mothers. In R. Lerman & T. Ooms (Eds.), *Young unwed fathers: Changing roles and emerging policies* (pp. 117-138). Philadelphia, Pa: Temple University Press.

Furstenberg, F. F., Brooks-Gunn, J., & Chase-Lansdale, L. (1989). Teenaged pregnancy and childbearing. *American Psychologist, 44,* 313-320.

Furstenberg, F. F., Brooks-Gunn, J., & Morgan, S. P. (1987). *Adolescent mothers in later life.* Cambridge, MA: Cambridge University Press.

Garasky, S., & Meyer, D. R. (1996). Reconsidering the increase in father-only families. *Demography, 33,* 385-393.

Garbarino, J., Dubrow, N., Kostelny, K., & Pardo, C. (1992). *Children in danger: Coping with the consequences of community violence.* San Francisco: Jossey-Bass.

Garbarino, J., Kostelny, K., & Dubrow, N. (1991). *No place to be a child: Growing up in a war zone.* Lexington, MA: Lexington Books.

Garfinkel, I., & McLanahan, S. S. (1986). *Single mothers and their children: A new American dilemma.* Washington, DC: Urban Institute Press.

Gary, L. E. (1981). *Black men.* Beverly Hills, CA: Sage.

Gary, L. E., & Leashore, B. R. (1982). High-risk status of black men. *Social Work, 27*(1), 54-58.

Gecas, V. (1976). The socialization and child care roles. In F. I. Nye (Ed.), *Role structure and analysis of the family* (pp. 33-59). Beverly Hills, CA: Sage.

Genovese, E. (1974). *Roll, Jordan, roll: The world the slaves made.* New York: Pantheon.

George, L. (1989). Stress, social support, and depression over the life-course. In K. Markides & C. Cooper (Eds.), *Aging, stress, and health* (pp. 241-267). New York: John Wiley.

Geronimus, A. T. (1991). Teenage childbearing and social and reproductive disadvantage: The evolution of complex questions and the demise of simple answers. *Family Relations, 40,* 463-471.

Geronimus, A. T., & Korenman, S. (1992). The socioeconomic consequences of teen childbearing reconsidered. *Quarterly Journal of Economics, 107,* 1187-1214.

Geronimus, A. T., & Korenman, S. (1993). The socioeconomic costs of teen childbearing: Evidence and interpretation. *Demography, 30,* 281-290.

Gertsel, N. (1988). Divorce and kin ties: The importance of gender. *Journal of Marriage and the Family, 50,* 209-219.

Gibson, R. (1972). Kin family network: Overheralded structure in past conceptualization of family functioning. *Journal of Marriage and the Family, 34,* 13-23.

Gibson, R. (1991). Retirement. In J. S. Jackson (Ed.), *Life in black America* (pp. 179-198). Newbury Park, CA: Sage.

Gibson, R. C. (1982). Blacks at middle and late life: Resources and coping. *Annals of the American Academy of Political and Social Science, 464,* 79-90.

Gibson, R. C., & Jackson, J. S. (1992). The black oldest old: Health functioning and informal support. In K. Suzman, D. Willes, & K. Manton (Eds.), *The oldest old* (pp. 321-340). New York: Oxford University Press.

Gibson, R. C., & Jackson, J. S. (in press). *Health in black America.* Thousand Oaks, CA: Sage.

Gilkes, C. (1980). The black church as a therapeutic community: Suggested areas for research into the black religious experience. *Journal of the Interdenominational Theological Center, 8*(1), 29-44.

Glasgow, D. G. (1980). *The black underclass.* San Francisco: Jossey-Bass.

Glen, N. (1975). The contribution of marriage to the psychological well-being of males and females. *Journal of Marriage and the Family, 37,* 594-600.

Glick, P. C. (1984). A demographic picture of black families. In H. P. McAdoo (Ed.), *Black families* (pp. 111-132). Beverly Hills, CA: Sage.

Glick, P. C. (1988). Demographic pictures of black families. In H. McAdoo. (Ed.), *Black families* (2nd ed., pp. 107-110). Beverly Hills, CA: Sage.

Glick, P. C., Heer, D. M., & Beresford, J. C. (1963). Family formation and family composition: Trends and prospects. In M. B. Sussman (Ed.), *Sourcebook in marriage and the family* (pp. 30-40). New York: Houghton Mifflin.

Goetting, A. (1986). Parental satisfaction: A review of the research. *Journal of Family Issues, 7,* 83-109.

Goldman, N., Westoff, C. F., & Hammerslough, C. (1984). Demography of the marriage market in the United States. *Population Index, 50*(1), 5-25.

Goldscheider, F. K., & Waite, L. J. (1986). Sex differentials in the entry into marriage. *American Journal of Sociology, 92*(1), 91-109.

Gooden, W. (1989). Development of black men in early adulthood. In R. L. Jones (Ed.), *Black adult development and aging* (pp. 63-90). Berkeley, CA: Cobbs & Henry.

Gordon, E. T., Gordon, E. W., & Nembhard, J. G. (1994). Social science literature concerning African American men. *Journal of Negro Education, 63*(4), 508-531.

Gordon, L., & McLanahan, S. S. (1991). Single parenthood in 1900. *Journal of Family History, 16*(2), 97-116.

Gore, S. L. (1978). The effects of social support in moderating the health consequences of unemployment. *Journal of Health and Social Behavior, 19,* 157-165.

Gottschalk, P., McLanahan, S., & Sandefur, G. D. (1994). The dynamics and intergenerational transmission of poverty and welfare participation. In S. H. Danziger, G. D. Sandefur, & D. W. Weinberg (Eds.), *Confronting poverty: Prescriptions for change* (pp. 85-108). Cambridge, MA: Harvard University Press.

Gould, R. (1976). Measuring masculinity by the size of a paycheck. In D. S. David & R. Brannon (Eds.), *The 49% majority: The male sex role* (pp. 113-117). Reading, MA: Addison-Wesley.

Gove, W. R. (1972). The relationship between sex roles, mental illness, and marital status. *Social Forces, 51*(1), 34-44.

Gove, W. R., & Tudor, J. (1973). Adult sex roles and mental illness. *American Journal of Sociology, 78,* 812-835.

Gove, W. R., Hughes, M., & Style, C. B. (1983). Does marriage have positive effects on the well-being of the individual? *Journal of Health and Social Behavior, 24,* 122-131.

Granovetter, M. (1973). The strength of weak ties. *American Journal of Sociology, 78,* 1360-1380.

Granovetter, M. (1974). *Getting a job: A study of contacts and careers.* Cambridge, MA: Harvard University Press.

Granovetter, M. (1995). *Getting a job: A study of contacts and careers* (2nd ed.). Chicago: University of Chicago Press.

Green, L. (1982). A learned helplessness analysis of problems confronting the black community. In S. Turner & R. T. Jones (Eds.), *Behavioral modification in black populations: Psychological issues and empirical findings* (pp. 73-93). New York: Plenum.

Greene, R. L., Jackson, J. S., & Neighbors, H. W. (1993). Mental health and health-seeking behavior. In J. S. Jackson, L. M. Chatters, & R. J. Taylor (Eds.), *Aging in black America* (pp. 185-200). Newbury Park, CA: Sage.

Greene, W. H. (1990). *Econometric analysis.* New York: Macmillan.

Grogger, J., & Bronars, S. (1993). The socioeconomic consequences of teenage childbearing: Findings from a natural experiment. *Family Planning Perspectives, 25,* 156-161, 174.

Gurin, G., Veroff, J., & Feld, S. (1960). *Americans view their mental health: A nationwide survey* (Joint Commission on Mental Illness and Health Monograph No. 4). New York: Basic Books.

Gutman, H. G. (1976). *The black family in slavery and freedom, 1750-1925.* New York: Pantheon.

Guttentag, M., & Secord, P. F. (1983). *Too many women: The sex ratio question.* Beverly Hills, CA: Sage.

Haavio, M. E. (1971). Satisfaction with family, work, leisure, and life among men and women. *Human Relations, 24,* 585-601.

Hakim, C. (1982). The social consequences of high unemployment. *Journal of Social Policy, 2,* 433-467.

Hamilton, V. L., Broman, C. L., Hoffman, W. S., & Renner, D. S. (1990). Hard times and vulnerable people: The initial effects of plant closings on mental health. *Journal of Health and Social Behavior, 31*(2), 123-140.

Hammen, C., Burge, D., & Stansbury, K. (1990). Relationship of mother and child variables to child outcomes in a high-risk sample: A causal modeling analysis. *Developmental Psychology, 26*(1), 24-30.

Hampton, R. (1991). Child abuse in the African American community. In J. Everett, S. Chipungu, & B. Leashore (Eds.), *Child welfare: An Afrocentric perspective* (pp. 187-219). New York: Rutgers University.

Hampton, R. L. (1979). Husband's characteristics and marital disruption in black families. *Sociological Quarterly, 20,* 255-266.

Hareven, T. (1977). Family time, historical time. *Daedalus, 106*(2), 57-70.

Harris, K. E. (1995). Public policy, the black community, and fathering. *Father Focus, 1*(1), 1-3.

Harris, K. E. (1996a). *Defining the social policy environment on fatherhood.* Chicago: Center of Fathers, Families, and Public Policy.

Harris, K. E. (1996b, November). *Social welfare policy reform: Creating barriers to father support and involvement.* Paper presented at the annual meeting of the National Council on Family Relations, Kansas City, MO.

Harrison, A. (1985). The black family's socializing environment. In H. McAdoo & J. McAdoo (Eds.), *Black children* (pp. 174-193). Beverly Hills, CA: Sage.

Harrison, A. O., Wilson, M. N., Pine, C. J., Chan, S. Q., & Buriel, R. (1990). Family ecologies of ethnic minority children. *Child Development, 61,* 347-362.

Hartmann, H. (1976). Capitalism, patriarchy, and job segregation by sex. *Signs, 1,* 137-168.

Hatchett, S. J. (1991). Women and men. In J. S. Jackson (Ed.), *Life in black America* (pp. 84-104). Newbury Park, CA: Sage.

Hatchett, S. J., Cochran, D. L., & Jackson, J. S. (1991). Family life. In J. S. Jackson (Ed.), *Life in black America* (pp. 46-83). Newbury Park, CA: Sage.

Hatchett, S. J., & Jackson, J. S. (1993). African American extended kin systems: An assessment. In H. P. McAdoo (Ed.), *Family ethnicity: Strengths in diversity* (pp. 90-118). Newbury Park, CA: Sage.

Hatchett, S., Veroff, J., & Douvan, E. (1995). Marital instability among black and white couples in early marriage. In M. B. Tucker & C. Mitchell- Kernan (Eds.), *The decline in marriage among African Americans—Causes, consequences, and policy implications* (pp. 177-218). New York: Russell Sage.

Hawkins, A. J., & Dollahite, D. C. (1997). *Generative fathering: Beyond deficit perspectives.* Thousand Oaks, CA: Sage.

Hawkins, A. J., & Eggebeen, D. J. (1990). Are fathers fungible? Patterns of coresident adult men in maritally disrupted families and young children's well-being. *Journal of Marriage and the Family, 53,* 958-972.

Hayes, C. D. (Ed.). (1987). *Risking the future: Adolescent sexuality, pregnancy, and childbearing* (Vol. 1). Washington, DC: National Academy Press.

Hays, W., & Mindel, C. (1973). Extended kinship relations in black and white families. *Journal of Marriage and the Family, 35*(1), 51-56.

Heaton, T. B., & Pratt, E. L. (1990). The effects of religious homogamy on marital satisfaction and stability. *Journal of Family Issues, 11,* 191-207.

Heckler, M. (1985). *Report of the Secretary's task force on black and minority health* (see also related subcommittee reports and commissioned papers). Washington, DC: U.S. Department of health and Human Services.

Heer, D., & Grossbard-Shechtman, A. (1981). The impact of the female marriage squeeze and the contraceptive revolution on sex roles and the women's liberation movement in the United States, 1960 to 1975. *Journal of Marriage and the Family, 34*(2), 49-65.

Henshaw, S. K. (1991). The accessibility of abortion services in the United States. *Family Planning Perspectives, 23,* 246-263.

Henshaw, S. K. (1992). Research note—Abortion trends in 1987 and 1988. In S. K. Henshaw & J. Van Hort (Eds.), *Age and race abortion fact book—Readings, trends, and state and local data to 1988* (pp. 68-70). New York: Alan Guttmacher Institute.

Henshaw, S. K., Koonin, L. M., & Smith, J. C. (1992). Characteristics of U.S. women having abortions, 1987. In S. K. Henshaw & J. Van Hort (Eds.), *Age and race abortion fact book—Readings, trends, and state and local data to 1988* (pp. 61-67). New York: Alan Guttmacher Institute.

Henshaw, S. K., & Silverman, J. (1988). The characteristics and prior contraceptive use of U.S. abortion patients. *Family Planning Perspectives, 20,* 158-168.

Hepworth, S. J. (1980). Moderating factors of the psychological impact of unemployment. *Journal of Occupational Psychology, 53,* 139-145.

Hernandez, D. (1993). *American's children: Resources from family, government, and the economy.* New York: Russell Sage.

Hill, M. S. (1990). *Shared housing as a form of economic support for young, unmarried mothers* (Working Paper). Ann Arbor: University of Michigan, Institute for Social Research.

Hill, R. (1971). *The strengths of black families.* New York: Emerson Hall.

Hill, R. (1993). *Research on the African American family: A holistic perspective.* Westport, CT: Auburn House.

Hill, R. B. (1972). *Strengths of black families.* New York: Emerson-Hall.

Hill, R. B., Billingsley, A., Ingram, E., Malson, M. R., Rubin, R. H., Stack, C., Stewart, J. B., & Teele, J. E. (1989). *Research on African American families: A holistic perspective.* Boston: William Monroe Trotter Institute.

Hill, R., & Mattessich, P. (1979). Family development theory and life span development. In P. Baltes & O. Brim (Eds.), *Life-span development and behavior* (Vol. 3). New York: Academic Press.

Hiller, D. V., & Philliber, W. W. (1986). The division of labor in contemporary marriage: Expectations, perceptions, and performance. *Social Problems, 33*(3), 191-201.

Hochschild, A. (1989). *The second shift.* New York: Avon Books.

Hochschild, A. R. (1989). *The second shift: Working parents and the revolution at home.* Viking: New York.

Hodson, R. (1983). *Workers' earnings and corporate economic structure.* New York: Academic Press.

Hofferth, S. (1984). Kin networks, race, and family structure. *Journal of Marriage and the Family, 46,* 791-806.

Hofferth, S. L. (1985). Children's life course: Family structure and living arrangements in cohort perspective. In G. H. Elder, Jr. (Ed.), *Life course dynamics: Trajectories and transitions, 1968-1980* (pp. 75-112). Ithaca, NY: Cornell University Press.

Hofferth, S. L. (1987). Social and economic consequences of teenage childbearing. In National Research Council (Ed.), *Risking the future: Adolescent sexuality, pregnancy, and childbearing* (pp. 123-144). Washington, DC: National Academy Press.

Hoffman, S. D., Foster, E. M., & Furstenberg, F. F., Jr. (1993a). Reevaluating the costs of teenage childbearing. *Demography, 30*(1), 1-14.

Hoffman, S. D., Foster, E. M., & Furstenberg, F. F., Jr. (1993b). Reevaluating the costs of teenage childbearing: Response to Geronimus and Korenman. *Demography, 30,* 291-296.

Hogan, D. P., Eggebeen, D. J., & Clogg, C. C. (1993). The structure of intergeneratinal exchanges in American families. *American Journal of Sociology, 98,* 1428-1458.

Hogan, D. P., Hao, L.-X., & Parish, W. L. (1990). Race, kin networks, and assistance to mother-only families. *Social Forces, 68*(3), 797-812.

Hogan, D. P., & Kitagawa, E. M. (1985). The impact of social status, family structure, and neighborhood on the fertility of black adolescents. *American Journal of Sociology, 90,* 825-855.

Hogan, D. P., & Lichter, D. T. (1995). Children and youth: Living arrangements and welfare. In R. Farley (Ed.), *State of the union: America in the 1990s. Vol. 2: Social trends* (pp. 93-139). New York: Russell Sage.

Honig, A. S., & Mayne, G. (1982). Black fathering in three social class groups. *Ethnic Groups, 4,* 229-238.

Hood, J. C. (1986). The provider role: Its meaning and measurement. *Journal of Marriage and the Family, 48,* 349-359.

Horton, H. D., & Burgess, N. (1992). Where are the black men? Regional differences in the pool of marriageable black males in the United States. *National Journal of Sociology, 6*(1), 3-19.

Hossain, Z., & Roopnarine, J. L. (1993). Division of household labor and child care in dual-earner African American families with infants. *Sex Roles, 28,* 571-583.

House, J. S. (1981). *Work stress and social support.* Reading, MA: Addison-Wesley.

House, J. S., & Robbins, C. (1983). Age, psychosocial stress, and health. In M. W. Riley, B. Hess, & K. Bond (Eds.), *Aging in society: Selected reviews of recent research* (pp. 175-197). Hillsdale, NJ: Lawrence Erlbaum.

House, J. S., Umberson, D., & Landis, K. R. (1988). Structures and processes of social support. *Annual Review of Sociology 2,* 293-318.

Hughes, F. P., & Noppe, L. D. (1985). *Human development across the life span.* New York: West.

Hunter, A. G. (1993). Making a way: Strategies of Southern urban African American families, 1900 and 1936. *Journal of Family History, 18*(3), 231-248.

Hunter, A. G., & Davis, J. E. (1992). Constructing gender: An exploration of Afro-American men's conceptualization of manhood. *Gender and Society, 6,* 464-479.

Hunter, A. G., & Ensminger, M. E. (1992). Diversity and fluidity in children's living arrangements: Family transitions in an urban Afro-American community. *Journal of Marriage and the Family 54,* 418-426.

Hunter, A. G., & Sellers, S. L. (1996). *Feminist attitudes among African American women and men.* Unpublished manuscript, University of Michigan, Institute for Social Research, Ann Arbor.

Hurd, E. P., Moore, C., & Rogers, R. (1995). Quiet success: Parenting strengths among African Americans. *Families in society, 76,* 434-443.

Jackson, J. (1971). But where are all the men? *Black Scholar, 3*(4), 34-41.

Jackson, J. J. (1973). Family organization and technology. In K. S. Miller & R. M. Dreger (Eds.), *Comparative studies of blacks and whites in the United States* (pp. 405-445). New York: Seminar Press.

Jackson, J., McCullough, W., & Gurin, G. (1988). Family, socialization environment, and identity development in black Americans. In H. McAdoo (Ed.), *Black families* (2nd ed., pp. 242-256). Beverly Hills, CA: Sage.

Jackson, J. S. (Ed.). (1991). *Life in black America.* Newbury Park, CA: Sage.

Jackson, J. S., Chatters, L. M., & Neighbors, H. (1986). The subjective life quality of black Americans. In F. Andrews (Ed.), *Research on the quality of life* (pp. 193-213). Ann Arbor: University of Michigan, Institute for Social Research.

Jackson, J. S., Chatters, L. M., & Taylor, R. J. (Eds.). (1993). *Aging in black America.* Newbury Park, CA: Sage.

Jackson, J. S., Jayakody, R., & Antonucci, T. (1996). Exchanges within black American three-generation families: The family environment context model. In T. Hareven (Ed.), *Aging and generational relations over the life course* (pp. 351-381). New York: Walter de Gruyter.

Jackson, J. S., Tucker, M. B., & Gurin, G. (1980). *National Survey of Black Americans* [Machine-readable data file]. Ann Arbor, MI: Institute for Social Research [Producer], Inter-University Consortium for Political and Social Research [Distributor].

Jackson, J. S., & Wolford, M. L. (1992). Changes from 1979 to 1987 in mental health status and help seeking among African Americans. *Journal of Geriatric Psychiatry, 25*(1), 15-67.

Jahoda, M. (1982). *Employment and unemployment: A social-psychological analysis.* Cambridge, MA: Harvard University Press.

Jayakody, R. T. (1996). *Time of transition: Living arrangement and family status transitions after a marital disruption.* Unpublished doctoral dissertation, University of Michigan.

Jayakody, R. T., Chatters, L. M., & Taylor, R. J. (1993). Family support to single and married African American mothers: The provision of financial, emotional, and child care assistance. *Journal of Marriage and the Family, 55,* 261-276.

Jaynes, G. D., & Williams, R. M., Jr. (Eds.). (1989). *A common destiny: Blacks and American society.* Washington, DC: National Academy Press.

Jemmott, J. B., Ashby, K. L, & Lindenfeld, K. (1989). Romantic commitment and the perceived availability of opposite sex persons: On loving the one you're with. *Journal of Applied Social Psychology, 19,* 1198-1211.

Jenkins, S., & Diamond, B. (1985). Ethnicity and foster care: Census data as predictors of placement variables. *American Journal of Orthopsychiatry, 55,* 267-276.

Johnson, J. H., & Oliver, M. L. (1991). Economic restructuring and black male joblessness in U.S. metropolitan areas. *Urban Geography, 12*(6), 542-562.

Johnson, J. H., & Oliver, M. L. (1992). Structural changes in the U.S. economy and black male joblessness: A reassessment. In G. E. Peterson & W. Vroman (Eds.), *Urban labor markets and job opportunity* (pp. 113-147). Washington, DC: Urban Institute Press.

Johnson, W. (in press). Family and peer influence affecting child support provision among urban, poor young African American males. In I. Garfinkel & S. McLanahan (Eds.), *Child support enforcement and nonresident fathers.* New York: Russell Sage.

Johnson, W. E. (1993). *Perceptions and patterns of paternal role functioning among lower socioeconomic status adolescent and young adult African American males: A social choice/social norms perspective.* Unpublished doctoral dissertation, University of Chicago.

Johnson, W. E. (1995). Paternal identity among urban adolescent males. *African American Research Perspectives, 2*(1), 82-86.

Johnson, W. E. (1996). *Socially contextualized paternal identity: The construction of possible selves among urban poor adolescent African American males.* Unpublished manuscript, University of Michigan, Institute for Social Research, Ann Arbor.

Jones, E. G., & Forrest, H. D. (1992). Contraceptive failure rates based on the 1988 NSFG. *Family Planning Perspectives, 22,* 12-19.

Jones, J. (1979). Conceptual and strategic issues in the relationship of black psychology to American social science. In A. W. Boykin, A. J. Franklin, & J. F. Yates (Eds.), *Research directions of black psychologists* (pp. 390-432). New York: Russell Sage.

Kahn, R. (1974). Conflict, ambiguity, and overload: Three elements in job stress. In A. McLean (Ed.), *Occupational stress* (pp. 47-61). Springfield, IL: Charles C Thomas.

Kahn, R. L., & Antonucci, T. C. (1980). Convoys over the live course: Attachment, roles, and social support. In P. B. Baltes & O. Brim (Eds.), *Life-span development and behavior* (Vol. 3, pp. 253-286). Lexington, MA: Lexington Books.

Kallenberg, A. (1983). Work and stratification. *Work & Occupations, 10*(3), 251-259.

Kallenberg, A., & Sorenson, A. (1979). The sociology of labor markets. *Annual Review of Sociology, 5,* 351-379.

Kalmuss, D. S., & Namerow, P. B. (1994). Subsequent childbearing among teenage mothers: The determinants of a closely spaced second birth. *Family Planning Perspectives, 26,* 149-153.

Kando, T. M., & Summers W. C. (1971). The impact of work on leisure: Toward a paradigm and research strategy. *Pacific Sociological Review, 14,* 310-327.

Kane, E. (1992). Race, gender, and attitudes toward gender stratification. *Social Psychology Quarterly, 55*(3), 311-320.

Kane, E., & Sanchez, L. (1994). Family status and criticism of gender inequality at home and at work. *Social Forces, 72*(4), 1079-1102.

Kasl, S. V., & Cobb, S. (1970). Blood pressure changes in men undergoing job loss: A preliminary report. *Psychosomatic Medicine, 32,* 19-38.

Kellam, S. G., Adams, R. G., Brown, C. H., & Ensminger, M. E. (1982). The long-term evolution of the family structure of teenage and older mothers. *Journal of Marriage and the Family, 44,* 539-554.

Kellam, S. G., Ensminger, M. E., & Turner, R. J. (1977). Family structure and the mental health of children: Concurrent and longitudinal communitywide studies. *Archives of General Psychiatry, 34*(9), 1012-1022.

Kelley, H. H. (1983). Love and commitment. In H. H. Kelley, E. Berscheid, A. Christensen, J. H. Harvey, T. L. Huston, G. Levinger, E. McClintock, L. A. Peplau, & D. R. Peterson (Eds.), *Close relationships* (pp. 265-314). New York: W. H. Freeman.

Kelley, M. L., & Colburn, C. B. (1995). Economically disadvantaged African American fathers: Social policy and fathering. *Journal of African American Men, 1*(1), 63-74.

Kelley, M. L., Power, T. G., & Wimbush, D. D. (1992). Determinants of disciplinary practices in low-income black mothers. *Child Development, 63,* 573-582.

Kennedy, T. R. (1980). *You gotta deal with it: Black family relations on a Southern community.* New York: Oxford University Press.

Kessler, R. C. (1979). Stress, social status, and psychological distress. *Journal of Health and Social Behavior, 20,* 259-272.

Kessler, R. C. (1982). A disaggregation of the relationship between socioeconomic status and psychological distress. *American Sociological Review, 47,* 752-764.

Kessler, R. C., & Essex, M. (1982). Marital status and depression: The importance of coping resources. *Social Forces, 61,* 484-507.

Kessler, R. C., House, J. S., & Turner, J. B. (1987). Unemployment and health in a community sample. *Journal of Health and Social Behavior, 28*(4), 51-59.

Kessler, R. C., Price, R. H., & Wortman, C. G. (1985). Social factors in psychopathology: Stress, social support, and coping processes. *Annual Review of Psychology, 36,* 531-572.

Kessler, R. C., Turner, J. B., & House, J. S. (1989). Unemployment, reemployment, and emotional functioning in a community sample. *American Sociological Review, 54,* 648-657.

Kiecolt, K. J. (1988). Recent developments in attitudes and social structure. *Annual Review of Sociology, 14,* 381-403.

Kiecolt, K. J., & Fossett, A. M. (1995). Mate availability and marriage among African Americans: Aggregate- and individual-level analyses. In M. B. Tucker & C. Mitchell-Kernan (Eds.), *The decline in marriage among African Americans: Causes, consequences, and policy implications* (pp. 121-135). New York: Russell Sage.

Kissman, K. (1989). Social support, parental belief systems, and well-being. *Youth & Society, 21*(1), 120-130.

Klepinger, D. H., Lundberg, S., & Plotnick, R. D. (1995). Adolescent fertility and the educational attainment of young women. *Family Planning Perspectives, 27*(1), 23-28.

Kletzer, L. G. (1991). Job displacement: Black and white workers compared. *Monthly Labor Review, 144*(7), 17-25.

Koeske, G. F., & Koeske, R. D. (1990). The buffering effect of social support on parental stress. *American Journal of Orthopsychiatry, 60,* 440-451.

Korenman, S., & Turner, S. (1996). Employment contacts and minority-white wage differences. *Industrial Relations, 35*(1), 106-122.

Kost, K., & Forrest, J. D. (1992). American women's sexual behavior and exposure to risk of sexually transmitted diseases. *Family Planning Perspectives, 24,* 244-254.

Kosterlitz, J. (1992). The marriage penalty. *National Journal, 24,* 1454-1457.

Krause, N., & Borawski-Clark, E. (1995). Social class differences in social support among older adults. *The Gerontologist, 35,* 498-508.

Lamb, M. E., Pleck, J. H., & Levine, J. A. (1986). Effects of increased paternal involvement on children in two-parent families. In R. Lewis & R. A. Salt (Eds.), *Men in families* (pp. 141-158). Newbury Park, CA: Sage.

Lamb, M., & Lamb, V. (1976). The nature and importance of the father-infant relationship. *Family Coordinator, 25,* 379-385.

Lamb, M., & Sagi, A. (Eds.). (1983). *Fatherhood and family policy.* Hillsdale, NJ: Lawrence Erlbaum.

Landale, N. S., & Tolnay, S. E. (1991). Group differences in economic opportunity and the timing of marriage: Blacks and whites in the rural South, 1910. *American Sociological Review, 56*(1), 33-45.

Landry, D. J., & Forrest, J. D. (1995). How old are U.S. fathers? *Family Planning Perspectives, 27,* 159-161, 165.

LaRossa, R. (1988). Fatherhood and social change. *Family Relations, 37,* 451-457.

Larson, L. E., & Goltz, J. W. (1989). Religious participation and marital commitment. *Review of Religious Research, 30,* 387-400.

Lemme, B. H. (1995). *Development in adulthood.* Boston: Allyn & Bacon.

Lerman, R. I. (1986). Who are the young absent fathers? *Youth & Society, 18*(1), 3-27.

Lerman, R. I. (1993). A national profile of young unwed fathers. In R. I. Lerman & T. J. Ooms (Eds.), *Young unwed fathers: Changing roles and emerging policies* (pp. 27-51). Philadelphia, PA: Temple University Press.

Levant, R., & Kelly, J. (1989). *Between father and child.* New York: Viking.

Levin, J. S., Chatters, L. M., & Taylor, R. J. (1995). Religious effects on health status and life satisfaction among black Americans. *Journal of Gerontology: Social Sciences, 50B,* S154-S163.

Levin, J. S., Taylor, R. J., & Chatters, L. M. (1994). Race and gender differences in religiosity among older adults: Findings from four national surveys. *Journal of Gerontology: Social Sciences, 49*(3), S137-S145.

Levine, L. (1977). *Black culture and black consciousness: Afro-American folk thought from slavery to freedom.* Oxford, UK: Oxford University Press.

Levitt, M., Guacci, N., & Weber, R. A. (1991). Intergenerational support, relationship quality, and well-being: A bicultural analysis. *Journal of Family Issues, 13,* 465-481.

Lewis, C., & O'Brien, M. (Eds.). (1987). *Reassessing fatherhood: New observations on fathers and the modern family.* London: Sage.

Lewis, H. (1955). *Blackways of Kent.* Chapel Hill: University of North Carolina Press.

Liao, T. F. (1994). *Interpreting probability models: Logit, probit, and other generalized linear models.* Thousand Oaks, CA: Sage.

Lichter, D. T., LeClere, F. B., & McLaughlin, D. K. (1991). Local marriage market conditions and the marital behavior of black and white women. *American Journal of Sociology, 96,* 843-867.

Lichter, D. T., McLaughlin, D. K., Kephart, G., & Landry, D. J. (1992). Race and the retreat from marriage: A shortage of marriageable men? *American Sociological Review, 57,* 781-799.

Lieberson, S., & Waters, M. C. (1988). *From many strands: Ethnic and racial groups in contemporary America.* New York: Russell Sage.

Liebow, E. (1967). *Tally's corner.* Boston: Little, Brown.

Liem, R., & Liem, J. H. (1988). Psychological effects of unemployment on workers and their families. *Journal of Social Issues, 44*(4), 87-106.

Lin, N., Ensel, W., & Vaughn, J. (1981). Social resources and strength of ties: Structural factors in occupational status attainment. *American Sociological Review, 46,* 393-405.

Lincoln, C. E., & Mamiya, L. H. (1990). *The black church in the African American experience.* Durham, NC: Duke University Press.

Linn, M. W., Sandifer, R., & Stein, S. (1985). Effects of unemployment on mental and physical health. *American Journal of Public Health, 75,* 502-506.

Litwak, E., & Kulis, S. (1987). Technology, proximity, and measures of kin support. *Journal of Marriage and the Family, 49,* 649-661.

Lloyd, K. M., & South, S. J. (1996). Contextual influences on young men's transition to first marriage. *Social Forces, 74,* 1097-1119.

Mack, D. E. (1978). Power relationships in black families. *Journal of Personality and Social Psychology, 30,* 409-413.

Macpherson, D., & Stewart, J. B. (1991). The effects of extended families and marital status on housing consumption by black female-headed families. *Review of Black Political Economy, 41*(Winter/Spring), 65-83.

Manning, W. D., & Smock, P. J. (1995). Why marry? Race and the transition to marriage among cohabitors. *Demography, 32*(4), 509-520.

Marciano, T. D. (1987). Families and religions. In M. B. Sussman & S. K. Steinmetz (Eds.), *Handbook of marriage and the family* (pp. 285-316). New York: Plenum.

Mare, R. D., & Winship, C. (1991). Socioeconomic change and the decline of marriage for blacks and whites. In C. Jencks & P. Peterson (Eds.), *The urban underclass* (pp. 175-202). Washington, DC: Brookings Institution.

Marini, M. M. (1978). The transition to adulthood: Sex differences in educational attainment and age at marriage. *American Sociological Review, 43,* 483-507.

Marriage: 800,000 Negro girls will never get to altar, experts predict. (1947, June). *Ebony, 4,* 21-24.

Marsden, P., & Hurlbert, J. (1988). Social resources and mobility outcomes: A replication and extension. *Social Forces, 66,* 1038-1059.

Marsiglio, W. (1987). Adolescent fathers in the United States: Their initial living arrangements, marital experience, and educational outcomes. *Family Planning Perspective, 19,* 240-251.

Marsiglio, W. (1988). Commitment to social fatherhood: Predicting adolescent males' intentions to live with their child and partner. *Journal of Marriage and the Family, 50,* 427-441.

Marsiglio, W. (1991). Paternal engagement activities with minor children. *Journal of Marriage and the Family, 53,* 973-986.

Marsiglio, W. (1993). Adolescent males' orientation toward paternity and contraception. *Family Planning Perspectives, 25*(1), 22-31.

Marsiglio, W. (1995a). Fatherhood scholarship: An overview and agenda for the future. In W. Marsiglio (Ed.), *Fatherhood: Contemporary theory, research, and social policy* (pp. 1-21). Thousand Oaks, CA: Sage.

Marsiglio, W. (1995b). Fathers' diverse life course patterns and roles: Theory and social interventions. In W. Marsiglio (Ed.), *Fatherhood: Contemporary theory, research, and social policy* (pp. 78-101). Thousand Oaks, CA: Sage.

Marsiglio, W., & Scanzoni, J. H. (1990). Pregnant and parenting black adolescents: Theoretical and policy perspectives. In A. R. Stiffman & L. E. Davis (Eds.), *Ethnic issues in adolescent mental health* (pp. 220-244). Newbury Park, CA: Sage.

Marsiglio, W., & Shehan, C. (1993). Adolescent males' abortion attitudes: Data from a national survey. *Family Planning Perspectives, 25,* 162-169.

Martin, E., & Martin, J. (1978). *The black extended family.* Chicago: University of Chicago Press.

Martin, T. C., & Bumpass, L. L. (1989). Recent trends in marital disruption. *Demography, 26*(1), 37-51.

Martineau, W. (1977). Informal social ties among urban black Americans. *Journal of Black Studies, 8*(1), 83-104.

Marx, J., & Leicht, K. (1992). Formality of recruitment to 229 jobs: Variations by race, sex, and job characteristics. *Sociology and Social Research, 76,* 190-196.

Matsueda, R. L., & Heimer, K. (1987). Race, family structure, and delinquency: A test of differential association and social control theories. *American Sociological Review, 52,* 826-840.

Mayer, S. E., & Jencks, C. (1989). Growing up in poor neighborhoods: How much does it matter? *Science, 243,* 1441-1145.

Mays, B. E., & Nicholson, J. W. (1933). *The Negro's church.* New York: Russell and Russell.

McAdoo, H. P. (1977). The impact of upward mobility on kin-help patterns and the reciprocal obligations in black families. *Journal of Marriage and the Family.*

McAdoo, H. P. (1978). Factors related to stability in upwardly mobile black families. *Journal of Marriage and the Family, 40*(4), 761-776.

McAdoo, H. P. (1980). Black mothers and the extended family support network. In L. F. Rodgers-Rose (Ed.), *The black woman* (pp. 125-144). Beverly Hills, CA: Sage.

McAdoo, H. P. (Ed.). (1981). *Black families.* Newbury Park, CA: Sage.

McAdoo, H. P. (1984). Poverty equals women and their children. *Point of View, 8,* 9.

McAdoo, H. P. (1993). *Family ethnicity: Strength and diversity.* Newbury Park, CA: Sage.

McAdoo, H. P. (1996). *Black families* (2nd ed.). Thousand Oaks, CA: Sage.

McAdoo, H. P., & Crawford, V. (1990). The black church and family support programs. *Prevention and Human Services, 9,* 193-203.

McAdoo, J. (1981). Black fathers and child interaction. In L. Gray (Ed.), *Black men* (pp. 115-130). Newbury Park, CA: Sage.

McAdoo, J. (1986). Black father's relationships with their preschool children and the children's development of ethnic identity. In R. A. Lewis & R. E. Salt (Eds.), *Men in families* (pp. 169-180). Newbury Park, CA: Sage.

McAdoo, J. (1988a). The roles of black fathers in the socialization of Black children. In H. P. McAdoo (Ed.), *Black families* (pp. 257-269). Newbury Park, CA: Sage.

McAdoo, J. (1988b). Changing perspectives on the role of the black father. In P. Bronstein & C. P. Cowan (Eds.), *Fatherhood today: Men's changing role in the family* (pp. 79-92). New York: John Wiley.

McAdoo, J. (1993). The role of African American fathers: An ecological perspective. *Families in Society, 74,* 28-35.

McAdoo, J., & McAdoo, J. B. (1994). The African American father's role within the family. In R. G. Majors & J. U. Gordon (Eds.), *The American black male: His present status and his future* (pp. 286-297). Chicago: Nelson Hall.

McDaniel, A. (1990). The power of culture: A review of the idea of Africa's influence on family structure in antebellum American. *Journal of Family History, 15,* 225-238.

McKelvey, R. D., & Zavoina, W. (1975). A statistical model for the analysis of ordinal level dependent variables. *Journal of Mathematical Sociology, 4,* 103-120.

McKenry, P. C., Price, J., & Sharon, J. (Eds.). (1994). *Families and change: Coping with stressful events.* Thousand Oaks, CA: Sage.

McLanahan, S. S. (1985). Family structure and the reproduction of poverty. *American Journal of Sociology, 90,* 873-901.

McLanahan, S. S. (1988). Family structure and dependency: Early transitions to female household headship. *Demography, 25*(1), 1-16.

McLanahan, S. S, & Booth, K. (1989). Mother-only families: Problems, prospects, and politics. *Journal of Marriage and the Family, 51,* 557-580.

McLanahan, S. S., & Bumpass, L. (1988). Intergenerational consequences of family disruption. *American Journal of Sociology, 94,* 130-152.

McLanahan, S. S., & Casper, L. (1995). Growing diversity and inequality in the American family. In R. Farley (Ed.), *State of the union: America in the 1990s. Vol. 2: Social trends* (pp. 1-45). New York: Russell Sage.

McLaughlin, D. K., Lichter, D. T., & Johnston, G. M. (1993). Some women marry young: Transitions to first marriage in metropolitan and nonmetropolitan areas. *Journal of Marriage and the Family, 55,* 827-838.

McLoyd, V. (1989). Socialization and development in a changing economy: The effects of paternal job and income loss on children. *American Psychologist, 44*(2), 293-302.

McLoyd, V. C. (1990). The impact of economic hardship on Black families and children: Psychological distress, parenting, and socioemotional development [Special Issue: Minority Children]. *Child Development, 61,* 311-346.

McQueen, A. J. (1979). The adaptations of urban black families: Trends, problems, and issues. In D. Reiss & H. A. Hoffman (Eds.), *The American family: Dying or developing* (pp. 79-101). New York: Plenum.

Meadow, K. (1962). Negro-white differences among newcomers to a transitional urban area. *Journal of Intergroup Relations, 3,* 320-330.

Mercer, R. T., & Ferketich, S. L. (1995). Experienced and inexperienced mothers' maternal competence during infancy. *Research in Nursing & Health, 18,* 333-343.

Merton, R. K. (1941). Intermarriage and social structure: Fact and theory. *Psychiatry, 4,* 361-374.

Merton, R. K. (1968). *Social theory and social structure.* New York: Free Press.

Miller, D. B. (1994). Influences on parental involvement of African American adolescent fathers. *Child and Adolescent Social Work Journal, 11*(5), 363-378.

Milner, D. (1983). *Children and race.* Beverly Hills, CA: Sage.

Mincy, R. B. (Ed.). (1994a). *Nurturing young black males.* Washington, DC: Urban Institute Press.

Mincy, R. B. (1994b). The underclass: Concept, controversy, and evidence. In S. H. Danziger, G. D. Sandefur, & D. W. Weinberg (Eds.), *Confronting poverty: Prescriptions for change* (pp. 109-146). Cambridge, MA: Harvard University Press.

Mincy, R. B., & Sorenson, E. (1994, October). *Deadbeats and turnips in child support reform.* Paper presented at the annual meeting of the Association for Public Policy Analysis and Management, Chicago.

Moffitt, R. (1992). Incentive effects of the U.S. welfare system: A review. *Journal of Economic Literature, 30*(March), 1-61.

Montaga, P. D. (1977). *Occupations and society: Toward a sociology of the labor market.* New York: John Wiley.

Montgomery, J. D. (1991). Social networks and labor-market outcomes: Toward an economic analysis. *American Economic Review, 81,* 1408-1418.

Moore, K. A., Simms, M. C., & Betsey, C. L. (1989). *Choice and circumstance: Racial differences in adolescent sexuality and fertility.* New Brunswick, NJ: Transaction Publishers.

Morgan, J. N. (1991). Panel study of income dynamics 1968-1988 (Waves I-XXI). Ann Arbor, MI: Inter-University Consortium for Political and Social Research.

Morgan, S. P., McDaniel, A., Miller, A. T., & Preston, S. H. (1993). Racial differences in household and family structure at the turn of the century. *American Journal of Sociology, 98*(4), 798-828.

Morisey, P. G. (1990). Black children in foster care. In S. M. L. Logan, E. M. Freeman, & R. G. McRoy (Eds.), *Social work practice with black families* (pp. 133-147). New York: Longman.

Morris, A. D. (1984). *The origins of the civil rights movement: Black communities organizing for change.* New York: Free Press.

Mosher, W. D. (1990). Contraceptive practice in the United States, 1982-1988. *Family Planning Perspectives, 22,* 198-205.

Mosher, W. D., & McNally, J. W. (1991). Contraceptive use at first premarital intercourse: United States, 1965-1988. *Family Planning Perspectives, 23*(3), 108-116.

Mott, F. L. (1990). When is a father really gone? Paternal-child contact in father-absent homes. *Demography, 27,* 499-517.

Moynihan, D. (1965). *The Negro family: The case for national action.* Washington, DC: Government Printing Office.

Mukenge, I. R. (1983). *The black church in urban America: A case study in political economy.* Lanham, MD: University Press of America.

Nath, P. S., Borkowski, J. G., Whitman, T. L., & Schellenbach, C. J. (1991). Understanding adolescent parenting: The dimensions and functions of social support. *Family Relations, 40,* 411-420.

National Center for Health Statistics. (1988). Advanced data from vital and health statistics. *Monthly Vital Statistics Report* (No. 194). Washington, DC: Government Printing Office.

National Center for Health Statistics. (1993). *Monthly Vital Statistics Report* (Suppl. 41). Washington, DC: Government Printing Office.

National Center for Health Statistics. (1995a). Advance report of final divorce statistics, 1989 and 1990. *Monthly Vital Statistics Report* (No. 43, 1). Washington, DC: Government Printing Office.

National Center for Health Statistics. (1995b). Contraceptive use in the United States: 1982-1990, advance data. *Monthly Vital Statistics Report* (No. 260, 1-16). Washington, DC: Government Printing Office.

National Center for Health Statistics. (1995c). Trends in pregnancies and pregnancy rates: Estimates for the United States, 1980-1992. *Monthly Vital Statistics Report* (No. 43, 1-8). Washington, DC: Government Printing Office.

National Center for Health Statistics. (1996). Advance report of final natality statistics, 1994. *Monthly Vital Statistics Report* (No. 44, 1-30). Washington, DC: Government Printing Office.

National Child Abuse and Neglect Data System. (1996). *Child maltreatment, 1994: Reports from the states to the National Center on Child Abuse and Neglect, U.S. Department of Health and Human Services.* Washington, DC: Government Printing Office.

Neighbors, H. W. (1985). Seeking professional help for personal problems: Black Americans' use of health and mental health services. *Community Mental Health Journal, 21*(3), 156-166.

Neighbors, H. W. (1986). Socioeconomic status and psychologic distress in adult blacks. *American Journal of Epidemiology, 124,* 779-793.

Neighbors, H. W. (1991). Mental health. In J. S. Jackson (Ed.), *Life in black America* (pp. 221-237). Newbury Park, CA: Sage.

Neighbors, H. W. (1996). The use of help resources: A method for studying help-seeking from the National Survey of Black Americans. In R. Jones (Ed.), *Handbook of tests and measurements* (Vol. 2, pp. 579-586). Hampton, VA: Cobb & Henry.

Neighbors, H. W., & Howard, C. S. (1987). Sex differences in professional help seeking among adult black Americans. *American Journal of Community Psychology, 15*(4), 403-417.

Neighbors, H. W., & Jackson, J. S. (1984). The use of informal and formal help: Four patterns of illness behavior in the black community. *American Journal of Community Psychology, 12,* 629-644.

Neighbors, H. W., & Jackson, J. S. (Eds.). (1996a). *Mental health in black America.* Thousand Oaks, CA: Sage.

Neighbors, H. W., & Jackson, J. S. (1996b). Mental health in black America: Psychosocial problems and help-seeking behavior. In H. W. Neighbors & J. S. Jackson (Eds.), *Mental health in black America* (pp. 1-13). Thousand Oaks, CA: Sage.

Neighbors, H. W., & LaVeist, T. A. (1989). Socioeconomic status and psychological distress: The impact of material aid on economic problem severity. *Journal of Primary Prevention, 10,* 149-165.

Neighbors, H. W., & Taylor, R. J. (1985). The use of social service agencies by black Americans. *Social Service Review, 59,* 258-268.

Neighbors, H. W., Jackson, J. S., Bowman, P. J., & Gurin, G. (1983). Stress, coping, and black mental health: Preliminary findings from a national study. *Prevention in Human Services, 2*(3), 5-29.

Nelsen, H. M. (1988). Unchurched black Americans: Patterns of religiosity and affiliation. *Review of Religious Research, 29,* 398-412.

Nelsen, H. M., & Nelsen, A. K. (1975). *Black church in the sixties.* Lexington: University Press of Kentucky.

Newman, K. (1988). *Declining fortunes: The experience of downward mobility in the American middle class.* New York: Free Press.

Nitz, K., Ketterlinus, R. D., & Brandt, L. J. (1995) The role of stress, social support, and family environment in adolescent mothers' parenting. *Journal of Adolescent Research, 10,* 358-382.

Nobles, W. W. (1978). Psychological research and the black self-concept: A critical review. *Journal of Social Issues, 29*(1), 11-31.

Norton, A., & Moorman, J. (1987). Current trends in marriage and divorce among American women. *Journal of Marriage and the Family, 49*(1), 3-14.

Oakley, A. (1974). *The sociology of housework.* New York: Pantheon.

Ogbu, J. O. (1983). Socialization: A cultural ecological approach. In K. Borman (Ed.), *The social life of children in a changing society* (pp. 253-267). Hillsdale, NJ: Lawrence Erlbaum.

Ogbu, J. O. (1985). A cultural ecology of competence among inner-city blacks. In M. B. Spencer, G. K. Brookins, & W. R. Allen (Eds.), *Beginnings: The social and affective development of black children* (pp. 45-66). Hillsdale, NJ: Lawrence Erlbaum.

O'Hare, W. (1988). An evaluation of three theories regarding the growth of black female-headed families. *Journal of Urban Affairs, 10,* 183-197.

Oliver, M. (1988). The urban black community as network: Toward a social network perspective. *Sociological Perspective, 29,* 623-645.

Oliver, M. L., & Shapiro, T. M. (1989). Race and wealth. *Review of Black Political Economy, 17*(4), 5-25.

O'Muircheartaigh, C. (1989). Sources of nonsampling error: Discussion. In D. Kasprzyk, G. Duncan, G. Kalton, & M. P. Singh (Eds.), *Panel surveys* (pp. 271-288). New York: John Wiley.

Oppenheimer, V. K. (1988). A theory of marriage timing. *American Journal of Sociology, 94,* 563-591.

Oppenheimer, V. K., Blossfeld, H.-P., & Wackerow, A. (1995). United States of America. In H.-P. Blossfeld (Ed.), *The new role of women: Family formation in modern societies* (pp. 150-173). Boulder, CO: Westview.

Orshansky, M. (1965). Counting the poor: Another look at the poverty profile. *Social Security Bulletin, 28*(1), 3-29.

Ortega, S., Crutchfield, R. D., & Rushing, W. A. (1983). Race differences in elderly personal well-being: Friendship, family, and church. *Research on Aging, 4*(1), 101-117.

Ortega, S., Whitt, H. P., & Williams, J. A. (1988). Religious homogamy and marital happiness. *Journal of Family Issues, 9,* 224-239.

Owen, M., Chase-Lansdale, P., & Lamb, M. (1982). *Mothers' and fathers' attitudes, maternal employment and the security of infant-parent attachment.* Unpublished manuscript.

Parish, W. L., Hao, L.-X., & Hogan, D. P. (1991). Family support networks, welfare, and work among young mothers. *Journal of Marriage and the Family, 53,* 203-215.

Parke, R. D. (1981). *Fathers.* Cambridge, MA: Harvard University Press.

Parke, R. D., & Neville, B. (1987). Teenage fatherhood. In S. L. Hofferth & C. D. Hayes (Eds.), *Risking the future: Adolescent sexuality, pregnancy, and childbearing* (Vol. 2, pp. 145-173). Washington, DC: National Academy Press.

Parsons, T., & Bales, R. F. (1955). *Family, socialization, and interaction process.* Glencoe, IL: Free Press.

Passel, J. S., & Robinson, J. G. (1985). Factors associated with variation in sex ratios of the population across states and MSAs: Findings based on regression analysis of 1980 census data. In *Proceedings of the Social Statistics Section of the Annual Meeting of the American Statistical Association* (pp. 624-28). Washington, DC: Government Printing Office.

Pearlin, L. I. (1983). Role strains and personal stress. In H. B. Kaplan (Ed.), *Psychosocial stress: Trends in theory and research* (pp. 3-32). New York: Academic Press.

Pearlin, L. I., & Johnson, J. (1977). Marital status, life strains, and depression. *American Sociological Review, 42,* 704-715.

Pearlin, L. I., Lieberman, M. I., Menaghan, E. G., & Mullan, J. T. (1981). The stress process. *Journal of Health and Social Behavior, 22,* 337-356.

Perrucci, C. C., Perruci, R., Targ, D. B., & Targ, H. R. (1988). *Plant closing.* New York: Aldine de Gruyter.

Perrucci, C. C., & Targ, D. B. (1988). Effects of a plant closing on marriage and family life. In P. Voydanoff & L. C. Majka (Eds.), *Families and economic distress: Coping strategies and social policy* (pp. 55-72). Newbury Park, CA: Sage.

Peters, M. (1985). Racial socialization of young black children. In H. McAdoo & J. McAdoo (Eds.), *Black children* (pp. 159-173). Beverly Hills, CA: Sage.

Peters, M., & Massey G. (1983). Chronic versus mundane stress in family stress theories: The case of black families in white America. *Marriage and Family Review, 6,* 193-218.

Pierce, C. (1975). The mundane extreme environment and its effect on learning. In S. Brainard (Ed.), *Learning disabilities: Issues and recommendations for research.* Washington, DC: National Institute of Education.

Pierce, L. H., & Pierce, R. L. (1984). Race as a factor in the sexual abuse of children. *Social Work Research and Abstracts, 20*(2), 9-14.

Pietromonaco, P., Manis, J., & Frohardy-Lane, K. (1984, August). *Psychological consequences of multiple social roles.* Paper presented at the annual meeting of the American Psychological Association, Toronto, Canada.

Piore, M. (1975). Notes on a theory of labor market stratification. In R. Edwards, M. Reich, & D. Gordon (Eds.), *Labor market segmentation* (pp. 125-150). Lexington, MA: D. C. Heath.

Pitrkowski, C. S. (1978). *Work and the family system: A naturalistic study of working class and lower middle.* New York: Free Press.

Pleck, J. H. (1983). Husbands' paid work and family roles: Current research issues. In H. Lopata & J. Pleck (Eds), *Research in the interweave of social roles: Vol. 3. Families and jobs* (pp. 251-333). Greenwich, CT: JAI.

Pleck, J. H. (1985). *Working wives/working husbands.* Beverly Hills, CA: Sage.

Pleck, J. H. (1987). American fathering in historical perspective. In M. S. Kimmel (Ed.), *Changing men: New directions in research on men and masculinity* (pp. 83-97). Newbury Park, CA: Sage.

Pleck, J. H., Sonenstein, F. L., & Ku, L. (1993). Masculinity ideology: Its impact on adolescent males' heterosexual relationships. *Journal of Social Issues, 49*(3), 11-29.

Pleck, J., & Lange, L. (1978). *Men's family role: Its nature and consequences* (Working Paper). Wellesley, MA: Wellesley College Center for Research on Women.

Polit, D. F. (1989). Effects of a comprehensive program for teenage parents: Five years after project redirection. *Family Planning Perspectives, 21,* 164-187.

Pollner, M. (1989). Divine relations, Social relations, and well-being. *Journal of Health and Social Behavior, 30*(1), 92-104.

Porter, J., & Washington, R. (1993). Minority identity and self-esteem. *Annual Review of Sociology, 19,* 139-161.

Preston, S., & Richards, A. T. (1975). The influence of women's work opportunities on marriages rates. *Demography, 12,* 209-222.

Quinn, R. E. (1997). Coping with cupid: The formation, impact, and management of romantic relationships in organizations. *Administrative Science Quarterly, 22*(1), 30-45.

Quinn, R. P., & Staines, G. L. (1979). *The 1977 Quality of Employment Survey.* Ann Arbor: University of Michigan, Institute for Social Research.

Radin, N., & Kamii, C. (1965). The child-rearing attitudes of disadvantaged Negro mothers and some educational implications. *Journal of Negro Education 34,* 138-146.

Rapp, R., Ross, E., & Bridenthal, R. (1979). Examining family history. *Feminist Studies, 5,* 174-200.

Ray, S. A., & McLoyd, V. C. (1986). Fathers in hard times: The impact of unemployment and poverty on paternal and marital relations. In M. E. Lamb (Ed.), *The father's role: Applied perspectives* (pp. 339-383). New York: John Wiley.

Reis, J. (1989). A comparison of young teenage, older teenage, and adult mothers on determinants of parenting. *Journal of Psychology, 123*(2), 141-151.

Renne, K. (1970). Correlates of dissatisfaction in marriage. *Journal of Marriage and the Family, 32,* 54-67.

Reskin, B., & Coverman, S. (1985). Sex and race in the determinants of psychophysical distress: A reappraisal of the sex-role hypothesis. *Social Forces, 63,* 1038-1059.

Richards, T., White, M. J., & Tsui, A. O. (1987.) Changing living arrangements: A Hazard model of transitions among household types. *Demography 24,* 75-81.

Richardson, B. (1981). Racism and child-rearing: A study of black mothers (Doctoral Dissertation, Claremont Graduate School, 1981). *Dissertation Abstracts International, 42,* 15A.

Richardson, R. A., Barbour, N. B., & Bubenzer, D. L. (1991). Bittersweet connections: Informal social networks as sources of support and interference for adolescent mothers. *Family Relations, 40,* 430-434.

Riley, M. W. (1986). Overview and highlights of a sociological perspective. In A. B. Sorensen, F. Weinhart, & L. R. Sherrod (Eds.), *Human development and the life course* (pp. 153-175). Hillsdale, NJ: Lawrence Erlbaum.

Roberts, J. D. (1980). *Roots of a black future: Family and church.* Philadelphia: Westminster.

Rodgers, W. L., & Thornton, A. (1985). Changing patterns of first marriage in the United States. *Demography, 22,* 265-279.

Roof, W. C., & McKinney, W. (1987). *American mainline religion.* New Brunswick, NJ: Rutgers University Press.

Rosenberg, M. (1965). *Society and the adolescent self image.* Princeton, NJ: Princeton University Press.

Ross, C. E., & Huber, J. (1985). Hardship and depression. *Journal of Health and Social Behavior, 26,* 312-327.

Ross, C. E., Mirowsky, J., & Goldsteen, K. (1990). The impact of family on health: The decade in review. *Journal of Marriage and the Family, 52,* 1059-1078.

Ross, H. L., & Sawhill, I. (1975). *Time of transition: The growth of families headed by women.* Washington, DC: Urban Institute Press.

Ross, J. C., & Wheeler, R. (1971). *Black belonging.* Westport, CT: Greenwood.

Rubin, L. (1994). *Families on the faultline.* New York: HarperCollins.

Russell, G. (1982). Shared-caregiving families: An Australian study. In M. Lamb (Ed.), *Nontraditional families: Parenting and child development.* Hillsdale, NJ: Lawrence Erlbaum.

Russell, G., & Radin, N. (1983). Increased paternal participation: The fathers' perspective. In M. Lamb & A. Sagi (Eds.), *Fatherhood and family policy* (pp. 139-167). Hillsdale, NJ: Lawrence Erlbaum.

Ryan, P. (1981). Segmentation, duality, and the internal labor market. In F. Wilkinson (Ed.), *The dynamics of labor market segmentation* (pp. 3-20). New York: Academic Press.

Sampson, R. (1987). Urban black violence: The effects of male joblessness and family disruption. *American Journal of Sociology, 93,* 348-405.

Sampson, R. (1995). Unemployment and imbalanced sex ratios: Race- specific consequences for family structure and crime. In M. B. Tucker & C. Mitchell-Kernan (Eds.), *The decline in marriage among African Americans: Causes, consequences, and policy implications* (pp. 229-254). New York: Russell Sage.

Scanzoni, J., & Arnett, C. (1987). Enlarging the understanding of marital commitment via religious devoutness, gender role preferences, and locus of marital control. *Journal of Family Issues, 8*(1), 136-156.

Schilmoeller, G. L., Baranowski, M. D., & Higgins, B. S. (1991). Long-term support and personal adjustment of adolescent and older mothers. *Adolescence, 26,* 787-797.

Schoen, R. (1983). Measuring the tightness of the marriage squeeze. *Demography, 20*(1), 61-78.

Schoen, R., & Kluegel, J. R. (1988). The widening gap in black and white marriage rates: The impact of population composition and differential marriage propensities. *American Sociological Review, 53,* 895-907.

Schoen, R., & Wooldredge, J. (1989). Marriage choices in North Carolina and Virginia, 1969-1971 and 1979-1981. *Journal of Marriage and the Family, 51,* 465-481.

Schumm, W. R. (1985). Beyond relationship characteristics of strong families: Constructing a model of family strengths. *Family Perspective, 19*(1), 1-9.

Schwab, J. J., & Schwab, M. E. (1978). *Sociocultural roots of mental illness: An epidemiologic survey.* New York: Plenum Medical.

Secord, P., & Ghee, K. (1986). Implications of the black marriage market for marital conflict. *Journal of Family Issues, 7*(1), 21-30.

Seltzer, J. A., & Bianchi, S. M. (1988). Children's contact with absent fathers. *Journal of Marriage and the Family, 50,* 663-667.

Shimikin, D. B., Shimikin, E. M., & Frate, D. A. (Eds.). (1978). *The extended family in black societies.* Paris: Mouton.

Sieber, S. D. (1974). Toward a theory of role acclamation. *American Sociological Review, 39,* 567-578.

Simmons, W. (1979). The relationship between academic status and future expectations among low-income blacks. *Journal of Black Psychology 6,* 7-16.

Simons, R. L., Beaman, J., Conger, R. D., & Chao, W. (1993). Stress, support, and antisocial behavior trait as determinants of emotional well-being and parenting practices among single mothers. *Journal of Marriage and the Family, 55,* 385-398.

Simons, R. L., Lorenz, F. O., Wu, C., & Conger, R. D. (1993). Marital and spouse support as me-
diator and moderator of the impact of economic strain upon parenting. *Developmental Psychology, 29,* 368-381.

Slaughter, D. (1981). *Perspectives on the development of Afro-American children and their families: Part II* (Afro Scholar Working Papers). Urbana: University of Illinois Afro-American
Studies and Research Program.

Slaughter, D. T. (1988). *Black children and poverty: A developmental perspective.* San Francisco:
Jossey-Bass.

Slesinger, D. (1980). Rapid changes in household composition among low-income mothers. *Family Relations, 29*(2), 75-81.

Slocum, W. L., & Nye, F. I. (1976). Provider and housekeeper roles. In F. I. Nye (Ed.), *Role structure and analysis of the family* (pp. 81-99). Beverly Hills, CA: Sage.

Smith, K. R., Zick, C. D., & Duncan, G. J. (1991). Remarriage patterns among recent widows and
widowers. *Demography, 28,* 361-374.

Smith, R., & Thornton, M. C. (1993). Identity and consciousness: Group solidarity. In J. Jackson,
L. Chatters, & R. J. Taylor (Eds.), *Aging in black America* (pp. 203-216). Newbury Park, CA:
Sage.

Smith, T. E., & Graham, P. (1995). Socioeconomic stratification in family research. *Journal of
Marriage and the Family, 57,* 930-940.

Smock, P. J. (1990). Remarriage patterns of black and white women: Reassessing the role of educational attainment. *Demography, 27,* 467-473.

Snarey, J., & Pleck, J. (1988, August). *Father's participation in child rearing: The consequences
for fathers midlife outcomes.* Paper presented at the annual meeting of the American Psychological Association, Boston.

South, S. J. (1988). Sex ratios, economic power, and women's roles: A theoretical extension and
empirical test. *Journal of Marriage and the Family, 50*(1), 19-31.

South, S. J. (1991). Sociodemographic differentials in mate selection preferences. *Journal of Marriage and the Family, 53,* 928-940.

South, S. J., & Lloyd, K. M. (1992). Marriage opportunities and family formation: Further implications of imbalanced sex ratios. *Journal of Marriage and the Family, 54,* 440-451.

Spanier, G. B., & Glick, P. C. (1980). Mate selection differentials between whites and blacks in the
United States. *Social Forces, 58,* 707-725.

Spencer, M. (1983). Children's cultural values and parental rearing strategies. *Developmental Review, 4,* 351-370.

Spencer, M. (1985). Cultural cognition and social cognition as identity correlates of black children's personal-social development. In M. Spencer, G. Brookins, & W. Allen (Eds.), *Beginnings: The social and affective development of black children* (pp. 215-230). Hillsdale, NJ:
Lawrence Erlbaum.

Spencer, M. B. (1990). Parental values transmission: Implications for the development of African
American children. In H. E. Cheatham & J. B. Stewart (Eds.), *Black families: Interdisciplinary
perspectives* (pp. 111-129). New Brunswick, NJ: Transaction Publications.

Stack, C. B. (1972). Black kindreds: Parenthood and personal kindreds among urban blacks. *Journal of Comparative Family Studies, 3,* 194-206.

Stack, C. B. (1974). *All our kin: Strategies for survival in a black community.* New York: Harper &
Row.

Stack, C., & Burton, L. (1993). Kinscripts. *Journal of Comparative Family Studies,, 24,* 157-170.

Staines, G. L. (1980). Spillover versus compensation: A review of the literature on the relationship
between work and nonwork. *Human Relations, 33*(2), 111-129.

Staples, R. (1981a). Race and marital status: An overview. In H. P. McAdoo (Ed.), *Black families*
(pp. 173-175). Beverly Hills, CA: Sage.

Staples, R. (1981b). *The world of black singles.* Westport, CT: Greenwood.

Staples, R. (1982). *Black masculinity: The black man's role in American society.* San Francisco: Black Scholar Press.

Staples, R. (1985). Changes in black family structure: The conflict between family ideology and structural conditions. *Journal of Marriage and the Family, 47,* 1005-1013.

Staples, R. (1994). *The black family: Essays and studies* (5th ed.). Belmont, CA: Wadsworth.

Staples, R., & Johnson, L. B. (1993). *Black families at the crossroads: Challenges and prospects.* San Francisco: Jossey-Bass.

Staples, R., & Mirande, A. (1980). Racial and cultural variations in American families: A decennial review of the literature on minority families. *Journal of Marriage and the Family, 42,* 157-174.

Steckel, R. H. (1980). Slave marriage and the family. *Journal of Family History, 5*(4), 406-421.

Stevens, J. H., Jr. (1984). Black grandmothers' and black adolescents' mothers' knowledge about parenting. *Developmental Psychology, 20,* 1017-1025.

Stevens, J. H., Jr. (1988). Social support, locus of control, and parenting in three low-income groups of mothers: Black teenagers, blacks adults, and white adults. *Child Development, 59,* 635-642.

Stier, H., & Tienda, M. (1993). Are men marginal to the family?: Insights from Chicago's inner city. In J. C. Hood (Ed.), *Men, work, and family* (pp. 23-44). Newbury Park, CA: Sage.

Strom, R., Strom, S., Collinsworth, R., & Schmid, J. (1990). Perceptions of parenting success by black mothers and their preadolescent children. *Journal of Negro Education, 59,* 611-622.

Sudarkasa, N. (1981). Interpreting the African heritage in Afro-American family organizations. In H. McAdoo (Ed.), *Black families* (pp. 37-53). Beverly Hills, CA: Sage.

Sullivan, M. (1985). *Teen fathers in the inner city: An exploratory ethnographic study.* New York: Ford Foundation, Urban Poverty Program.

Sullivan, M. L. (1986). *Ethnographic research on young fathers and parenting.* New York: Vera Institute.

Sweet, J., & Bumpass, L. (1987). *American families and households.* New York: Russell Sage.

Tanfer, K., Grady, W. R., Klepinger, D., & Billy, J. O. G. (1993). Condom use among U.S. men, 1991. *Family Planning Perspectives, 25*(2), 61-66.

Tatara, T. (1991). Overview of child abuse and neglect. In J. Everett, S. S. Chipungu, & B. Leashore (Eds.), *Child welfare: An Afrocentric perspective* (pp.187-219). New York: Rutgers University.

Tatum, B. (1987). *Assimilation blues.* Westport, CT: Greenwood.

Taylor, R. D. (1996). Adolescent's perceptions of kinship support and family management practices: Associations with adolescent adjustment in African American families. *Developmental Psychology, 32,* 687-695.

Taylor, R. J. (1985). The extended family as a source of support to elderly blacks. *The Gerontologist, 25*(5), 488-495.

Taylor, R. J. (1986). Receipt of support from family among black Americans: Demographic and familial differences. *Journal of Marriage and the Family, 48*(1), 67-77.

Taylor, R. J. (1988). Aging and supportive relationships among blacks Americans. In J. S. Jackson (Ed.), *The black American elderly: Research on physical and psychosocial health* (pp. 259-281). New York: Springer.

Taylor, R. J. (1990). Need for support and family involvement among black Americans. *Journal of Marriage and the Family, 52,* 584-590.

Taylor, R. J., & Chatters, L. M. (1986a). Church-based informal support among elderly blacks. *The Gerontologist, 26,* 637-642.

Taylor, R. J., & Chatters, L. M. (1986b). Patterns of informal support to elderly black adults: Family, friends, and church members. *Social Work, 31*(6), 432-438.

Taylor, R. J., & Chatters, L. M. (1988). Church members as a source of informal social support. *Review of Religious Research, 30,* 193-203.

Taylor, R. J., & Chatters, L. M. (1991a). Extended family networks of older black adults. *Journal of Gerontology: Social Sciences, 46*(4), S210-S217.

Taylor, R. J., & Chatters, L. M. (1991b). Religious life. In J. S. Jackson (Ed.), *Life in black America* (pp. 105-123). Newbury Park, CA: Sage.

Taylor, R. J., Chatters, L. M., & Jackson, J. S. (1993). A profile of familial relations among three generation black families. *Family Relations, 42,* 332-341.

Taylor, R. J., Chatters, L. M., & Mays, V. (1988). Parents, children, siblings, in-laws, and nonkin as sources of emergency assistance to black Americans. *Family Relations, 37,* 298-304.

Taylor, R. J., Chatters, L. M., Tucker, M. B., & Lewis, E. (1990). Developments in research on black families: A decade review. *Journal of Marriage and the Family, 52,* 993-1014.

Taylor, R. J., Hardison, C. B., & Chatters, L. M. (1996). Kin and nonkin as sources of informal assistance. In H. W. Neighbors & J. S. Jackson (Ed.), *Mental health in black America* (pp. 130-145). Newbury Park, CA: Sage.

Taylor, R. J., Leashore, B. R., & Toliver, S. (1988). An assessment of the provider role as perceived by black males. *Family Relations, 37,* 426-431.

Taylor, R. J., Luckey, I., & Smith, J. M. (1990). Delivering service in black churches. In D. S. R. Garland & D. L. Pancoast (Eds.), *The church's ministry with families: A practical guide* (pp. 194-209). Waco, TX: Word.

Taylor, R. J., Neighbors, H. W., & Broman, C. L. (1989). Evaluation by black Americans of the social service encounter during a serious personal problem. *Social Work, 34*(3), 205-211.

Teachman, J. D., Polonko, K. A., & Leigh, G. K. (1987). Marital timing: Race and sex comparisons. *Social Forces, 66,* 239-268.

Telleen, S., Herzog, A., & Kilbane, T. L. (1989). Impact of a family support program on mothers' social support and parenting stress. *American Journal of Orthopsychiatry, 59,* 410-419.

Testa, M., Astone, N. M., Krogh, M., & Neckerman, K. (1989). Employment and marriage among inner-city fathers. *Annals of the American Academy of Political and Social Science, 501,* 79-91.

Testa, M., Astone, N. M., Krogh, M., & Neckerman, K. M. (1993). Employment and marriage among inner-city fathers. In W. J. Wilson (Ed.), *The ghetto underclass* (pp. 96-108). Newbury Park, CA: Sage.

Teti, D. M., & Gelfand, D. M. (1991). Behavioral competence among mothers of infants in the first year: The mediational role of maternal self-efficacy. *Child Development, 62,* 918-929.

Thoits, P. (1983). Dimensions of life events that influence psychological distress: An evaluation and synthesis of the literature. In H. B. Kaplan (Ed.), *Psychosocial stress: Trends in theory and research* (pp. 33-103). New York: Academic Press.

Thoits, P. (1987). Gender and marital status differences in control and distress: Common stress versus unique stress explanations. *Journal of Health and Social Behavior, 28*(1), 7-22.

Thomas, D. L., & Cornwall, M. (1990). Religion and family in the 1980s: Discovery and development. *Journal of Marriage and the Family, 52,* 983-992.

Thomas, M. E., & Holmes, B. J. (1992). Determinants of satisfaction for blacks and whites. *Sociological Quarterly, 33,* 459-472.

Thomas, V., Milburn, N. G., Brown, D. R., & Gary, L. E. (1988). Social support and depressive symptoms among blacks. *Journal of Black Psychology, 14*(2), 35-45.

Thompson, L., & Walker, A. J. (1989). Gender in families: Women and men in marriage, work, and parenthood. *Journal of Marriage and the Family, 51,* 845-871.

Thompson, M., & Ensminger, M. (1989). Psychological well-being among mothers with school age children: Evolving family structures. *Social Forces, 67,* 715-730.

Thornton, A. (1988). Cohabitation and marriage in the 1980s. *Demography, 25,* 497-508.

Thornton, A. (1989). Changing attitudes toward family issues in the United States. *Journal of Marriage and the Family, 51,* 873-893.

Thornton, A., & Freedman, D. (1983). The changing American family. *Population Bulletin, 38*(4), 3-39.

Thornton, M. C., Chatters, L., Taylor, R. J., & Allen, W. (1990). Sociodemographic and environmental correlates to racial socialization by black parents. *Child Development, 61,* 401-409.

Tienda, M., & Angel, R. (1982). Headship and household composition among blacks, Hispanics, and other whites. *Social Forces, 61,* 508-531.

Tienda, M., & Glass, J. (1985). Household structure and labor force participation of black, Hispanic, and white mothers. *Demography, 22*(3), 381-395.

Torres, A., & Forrest, J. D. (1988). Why do women have abortions? In S. K. Henshaw & J. Van Hort (Eds.), *Age and race abortion fact book—Readings, trends, and state and local data to 1988* (pp. 84-91). New York: Alan Guttmacher Institute.

Tran, T. V., Wright, R., & Chatters, L. M. (1991). Health, stress, psychological resources, and subjective well-being among older blacks. *Psychology and Aging, 6*(1), 100-108.

Trent, K., & Powell-Griner, E. (1991). Differences in race, marital status, and education among women obtaining abortions. *Social Forces, 69,* 1121-1141.

Troll, L. E. (1971). The family in later life: A decade review. *Journal of Marriage and the Family, 33,* 263-290.

Trussell, J. (1988). Teenage abortion, birth, and pregnancy statistics: An update. *Family Planning Perspectives, 20*(6), 65-76.

Tucker, M. B. (1987). The black male shortage in Los Angeles. *Sociology and Social Research, 71,* 221-227.

Tucker, M. B., & Mitchell-Kernan, C. (1990). New trends in black American interracial marriage: The social structural context. *Journal of Marriage and the Family, 52,* 209-218.

Tucker, M. B., & Mitchell-Kernan, C. (Eds.). (1995a). *The decline in marriage among African Americans: Causes, consequences, and policy implications.* New York: Russell Sage.

Tucker, M. B., & Mitchell-Kernan, C. (1995b). Interracial dating and marriage in Southern California. *Journal of Social and Personal Relationships, 12,* 341-361.

Tucker, M. B., & Mitchell-Kernan, C. (1995c). Marital behavior and expectations: Attitudinal and structural correlates. In M. B. Tucker & C. Mitchell-Kernan (Eds.), *The decline in marriage among African Americans: Causes, consequences, and policy implications* (pp. 145-171). New York: Russell Sage.

Tucker, M. B., & Mitchell-Kernan, C. (1995d). African American marital trends in context: Toward a synthesis. In M. B. Tucker & C. Mitchell-Kernan (Eds.), *The decline in marriage among African Americans: Causes, consequences, and policy implications* (pp. 345-362). New York: Russell Sage.

Tucker, M. B., & Mitchell-Kernan, C. (1995e). Trends in African American family formation: A theoretical and statistical overview. In M. B. Tucker & C. Mitchell-Kernan (Eds.), *The decline in marriage among African Americans: Causes, consequences, and policy implications* (pp. 3-26). New York: Russell Sage.

Tucker, M. B., & Taylor, R. T. (1987). Demographic correlates of relationship status among black Americans. *Journal of Marriage and the Family, 51,* 655-665.

Tucker, M. B., Taylor, R., & Mitchell-Kernan, C. (1993). Marriage and romantic involvement among aged African Americans. *Journal of Gerontology: Social Sciences, 48*(3), S123-S132.

Ulbrich, P., Warheit, G., & Zimmerman, R. (1989). Race, socioeconomic status, and psychological distress: An examination of differential vulnerability. *Journal of Health and Social Behavior, 30*(1), 131-146.

U.S. Bureau of the Census. (1980). *1980 census of population, Vol. 1* (Characteristics of the population, Chapter C, general social and economic characteristics). Washington, DC: Department of Commerce.

U.S. Bureau of the Census. (1982). *State and metropolitan area data book, 1982.* Washington, DC: Department of Commerce.

U.S. Bureau of the Census. (1983). Child support and alimony: 1981 advanced report. *Current population reports* (Series P-23, No. 124). Washington, DC: Government Printing Office.

U.S. Bureau of the Census. (1985). *1980 census of the population, subject reports, marital characteristics.* Washington, DC: Government Printing Office.

U.S. Bureau of the Census. (1986). Household and family characteristics: March, 1985. *Current population reports* (Series P-20, No. 411). Washington, DC: Government Printing Office.

U.S. Bureau of the Census. (1989a). Studies in marriage and the family. *Current population reports, special studies* (Series P-23, No. 162). Washington, DC: Government Printing Office.

U.S. Bureau of the Census. (1989b). The black population in the United States: March, 1988. *Current population reports* (Series P-20, No. 422). Washington, DC: Government Printing Office.

U.S. Bureau of the Census. (1991a). Fertility of American women: 1990. *Current population reports, population characteristics* (Series P-20, No. 454). Washington, DC: Government Printing Office.

U.S. Bureau of the Census. (1991b). *Statistical abstracts of the United States: 1991* (11th ed.). Washington, DC: Government Printing Office.

U.S. Bureau of the Census. (1991c). Money income and poverty status in the United States, 1989. *Current population reports* (Series P-60, No. 168). Washington, DC: Government Printing Office.

U.S. Bureau of the Census. (1991d). Marital status and living arrangements. *Current population reports* (Series P-20, No. 450). Washington, DC: Government Printing Office.

U.S. Bureau of the Census. (1992a). Marital status and living arrangements: March, 1991. *Current population reports* (Series P-20, No. 461). Washington, DC: Government Printing Office.

U.S. Bureau of the Census. (1992b). Household and family characteristics: March, 1991. *Current population reports, population characteristics* (Series P-20, No. 458). Washington, DC: Government Printing Office.

U.S. Bureau of the Census. (1992c). *Census of the population and housing, 1990: Summary tape file 3* [CD-ROM, machine-readable data file]. Washington, DC: Author.

U.S. Bureau of the Census. (1992d). Marriage, divorce, and remarriage in the 1990s. *Current population reports* (Series P-23, No. 180). Washington, DC: Government Printing Office.

U.S. Bureau of the Census. (1992e). Marital status and living arrangements: March, 1992. *Current population reports* (Series P-20, No. 468). Washington, DC: Government Printing Office.

U.S. Bureau of the Census. (1992f). *Public use microdata sample U.S. technical documentation.* Washington, DC: Government Printing Office.

U.S. Bureau of the Census. (1994a). Household and family characteristics: March, 1994. *Current population reports* (Series P-20, No. 483). Washington, DC: Government Printing Office.

U.S. Bureau of the Census. (1994b). Marital status and living arrangements: March, 1994. *Current population reports* (Series P-20, No. 484). Washington, DC: Government Printing Office.

U.S. Bureau of the Census. (1995a). Child support for custodial mothers and fathers: 1991. *Current population reports* (Series P-60, No. 187). Washington, DC: Government Printing Office.

U.S. Bureau of the Census. (1995b). *Report to congress on out-of-wedlock childbearing* (DHHS Publication No. PHS. 95-1257). Hyattsville, MD: Government Printing Office.

U.S. Bureau of the Census. (1996a). Families by median income, race, and Hispanic origin of householder: 1947-1994 [On-line *Current population reports* (Series P-60, Table F-4a)]. Available at U.S. Bureau of the Census, World Wide Web Site.

U.S. Bureau of the Census. (1996b). Living arrangements of white and black children under 18 years old: 1960 to the present. Marital status and living arrangements [On-line *Current population reports* (Series P-20)]. Available at U.S. Bureau of the Census, World Wide Web Site.

U.S. Bureau of the Census. (1996c). Marital status of persons 15 years old and over by age, sex, region, and race: March, 1995. Marital status and living arrangements [On-line *Current population reports* (Series P-20)]. Available at U.S. Bureau of the Census, World Wide Web Site.

U.S. Bureau of the Census. (1996d). Poverty in the United States: 1995. *Current population reports* (Series P-60, No. 194). Washington, DC: Government Printing Office.

U.S. Bureau of the Census. (1996e). Poverty status of families by type of family: Presence of related children, race, and Hispanic origin. Historical poverty tables-families [On-line *Current population survey* (March)]. Available at U.S. Bureau of the Census, World Wide Web Site.

U.S. Bureau of the Census. (1996f). The black population in the United States: March, 1995. *Current population reports* (Series P-20, Table 15). Washington, DC: Author.

Veroff, J., Douvan, E., & Kulka, R. (1981a). *The inner American*. New York: Basic Books.

Veroff, J., Douvan, E., & Kulka, R. (1981b). *Mental health in America*. New York: Basic Books.

Voight, J. D., Hans, S. L., & Bernstein, V. J. (1996). Support networks of adolescent mothers: Effects on parenting experience and behavior. *Infant Mental Health Journal, 17*(1), 58-73.

Waite, L. J. (1995). Does marriage matter? *Demography, 32*, 483-507.

Walker, H. A. (1988). Black-white differences in marriage and family patterns. In S. M. Dornbusch & M. H. Strober (Eds.), *Feminism, children, and the new families* (pp. 87-112). New York: Guilford.

Wan, C. K., Jaccard, J., & Ramey, S. L. (1996). The relationship between social support and life satisfaction as a function of family structure. *Journal of Marriage and the Family, 58*, 502-513.

Warr, P. B. (1987). *Work, unemployment, and mental health*. Oxford, UK: Oxford University Press.

Warr, P. B., & Jackson, P. (1985). Factors influencing the psychological impact of prolonged unemployment and of reemployment. *Psychological Medicine, 15*, 795-807.

Washington, J. M. (1985). Jesse Jackson and the symbolic politics of black Christendom. *Annals of the American Academy of Political and Social Science, 480*, 89-105.

Washington, P. A. (1996). The police: A reluctant social service agency in the African American community. In H. W. Neighbors & J. S. Jackson (Eds.), *Mental health in black America* (pp. 177-188). Thousand Oaks, CA: Sage.

Wegener, B. (1991). Job mobility and social ties: Social resources, prior job, and status attainment. *American Sociological Review, 56*(1), 60-71.

Weissman, M. M., Myers, J. K., & Ross, C. E. (Eds.). (1986). *Community surveys of psychiatric disorders*. New Brunswick, NJ: Rutgers University Press.

Weitz, J. A. (1952). A neglected concept in the study of job satisfaction, *Personnel Psychology, 5*, 201-205.

Wells, A. J. (1988). Variations in mothers' self-esteem in daily life. *Journal of Personality and Social Psychology, 55*, 661-668.

Wheaton, B. (1980). The sociogenesis of psychological disorder: An attributional theory. *Journal of Health and Social Behavior, 21*(2), 100-124.

Wheaton, B. (1985). Models for the stress-buffering functions of coping resources. *Journal of Health and Social Behavior, 26*, 352-364.

White, L. K. (1981). A note on racial differences in the effect of female economic opportunity on marriage rates. *Demography, 18*, 349-354.

White, M. J., & Tsui, A. O. (1986). A panel study of family-level structural change. *Journal of Marriage and the Family 4*, 435-446.

Wikstrom, O. (1987). Attribution, roles, and religion: A theoretical analysis of Sunden's role theory and the attributional approach to religious experience. *Journal for the Scientific Study of Religion, 26*, 390-400.

Wilkie, J. R. (1991). The decline in men's labor force participation and income and the changing structure of family economic support. *Journal of Marriage and the Family, 53*(1), 111-122.

Wilkie, J. R. (1993). Changes in U.S. men's attitudes toward the family provider role, 1972-1989. *Gender & Society, 7*(2), 261-279.

Wilkinson, D. Y., & Taylor, R. L. (Eds.). (1977). *The black male in America*. Chicago: Nelson Hall.

Williams, D. R., & Griffith, E. (1993, March). *African American churches in New Haven: Organizational correlates of performance.* Paper presented at the Project on Non-Profit Organizations (PONPO) Seminar, Yale University.

Williams, D., Takeuchi, D., & Adair, R. (1992). Marital status and psychiatric disorders among blacks and whites. *Journal of Health and Social Behavior, 33*(2), 140-157.

Williams, M. D. (1974). *Community in a black Pentecostal church.* Pittsburgh: University of Pittsburgh Press.

Willie, C. V., & Greenblatt, S. L. (1978). Four "classic" studies of power relationships in black families: A review and look to the future. *Journal of Marriage and the Family, 40*(4), 691-694.

Wilson, M. N. (1986). The black extended family: An analytical consideration. *Developmental Psychology, 22,* 246-259.

Wilson, M. N. (1989). Child development in the context of the black extended family. *American Psychologist, 44,* 380-385.

Wilson, M. N., & Tolson, T. F. J. (1990) . Familial support in the black community. *Journal of Clinical Child Psychology, 19,* 347-355.

Wilson, M. N., Tolson, T. J. F., Hinton, I. D., & Kiernan, M. (1990). Flexibility and sharing of child care duties in black families. *Sex Roles, 22*(7/8), 409-425.

Wilson, W. J. (1978). *The declining significance of race.* Chicago: University of Chicago Press.

Wilson, W. J. (1987). *The truly disadvantaged: The inner city, the underclass, and public policy.* Chicago: University of Chicago Press.

Wilson, W. J. (1996). *When work disappears: The world of the new urban poor.* New York: Random House.

Wilson, W. J., & Neckerman, K. M. (1987). Poverty and family structure: The widening gap between evidence and public policy issues. In W. J. Wilson (Ed.), *The truly disadvantaged* (pp. 232-259). Chicago: University of Chicago Press.

Wineberg, H. (1996). The prevalence and characteristics of blacks having a successful marital reconciliation. *Journal of Divorce & Remarriage, 25*(1/2), 75-86.

Wineberg, H., & McCarthy, J. (1993). Separation and reconciliation in American marriages. *Journal of Divorce & Remarriage, 20*(1), 21-42.

Winkler, A. E. (1993). The living arrangements of single mothers with dependent children: An added perspective. *American Journal of Economics and Sociology, 52*(1), 1-18.

Wojkiewicz, R. A., McLanahan, S. S., & Garfinkel, I. (1990). The growth of families headed by women: 1950-1980. *Demography, 27,* 19-30.

Worobey, J. L., & Angel, R. J. (1990). Poverty and health: Older minority women and the rise of the female-headed household. *Journal of Health and Social Behavior, 31,* 370-383.

Wyatt, G. E. (1985). The sexual abuse of Afro-American and white American women in childhood. *Child Abuse & Neglect, 9,* 507-519.

Zabin, L. B., Hirsch, M. B., & Emerson, M. R. (1989). When urban adolescents choose abortion: Effects on education, psychological status, and subsequent pregnancy. *Family Planning Perspectives, 21,* 248-255.

Zimmerman, M. A., Salem, D. A., & Maton, K. I. (1995). Family structure and psychosocial correlates among urban African American adolescent males. *Child Development, 66,* 1598-1613.

Zollard, A., & Williams, J. S. (1987). The contribution of marriage to the life satisfaction of black adults. *Journal of Marriage and the Family, 49*(1), 87-92.

NAME INDEX

Abell, E., 185, 186
Abrahamse, A., 27
Adair, R., 95, 97
Adams, R. G., 260
Adams, T. K., 221
Adelmann, P. K., 7, 296
Affleck, G., 192
Ahmeduzzaman, M., 216
Ahn, N., 30
Albrecht, C., 69
Aldous, J., 263, 264
Aldrich, J. H., 129
Alejandro-Wright, M., 201
Allen, D. A., 192
Allen, R., 201, 217
Allen, W. D., 7, 216, 217, 238
Allen, W. R., 3, 39, 40, 41, 43, 170, 176, 185, 201, 205, 207, 216, 218, 222-224, 239, 240, 243, 244, 246, 247, 264
Alwin, D. F., 179
Anderson, P. A., 191
Andrews, F., 97, 144
Angel, R., 44, 56, 170-179, 185-187, 271
Anthony, E., 21
Antonucci, T. C., 7, 191, 202, 260, 264, 296

Arnett, C., 126
Aronoff, J., 216
Aschenbrenner, J., 6, 144
Ashby, K. L., 87
Astone, N. M., 59, 219
Auletta, K., 242
Austin, R. L., 46
Averitt, R. T., 241

Bachrach, C. L., 41
Bales, R. F., 217, 218
Ball, R., 97
Baltes, P. B., 222
Bane, M. J., 170, 176
Baranowski, M. D., 193
Barbour, N. B., 202, 203
Barnett, R. C., 138, 139, 143, 217, 218
Bartolome, F., 132, 139, 141
Baruch, G. K., 138, 139, 143, 217, 218
Beaman, J., 191, 192, 193
Beck, R. W., 176, 257, 260, 277
Beck, S. H., 176, 257, 260, 277
Becker, G. S., 65, 68, 76, 217
Bell, C. C., 21
Belsky, J., 186, 191, 202

Bengtson, V. L., 194, 260, 264, 282, 290, 296, 316
Bennett, N. E., 63
Beresford, J. C., 86
Berman, P. W., 216
Bernard, J., 217, 218
Bernstein, V. J., 193
Besharov, D. J., 170
Best, K. K., 186, 192
Betsey, C. L., 27
Bianchi, S., 17, 65, 68, 69, 76, 264, 271
Biller, H., 216, 217, 239
Billingsley, A., 3, 7, 124, 191, 216-217, 218-219, 238, 239, 243-240, 247, 294
Billy, J. O. G., 33
Blankehnorn, D., 218
Blee, K. M., 217
Bloom, D. E., 63
Blossfeld, H. P., 68
Bluestone, B., 162, 218, 224
Blumstein, P., 76
Booth, K., 43, 44
Borawski-Clark, E., 191, 192
Borkowski, J. G., 191, 192, 194
Bowman, P., 7, 132, 142, 141, 154, 155, 186, 192, 201, 205, 216, 219-225, 227-229, 227, 238-247, 250, 251, 254, 257, 261, 282, 288, 289
Bowser, B., 217, 239
Boykin, A. W., 205-208, 216, 217
Bozett, F. W., 222, 240
Braddock, J., 153, 159, 161
Brandt, L. J., 193
Bridenthal, R., 263
Bridges, W., 152
Broman, C., 7, 95, 97, 98, 98, 163, 217, 253, 258, 288
Bromet, E. J., 162
Bronars, S., 30
Bronfenbrenner, U., 201
Bronstein, P., 216
Brooks-Gunn, J., 29, 179, 194, 201
Brown, C. H., 260
Brown, D., 101, 194, 289, 288
Bubenzer, D. L., 202, 203
Bumpass, L. L., 16, 44, 45, 49-55, 88, 97, 170, 176, 252
Burge, D., 191
Burgess, N., 65
Buriel, R., 186

Burton, L. M., 3, 144, 176, 194, 260, 264, 271, 282, 290, 294, 296, 313
Bushwall, S., 216

Caldwell, C. H., 124
Callan, A., 124
Campbell, A., 97, 98, 102, 138, 144
Campbell, S. B., 191
Cancian, F., 217, 218
Carlsmith, J., 216
Carson, E., 153
Casper, L., 40, 42, 43, 45, 47-51, 53, 54
Cates, W., Jr., 35
Cazenave, N., 217-218, 238, 240, 244, 249, 250, 257, 261
Chadiha, L. A., 218, 251
Champoux, J. E., 138, 141, 141
Chan, S. Q., 186
Chao, W., 191, 192, 193
Chase-Lansdale, P. L., 29, 179, 194, 249
Chatters, L. M., 3, 6, 7, 15, 56, 95, 98, 99, 100, 117, 120, 117, 124, 127, 132, 144, 170, 179, 178, 180, 191, 192, 194, 202, 201, 205, 207, 216, 218, 253, 258-261, 274, 282, 288, 296, 297, 313-316
Chaves, M., 124
Cherlin, A. J., 48-50, 52, 53, 179
Chevan, A., 263, 260, 278
Chiriboga, D. A., 99
Christmon, K., 249
Clawson, M., 186, 192
Clogg, C. C., 296, 313, 316
Cobb, S., 162
Cochran, D. L., 6, 274, 283, 289
Cohen, S., 96, 100
Cohen, T. F., 217, 238
Cohler, B., 21
Cohn, J. F., 191
Cohn, R. M., 222
Colburn, C. B., 218, 244
Cole, J., 206
Coleman, L. M., 7, 296
Colleta, N. D., 194
Collins, P., 158, 160, 194, 216, 218, 242
Collinsworth, R., 186
Conger, R. D., 191-18
Connor, M., 216
Converse, P. E., 97, 98, 138, 144, 179
Cooper, C. S., 192, 202
Cooper-Lewter, N.C., 125

Corcoran, M., 152-154, 155-156
Cornwall, M., 117, 124
Corter, C., 191, 193, 198
Cosby, B., 216
Coverman, S., 97
Cowan, C. P., 216
Cox, O. C., 66, 69, 74, 79, 80
Craig, P. H., 63
Crano, W. D., 216
Crawford, A. G., 179, 186, 187
Crawford, V., 124
Cready, C. M., 69
Crnic, K. A., 193, 198
Crockenberg, S. B., 201
Crohan, S. E., 7, 296
Crosby, F., 138
Cross, T. L., 219, 242
Crowne, D. P., 134
Crutchfield, R. D., 124
Cutler, N., 316

Daniel, J., 201
Daniels, P., 240
Danziger, S.D., 62
Danziger, S. H., 2
Danziger, S. K., 31, 62, 217
Darity, W., 59, 63, 218, 219, 242, 243, 251, 271
Datcher, L., 152-154, 158-15
Davis, A. G., 217
Davis, A. J., 240
Davis, J. E., 249
Davis, K., 58
Deehter, A., 239
DeLuccie, M. F., 217, 240
DeMaris, A., 180
Dew, M. A., 162
Diamond, B., 17
Dilworth-Anderson, P., 3, 176, 294
Doherty, W. J., 216, 217, 218, 238
Dollahite, D. C., 240
Dornbusch, J., 216
Douvan, E., 60, 97, 98, 144-141, 252
Dressler, W., 101, 264
DuBois, W. E. B., ix
Dubrow, N., 20-2
Duck, S., 80
Duncan, G., 17, 30, 55, 152-154, 158-160, 221, 244
Dunst, C. J., 192, 193, 202

Edwards, R., 241, 242
Eggebeen, D. J., 18, 47, 260, 296, 313
Elder, G. H., 263, 264, 271
Ellison, C. G., 7, 99, 101, 123-125, 132, 133, 253, 258
Ellwood, D. T., 46, 170, 176
Emerson, M. R., 27
Eng, E., 124
England, P., 65, 68
Ensel, W., 152
Ensminger, M. E., 46, 99, 179, 264, 260, 277
Epenshade, T. J., 83, 87, 274
Ericksen, E. P., 232
Ericksen, J. A., 232
Erikson, E. H., 240
Eron, L. D., 222
Essex, M., 97, 100
Evans, B., 216
Evans, P., 132, 139, 141

Fagan, J., 217
Farkas, G., 65, 68
Farley, R., 39-41, 43, 65, 68, 69, 76, 176, 218, 224, 239, 243, 244, 246, 264
Feagin, J., 297
Ferketich, S. L., 202
Filene, P. G., 218
Fleming, A. S., 191, 193, 198
Forman, T. A., 217-218, 239, 244-247, 251
Forrest, H. D., 25, 35
Forrest, J. D., 22, 23, 32, 33
Fossett, A. M., 7, 59, 65, 67-75, 80, 81, 87
Foster, E. M., 30, 31
Frank, S., 202
Franklin, C. W., 250
Frate, D. A., 271
Frazier, E. F., 123, 219, 260
Freedman, D., 50, 52
Frohardy-Lane, K., 143
Furstenberg, F. F., 23, 24, 29, 30, 179, 186, 187, 201, 216, 249, 260

Garasky, S., 47
Garbarino, J., 20-22
Garfinkel, I., 39, 42, 43, 170
Gary, L. E., 101, 194, 217, 218, 221, 222, 238, 239, 244, 249, 288
Gecas, V., 218
Gelfand, D. M., 193, 202

Genovese, E., 217
George, L., 99
Geronimus, A. T., 30
Gershman, K., 192
Gertsel, N., 101
Ghee, K., 59, 87
Gibson, R. C., 7, 170, 185, 240
Gilkes, C., 118
Gilmore, R., 80
Glasgow, D. G., 242
Glass, J., 179, 185
Glen, N., 97
Glick, P. C., 58, 65, 86, 88, 96
Goetting, A., 179, 191
Goldman, N., 74, 80
Goldscheider, F. K., 69, 81
Goldstein, K., 99
Goltz, J. W., 126
Gooden, W., 240
Gordon, E. T., 216
Gordon, E. W., 216
Gordon, L., 172
Gore, S. L., 162
Gottschalk, P., 221
Gould, R., 217, 239
Gove, W. R., 97, 98, 100
Grady, W. R., 33
Graham, P., 247
Granovetter, M., 152, 153, 161
Green, L., 239
Greenberg, M. T., 193
Greenblatt, S. L., 218, 240
Greenburg, M. T., 198
Greene, A. D., 124
Greene, R. J., 6
Greene, W. H., 181
Grogger, J., 30
Gross, R., 216
Grossbard-Schechtman, A., 63-6
Guacci, N., 191
Gurin, G., x, 5, 7, 65, 74, 201, 205, 217, 246, 282
Guttentag, M., 59, 63-67, 80, 81, 86, 87, 271
Guttman, H. G., 144, 217

Haavio, M. E., 143
Hakim, C., 162
Hamilton, V. L., 163
Hammen, C., 191
Hammerslough, C., 74, 80

Hampton, R., 20
Hans, S. L., 193
Hao, L. X., 170, 176-178, 185, 187, 191, 192, 194
Hardison, C. B., 144, 261, 282, 298
Hareven, T., 263, 278
Harris, K., 216, 219, 218, 218, 260
Harrison, A., 186, 201
Harrison, B., 162
Hartmann, H., 218
Hastorf, A., 216
Hatch, J., 124
Hatchett, S., 6, 7, 60, 201, 246, 252, 274, 283, 289, 313
Hawkins, A. J., 240, 260
Hayes, C. D., 30
Hays, W., 100, 191
Heaton, T. B., 132
Heckler, M., 222
Heer, D., 63-67, 86
Heimer, K., 46
Henshaw, S. K., 35-3
Hepworth, S. J., 162
Hernandez, D., 16, 18
Herzog, A., 193
Higgins, B. S., 193
Higgins, L. H., 124
Hill, M. S., 179
Hill, R. B., 3, 194, 217, 239, 240, 242, 244, 278
Hiller, D. V., 217
Hinton, I. D., 217
Hirsch, M. B., 27
Hochschild, A. R., 218
Hodson, R., 241
Hoeppner, S. H., 264
Hofferth, S. L., 30, 170, 176, 185, 277
Hoffman, S. D., 30, 31
Hoffman, W. S., 163
Hogan, D. P., 18, 45, 61, 170, 176-178, 185, 187, 191-192, 194, 296, 310, 313
Hole, C. B., 202
Holmes, B. J., 253, 258
Honig, A. S., 244
Hood, J. C., 218, 221
Hopkins, J., 191
Horton, H. D., 65
Hoschschild, A. R., 258
Hossain, Z., 218
House, J. S., 96, 99, 100, 162
Howard, C. S., 7, 186, 201, 205, 216, 280

Huber, J., 98, 99
Hughes, F. P., 222
Hughes, M., 97, 98
Hunter, A. G., 217, 249, 264, 260, 277
Hurd, E. P., 186
Hurlbert, J., 152
Huyck, M., 202

Ingram, E., 3

Jaccard, J., 191
Jackson, J., x, 5, 6, 56, 58, 63, 65, 67, 74, 86, 95,
    117, 176, 191, 194, 201, 205, 217, 246, 253,
    258, 260, 264, 280-284, 289, 298, 313
Jacobson, S., 202
Jahoda, M., 162
Jayakody, R., 6, 7, 144, 170, 179, 178, 192,
    202, 264, 274, 296, 313-316
Jaynes, G. D., 14, 18, 39, 40, 43, 46, 217, 219,
    220, 239, 243, 244, 246
Jemmott, J. B., 87
Jencks, C., 180, 209, 229
Jenkins, E. J., 21
Jenkins, S., 17
Johnson, J., 99, 218
Johnson, L. B., 3, 7, 176, 217-218, 219, 238,
    239, 240, 243, 294
Johnson, W., 249
Johnston, G. M., 69
Jones, E. G., 25, 35
Jones, J., 206
Justkowski, R., 202

Kahn, R., 139, 141, 191, 202
Kallenberg, A., 241
Kamii, C., 206
Kando, T. M., 138, 139
Kane, E., 217
Kasl, S. V., 162
Kellam, S. G., 46, 179, 260
Kelley, H. H., 80
Kelley, M. L., 193, 218, 244
Kelly, J., 216
Kelly, M. L., 191
Kephart, G., 59, 63, 65, 68, 69, 80, 81
Kessler, R. C., 96-100, 120, 162, 222
Ketterlinus, R. D., 193
Kiecolt, K. J., 7, 59, 65, 67-75, 80, 81, 87, 251
Kiernan, M., 217
Kilbane, T. L., 193

Kissman, K., 191
Kitagawa, E. M., 45
Klein, E., 191, 193, 198
Klepinger, D. H., 30, 33
Kletzer, L. G., 218
Kluegel, J. R., 67
Koeske, G. F., 193, 198, 202
Koeske, R. D., 193, 198, 202
Kollock, P., 80
Koonin, L. M., 37, 38
Korenman, S., 30, 161
Kost, K., 33
Kosteiny, K., 20-2
Kosterlitz, J., 69, 81
Krause, N., 191, 192
Krogh, M., 59, 219
Ku, L., 25
Kulis, S., 198
Kulka, R., 97, 98, 144-14
Kuypers, J. A., 316

Lamb, M., 205, 216, 218, 249
Lamb, V., 205, 216
Landale, N. S., 63, 67
Landis, K. R., 96, 100
Landry, D. J., 32, 59, 63, 65, 68, 69, 80, 81
Lang, L., 248
LaRossa, R., 217
Larson, L. E., 126
LaVeist, T. A., 282
Leashore, B. R., 222, 239, 244, 254, 261
LeClere, F. B., 59, 65, 67-69, 80, 81
Lee, D., 194
Leicht, K., 158, 161
Leiderman, H., 216
Leigh, G. K., 68
Lemme, B. H., 222
Lerman, R. I., 31, 218
Levant, R., 216
Levin, J. S., 117, 253
Levine, J. A., 249
Levine, L., 271
Levitt, M., 191
Lewis, C., 216
Lewis, E., 3, 15, 274
Lewis, H., 124, 216
Liao, T. F., 180
Lichter, D. T., 18, 59, 61, 63, 65, 67-69, 80, 81,
    80
Lieberman, M. I., 99, 222

Lieberson, S., 57
Liebow, E., 218, 218, 219, 238, 240, 244
Liem, J. H., 162
Liem, R., 162
Lin, N., 152
Lincoln, C. E., 124, 134
Lindenfeld, K., 87
Linn, M. W., 162
Lipsitt, L., 222
Litwak, E., 198
Lloyd, K. M., 63, 65, 67-69, 80, 81, 271
London, K. A., 41
Lorenz, F. O., 191
Lundberg, S., 30

Mack, D. E., 218, 240
Macpherson, D., 179
Malson, M. R., 3
Mamiya, L. H., 124, 134
Mangen, D. J., 260, 312
Manis, J., 143
Manning, W. D., 47, 219
Marciano, T. D., 117
Marini, M. M., 68
Marlowe, D., 134
Marsden, P., 152
Marsiglio, W., 27, 28, 36, 217, 218, 219, 238,
    249, 252, 260
Martin, E., 180, 264, 271
Martin, J., 180, 264, 271
Martin, S. S., 179
Martin, T. C., 50
Martineau, W., 297
Marx, J., 158, 161
Massey, G., 201
Matias, R., 191
Maton, K. I., 217
Matsueda, R. L., 46
Mattessich, P., 278
Mayer, S. E., 180, 209, 229
Mayne, G., 244
Mays, B. E., 123
Mays, V., 7, 100, 191
McAdoo, H. P., x, 3, 124, 144, 176, 185, 192,
    194, 216, 217, 221, 218, 224, 226, 229, 238,
    239, 241, 242
McAdoo, J. B., 217, 218, 229, 238, 252, 257,
    288
McCarthy, J., 49
McCullough, W., 201, 205, 217

McDaniel, A., 172, 173, 260
McKelvey, R. D., 180
McKenry, P. C., 288
McKinney, W., 117
McLanahan, S. S., 39, 40, 42-45, 47-51, 53, 54,
    172, 170, 216, 228
McLaughlin, D. K., 59, 63, 65, 67-69, 80, 81
McLoyd, V. C., 186, 218, 219, 240, 244
McNally, J. W., 34, 35
McPartland, J., 153, 159, 161
McQueen, A. J., 58, 86
Meadow, K., 297
Menaghan, E. G., 99, 229
Mercer, R. T., 202
Merton, R. K., 58, 217, 239
Meyer, D. R., 47
Milburn, N. G., 288
Miller, A. T., 172, 173
Miller, D. B., 217
Milner, D., 201
Mincy, R. B., 216, 217, 228, 239, 243
Mindel, C., 100, 191
Mirande, A., 260
Mirowsky, J., 99
Mitchell, H. H., 125
Mitchell-Kernan, C., 3, 7, 49, 56-58, 60, 68, 81,
    83, 84, 85, 87, 89, 97, 219, 243, 251, 289
Moffit, R., 44
Montaga, P. D., 241, 242
Montgomery, J. D., 153
Moore, C., 186
Moore, K. A., 27
Moorman, J., 96
Morgan, J. N., 209, 229, 230
Morgan, S. P., 29, 172, 173, 179, 201
Morisey, P. G., 17
Morris, A. D., 123, 153
Morrison, P., 27
Mosher, W. D., 34, 35
Mott, F. L., 31, 32, 252
Mukenge, I. R., 123
Mullan, J. T., 99, 229
Myers, J. K., 274
Myers, S., 59, 63, 218, 219, 242, 243, 251, 271

Nath, P. S., 191, 192, 194
Neckerman, K. M., 59, 63, 65, 80, 219
Neighbors, H. W., 6, 89, 95, 117, 144, 280-282,
    284, 285, 288
Nelsen, A. K., 123

Nelsen, H. M., 123, 134
Nelson, F. D., 129
Nembhard, J. G., 216
Neville, B., 31
Newman, K., 218
Nichols-Casebolt, A., 31
Nitz, K., 193
Nobles, W. W., 207
Noppe, L. D., 229
Norton, A., 96
Nye, F. I., 218

Oakley, A., 218
O'Brien, M., 216
Ogbu, J. O., 186, 216
O'Hare, W., 68
Oliver, M., 144, 218, 316
O'Muircheartaigh, C., 300
Oppenheimer, V. K., 63-66, 68, 69, 80, 81
Orshansky, M., 209, 230
Ortega, S., 124, 134
Owen, M., 249

Pardo, C., 20-2
Parish, W. L., 170, 176-178, 185, 187, 191, 194
Parke, R. D., 31, 216
Parrish, W. L., 192
Parson, T., 217, 218
Passel, J. S., 65, 79
Pearlin, L. I., 99, 217, 218, 229, 238
Pedersen, F. A., 216
Perrucci, C. C., 163
Perrucci, R., 163
Peters, M., 201, 205
Peterson, R. A., 229
Philliber, W. W., 217
Pierce, C., 201
Pierce, L. H., 19
Pierce, R. L., 19
Pietromonaco, P., 143
Pine, C. J., 186
Piore, M., 241, 242
Pitrkowski, C. S., 138
Pitts, B. J., 264
Pleck, J. H., 25, 217, 218, 224, 240, 248, 249
Plotnick, R. D., 30
Polit, D. F., 61, 62
Pollner, M., 125
Polonko, K. A., 68
Porter, J., 206

Powell-Griner, E., 37
Power, T. G., 191, 193
Pratt, E. L., 134
Preston, S., 65, 67, 172, 173
Price, J., 288
Price, R., 96, 229

Quinn, A. J., 170
Quinn, R. E., 144
Quinn, R. P., 141

Radin, N., 206, 217, 221
Raley, R. K., 52, 54, 55
Ramey, S. L., 191
Rapp, R., 263
Ray, S. A., 218, 244
Reese, H., 229
Reis, J., 191
Renne, K., 201
Renner, D. S., 163
Reskin, B., 97
Richards, A. T., 65, 67
Richards, T., 257-260, 278
Richardson, B., 206
Richardson, R. A., 202, 203
Riley, M. W., 263, 278
Ritter, P., 216
Robbins, C., 99
Roberts, J. D., 125
Robinson, J. G., 65, 79
Rodgers, W., 17, 98, 138, 144, 244
Rodgers, W. L., 86, 228
Rogers, R., 186
Rogers, W., 97
Roof, W. C., 117
Roopnarine, J. L., 216
Roopnarine, J. R., 218
Rosenthal, C., 282, 290
Ross, C. E., 98, 99, 274
Ross, E., 263
Ross, H. L., 88, 217, 219, 239
Ross, J. C., 124
Rubin, B., 46
Rubin, L., 218
Rubin, R. H., 3
Rushing, W. A., 124
Russell, G., 217, 249
Ryan, P., 241

Sagi, A., 216

Salem, D. A., 217
Sampson, R., 46, 59, 87, 219, 229
Sanchez, L., 217
Sandefur, G. D., 2, 228
Sanders, R., 229, 240
Sandifer, R., 162
Sawhill, I., 88, 217, 219, 239
Scanzoni, J., 126, 218, 238
Schellenbach, C. J., 191, 192, 194
Schilmoeller, G. L., 193
Schmid, J., 186
Schoen, R., 57, 67, 86, 87
Schulberg, H. C., 162
Schumm, W. R., 126
Schwab, J. J., 274
Schwab, M. E., 274
Secord, P. F., 59, 63-67, 80, 81, 86, 87, 97, 271
Sellers, S. L., 217
Seltzer, J. A., 17
Shapiro, T. M., 316
Shehan, C., 36
Sherkat, D. E., 124, 132, 133
Shimikin, D. B., 271
Shimikin, E. M., 271
Sieber, S. D., 138, 139, 143
Silverman, J., 35
Simmins, W., 206
Simms, M. C., 27
Simons, R. L., 191-18
Singh, S., 22, 23
Slaughter, D., 201
Slesinger, D., 257, 263, 260
Slocum, W. L., 218
Slough, N. M., 193, 198
Smith, J. C., 37, 38
Smith, K. R., 55
Smith, R., 217
Smith, T. E., 247
Smock, P. J., 51, 219, 239
Snarey, J., 240
Snyder, A. R., 47
Sonenstein, F. L., 25
Sorenson, A., 241
Sorenson, E., 228, 239, 243
South, S. J., 63, 65, 67-69, 80, 81, 87, 271
Spanier, G. B., 58, 65, 86
Spencer, M. B., xi, 186, 201, 206, 207
Stack, C. B., 3, 176, 178, 191, 194, 217-218, 263, 271, 288, 295, 313
Staines, G. L., 138, 141, 144, 141

Stansbury, K., 191
Staples, R., x, 3, 7, 58, 66, 84, 86, 98, 217, 221, 226, 229, 238, 239, 240, 243, 260
Stein, S., 162
Stevens, J. H., Jr., 179, 194, 296
Stewart, J. B., 3, 179
Stolley, K. S., 41
Stone, K. M., 35
Strom, R., 186
Strom, S., 186
Styles, C. B., 97, 98
Sudarkasa, N., 176
Sullivan, M., 218, 249
Summers, W. C., 138, 139
Sutton, G. H., 263, 260, 278
Sweet, J., 44, 49, 51-55, 88, 97, 170, 176

Takeuchi, D., 95, 97
Tanfer, K., 33
Targ, D. B., 163
Targ, H. R., 163
Tatara, T., 18, 19, 20
Tatum, B., 206, 207
Taylor, R., 3, 6, 7, 15, 56, 63, 67-69, 79, 78, 80, 84, 87-89, 97, 100, 117, 124, 127, 132, 144, 156, 161, 170, 179, 178, 180, 191, 192, 194, 202, 201, 205, 207, 216, 218, 225, 226, 239, 244, 251, 253, 254, 258-261, 271, 274-283, 289, 288, 296-298, 313, 316
Teachman, J. D., 68
Teele, J. E., 3
Telleen, S., 191, 193
Tennen, H., 192
Testa, M., 59, 219
Teti, D. M., 193, 202
Thoits, P., 96, 100, 102
Thomas, D. L., 117
Thomas, M. E., 253, 258
Thomas, V., 288
Thompson, L., 221, 238
Thompson, M., 99
Thornton, A., 50, 52, 53, 86, 221
Thornton, M. C., 7, 201, 205, 207, 216-21
Tickamyer, A. R., 221
Tienda, M., 44, 170, 176, 179, 185-187, 271
Toliver, S., 239, 244, 254
Tolnay, S. E., 67
Tolson, T. F. J., 194, 202, 221
Toms, F., 205-208, 216, 217
Tran, T. V., 258

Trent, K., 37
Trivette, C. M., 193
Troll, L. E., 260
Trussell, J., 23, 24, 28
Tsui, A. O., 257-260, 278
Tucker, M. B., x, 3, 5, 7, 15, 49, 56-60, 63, 65, 67-69, 79, 78, 80, 81, 83-89, 97, 219, 243, 251, 271, 274, 289
Tudor, J., 100
Turner, J. B., 99, 162
Turner, R. J., 179
Turner, S., 161

Ulbrich, P., 99
Umberson, D., 96, 100

Vance, S. D., 192, 202
Vaughn, B. E., 186, 192
Vaughn, J., 152
Veroff, J., 60, 97, 98, 144-141, 252
Villemez, W., 152
Voight, J. D., 193

Wackerow, A., 68
Waite, L., 27, 40, 48, 52, 53, 69
Walker, A. J., 221, 238
Walker, H. A., 264, 274
Wan, C. K., 191
Warheit, G., 99
Washesteem, R., 206
Washington, J. M., 123, 125
Washington, P. A., 283, 284
Washington, W. N., 186, 192
Waters, M. C., 57
Watkins, S., 217
Webber, R. A., 191
Wegener, B., 152
Weinberg, D. H., 2
Weingarten, K., 240
Weissman, M. M., 274
Weitz, J. A., 141, 141
Westoff, C. F., 74, 76
Wheaton, B., 99, 98, 121

Wheeler, R., 124
White, M. J., 257-260, 278
Whitfield, J., 216
Whitman, T. L., 191, 192, 194
Whitt, H. P., 134
Wikstrom, O., 125
Wilkie, J. R., 223, 224, 226, 239
Wilkinson, D. Y., 225
Williams, D., 95, 97
Williams, J. A., 134
Williams, J. S., 95, 97
Williams, L., 97
Williams, M. D., 124
Williams, R. M., Jr., 14, 18, 39, 40, 43, 46, 221, 226, 227, 239, 243, 244, 246
Willie, C. V., 223, 240
Wills, T., 96, 100
Wilson, H., 2
Wilson, M. N., 3, 186, 192, 194, 202, 203, 221
Wilson, W. J., 14, 46, 59, 63, 65, 76, 87, 154, 218, 224-226, 228, 242, 243, 244, 246, 251
Wimbush, D. D., 191, 193
Wineberg, H., 49
Winkler, A. E., 179, 178
Withey, S., 97, 144
Wojkiewicz, R. A., 42
Wolford, M. L., 6, 284
Wooldredge, J., 57
Worobey, J. L., 56
Wortman, C., 96, 229
Wright, R., 258
Wu, C., 191
Wyatt, G. E., 19

Yancey, W. L., 223

Zabin, L. B., 27
Zamsky, E. S., 194
Zavoina, W., 180
Zick, C. D., 55
Zimmerman, M. A., 220
Zimmerman, R., 99
Zolard, A., 95, 97

SUBJECT INDEX

Abortions and fetal losses, 26-27, 36-39
Abuse and neglect, child, 18-20
Adaptive reactions, 206
Adjustment techniques, 206
Adolescent reproductive behavior, 22-23
    abortions and fetal losses, 26-27
    attitudes toward childbearing, 27-28
    contraceptives, 25
    fathers, adolescent and nonresident, 31-32
    mothers, future consequences for, 29-31
    pregnancies, 25-26, 28-29
    sexual activity, 24
Adoption, 41
African cultural ethos, 207, 210, 216-217
Age:
    elderly adults, 56, 217
    fathers and coping mechanisms, 222-223
    fathers and life cycle stages, 240-246
    life satisfaction for men, 258-260
    living arrangements, 263-264, 268, 270-278
    racial socialization, 209, 217
    referrals, job, 159
    stress, 98

supportive networks, 300, 307-312, 313, 316
AIDS (acquired immune deficiency syndrome), 25
Aid to Families with Dependent Children (AFDC). See Welfare
Alan Guttmacher Institute (AGI), 23, 24, 37
Alimony payments, 44
All My Kin (Stack), 289
Americans View Their Mental Health (Gurin, Veroff & Feld), 275

Bible, 126
Black cultural expressions, 206-207, 209
Black Families at the Crossroads: Challenges and Prospects (Staples & Johnson), 7
Black Families in White America (Billingsley), 289

Census, U.S. Bureau of the, 100
Centers for Disease Control and Prevention (CDC), 37
Challenge: A Journal of Research on African American Men, 250

Child protective services (CPS), 19
Children:
 abusing, 18-20
 child care, 43
 custody and divorce, 50-51
 foster care, 16-17, 19
 infants, social support and responsibility to, 193
 living arrangements, 15-16
 minority experiences passed on to, 208
 poverty, 17-18, 220
 resilient, 21-22
 single-parent families, 252
 socialization of, 203-201
 violence and psychological development of, 20-22
 See also Parental competence; Racial socialization
Church, centrality of the Black, 123-124, 291-292, 312
Climbing Jacob's Ladder (Bilingsley), 7
Cohabitation, 51-55, 278
Communal networks, 152-153
 See also Informal social support networks and employment; Supportive network
Condom use, 33
Contraceptives, 25, 33-3
Coping styles/resources, 144-146, 206
Coresident living arrangements, 44, 176-177, 188
Crime and female-headed families, 46
Cultural expressions, black, 206-207, 209
Current Population Survey, 57, 179, 220
Custody and divorce, 50-51

Decline in Marriage Among African-Americans, The (Tucker & Mitchell-Kernan), 7
Deindustrialization, 242
Demographic trends, 8, 14
 adolescent reproductive behavior, 22-32
 children's well-being, 15-22
 conclusions, 60-63
 family structure/patterns, 39-47, 288-289
 marital patterns/status, 48-60
 postindustrial trends, 219-219
 sexual prevalence and contraceptive use, 33-3
Devotional activities, private, 125-126, 127
Divorce, 49-51, 98, 100-97, 169-170, 260
DuBois, W. E. B., ix

Education:
 fathers, 223-224
 marital patterns/status, 68-69, 170
 mate availability, 76
 mental health and marital status, 98
 parental competence, 198, 197, 203-201
 racial socialization, 209, 212, 216
 referrals, job, 159
 single mothers, 187
 spousal role for men, 255-256, 258
 widowhood, 55
 work and family role strain, 146
Elderly adults, 56, 217
Employment:
 fathers, 227-227, 240-242
 informal social support networks, 11, 146-161, 191-195
 job categories, 155, 158
 manufacturing sector, 242
 marital patterns/status, 43, 251-252
 occupational prestige, 148
 postindustrial trends, 219-219
 unemployment impacting families, 162-171
Ethnographic methodologies, 289-291, 312-319
Expressive family roles, 217-218, 251-252
 See also Fathers
Extended families:
 female-headed families, 44
 married couples, 276-277
 single mothers, 173, 176-177, 188
 single-parent families, 277-278

Family structure/patterns:
 extended families, 44, 173, 176-177, 188, 276-278
 flexible family roles, 238-240
 frequency of contact, 281
 household types, 266-267, 268-278
 informal social support networks and employment, 154-155
 instrumental and expressive family roles, 217-218, 250-251
 mate availability and marital patterns/status, 79
 nonmarital childbearing, 39-41
 referrals, job, 159-160
 regional differences, 216, 260-261
 single-father families, 46-47, 174
 stress buffering, 99-101

support networks, 11-12
unemployment impacting, 162-171, 242
See also Demographic trends; Living arrangements; Racial socialization; *various subject headings*; Work and family role strain
Fatalism, sense of, 21
Fathers, 216
  adolescent and nonresident, 31-32
  critical trends and issues, 218-219
  expressive and instrumental roles, links between, 225-227
  flexibility of family roles, increasing, 238-240
  instrumental and expressive family roles, 217-218
  labor market status and role of, 227-227
  life cycle stages, adult, 235-237
  marital patterns/status, 219-220, 227-229
  mothers' roles vs. role of, 224-225
  parental roles, 217
  postindustrial trends, 219-219, 240-247
  poverty, 220-221, 224, 229-232, 243-244
  psychosocial development issues, 221-223
  single-father families, 46-47, 174
  uncoupling instrumental and expressive roles, 240-240
  See also Men
Female-headed families, 11
  coresident living arrangements, 44
  crime, 46
  friends and family, importance of, 281
  increase in, 41-42
  intergenerational consequences, 45
  poverty, 42-44, 220
  single mothers contrasted with, 170-171
  welfare and black family structure, 44-45
Fetal loss, 38-39
Foster care, 16-17, 19
Friendships, 12
  female-headed families, 281
  job referrals, informal, 156, 158
  stress buffering, 99-101
  supportive networks, 292-293, 296

Gender differences. *See* Men; Women
Geographic location and family interactions, 216, 260-261
God role, 126

Good Dads-Bad Dads: Two Faces of Fatherhood (Furstenberg), 249
Grandparents, 16, 194, 253-254
Group self-esteem, 216-217
Growth of American Families Survey (1955), 23

Happiness, personal, 100, 103-116
Health insurance, 43
Help seeking, 285
Hispanic Americans:
  abortions and fetal losses, 26, 38, 39
  adolescent reproductive behavior, 26
  children's living arrangements, 15-16
  extended family households, 44
  fathers, adolescent and nonresident, 31
  pregnancies, 36
HIV (human immunodeficiency virus), 25
Household types, overview of, 266-267
  See also Living arrangements

Infants, social support and responsibility to, 193
Informal social support networks and employment, 11
  conclusions, 160-161
  methods used in researching, 154-155
  parental competence, 191-195
  referrals, job, 156-160
  research, previous, 146-153
Instrumental family roles, 217-218, 250-251
  See also Fathers
Intergenerational consequences of female-headed families, 45
Intergenerational family life cycle, 263-264
Intergenerational transmission of religious beliefs, 128
Interpersonal problems, 286-287, 289
Interracial marriage, 56-58
Intervention programs to improve maternal capabilities, 201

Job(s):
  categories, 155, 158
  displacement, industrial, 219
  referrals, 156-160
  structural joblessness, 242
  See also Employment
Journal of African American Males, 250

Labor market status and role of fathers, 227
Life cycle, intergenerational family, 263-264
Life cycle stages, adult, 222-223, 235-237, 240-246
Life satisfaction:
    men, 243-254, 257, 258-261
    mental health and marital status, 100, 103-100, 116-117
    religious involvement, 126, 131
    single mothers, 187
    unemployment impacting families, 169-170
    work and family role strain, 144
Living arrangements:
    children, 15-16
    cohabitation, 51-55, 278
    complexities of residential patterns, 257-263
    extended households, 44, 173, 176-177, 188, 276-278
    household types, overview of, 266-267
    intergenerational family life cycle, 263-264
    nonfamily households, 270-271
    nuclear married-couple households, 271-266
    nuclear single-parent households, 275-276
    parental competence, 198, 199, 202
    race/gender and family trajectories, 264-260
    single mothers, 170-173, 182-184, 186-187
    summary and conclusions, 278-271
    variations by age/gender and family status, 267-270
Logistic regression models, multivariate, 129-132

Mainstream goals and values, 207-209
Manufacturing sector, 242
Marital patterns/status, 8-9
    cohabitation, 51-55
    elderly adults, 56
    emotional well-being, 289-290
    extended households, 276-277
    fathers, 219-220, 227-229
    interpersonal problems, 287
    interracial marriage, 56-58
    living arrangements, 182-184
    mate availability influencing, 63-81
    nonmarital childbearing, 39-41
    racial socialization, 212

referrals, job, 158, 159
relationship opportunities, 88
remarriage, 51, 88
romantic opportunities, 97
separation/reconciliation and divorce, 49-51
single mothers, 169-170, 185-186, 188
spousal role for men, 43, 251-252
theories on declining rates of marriage, 58-60
whites and blacks, marriage gap between, 48-49
widowhood, 55, 260
work and family role strain, 144, 145
See also Mental health and marital status
Mate availability and marital patterns/status, 63-81, 86-87
Media image of black family life, 2-3
Men:
    discussion of results, 257-261
    extended households, 268
    familial roles and perceptions of, 10-11
    interracial marriage, 57-58
    life satisfaction, 243-254, 257, 258-261
    living arrangements, 268, 270-278
    marital patterns/status, 59-60, 290
    mate availability influencing marital patterns/status, 63-81
    methods used in researching, 254-255
    parental role, 252
    provider role, 250-251
    psychological involvement, self-rated, 248-249
    racial socialization, 212
    referrals, job, 158, 160
    religious involvement, 134
    results of research, 255-257
    sexuality and condom use, 33
    single-father families, 46-47
    spousal role, 251-252
    stereotypical perceptions of, 249
    stress, 99
    supportive networks, 300-307, 312, 316
    widowhood, 55
    See also Fathers; Marital patterns/status; Romantic relationships, unmarried people in
Mental health and marital status, 100-96
    conclusions, 117-121
    data analysis, 101
    factors affecting stress exposure, 98-101
    fathers, 221-223

friends, importance of family and, 99-99
happiness, personal, 101-116
life satisfaction, 116-117
methods used in researching, 99-101
research on, previous, 97-99
results of research, 102-98
See also Work and family role strain
Mental health needs:
    conclusions, 290
    discussion of results, 288-290
    family difficulties, 282-284
    fathers, 221-223
    friends and family, importance of, 281-284
    introduction and overview, 280
    methods used in researching, 284-285
    parental responsibilities, 98
    results of research, 286-287
    socioeconomic achievement, 282
Minority experiences passed on to children, 208
Model family form, 3
Mothers, 224-225
    See also Adolescent reproductive behavior;
        Female-headed families; Parental com-
        petence, mothers' perceptions of; Single
        mothers
Moynihan Report (1965), 289

National Center for Health Statistics (NCHS),
    23, 25, 37
National Child Abuse and Neglect Data Sys-
    tem (NCANDS), 19
National Incidence Studies (NIS), 19
National Institute of Mental Health, 5
National Survey of Adolescent Males (1988),
    23, 27
National Survey of Black Americans (NSBA),
    x, 4, 5-7
    fathers, 223, 247
    informal social support networks and em-
        ployment, 154
    living arrangements, 260
    marital patterns/status, 74
    men, 254
    mental health needs, 281-284
    parental competence, 195
    provider role for men, 250
    racial socialization, 208
    religious involvement, 127-128
    survey-based research, 291

unemployment impacting families, 163
work and family role strain, 140
National Surveys of Family Growth (NSFG),
    23, 25, 34
1980s and African American fathers, 246-247
Nonfamily households, 270-271
Nonmarital childbearing, 39-41
Nontraditional family statuses, 41-42
Nuclear single-parent/married couple house-
    holds, 271-276

Occupational prestige, 148
Open systems perspective, 138-139

Panel Study of Income Dynamics (1978), 154,
    209, 230
Parental competence, mothers' perception of,
    186-192
    attitudes/behaviors, social support and par-
        enting, 192-195
    conclusions and implications, 201-202
    discussion of results, 201-201
    methods used in researching, 195-200
    multivariate analyses, 200-201
Parental responsibilities:
    interrelated functions, five, 217
    men, roles for, 252, 256-257
    mental health, 98
    performance and role perception, 9-10
    See also Fathers; Female-headed families;
        Parental competence, mothers' percep-
        tions of; Single mothers
Pathological portrayal of black families, 3
Postindustrial trends and African American fa-
    thers, 219-219, 240-247
Posttraumatic stress disorder (PTDS), 21
Poverty:
    child abuse, 19-20
    childhood, 17-18, 220
    elderly adults, 56
    fathers, 220-221, 224, 229-232, 243-244
    female-headed families, 42-44, 220
    national programs and policies, 62
    single-father families, 47
    structural arguments concerning causes of, 2
    violence related to, 20-22
    See also Socioeconomic achievement
Pregnancy:
    adolescent reproductive behavior, 25-26,
        28-29

demographic trends, 35-36
nonmarital childbearing, 39-41
Problem focus on the black family, 1-4
Project Redirection, 61-62
Provider role for men, 60, 250-251, 261
Psychological involvement in the family, men's self-rated, 248-249
Psychological well-being. *See* Mental health and marital status; Mental health needs; Work and family role strain

Racial composition, job, 155
Racial socialization:
    conclusions, 217-217
    cultural expressions, black, 206-207
    discussion of results, 216
    messages conveyed by parents, 10
    methods used in researching, 208-210
    parents view of their children, 201-205
    results of research, 210-216
    self-esteem, group, 216-217
    self-esteem, personal, 216-216
    triple quandary process, 205-206
Reagan, Ronald, 246-247
Reconciliation, marital, 49
Referrals, job, 156-160
Regional differences in family phenomena, 260-261
Religious involvement, 9, 117
    church, centrality of the Black, 123-124, 291-292, 312
    congregations as family support systems, 124-125
    devotional activities, private, 125-126
    discussion, 133-135
    dummy variables, 132-133
    logistic regression models, multivariate, 129-132
    quality of family life, subjective, 126-127
    socioeconomic achievement, 128
    supportive networks, 291-292
    work and family role strain, 144, 145, 147
Remarriage, 51, 88
Reproductive behavior. *See* Adolescent reproductive behavior; Sexual prevalence and contraceptive use
Research methods and sources, 8-9, 289-291, 312-319
    See also specific subject headings
Resilient children, 21-22

Robert Taylor Homes housing project (Chicago), 21
Romantic relationships, unmarried people in, 8-9, 83
    conceptual perspectives, 84-86
    conclusions, 99
    discussion, 95-98
    mate availability, 86-87
    method, 89-91
    research, previous, 88-89
    results, 91-95
    social structural position, 87-88

Secondary sector of the labor market, 242
Self-determination, 217
Self-efficacy beliefs, 240
Self-esteem:
    group, 216-217
    maternal, 193
    parental competence, 201-202
    personal, 216-216
    racial socialization, 206
Self-respect, 205
Separation/reconciliation and divorce, 49-51
Sex ratio hypothesis and marital patterns/status, 63-81, 81-82, 86-87
Sexual prevalence and contraceptive use:
    abortion, 36-38
    contraceptive failure, 35
    fetal loss, 38-39
    men, 33
    pregnancy, 35-36
    women, 33-35
Single-father families, 46-47
Single mothers:
    defining, 173-174
    discussion of results and conclusions, 184-185
    family support, 178
    inaccurate portrayals of, 174
    living arrangements, 170-173, 182-184
    marital patterns/status, 169-170
    methods used in researching, 179-181
    parental competence, 198, 201
Single-parent families:
    extended families, 277-278
    male headed, 46-47, 174
    nuclear, 275-276
    parental responsibilities, 252
    socializing children, 217-216

whites and blacks in, 172-173
  See also Female-headed families; Single
    mothers
Socialization:
  of children, 203-201, 217-216
  religious, 127-128, 133
  See also Racial socialization
Social structural position and romantic in-
    volvement, 87-88
Social support systems, 11-12, 99-99
  See also Informal social support networks
    and employment; Supportive networks
Socioeconomic achievement:
  adolescent reproductive behavior, 30
  ethnographic and survey research, contrast-
    ing, 313-316
  household types, 267
  informal social support networks and em-
    ployment, 154
  instrumental dimensions of fatherhood,
    217-218
  male-female bonds, 288
  marital patterns/status, 59-60, 170, 251-252
  mental health and marital status, 98, 101
  mental health needs, 282
  parental competence, 198, 203
  racial socialization, 209, 216
  religious involvement, 128
  single mothers, 179-180
  single-parent families, 173
  spousal role for men, 258
  See also Poverty
Spousal role for men, 43, 251-252, 255-256,
    258
Sterilization, female/male, 34
Strength of Black Families, The (Hill), 289
Stress, 9
  age, 98
  buffering, family resources for, 99-101
  family support networks, 12
  father-child and marital family, 240-240
  men, 258
  mundane extreme environmental, 201
  See also Mental health and marital status;
    Mental health needs
Supportive networks, 11-12, 292
  church support, 291-292
  discussion of results, 313-316
  employment and informal, 146-161,
    191-195

ethnographic and survey research, contrasting, 312-319
friendships, 292-293
methods used in researching, 294-296
multiple sources, 293
research, previous, 289-291
results of research, 297-307
survey approaches, 291
transition, families in, 288-289
See also Informal social support networks
  and employment
Survey-based research, 291, 312-319
Survey of Men (1991), 23

Teenagers. *See* Adolescent reproductive
  behavior
Transition, families in, 288-289
Triple quandary process, 205-206

Underemployment, 219
Unemployment impacting families, 162
  discussion of results, 171
  methods used in researching, 163-165
  results of research, 165-170
  structural joblessness, 242

Violence and psychological development of
  children, 20-22

Walk-in applications, 158
Weak ties theory, 152
Welfare:
  fathers, 221, 244
  female-headed families, 43, 44-45
  mate availability and marital patterns/status,
    75, 76-77
  single mothers, 188-180
White Americans:
  abortions and fetal losses, 26, 37-39
  adolescent reproductive behavior, 26, 28
  adoption, 41
  attitudes toward childbearing, 27
  children in poverty, 220
  children's living arrangements, 15-16
  contraceptives, 25
  divorce, 170
  extended households, 44, 176
  fathers, adolescent and nonresident, 31
  marital patterns/status, 48-49
  nonmarital childbearing, 40

nontraditional family statuses, 41
poverty, 221
pregnancies, 36
racial socialization, 210, 217
referrals for blacks, informal job, 156, 158
sexual prevalence and contraceptive practices, 33-35
single mothers, 174
socioeconomic achievement, 30
widowhood, 55
Widowhood, 55, 260
Women:
economic independence, 68
extended households, 268
interracial marriage, 57-58
living arrangements, 264-260, 268, 270-278
marital patterns/status, 59-60, 290
mate availability influencing marital patterns/status, 63-81

mothers, future consequences for adolescent, 29-31
racial socialization, 212
referrals, job, 158, 160
sexual prevalence and contraceptive practices, 33
stress, 99
supportive networks, 300-307, 313, 316
widowhood, 55
See also Female-headed families; Marital patterns/status; Romantic relationships, unmarried people in; Single mothers
Work and family role strain:
conclusions and implications, 149-150
discussion of results, 144, 146
interaction effects, 144, 147-148
methods used in researching, 140-142
minorities and women, 141-142
open systems perspective, 138-139
results of research, 142-145f
research, 138-144

About the Editors

Robert Joseph Taylor is Associate Professor of Social Work and Faculty Associate at the Institute for Social Research at the University of Michigan. His research, funded by the National Institutes of Health, focuses on family and friend social support networks across the life span, with a particular emphasis on the networks of older adults. Another major research area is the investigation of the correlates of religious participation and church support among African Americans. He has published articles on these topics in the *Journal of Gerontology: Social Sciences, Journal of Marriage and the Family, Family Relations, Review of Religious Research,* and *Social Work.*

James S. Jackson holds a Ph.D. in social psychology from Wayne State University and has been a faculty member of the University of Michigan since 1971. He is the Daniel Katz Distinguished University Professor of Psychology, Director of the Research Center for Group Dynamics, and Research Scientist at the Institute for Social Research, Professor of Health Behavior and Health Education in the School of Public Health, and Faculty Associate at the Center for Afro-American and African Studies and at the Institute of Gerontology. He is a Fellow of the American Psychological Society, American Psychological Association, and Gerontological Society of America. In addition, he was a recipient of a 1993-1994 Fogarty Senior Postdoctoral International Fellowship for study in France, where he holds the position of *Chercheur Invité, Groupe d'Etudes et de Recherches sur la Science, Ecole des Hautes Etudes en Sciences Sociales.* In 1990, he helped to establish, and continues to direct, the African American Mental Health Research Center, funded by the National Institute of Mental Health. His research interests and areas of publication include race and ethnic relations, health and mental health, adult development and aging, attitudes and attitude change, and African American politics.

Linda M. Chatters is Associate Professor in the Department of Health Behavior and Health Education of the School of Public Health and Faculty Associate with the Institute for Social Research at the University of Michigan. Her research, funded by the National Institutes of Health, focuses on psychological and social-structural determinants and correlates of subjective well-being in African Americans, as well as on the uses of survey data in this population. She has published extensively in the areas of subjective well-being, informal social support networks, and the measurement of religious participation. She received her Ph.D. in developmental psychology from the University of Michigan.

About the Contributors

Andrew Billingsley is among the nation's leading scholars of the African American experience. He is Professor and Chair of the Department of Family Studies at the University of Maryland, College Park, and Visiting Scholar-in-Residence at Spelman College in Atlanta. He is the recipient of the 1992 Du Bois, Johnson, Frazier Award, given by the American Sociological Association; the 1990 Marie Peters Award, given by the National Council on Family Relations; and the 1991 Distinguished Scholar Award, given by the Association of Black Sociologists. He is the author of several books including *Climbing Jacob's Ladder, Black Families in White America* (with Amy Tate Billingsley), *Children of the Storm* (with Jeanne Giovannoni), and *Black Families and the Struggle for Survival.*

Ruby L. Beale received her Ph.D. and M.A. degrees from the University of Michigan. She is currently on the faculty in the psychology department and the School of Business Administration and has a research scientist appointment at the Center for Education of Women at the University of Michigan. She is also a principal in a human resource management firm specializing in managing and enhancing work productivity, job and school performance with diverse populations. She has designed and implemented workshops on the psychological, interpersonal, organizational, and societal factors that can inhibit or facilitate the performance of employees and students. She is a specialist in diversity and multicultural programming and trains trainers to successfully implement programs with a diverse audience. She has provided consultation for organizational development to corporations, educational programs, professional associations and networks, municipalities, and grassroots community organizations. Her clients include Exxon; Dow; Citizen's Insurance Co.; NYNNEX of New England; America West; Michigan County Social Services Association; Washtenaw County Private and Public Social Service Agency Directors Council; Community Development Programs in Ann Arbor and Detroit; University of Virginia Law School; Great Lakes Region College Association; numerous school districts; and the University of Michigan's Medical School, Counseling Services, Athletic Department, Engineering School, and Comprehensive Studies Program.

Phillip J. Bowman is Associate Professor of Education and Social Policy and Faculty Fellow in the Institute for Policy Research at Northwestern University. He received his Ph.D in social psychology from the University of Michigan and was awarded both the Rockefeller and Senior Ford/National Research Council Postdoctoral Fellowships. While a study director at Michigan's Institute for Social Research, he worked on a series of innovative national surveys and directed a related postdoctoral training program. He has also held joint appointments in psychology and African American studies at both Michigan and the University of Illinois. His publications focus on the social psychology of chronic role strain, with an emphasis on race and cultural diversity issues in major life roles. He is especially interested in bridging role strain theory and related empirical research among at-risk African American populations to address pressing family, work, and educational policy issues.

Clifford L. Broman is Associate Professor of Sociology at Michigan State University. In 1984, he received his Ph.D. in sociology from the University of Michigan. He was a National Institute of Mental Health Postdoctoral Scholar from 1984-1985. He conducts research and publishes primarily in the areas of health-related behavior and psychological well-being.

Cleopatra Howard Caldwell is Assistant Professor in the Department of Health Behavior and Health Education and a Research Investigator with the African American Mental Health Research Center, Research Center for Group Dynamics, Institute for Social Research, University of Michigan. She has published journal articles in the areas of help-seeking behaviors and informal social support among African Americans, the black church as a social service institution, and race-related socialization and academic achievement among African American youth. Her current research focuses on two areas: (a) intergenerational family influences on early childbearing; and (b) self-efficacy, exercise, and the sexual behaviors of African American adolescent females. She received her Ph.D. in social psychology from the University of Michigan.

Christopher G. Ellison is Associate Professor of Sociology at the University of Texas at Austin, where he is affiliated with the African and Afro-American Studies and Religious Studies Programs, and is also a faculty research associate at the Population Research Center there. Much of his work focuses on contemporary African American religious life, with particular attention to the following: (a) the patterns and correlates of denominational switching, apostasy, and religious participation; (b) the implications of religious involvement for mental and physical health; and (c) religious variations in African American racial orientations and attitudes. He has also studied patterns and correlates of black social and political participation, as well as the implications of family life and social ties for individual well-being among African Americans. His work on these various topics has appeared in *Social Forces, Sociological Quarterly, Social Science Quarterly, Journal of Marriage and the Family, Social Science and Medicine, Review of Religious Research,* and various other publications.

Tyrone A. Forman is a doctoral student in the Department of Sociology at the University of Michigan, Ann Arbor, Michigan. He holds a master's degree in human development and social policy from Northwestern University, Evanston, Illinois. He is the coauthor with Phillip J. Bowman of a study titled *Race Differences in Family Role Strain,* which examines the performance of family roles in a national sample of African American and white fathers. His current teaching and research interests include the psychosocial consequences of racial stratification, the social psychology of work, African American fathers and families, life course patterns among African Americans, and social policy issues.

Mark A. Fossett is Associate Professor of Sociology at Texas A&M University at College Station, Texas, where he teaches in the areas of racial and ethnic relations, social demography of racial and ethnic groups, and quantitative methods. His published research focuses on the topics such as the measurement of racial inequality, trends in racial inequality over time and variation in racial inequality across areas, variation and trends in African American family structure especially as it is affected by mate availability, and racial residential segregation and the spatial distribution of employment opportunities for African Americans. His forthcoming book, *Long Time Coming: Racial Inequality in the Rural South, 1940-1990* (with M. Therese Seibert), examines trends over time in racial inequality in southern nonmetropolitan counties. He is presently working on a monograph that uses computer simulation models to investigate the role of ethnic preferences in racial residential segregation processes.

Andrea G. Hunter is Assistant Professor in the Department of Psychology and Women's Studies Program and is Faculty Associate at the Institute for Social Research at the University of Michigan. She received her Ph.D. in human development and family studies from Cornell University and continued postdoctoral work as a National Institute of Mental Health Fellow in Family Process and Psychopathology. Her research areas include African American families; grandparenting and intergenerational family relationships; African American men and gender constructions; feminist ideology among African Americans; race, gender, and the life course; and families and social change.

Rukmalie Jayakody is Assistant Professor in the Department of Human Development and Family Studies and a research affiliate at the Population Research Institute at Pennsylvania State University. She received her doctoral degree in 1996 from the University of Michigan. Her research focuses on single-mother families and kin assistance, living arrangements, and marital transitions.

Waldo E. Johnson, Jr. is Assistant Professor at the School of Social Service Administration, University of Chicago. He received his Ph.D. in social work from the School of Social Service Administration at the University of Chicago in 1993. He was a postdoctoral fellow in the Research and Training Program on Poverty, the Underclass, and Public Policy at the School of Social Work at the University of Michigan. His research interests and areas of publication include adolescent paternity among African American fathers and contextual factors affecting the physical and mental health status of African American males.

Verna M. Keith is Associate Professor in the Department of Sociology at Arizona State University. She received her Ph.D. from the University of Kentucky and did postdoctoral work in the School of Public Health and the Institute of Gerontology at the University of Michigan. She has authored and coauthored several articles on stress and mental health and has written on the use of health care services by racial-ethnic minorities. Her current research focuses on gender, stress, and mental health among African Americans.

K. Jill Kiecolt is Associate Professor of Sociology at Virginia Polytechnic Institute and State University. She received her Ph.D. from the University of California, Los Angeles, and later completed a postdoctoral fellowship in the Training Program in Social Psychology at Indiana University. She is continuing her research on the social structural determinants of marriage and family structure. She also is currently investigating the antecedents of attempts at life change.

Lilah Raynor Koski was a Research Assistant with the Family Transitions to Early Child Bearing Project at the Program for Research on Black Americans, Institute for Social Research at the University of Michigan. She received a B.S. degree in developmental psychology from the University of Michigan and is pursuing a graduate degree in psychology.

Harold W. Neighbors is Associate Professor in the Department of Health Behavior and Health Education, School of Public Health at the University of

Michigan. He is also an Adjunct Research Scientist with the Program for Research on Black Americans at the Institute for Social Research, where he is Associate Director of the African American Mental Health Research Center. He received his Ph.D. in social psychology from the University of Michigan in 1982. He did postdoctoral work at the Institute for Social Research where he was supported by the Rockefeller Foundation and the National Institute of Mental Health (New Investigator Research Award). His current research interests and areas of publication include psychiatric epidemiologic field methods, cultural influences on the diagnosis of mental disorder, and the use of services. He has directed both community and institutional surveys of African American mental health and is currently the recipient of a Research Scientist Development Award from the National Institute of Mental Health, where he is studying ethnic differences in the social epidemiology of mental disorder.

Sherrill L. Sellers is a graduate student in the Joint Doctoral Program in Social Work and Sociology at the University of Michigan. She is a Council on Social Work Education (CSWE) Research Fellow. Her research interests include life course development, health consequences of social inequality, intergenerational relations, and social policy. Her specialization is in social mobility and mental health.

Michael C. Thornton teaches in Afro-American Studies at the University of Wisconsin-Madison (on leave to the University of Massachusetts-Boston 1996-1997, Department of Sociology and Ph.D. Program in Gerontology). His research focuses on ethnic identity and race relations among groups of color. Recent publications deal with the role of religion in black attitudes toward Asian Americans, Africans, and Hispanics; interracial marriage and people; mass media depictions of Asian American and black relations; and racial and ethnic patterns of hospital emergency room use.

M. Belinda Tucker is a social psychologist and Professor of Psychiatry and Biobehavioral Sciences at the University of California, Los Angeles. She received her undergraduate training at the University of Chicago and her Ph.D. from the University of Michigan. Prior to coming to UCLA, she served as

Study Director in the University of Michigan's Institute for Social Research. From 1978 to 1989, she directed the research programs of the UCLA Center for Afro-American Studies. She has authored numerous articles on marriage and personal relationships, including a volume titled *The Decline in Marriage Among African Americans: Causes, Consequences, and Policy Implications.* She has participated in the direction of a number of landmark studies, including the National Women's Drug Abuse Project in 1976, the National Survey of Black Americans in 1979, and the Jamaica AIDS Project—a national survey of the Jamaican population completed in 1994. She is currently directing a 21-city national survey, which examines the social context and social and psychological correlates of family formation behaviors and attitudes. She serves on a number of national panels, including the Social and Group Processes Review Committee for the National Institute of Mental Health, and the Advisory Board of University of Michigan's African American Mental Health Research Center. She recently received a prestigious 5-year Independent Scientist Award from the National Institute of Mental Health. Her research interests include the causes and consequences of changing patterns of family formation in the United States and the Caribbean, the psychological and social structural implications of constrained mate availability, and interethnic relations.